A MODERN APPROACH
TO TAX LAW

To John,

Wishing you the best
of luck in your
Bar Finals.

[signature]

2 Nov. 1973.

A Modern Approach
to Tax Law

MICHAEL Z. HEPKER
LL.B. LL.M.(London)
Of Gray's Inn, Barrister:
Lecturer at The College of Law

HEINEMANN : LONDON

William Heinemann Ltd

15 Queen St, Mayfair, London W1X 8BE

LONDON MELBOURNE TORONTO
JOHANNESBURG AUCKLAND

First published 1973

434 90734 0 (hardback)
434 90735 9 (limp)

Printed in Great Britain by
Butler & Tanner Ltd
Frome and London

TO PATRICIA,

in the hope that she will
never stop trying 'to
understand the other in
all his otherness'.

Preface

This book is intended primarily for law students preparing for the Bar or Law Society Finals or for the various University and Polytechnic courses in revenue law that have sprung into being over the past five or six years. Hopefully the book may prove useful also to students of accountancy or of business and to those in commerce or industry, perhaps even to those in practice, who are looking for a readable treatment of the general principles of tax law.

So manifest is the need for it that a new students' textbook on tax law is hardly called upon to justify its existence in the customary way. There are only two books available to students at the moment. The one is impeccably written but its author, an eminent QC, is no longer able to edit it himself and it is now out of date. Indeed, the current edition has become—in the light of Mr Barber's innovations—largely a work of history. The other book is admirably comprehensive but—at least to my students—perhaps not quite so comprehensible.

What does call for some explanation is this book's manner of presentation. Law books are not noted for their levity of style but there is really no reason why students' textbooks should not be more lively. If I were stuck on a desert island with nothing to read but the books I used as an undergraduate, I would probably refer to Farrand's *Contents of a Conveyance* as often as any. Conveyancing is hardly music hall material but *Farrand* sugars the pill with a line in humour that ranges from detached irony to almost prep school stuff: and it is all the more interesting a book for it. I have tried to achieve much the same sort of result in this book.

I have ventured also to make suggestions as to possible reforms where they seemed to me appropriate. A writer on tax would need a truly Shakespearean gift for suppressing his own personality if he were to avoid disclosing his value bias. I have preferred to make mine fairly explicit. To some extent I go along with Aneurin Bevan, who once said: 'I know what happens to people who stay in the middle of the road. They get run over.'

Perhaps the greatest difference between this and other tax books lies in the lengthy introductory section dealing *inter alia* with some aspects of the economics, sociology, and history of taxation. It seems to me, as a convinced interdisciplinarian, that tax ought ideally to be studied from the viewpoint of all the social sciences. Although I am equipped by training to deal only with the legal aspects of taxation, I offer the introductory section as a small contribution towards what I hope will eventually become a new approach to the study of taxation.

A final word of explanation. The manuscript was completed in early April 1973. The book went to press on 9 July. Even in that short period there were a number of significant developments: the Courts were regrettably no less active than usual in shifting the clichéd sands of tax law while Parliament had been busily licking the Finance Bill into shape. When the book was in proof it was decided to meet this difficulty by adding a new section that would allow the latest happenings to be included without disruption of the original text. This new section ('Recent Developments') is not merely a list of stop-press items: it is—or at any rate is intended to be— an integrated discussion of the principles affected by recent changes, and has provided the opportunity for a much fuller discussion of them than would otherwise have been possible. The text and the 'Recent Developments' are cross-referenced: where affected the text is marked ●, while the 'Recent Developments' are page-referenced to the text. In the result, the law is stated as at 9 July 1973.

At that date the Finance Bill 1973 had not yet received the Royal Assent. However, it had been amended in Committee and by Standing Committee H and was unlikely to be amended significantly before Assent. References in the text are therefore to sections of the Finance Act 1973 rather than clauses of the Bill.

I am extremely grateful to the publishers—to John St. John, James Negus, and Malcolm Stern in particular—as much for their unfailing kindness as for their efficiency. I would like to thank my friends, David Harrison of the University of Rhodesia, David Rippin of the Open University, Roger Kaye of the Chancery Bar, who read and commented on the typescript, and Vernon McCulloch, who checked the computations; my colleagues at The College of Law, Miss Hilary Jackson in particular, for their encouragement and helpful advice; *Punch*, *The Times*, and the *Sunday Express* for their permission to reproduce the various cartoons; and Miss Ruth Planner whose ingenuity and typing skills proved more than a match for the paperchase my manuscript set her.

And finally, indulgent readers, may I urge you to have in mind throughout the book Cervantes' sage advice: 'There is no book so bad but there is something good in it.'

M. Z. H.

Contents

3 Capital Gains Tax

Recent Developments

Table of Abbreviations

GENERAL

ACT	advance corporation tax
F.A.	Finance Act
TA	Income and Corporation Taxes Act 1970
TMA	Taxes Management Act 1970
VAT	Value Added Tax

REPORTS

A.C.	Appeal Cases
A.E.R.	All England Reports (officially cited "All E.R.")
A.T.C.	Annotated Tax Cases
Ch.	Chancery Division
K.B.	King's Bench
L.J.K.B.	Law Journal King's Bench
L.J.Q.B.	Law Journal Queen's Bench
L.T.	Law Times
Q.B.	Queen's Bench
S.J.	Solicitors' Journal
S.T.C.	Simon's Tax Cases
T.C.	Reports of Tax Cases
T.L.R.	Times Law Reports
T.R.	Taxation Reports
W.L.R.	Weekly Law Reports
W.N.	Weekly Notes

LITERATURE

B.T.E.	*British Tax Encyclopaedia* (Sweet & Maxwell)
B.T.R.	*British Tax Review* (Sweet & Maxwell)
Beattie	*Elements of the Law of Income and Capital Gains Taxation* by C. N. Beattie 9th ed. by N. Ross (Stevens & Sons 1970)
Bramwell	*Taxation of Companies* by R. M. Bramwell (Sweet & Maxwell 1973)
C.L.P.	*Current Legal Problems* (Stevens & Sons)

Cheshire	*Cheshire's Private International Law* 8th ed. by G. C. Cheshire and P. M. North (Butterworths 1970)
Dicey and Morris . . .	*Dicey and Morris on The Conflict of Laws* 8th ed. by J. H. C. Morris (Stevens & Sons 1967)
Econ. J.	*Economic Journal* (Macmillan)
Harvey	*Settlements of Land* by B. W. Harvey (Sweet & Maxwell 1973)
Pinson	*Revenue Law* 6th ed. by B. Pinson (Sweet & Maxwell 1972)
Simon	*Simon's Taxes* 3rd ed. (Butterworths 1970)
Talbot and Wheatcroft .	*Corporation Tax* by J. E. Talbot and G. S. A. Wheatcroft (Sweet & Maxwell 1968)
Wheatcroft and Park . .	*Wheatcroft on Capital Gains Taxes* by G. S. A. Wheatcroft and A. E. W. Park (Sweet & Maxwell 1967)
Whiteman and Wheatcroft	*Whiteman and Wheatcroft on Income Tax and Surtax* by P. G. Whiteman and G. S. A. Wheatcroft (Sweet & Maxwell 1971)

Table of Cases

Table of Statutes

B

1
Generalities

The rich man in his castle,
The poor man at his gate,
We've kept them, high or lowly,
Applauded by the state.

Never put off until tomorrow what you can do today: by that time there may be a tax on it. *Transatlantic proverb.*

1.1 A high-flying bird's-eye view of the fiscal landscape

1.11 TAXONOMY: THE OFFICIAL CLASSIFICATION

UK taxes are officially classified according to tax base as follows:

(1) The taxes on *income* are income tax, estate duty, and corporation tax.
(2) The taxes on *capital* are capital gains tax, estate duty, and corporation tax.
(3) The taxes on *expenditure* comprise:
    (*a*) customs and excise duties;
    (*b*) value added tax (in this book cited as "VAT");
    (*c*) car tax;
    (*d*) stamp duties;
    (*e*) licence duties on motor vehicles, televisions, dogs, guns, gaming, etc; and
    (*f*) local rates.

By re-classifying the taxes on income and capital according to the type of person chargeable, we discover that individuals are liable to income tax, capital gains tax, and estate duty, while companies are liable only to corporation tax. For individuals the tax year, termed a "year of assessment", runs from 6 April in each calendar year to 5 April in the next; the year of assessment 1973–74, say, covers the period 6 April 1973 to 5 April 1974. For companies the tax year is the "financial year" from 1 April to 31 March; one refers, for example, to "the financial year 1973", meaning the period 1 April 1973 to 31 March 1974.

1.12 ANOTHER CLASSIFICATION: DIRECT AND INDIRECT TAXES

The taxes on income and capital are levied *directly* on chargeable persons. By contrast, the taxes on expenditure are levied on the ownership or use of goods and on services; while they may be collected from the person providing the goods or services (importer, manufacturer, wholesaler), their burden is usually borne *indirectly* by the ultimate consumer or user in the form of higher prices. Expenditure (or "outlay") taxes are sometimes colloquially referred to as "hidden taxes", a description which reflects their characteristic feature—a separation of what Hicks has called their formal and effective incidence ('The terminology of tax analysis' ((1946) *Econ. J.* vol. 56 no. 221, pp. 38–50)).

Some of the taxes on expenditure are *specific*. Others are *ad valorem*. A specific duty is one based on quantity (e.g. in 1972–73 customs duty on hydrocarbon oils was 22½p per gallon), while an *ad valorem* duty is one based on value (e.g. in 1972–73 general betting duty on off-course bets was 6% of the stake money).

If direct/indirect is the most usual classification—in the UK if not elsewhere—it is by no means the most useful. The major difficulty is to say of a particular tax who bears the final burden. Local rates, for example, are borne usually by the tenant, but sometimes by the landlord, depending on the state of the market in each locality. Economists are divided as to whether corporation tax on companies' profits are usually shifted on to the consumer (*pro* shifting are studies by Krzyaniak and Musgrave (1963) (USA), Roskamp (1965) (West Germany), Laumas (1966) (India), and the Canadian Royal Commission (1966); *contra* Cragg *et al.* (1967) and Gordon (1967)). Also, the classification is applied to methods of collection as well as to taxes, which is apt to cause confusion.

1.13 YET ANOTHER: PROGRESSIVE, PROPORTIONAL, AND REGRESSIVE

It is also possible to classify taxes, and indeed tax systems, according to their incidence among the intended class of taxpayers. One must, however, be careful to avoid any confusion between formal and effective incidence. Looking at formal rates, it would be accurate to say that a tax is *progressive* if the ratio of tax liability to income (or other tax base) rises as income (or other tax base) increases, *proportional* if the ratio remains constant, and *regressive* if it falls. But the formal rates may conceal rather than reveal a tax's true impact (i.e. its effective incidence), a theme we will return to in 1.2 below. For instance, in 1972–73 customs duty on tobacco was normally levied at a flat (i.e. proportional) rate of £5·041 per lb, representing about two-thirds of the retail price of a packet of cigarettes. Yet it is precisely because the formal incidence of duty was proportional (in the sense that everyone buying cigarettes paid the same percentage of the cost in tax) that its effective incidence was so markedly regressive (since cigarettes —and hence the duty on tobacco—undoubtedly accounted for a much larger slice of small than of large incomes). In terms of effective incidence, a progressive/proportional/regressive tax is not simply one of which the rich pay more/the same/less of respectively than do the poor, but rather one which accounts for a greater/the same/a smaller percentage respectively of large than of small incomes.

The economist Adam Smith considered the proportional principle the most equitable basis of taxation, since it seemed fair that, if a man with income of £1,000 paid £100 in tax, a man with £4,000 should pay £400. Since his day it has come to be acknowledged that £1 is worth more to a man with £1,000 than to a man with £100,000, a simple notion which economists flushed with success have dignified with an imposing title—the law of diminishing marginal utility. Progression is now seen to accord better with the traditional view that taxation should be related to ability to pay.

We have seen that formal rates invite misleading conclusions as to a tax's effective incidence. They are, moreover, ambiguous. Let us, for the sake of argument, consider Ivor Fortune, a single man whose income, entirely earned, in 1973–74 is £30,000. (He is, presumably, a conscientious objector to tax planning!) Earned income is taxed in the UK at steeply progressive rates rising to 75% above £20,000. The statement seems plausible that: 'Ivor pays income tax at the rate of 75%'. Yet, although the slice of his income above £20,000 is admittedly taxable at 75%, his income tax bill for 1973–74 of £17,653·75 would amount to no more than 58·8% of his earnings. It is therefore equally plausible to assert that: 'Ivor pays income tax at the rate of 58·8%'. Ambiguity can be removed by distinguishing, in statements of tax rates, between "marginal" rates applicable to particular slices of income (here 75%) and "average" rates applicable to its entirety (here 58·8%). Many of the complaints about rates of tax in this country trade on this ambiguity.

1.14 A LOOK AT SOME OF THE TAXES NOT TREATED AT LENGTH IN THIS BOOK

Chapter 1 of this book deals with a number of general matters: the economics and history of taxation; tax legislation, administration, and litigation; the interpretation of tax statutes; and the basic concepts of residence and domicile. Some of the specific taxes are then dealt with in some detail—income tax in Chapter 2, capital gains tax in Chapter 3, corporation tax in Chapter 4, and VAT in Chapter 5. As for the others, our high-flying bird has been persuaded to take a turn over them now; limited space unfortunately allows him no more than this quick look.

Estate duty

Estate duty is payable on the value of all property which passes on death. The charge is not limited to property owned by the deceased but may extend also to other property, e.g. settled property from which the deceased was entitled to the income during his lifetime, the deceased's share of partnership property, property comprised in a *donatio mortis causa* made by the deceased, and indeed any gifts made by the deceased within seven years of his death. The exemptions include property in which the deceased was interested only in a fiduciary or representative capacity or by way of security (e.g. as trustee, executor, or mortgagee), property settled on the deceased for life which reverts on his death to the settlor, gifts up to £15,000 in value to the surviving spouse, gifts up to £50,000 in value to charities, and unlimited gifts to certain national institutions. The amount of duty is computed by first aggregating all property liable to estate duty so as to form one "estate", and then applying a progressive scale of percentage rates. At present the scale ascends in successive "slices", above the initial exempt slice of £15,000, from 25% on estates of between £15,000 and £20,000 to 75% on estates above £500,000. Industrial land and buildings, machinery and plant, and agricultural property are charged at 55% of the estate rate. It follows that, where a man's entire estate passes to his widow, no duty is payable unless the estate exceeds £30,000.

Customs and excise duties

Customs duties are levied on goods imported from abroad and on goods manufactured in bond from imported dutiable materials. They comprise "protective" duties, which serve to shield home industries from trade competition (and formerly served as a means of giving trade preference to Commonwealth and EFTA countries), and the "revenue" duties, principally on tobacco, alcoholic drinks, hydrocarbon oils, and matches and mechanical lighters. On the other hand, excise duties are levied on goods produced in the UK (other than those manufactured in bond from imported dutiable materials) and on services—principally on alcoholic drinks, betting and gaming, and matches and mechanical lighters.

During the transitional period of our EEC entry—1 April 1973 to 1 July 1977—customs tariffs between the Six and the Three (UK, Republic of Ireland, Denmark) will gradually be abolished. Each of the Three will also be adjusting its individual external tariff rates upwards or downwards, as the case may be, so as to bring them into alignment with the Community's Common Customs Tariff (CCT) on "third country" goods, i.e. goods from outside the Community.

The Chancellor of the Exchequer has a power, which is known as the "Regulator" and must be renewed annually, to vary the rates of the main customs and excise duties by up to 10%.

Stamp duties

● Stamp duties are imposed by the Stamp Act 1891, as amended, on the execution of a variety of commercial and legal documents, such as conveyances and transfers of property, settlements, leases, mortgages, life insurance policies, and contracts under seal.

Local rates

Rates are a local tax levied on occupiers of "rateable property" as a contribution towards the cost of local services. Local authority expenditure currently runs at about £8,000 million annually. About a third is capital expenditure, e.g. on housing, roads, etc, the remainder current expenditure, principally on education, also on the police and fire services, health and welfare, sewerage, etc. Capital expenditure is normally financed by borrowing. Rates contribute about a third of current expenditure, the remainder being met by government grants (approaching a half) and rents from municipal houses, dividends, and interest (one-fifth).

The rating authority, i.e. the local council—and, curiously enough, only since 1925 has there been a single rating authority for each area—calculates an occupier's payment annually by multiplying the "rateable value" of his property by the rate poundage—a percentage fixed by the authority according to its projected financial needs. The rateable value of a property is the notional annual rent it will command in the open market. At one time valuations were not made regularly and inter-local disparities developed. The Local Government Act 1948 improved matters by assigning the task of valuation throughout England and Wales to the Department of Inland Revenue. The Board's Valuation Department prepares new valuation lists quinquennially and sends them to the local councils, where they are available for public inspection. The Labour Government dispensed with the revaluation due in 1968, so that the latest valuation at the end of 1972 was the first for ten years. The new valuation lists came into force on 1 April 1973. Disputes about rating assessments are heard by local valuation courts, each consisting of three members of an independent local valuation panel; and, on appeal, by the Lands Tribunal.

Rateable property is widely defined to include land, houses, buildings, and also mines, quarries, structures of all kinds, and even some plant and machinery; councils even have power to half-rate unoccupied property. Agricultural property, however, is exempt. The rateable person is normally the occupier, i.e. in the case of leased premises the tenant, but councils may rate the owners of small properties or make arrangements with the owners of properties let on weekly or monthly tenancies for the owners to pay the rates and then recover them from the tenants along with their rent. Charities pay half rate on property occupied for charitable purposes. Councils are empowered to reduce or remit the rates for a wide range of non-profit-making bodies.

If all economists were laid end to end, they would not reach a conclusion. *Bernard Shaw.*

1.2 Economic aims and effects of taxation

The nineteenth century regarded taxation simply as a means of raising revenue and believed that money spent privately did more good than money spent by government. (This belief has not yet died—'If you want to show that crime doesn't pay,' a taxi-driver advised the author recently, 'put it in the hands of the government.') Economists therefore suggested that taxation and government expenditure ought ideally to be minimized. With the introduction of health and unemployment insurance and old age pensions by the Liberals of 1906–14 this outlook was jettisoned. It gradually came to be realized that, given a certain level of government expenditure, increases in taxation would tend to dampen consumer expenditure and countervail against inflation, while decreases in taxation would tend to have the opposite effect. Keynes and his followers argued that taxation could be used *deliberately* for these purposes, a view which has revolutionized Budgetary policy since its explicit acceptance in the 1944 White Paper "Employment Policy" and inauguration in the interim Budget of November 1947.

The Budget is now seen, in the words of the Plowden Report, 'not as a simple balancing of tax receipts against expenditure, but as a sophisticated process in which the instruments of taxation and expenditure are used to influence the course of the economy'. Before the War it would have seemed trite to suggest that the primary aim of taxation was to raise the finance needed for government spending. Today the suggestion is seen as deceptively simple. As one economist has put it: 'If that were all that was required of taxation, a benevolent government would abolish taxation and finance all its expenditure by printing money or borrowing it' (C. M. Allan *The Theory of Taxation* Penguin Books 1971 p. 23). Since this is likely to be inflationary, the basic function of taxation is 'to reduce private expenditure in order to allow governments to spend without causing inflation' (ibid. p. 26). Thus 'taxation is basically a deflationary device' (ibid. p. 23). There are of course subsidiary objectives: to redistribute income or wealth, to influence the balance of payments, to encourage exports and discourage imports, to promote long-term economic growth, etc. And apart from these general aims, specific taxes continue to be introduced in order to produce specific effects, e.g. in the case of Selective Employment Tax (1966–73) to encourage labour migration from service into manufacturing industries.

A Chancellor of the Exchequer, in deciding between taxes or tax bases, has recourse to a tradition of opinion as to the relevant criteria that stretches back at least to Adam Smith's *The Wealth of Nations* (1776). His celebrated "canons of taxation"—equity, certainty, convenience to the taxpayer, and administrative efficiency—have survived remarkably well. Economists have also emphasized such criteria as *neutrality*, i.e. the extent to which a tax avoids distortions in the working of the market mechanism, and *ability to pay*. Their analyses have tended, however, to be inconclusive. For example, J. R. Hicks (*Value and Capital* Oxford University Press 1939) demonstrated the superior neutrality of income taxes over taxes on specific goods in so far as they do not distort the consumer's choice between goods. Morag ((1959) *Econ. J.* vol. 69 no. 273 pp. 87–94), by challenging Hicks's assumption of a required yield, has managed to turn the Hicks conclusion on its head. Again, the ability-to-pay criterion has given rise to a proliferation of equal sacrifice theories, none of which seems entirely satisfactory.

Turning to the effects of taxation, economists have pointed out that, if a specific tax of £2 were to be levied on a commodity costing £10, the price would be raised to £12 if demand for the commodity were perfectly inelastic. The tax's effective incidence would be on the purchaser. Conversely, if demand were perfectly elastic, the price would have to remain at £10 since at any price above £10 demand would drop to zero. The tax's effective incidence would then be on the seller. Between these extremes, economists tell us that in general the price of a commodity rises to accommodate a tax increase in inverse proportion to the elasticity of demand. Unfortunately this theoretical model is almost impossible to apply accurately in practice.

In the face of burgeoning taxation over the past century in all countries, there have been innumerable protests that saturation point has been reached. Economists have developed and analysed the concept of "taxable capacity", said to be 25% of national income, but have not yet established what it is or at what point a country is likely to reach it. Clearly the more a government provides for its citizens, the greater will be the nation's taxable capacity. Despite the protests, taxation in the UK has increased its slice of the national income from 10% in 1913 to over a third in 1972–73. Whether or not counter-productive economic effects have set in as a result of heavy taxation in the UK is still very much an open question.

By far the most important tax, in terms of yield, is income tax, which in 1972–73 raised £7,264,026,744 (excluding surtax, which raised a further £356,764,722). This was followed by corporation tax (£1,600,193,163), customs and excise duties on hydrocarbon oils (£1,570 million (estimated)), tobacco (£1,140 million (estimated)), and alcoholic drinks (£1,065 million), death duties (£462,837,460), the protective duties (£305 million (estimated)), excise duties on betting and gaming (£175 million (estimated)), stamp duties (£168,476,067), and capital gains tax (£157,173,949). Purchase tax, now replaced by VAT, raised £1,315 million (estimated).

The law, in its majestic equality, forbids the rich as well as the poor to sleep under bridges. *Anatole France.*

1.3 Fact and myth: our tax system and its social effects

The path to a clear, unmuddled account of our tax system has become overgrown with a profusion of misconceptions, some of them deliberately planted for political reasons. A particularly deep-rooted perennial is the belief that the overall burden of taxation on the UK economy is high relative to other comparable countries. This belief derives some support from the figures showing taxation receipts in different countries. But a taxpayer's situation can fairly be judged only by comparing what he pays with what he receives. Until the economists provide us with a comparative table showing government services against taxation receipts in the various countries—quite an undertaking—any generalization in this area must be more an assertion than a conclusion. The author's impression is that nowadays most advanced industrialized countries have broadly similar fiscal structures built around a sharply progressive income tax. Even their relative yields from taxation do not differ as widely as is commonly supposed. A revealing parameter is the percentage that total tax receipts (including social security contributions) represent of the gross national product. In 1970 the figure for the UK was 42·7%, compared with 47·4% in Norway, 46·3% in Sweden, 45% in the Netherlands, 41·5% in Austria, 41·4% in France, 40·5% in West Germany, 38·2% in Belgium, 37·7% in Canada, 33% in the United States, 32·8% in Italy, and 21·3% in Japan.

Also misconceived is the notion, sometimes used to explain or justify the introduction of VAT, that the UK relies more on direct taxation than other countries. In reply to a parliamentary question on 10 June 1972, the Chancellor stated that taxes on income represented 40% of total taxation in the UK, while for the EEC countries the figures were rather lower: 37% (Luxembourg), 34·3% (Netherlands), 32·5% (Belgium), 29·9% (Germany), 21·3% (Italy), and 19·4% (France) (*H.C. Deb.* Vol. 835 col. 61). It is significant, however, that the UK relies less than most countries (Canada and Denmark excepted) on social security contributions. When these are added in with the taxes on income, the figures present a different story: 71·1% (Netherlands), 66·7% (Luxembourg), 62·5% (Belgium), 62·3% (Germany), 59·6% (France), 58·8% (Italy), 54·3% (UK). In fact very few countries raise a greater proportion of revenue than the UK by taxes on expenditure; in 1972–73 indirect taxes accounted for as much as 42·5% (estimated) of the total UK tax revenue (excluding social security contributions), which is almost the highest figure in the international table.

Looking at the formal rates of UK taxes, we notice that income tax and estate duty are steeply progressive, while capital gains tax, corporation tax, and most of the duties on expenditure are at flat rates, i.e. proportional. The effective incidence of these taxes is more difficult to ascertain. It is clear that our system of indirect taxation is relatively narrow, relying heavily on the revenue duties on tobacco, alcoholic drinks, and hydrocarbon oils; and that the duties on cigarettes and beer are markedly regressive. It is also clear—as the Allen Committee discovered in 1965—that local rates are highly regressive, though the extent of regression was mitigated by the General Rate Act 1967. This set up a system of rebates for cases of hardship, gave householders a lower rate in the pound than other ratepayers, and allowed them to pay their rates by ten instalments a year. (These improvements are welcome but peripheral. The hard truth is that local finance needs updating. When a local rate was first levied in English towns and villages in the fourteenth century, land—a permanent *indicium* of ability to pay—was the obvious tax base. The explanation for Exchequer grants, the other pillar of local finance, which date from 1825, lies in Parliament's desire to retain its hard-won control over the other modalities of taxation. Today it would surely be more appropriate for local authorities to levy a local income tax or some other form of progressive tax.) What is not clear is firstly whether our indirect taxes, overall, are regressive or progressive, and secondly the extent to which our direct taxes are progressive in effect.

Relative to other countries, the burden of taxation in the UK seems to fall more on the very high and very low income groups, with middle-range incomes bearing much the same burden as elsewhere. Since social security benefits lighten the burden for lower income groups, it is probably true to say that only the very high income groups are more heavily taxed than in most comparable countries. But, before we conclude that marginal rates on large incomes should be lowered, two points are worth considering. Firstly investigations indicate that high rates of tax are not a disincentive—though almost everyone *thinks* that the efforts of *others* are adversely affected. Secondly, discussion of rates of *income* taxation tends to obscure what many people regard as the real problem—inequality of *wealth* distribution.

The UK tax system is an undeniably effective instrument for the taxation of incomes. However, the Inland Revenue's latest quinquennial survey of personal incomes for 1969–70 shows that *even before tax* only 0·0023% of income earners received £10,000 a year or more. The top 1% of income earners account for less than 10% of total incomes, the top 10% for less than 30%. On the other hand, wealth in the UK is more unevenly distributed than in the United States. Indeed it is possible that 'Britain has the doubtful distinction of leading the international inequality league' (Atkinson *Unequal Shares* Allen Lane The Penguin Press 1972 p. 21). It is remarkable that throughout the era of high marginal rates of taxation dating from the First War—the maxima are currently 90% for income tax and 75% for estate duty—the gap between rich and poor has remained substantial. By treating the dead as a random sample of the living, Revell was able to estimate from the estate duty returns that in 1911–13 the top 1% of the adult population owned 69% of total personal wealth in Britain and that the top 5% then owned 87%. By 1960 the share of the top 1% had dropped to 42%—but the share of the next 4% had increased from 18% to 33% (indicating that redistribution had taken place not so much from rich to poor but, within rich families, from very rich to rich), and, moreover, the share of the top 1% had dropped to 43% by 1954. The estate duty figures are by no means exact. They omit pension rights, small estates, property held by the deceased as life tenant, etc. Nor do they adequately reflect avoidance practices (so simple and widespread that estate duty has come to be known as "the voluntary tax"; full duty is usually levied only when the deceased was so greedy or addled, or died so unexpectedly, that precautions were not put into effect). They understate the value of quoted shares—the total net value of all quoted companies' assets has been shown to be much more than the total stock market value of all those companies' shares. On the basis of investment incomes *The Economist* estimated (15 January 1966, reprinted in *Power in Britain* HEB 1973) that in 1960 the top 2% owned 55%, the top 7% 84% of wealth. It is safe to assume that in 1973 the top 1% owns over a quarter, the top 10% over half, of total personal wealth. The most that can be claimed for taxation and social security is that without them the disparity between rich and poor may have become even greater than it is. To those who accept the distributional objective of taxation—'money is like muck,' said Francis Bacon, 'not good except it be spread'—the case for some form of gift and/or wealth tax seems overwhelming.

Life must be lived forwards, but can only be understood backwards. *Kierkegaard.*

1.4 Brief historical conspectus

In early times taxation was to a large extent merely one of the instruments of oppression wielded by ruling classes over the subjugated. Many of the early exactions were not so much taxes as organized and legitimated forms of robbery. In the third century A.D., for example, the Romans filled their public coffers largely from the proceeds of "angareia" under which provincials were liable to conscription and their property to seizure on a purely *ad hoc* basis. A clay tablet found in Iraq was inscribed, an estimated 3,500 years ago, with the words: 'You can have a lord, you can have a king, but the man to fear is the tax collector.' If indirect taxes enjoyed at times a measure of stability, direct levies were invariably reserved for crises, usually to finance wars. The reliance of governments on taxation as the main source of public revenue is relatively recent.

Another modern development is the acceptance by Western democracies of the principle that taxes should be imposed on and collected from all sections of the community equitably on the basis of consent and representation. This principle has become a cornerstone of our constitution after centuries of bitter conflict. The landmarks are well known. Magna Carta (one should really say "the Great Charters", since there were in fact several), wrested from King John in 1215, and the Bill of Rights, promulgated in 1689 after the Civil War, embody the ascendancy of Parliament over the monarchy, the Parliament Act 1911 that of the Commons over the Lords. In 1767 a duty of 3d per pound was imposed on all tea entering America by the then Chancellor, Charles Townshend, of whom Burke remarked: 'To please universally was the object of his life, but to tax and to please, no more than to love and to be wise, is not given to men.' The colonists resisted, George III and Lord North obstinately refused to back down, and there followed the Boston tea party and the American War and Declaration of Independence. An oppressive tax system, under which the *ancien régime* had given over the task of tax collection to cruel and dishonest "tax farmers", helped also to ignite the smouldering anger of the French peasantry in 1789.

The institution of direct taxation as a more or less permanent feature of a tax system requires a degree of popular acceptance as well as a sound administrative structure capable of regular assessment and collection. These conditions were not satisfied in England before the end of the eighteenth century. Until then direct taxes were doomed to transience. The first was Danegeld, originally introduced to protect England against the Danish invaders and later continued as a land tax. To collect it William the Conqueror compiled Domesday Book. The advent of strict agrarian feudalism—each tenant bound to perform services for his hierarchical superior—left little room for taxation. It was not long, however, before the feudal dues were allowed to be commuted for money. The use, precursor of the trust, became a popular avoidance device: by enfeoffing several persons jointly to the use of the feoffer the tenant could acquire protection from most of the incidents of tenure. Dismayed at the resultant depletion of his feudal revenues, Henry VIII enacted the Statutes of Uses, which is not often thought of as a piece of anti-avoidance legislation. His unwilling subjects responded with a more sophisticated avoidance device—the "use upon a use"—which later came to be called a trust. How familiar this pattern has now become!

Other experiments in direct taxation followed. Henry II's tax on personal property was converted in the early fourteenth century into a subsidy granted by Parliament to the King. Poll taxes were levied in the late fourteenth century but evasion kept their yields low. Charles I took to issuing writs to various districts requiring them to supply and equip ships for stated periods. John Hampden, a wealthy landowner, refused to pay this "ship-money". (He appears in Gray's *Elegy*, with the benefit of a strong dash of poetic licence, as the "village-Hampden" who with dauntless breast the little tyrant of his fields withstood.) The Court gave judgment for the King but Parliament refused to accept the decision and impeached the judges. Eventually the Civil War ensued and Parliament, unsporting to the last, deprived Charles not only of his crown but of his head as well. During the Commonwealth Cromwell levied a "monthly assessment" on each district. Towards the end of the seventeenth century a system developed called "the General Aid". One of the Aids became a land tax which flourished during the eighteenth century and managed to survive, in an emasculated form, down to 1963.

Indirect taxation had its origins in the King's traditional right for life to impose customs duties on imports and exports, a tradition which came to an abrupt end when Parliament refused to grant them to Charles I for more than twelve months. In 1643 Pym, one of the Puritan leaders during the Civil War, levied "the excise", an unfairly regressive tax on food, drink, and other necessities imposed *vi et armis* on a hostile population. In the last decade of the seventeenth century the excise was extended to a curious array —hackney carriages, burials, births, marriages, bachelors, houses, and hawkers. Lacking an adequate administrative structure, Parliament aimed its imposts at the external signs of wealth. There arose such quaint expedients as window tax (1696), inhabited house duty (1778), and the duties on silver plate (1765), male servants (1777), female servants (1785), horses, sporting licences, and gamekeepers (all 1784). Pitt the younger ('Not merely a chip of the old block,' commented Burke, 'but the old block itself') was Prime Minister when the Napoleonic wars broke out in 1793. At first he turned to such bizarre taxes as those on hair powder (1795), on dogs (1796), on clocks and watches (1797), and on armorial bearings (1798). In 1798 he levied the "Triple Assessment". The various taxes on expenditure had come to be known as "the assessed taxes". Pitt's idea was to raise the rates of the assessed taxes by up to five times those of the previous year; and to prevent evasion by taxing those persons who had paid the assessed taxes in the previous year on the basis of the previous year's returns. His idea failed. The Triple Assessment yielded only half the anticipated sum. He could afford to delay no longer.

Pitt introduced income tax in January 1799. It was levied on the world-wide income of British residents and the British income of non-residents at the rate of 10%. Incomes up to £60 were exempt. Each taxpayer was required to make a general return of his income under nineteen heads called "cases" but in practice a lump sum return sufficed because there was no machinery for verifying returns. Not surprisingly evasion was rife; the yields of Pitt's Budgets of 1799, 1800, and 1801 all fell below the respective estimates. On the administrative front, Pitt empowered the "General Commissioners" to examine returns and make assessments and "Surveyors" to inspect the returns and make appropriate surcharges. (The Surveyors were eventually renamed "H.M. Inspectors of Taxes" in recognition of their services during the Great War.) The taxpayer or Surveyor, if dissatisfied with an assessment, could appeal to the "Commissioners of Appeal".

Pitt was succeeded as Chancellor by Addington. Pitt was undoubtedly one of England's great statesmen. Sir Walter Scott eulogized him along with Nelson and Fox: 'But search the land of living men, Where wilt thou find their like agen?' Addington's later career was undistinguished. As Home Secretary, for example, he is said to have used police spies. Pitt's pre-eminence caused historians to underrate Addington's achievement as Chancellor. Canning's jibe, 'Pitt is to Addington As London is to Paddington' had an undeniable ring of truth. Dr Farnsworth showed, however, that it is Addington and not Pitt who deserves to be dubbed 'the author of modern income tax'.

He accurately diagnosed the two main weaknesses of Pitt's tax—ease of evasion and the unpopularity of disclosure. The remedies which he devised in his 1803 Act have remained cardinal features of our system down to the present day. First, wherever practicable income was to be taxed at the source at which it arose rather than after receipt. Second, confidentiality was secured by requiring each taxpayer to make a separate return of each source of his income to different officials. For this purpose the various sources of income were classified into "Schedules" headed A, B, C, D, and E, Schedule D being sub-divided into six "Cases". Schedule A, called "the landlord's tax", was levied on the annual value of land; Schedule B, "the farmer's tax", on the occupation of farming land; and Schedule C on income payable out of any public revenue. Schedule D swept up income from "any kind of property" under:

Case I covering income from trades and manufactures,
Case II income from professions, employments, etc,
Case III profits of an uncertain annual value, e.g. from mines or canals,
Case IV interest from securities abroad,
Case V income from possessions abroad, and
Case VI annual profits not charged under any other Case or Schedule.

Schedule E charged emoluments of any public office or employment, pensions, annuities, etc.

This structure is extant today; though the income allocated to the various

Cases and Schedules has varied over the years, it is remarkable how similar the 1803 allocation is to that under the present system (*see* pp. 45–6 below). The exemption for incomes under £60 was retained; and there was an abatement of incomes between £60 and £150. Above that, tax was levied at the rate of 5%. Addington greatly improved the administration, dispensing with the Commissioners of Appeal and leaving the General Commissioners with both administrative and appellate functions. The new system brought in almost as much revenue as the old, though the rate had been halved. When Pitt was returned to power in 1805 he was shrewd enough to perform a *volte face* and adopt the new system virtually unchanged, though he created "Special Commissioners" to perform a variety of administrative tasks.

Lord Henry Petty's Act of 1806 was practically a reproduction of the 1803 and 1805 Acts with their provisions more logically arranged and the rate, following the disaster of Austerlitz, increased to 10%, at which it was to remain until 1816. The exemption limit was lowered to £50 and confined to "industrial incomes"—a first whiff of the principle of differentiation between earned and unearned income which has now become basic. The 1806 Act remained in force until 1816 when, over a year after Waterloo, the Government put an end to income tax. It was a short-sighted decision; the war-time expedient had been winning growing support among the more percipient, notably Ricardo, as a desirable permanent measure.

Between 1816 and 1842 there was no income tax. Public revenue was derived from customs and excise, the assessed taxes, and the land tax. The income tax was reimposed by Peel, that worthy but humourless reactionary whose smile O'Connell likened to 'moonlight falling upon the silver plate of a child's coffin' and Disraeli (independently) to 'the silver fittings on a coffin'. (On another occasion Disraeli remarked that Peel reminded him of a poker: 'The only difference is that a poker gives off occasional signs of warmth.') The 1842 Act was a virtual reproduction of the 1806 Act apart from the removal of any trace of differentiation and the raising of the exemption limit to £150. Peel intended the tax for three years only but it was reimposed every three years until Gladstone's masterly five-hour Budget speech of 1853. Declaring his conviction that income tax was an essentially temporary expedient—'an engine of gigantic power for great national purposes'—he proposed that the tax be continued for seven years at reducing rates until expiry in 1860. By 1860, however, the Crimean War had supervened (1854–56) and Gladstone had no choice but to eat humble pie and reimpose the tax indefinitely.

Between 1860 and the Liberal victory of 1906 there were few significant developments in the history of income taxation. The year 1874 saw income tax brought within the purview of the Courts of law. Both Surveyor and taxpayer were entitled to require the Commissioners determining an appeal against assessment to state a case for the opinion of the High Court. The year 1874 was also an election year. Both Gladstone and Disraeli could be heard courting the electorate with promises to abolish income tax. The promises were not kept, though the rate of income tax achieved its nadir that year of 2d in the £. The year 1880 witnessed the irony of Gladstone again having to raise the rate of income tax only a few years after his promise to abolish it. 'And so this temporary tax condemned to summary execution by Gladstone and to a lingering death by Disraeli survived on sufferance and was absorbed into the fiscal system in what might be described as a fit of parliamentary absence of mind' (Simon A1.412).

In 1894 Sir William Harcourt introduced estate duty, with rates rising from 1% on estates between £100 and £150 up to 8% on estates over £1 million. It was a brave measure, far ahead of its time. The Times denounced it as a means of holding families to "ransom" thrice in a century and the landed interests bitterly opposed it. One of Harcourt's neighbours, in an amusing letter to The Times, ventured to offer him some advice: 'When you are proposing to annex your neighbour's property, because you are the stronger and he is the weaker, leave metaphysics alone.'

The 1906–14 Liberal administration introduced two important principles into the income tax system. The first, the principle of graduation, featured in Lloyd George's famous 1909 Budget in the shape of a "super-tax" on incomes over £5,000 at the rate of $2\frac{1}{2}$%. In 1927 Churchill renamed this impost "surtax" and clarified its status as merely a deferred instalment of income tax rather than a tax in its own right. The second principle, differentiation, was reintroduced into the system when the 1907 Act subjected earned incomes not exceeding £2,000 to a lower rate.

The First World War ushered in the modern era of taxation. The rate of income tax had never previously exceeded $6\frac{2}{3}$%. In 1914 the standard rate was $6\frac{1}{4}$% and the maximum rate of supertax $6\frac{2}{3}$% on incomes above £8,000. By the end of the war standard rate had risen to 30% and super-tax to $22\frac{1}{2}$% on incomes over £10,000. A top marginal rate of less than 13% had become 55%. Moreover, McKenna had introduced a war tax called "Excess Profits Duty" at extremely high rates; up to its abolition in 1921 EPD accounted for no less than 25% of total revenue. Across the war years the total tax revenue had increased from about £100 million to £800 million. In the mid-nineteenth century it had been less than £30 million.

Income tax had therefore to adapt itself to its new rôle as a steeply progressive impost at high marginal rates. A consistent and equitable system of reliefs and allowances had to be developed, the rules for computing income elaborated, and avoidance countered by appropriate legislation. In 1916 a preliminary step was taken with the introduction of "marginal reliefs". Where relief was available, say, to a man with income of £100 or less, it was clearly unfair that a man with income of £99 should be entitled to full relief and a man with income of £101 to none at all. Justice demanded what the system of marginal reliefs now supplies, namely that the relief should slope off gradually above the limit. A more important preliminary was the consolidation of income tax law in the Income Tax Act 1918 which was the first of three consolidations, the others being the Income Tax Act 1952 and the Income and Corporation Taxes Act 1970 (currently in force).

The Royal Commission of 1920 produced a magisterial set of recommendations covering the whole field of income tax, the implementation of which accounted for a large proportion of the inter-war fiscal legislation. As a result of one of their recommendations, the Income Tax Management Act 1964 eventually deprived the General and Special Commissioners of their administrative functions and placed the Inspectorate at the fulcrum of a revamped administrative structure.

The Second World War produced even more dramatic increases in taxation than had the First. A standard rate of $27\frac{1}{2}\%$ and maximum surtax rate of $41\frac{3}{4}\%$ on incomes over £50,000 in 1939 were replaced as early as 1941 by a standard rate of 50% and a maximum surtax rate of $47\frac{1}{2}\%$ on incomes over £20,000. In the space of two years a top marginal rate of 68·75% on incomes over £50,000 had become 95% on incomes over £20,000. Total tax revenue leapt from under £900 million before the War to over £3,000 million after it. The fiscal exigencies of war included two new taxes—National Defence Contribution introduced by Chamberlain in 1937 and Excess Profits Tax by Simon in 1939. The 1941 increase in rates was accompanied by a reduction in the personal allowances. One of Keynes's ideas (in *How to Pay for the War* Macmillan 1940) was invoked in favour of the hard-pressed taxpayer: any additional income tax due to the reduced personal allowances was to be recorded and credited to the taxpayer for repayment after the War. These "post-war credits" were given also in respect of EPT.

During the War a new indirect tax called "purchase tax", levied on goods and collected at the wholesale stage, was introduced by Sir Kingsley Wood with effect from October 1940. An attractive yield earned the tax a settled place in our system until its replacement by VAT in April 1973. Also a cumulative "Pay As You Earn" scheme (PAYE) had been evolved which took effect from 1944. Employers were required to deduct from emoluments payable to employees whatever amounts would ensure that throughout the tax year deductions matched liability.

In the post-War era the massive problem of reconstruction brought two embryonic developments to maturity. In 1878 a "wear and tear" allowance had been given for depreciation of plant and machinery and in 1897 an administrative concession was made for obsolescence. The Income Tax Act 1945 moulded these into a comprehensive system of "capital allowances" for a wide range of capital expenditure. Since 1954 it has been overlaid by successive schemes for providing investment incentives which have been administered outside the fiscal system (apart from a brief period between 27 October 1970 and 21 March 1972 when no scheme of incentives existed, those dates marking Mr Barber's first and second thoughts on the matter).

Another post-War imperative was to resuscitate the export trade. The UK therefore concluded the first of about seventy double taxation treaties with the US in 1946. The main functions of these treaties are (i) to prevent double taxation either (a) by making certain classes of income taxable in one of the countries only, or (b) by granting a UK resident credit for foreign tax against his UK liability and vice versa; and (ii) to provide reciprocal assistance in the fight against evasion.

The Millard Tucker Committee, though hampered by its terms of reference, made a number of valuable recommendations in its Report in 1951. There followed the unfettered Radcliffe Commission, which produced a long and detailed Report in three instalments in 1953, 1954, and 1955. Many of its recommendations have been implemented.

Radcliffe was an essentially conservative document. However, a minority Report was appended which went virtually unnoticed at the time but has now come into prominence. The minority argued that income was itself an insufficient tax base and that the tax on income needed to be supplemented by both a capital gains tax and a corporation tax. Professor Titmuss's *Income Distribution and Social Change* (Allen & Unwin 1962) supported this thesis. In 1962 Selwyn Lloyd introduced a lightweight tax which, though commonly referred to as "capital gains tax", was in reality a new head of income tax—Case VII of Schedule D—aimed at short-term speculative gains.

Credit for broadening the base of direct taxation and for generating the current climate of radical reform must go to the Labour Government that came to power in 1964. When James Callaghan rose to deliver his Budget speech of 6 April 1965 the system of direct taxation was lopsided. Income was subjected to income tax and surtax, while capital, with two main exceptions, escaped tax altogether. The exceptions were (i) those capital receipts, e.g. lease premiums and the proceeds of sale of patent rights, which had been brought into charge from time to time as if they were income, and (ii) property passing on death, the value of which was liable to estate duty. Company profits were liable to two taxes—income tax and profits tax. The latter was Chamberlain's unpopular war baby, the National Defence Contribution, which in 1946 had been rechristened and confined to companies. Companies were assessed to income tax in the same way as individuals, except that they did not qualify for personal reliefs and were not normally liable to surtax.

Mr Callaghan announced the introduction of a genuine capital gains tax and a corporation tax. Individuals making disposals of assets within a year of acquiring them were to be liable under Case VII of Schedule D ("short-term" capital gains tax), otherwise to the new tax ("long-term" capital gains tax). Case VII was easily evaded and its yield was very low. In 1971 it was abolished. Since then the genuine capital gains tax has applied to all chargeable disposals. Mr Callaghan's system of corporation tax entailed the abolition of profits tax and the exemption of companies from income tax under Schedules A to E. A company was to pay corporation tax on its *total profits*, both income and capital gains, while its distributions were to be subjected also to income tax under the new Schedule F. Distributed profits were thus to be taxed twice.

To curb land speculation Mr Callaghan produced "betterment levy", a 40% charge on the net development value of land realized after 6 April 1967. The full value of land was treated as comprising (1) its value on the assumption that planning permission for development would not be given, its "current use value", and (2) its "development value". Increases in current use value attracted capital gains tax, increases in development value betterment levy. The 1970 Conservative Government wasted little time in abolishing the levy.

Mr Callaghan's reforms made for a much more balanced system of direct taxation. His major contribution to indirect taxation, Selective Employment Tax, introduced in 1966, was much less valuable. The tax was intended to counteract inflation and to encourage labour to move from the service industries into manufacturing. All employers were to bear the tax but those in manufacturing industries would receive it back with a premium. Unfortunately the Standard Industrial Classification was not updated and anomalies abounded. Moreover, some economists have suggested that labour migration into manufacturing may be a dubious virtue; in advanced economies an increase in the proportion of workers in service industries is inevitable.

The year 1964 was a victory of Mr Wilson's white heat of technology over Sir Alec's matchstick shuffling. Change was in the air, even if Mr Callaghan's changes were more radical than had been anticipated. On the other hand the Tories won power in 1970 with no stirring message: disenchantment with Labour left them little to do. It is therefore remarkable that Anthony Barber, the unheralded, second-string Chancellor, should have produced among the most far-reaching fiscal reforms since Pitt and Addington. In his 1971 Budget he announced that purchase tax and SET were to be replaced by VAT, income tax and surtax by a new unified income tax, and Mr Callaghan's system of corporation tax by a new system in which there would be no discrimination against distributed profits. These changes all took effect from April 1973. In his 1972 Budget Mr Barber announced his intention to reform the system of taxing capital on death. This has not yet been put into effect. His 1972 Speech also foreshadowed a revolutionary new tax-credit scheme under which tax is to be combined with social security in a single system and which may well prove as important a fiscal landmark as the introduction of income tax itself.

All money nowadays seems to be produced with a natural homing instinct for the Treasury. *The Duke of Edinburgh.*

1.5 Legislation and administration: the tax machine in motion

'Now, there are three stages in the imposition of a tax', declared Lord Dunedin in *Whitney* v. *IRC* (1925), 'there is the declaration of liability, that is the part of the statute which determines what persons in respect of what property are liable. Next, there is the assessment. Liability does not depend upon assessment. That, *ex hypothesi*, has already been fixed. But assessment particularizes the exact sum which a person liable has to pay. Lastly, come the methods of recovery, if the person taxed does not voluntarily pay' ([1926] A.C. 37 at 52). In this division (1.5) it is intended to present the *dramatis personae* involved in this three-act drama and to explain their interaction and dialogue.

1.51 ACT ONE: THE CHARGE

Someone, at least, has learnt the lesson of 1965. *John Chown* [1971] B.T.R. at 229.

Parliament has developed a unique legislative process for fiscal measures. By long-standing tradition changes in the tax laws are introduced annually in a single piece of legislation called the Finance Act (cited in this book as "F.A.", e.g. F.A. 1965). The task of preparing the contents of each forthcoming Act is assigned to the Treasury, that mysterious enclave of Whitehall's intellectual elite in which: 'It is not done to show enthusiasm for any idea.... The words "there is nothing new under the sun" seem to be written on the walls in invisible ink' (Brittan *Steering the Economy* Penguin 1971 p. 43). How they perform this task is obscure: 'The heart of decision-making remains the most opaque, least penetrable part of the British anatomy; the Treasury men have effectively defied parliament's stethoscopes, cardiograms or X-rays' (Sampson *The New Anatomy of Britain* Hodder & Stoughton 1971 p. 281). The treasury are at the helm of economic and fiscal policy—a relatively small department, yet so influential that the members of the Government are often referred to collectively as "the Treasury Bench". Nominally the heads of the Treasury are the Lords Commissioners: the First Lord of the Treasury (always the Prime Minister), the Chancellor of the Exchequer, and five Junior Lords. In practice, the Lords Commissioners never meet as a board. Their responsibilities are carried out by the Chancellor, assisted by the Chief Secretary to the Treasury, the Financial Secretary, and a Minister of State.

The Chancellor's annual proposals for financing Government expenditure are embodied in the "Budget", an old word meaning a bag containing papers or accounts. They remain a closely guarded secret until the fateful day, usually in late March or early April, when the Chancellor is photographed leaving No. 11 clutching his tattered black box. In it lies the Budget Speech he is to read in an atmosphere of hushed expectancy to an overflowing House of Commons. (Harold Macmillan once likened Budget day to a school prizegiving—'a bit of a bore, but the parents and old boys like it'.) The Speech outlines the proposals against the background of the Government's past and prospective revenue and expenditure. Normally it is the occasion for a general review of economic policy, though the proposals are concerned more with the means of financing expenditure than with expenditure itself. When opening the Budget—at 3.30 p.m.—the Chancellor lays before the House a *Financial Statement and Budget Report* which presents the economic background to the Budget and the transactions of the central Government and public sector as a whole. After the Speech the Budget proposals are embodied in Ways and Means resolutions passed by the House, whereupon they take immediate effect as law. The Budget proposals are reduced to statutory language and become the foundation of the Finance Bill, published a few weeks later. The decision in *Bowles* v. *Bank of England* [1913] 1 Ch. 57, that deductions of tax made between

Budget and Act were unauthorized, neccssitated the Provisional Collection of Taxes Act 1913, which was consolidated in 1968. This imbues each year's Budget resolution with statutory force until the Finance Act is passed, provided that this takes place within about four months. In practice the Finance Act receives the Royal Assent around the end of July each year. The curious result is that proposals having the force of law are subjected to amendment in the Ways and Means debates pending "re-enactment" in the Finance Act. Less curious, perhaps, when one considers that Finance Acts also provide the opportunity for non-Budgetary changes in the tax system and for certain other financial matters, such as provisions relating to Government borrowing.

When the Chancellor finds it expedient during the course of the year to introduce further fiscal proposals, he presents a supplementary "mini-Budget" which usually becomes the Finance (No. 2) Act of that year. Occasionally changes are effected by Acts other than Finance Acts, more often by delegated legislation emanating from either the Treasury or the Department of Trade and Industry in the form of statutory instruments called "Orders". Delegated authority is usually hedged about with strict legislative controls; in particular any Order imposing or increasing a tax invariably requires confirmation by affirmative resolution of the House of Commons.

Income tax and corporation tax are imposed annually and require renewal in each Finance Act. Hence the necessity for an annual Budget around the beginning of each financial year. The other taxes continue from year to year without the necessity for reimposition.

The tradition of secrecy is rooted in the need to prevent taxpayers improperly escaping or taking advantage of impending tax changes, but came to be a blanket rule applied even where this was not possible. Critics argued with increasing cogency that lack of prior consultation with informed opinion outside the Treasury rendered inevitable imperfectly researched and poorly drafted legislation. The Finance Act 1965 provided decisive testimony for their case; this seminal enactment, introducing two entirely new taxes as well as making important amendments to the existing code, was prepared by the Treasury behind closed doors in just a few months. Not surprisingly it bristled with errors both of conception and of execution requiring substantial remedial legislation in later Finance Acts.

Anthony Barber was the first Chancellor to take these criticisms to heart. His changes in the *manner* of introducing major tax reforms are as striking as those he has wrought in the substantive law itself. His announcement of VAT in 1971 was accompanied by the issue of a Green Paper as the basis for detailed discussions which then proceeded with representatives of trade and industry; Customs and Excise officials were despatched to countries operating VATs to obtain the benefit of their experience and insight; draft legislation was presented for public and Parliamentary discussion initially in a White Paper published at the time of the 1972 Budget and later in the Finance Bill; finally the basic VAT legislation was incorporated into the 1972 Act, with effect from April 1973. Next to F.A. 1965 the VAT provisions are a model of clarity. The new system of personal direct taxation which took effect in April 1973 was also announced in the 1971 Budget: implementary legislation was inserted into the Finance Bill 1971 and explained in a White Paper: F.A. 1972 s. 64 specified the rates of unified tax. A Green Paper setting out the alternative systems of corporation tax also accompanied the 1971 Budget announcement of a new corporation tax; on 10 May 1971 the House appointed a Select Committee to consider the Green Paper; it favoured the French "imputation" system, rather than the German "two-rate" system preferred by Mr Barber; in his 1972 Budget he deferred to the Committee's view; legislation was included in F.A. 1972 to take effect from April 1973.

The impending changes are to be brought about in the same open manner. The announcement in his 1972 Budget of a new system of taxing capital on death enabled Mr Barber to present yet another Green Paper to Parliament. Its first paragraph states: 'The Government believe that the time has come for a thorough-going review which should extend to possible alternative forms of death duty. A detailed examination of these alternatives must be carried out before there can be any question of changing and the Government do not intend to reach a decision on such an important matter without a full public discussion of the possibilities.' The 1972 Speech also contained proposals for the new tax-credit system: in October 1972 Mr Barber and Sir Keith Joseph, the social security Minister, presented—yes—a Green Paper to Parliament for examination by a Select Committee. It is expected to take about five years to implement the system.

Apart from its Parliamentary procedure, the most striking feature of revenue law is that, unlike other branches of the law, it is purely the creature of statute, the judicial function being confined to interpretation (*see* 1.7 below). Legislation is the sole source of tax law. Nevertheless attempts to codify tax law have failed and it is dispersed among a wide range of enactments. The legislation on direct taxation is to be found mainly in the annual crop of Finance Acts since 1842, of which, it will be recalled (from p. 17 above), there have been three substantive consolidations—in 1918, in 1952, and in the current Income and Corporation Taxes Act 1970 (hereafter cited as "TA"). Administrative and procedural provisions have been separately consolidated in the Taxes Management Act 1970 (hereafter cited as "TMA"). A self-explanatory consolidation is the Capital Allowances Act 1968, partly recast in F.A. 1971 Pt III. The substantive capital gains tax legislation was not included in the 1970 consolidation, except in relation to the capital gains of companies (which are chargeable not to capital gains tax but to corporation tax). To sum up, the income tax and corporation tax legislation is contained mainly in TA, TMA, and subsequent Finance Acts; the substantive capital gains tax legislation in F.A. 1965 and subsequent Acts; and the adjectival capital gains tax legislation in TMA and subsequent Acts. The legislation on VAT is to be found in F.A. 1972, F.A. 1973, and the already voluminous Regulations made thereunder.

1.52 ACT TWO: ASSESSMENT

While responsibility both for taxation and government expenditure rests with the Treasury, day-to-day administration of the tax system devolves upon two government departments answerable to the Treasury Ministers, namely the Board of Inland Revenue and the Board of Customs and Excise. The Revenue administer the direct taxes and stamp duties; and are responsible for the valuation of real property for such purposes as compensation for compulsory purchase, local rates, and estate duty. The Customs and Excise administer most indirect taxes; and also undertake for other departments a wide range of non-revenue work, such as the compilation of overseas trade statistics. Local rates are administered by local authorities, the larger pursuing an annual financial routine similar to the Budget ritual. Members of both Boards are styled "Commissioners". The Commissioners of Inland Revenue appoint the Inspectors and Collectors of Taxes, who act under their direction.

The functional separation of assessment and collection is a pivotal feature of the Revenue's administrative system. Assessment is the preserve of the Inspectorate, collection that of the Collector. Each Inspector is allocated to one of about 750 "tax districts" or to one of the Head Offices. The principal Head Office is at Somerset House in the Strand. Inspectors in charge of districts enjoy an enviable degree of autonomy. Most are Senior Inspectors. Heading the Inspectorate is a Chief Inspector.

At the beginning of every tax year the Inspector sends to each taxpayer allocated to his district, whether an individual or a company, a form called a "tax return" requiring details of chargeable receipts, to be completed and returned within a certain time, usually thirty days. There is a maximum penalty of £50 for failure to make the return. Even if the Inspector fails to send a return, every chargeable person who has not delivered a return is under an obligation to notify the Inspector of his chargeability, in the case of an individual within one year of the end of the year of assessment for which he is chargeable (TMA s. 7(1)) and in the case of a company within one year of the end of the accounting period for which the company is chargeable (ibid. s. 10(1)). There is a maximum penalty of £100 for failure to do so.

Returns may be required not only of persons chargeable on their own income but also persons such as trustees, personal representatives, agents, banks, and nominees, who are chargeable in a fiduciary capacity in respect of the income of others. Returns of companies must be made by the secretary, those of partnerships by the precedent partners, and those of unincorporated associations by the treasurer or equivalent officer. The income and gains of a married couple are included in a single return unless one of them has elected for separate assessment. In practice companies are not required to complete returns provided they continue to send in their annual accounts and tax computations.

The Inspector examines each taxpayer's completed return. If satisfied, he sends the taxpayer a "notice of assessment" indicating the amount of tax payable. This notice (unlike the return) is a pre-condition of liability. Where the manager of a company in *Berry* v. *Farrow* [1914] 1 K.B. 632 had not actually received the notice of assessment and written demand for payment left for him at the company's registered office, Bankes J. held invalid the Schedule E assessment that had been made on him. If not satisfied, the Inspector may resort to his increasingly wide powers for compelling disclosure of information or the production of books, accounts, or documents relating to taxable transactions. If still not satisfied, he has a trump card—the power under TMA s. 29(1)(*b*) to make an assessment 'to the best of his judgment', i.e. an estimated assessment. By making a deliberate over-estimate the Inspector is able to force the taxpayer to appeal (else year by year the over-estimate becomes wilder) and then the rule prevails that it is for an appellant taxpayer to displace the assessment, not for the Inspector to justify it.

Assessments are often the product of ongoing negotiations during the year between the Inspector and the taxpayer's accountant or other adviser. Employees are usually spared this by the PAYE system. In most cases they simply receive an assessment at the end of each tax year, though the Inspector has power to postpone their assessments or even in routine cases to dispense with them. Any sums over- or under-paid are recovered during the following year by an alteration of the "coding" which each employee is given on the basis of his personal allowances, unless either the Inspector or the employee insists upon immediate payment or repayment.

The Inspector also has power under TMA s. 29(3) to make a further assessment if he discovers that the taxpayer has been undercharged. The meaning of "discovers" in this context was a source of controversy for many years. Conflicting judicial authority was resolved *pro fisco publico* by *Cenlon Finance Co. Ltd* v. *Ellwood*. In that case the appellant company had agreed its Schedule D Case I computations for 1953–54 and 1955–56 with an Inspector on the basis that a dividend payment to the company of £25,000 should be left out of account. In 1956 a new Inspector was appointed who decided, after receiving a memorandum from the Chief Inspector, to raise a further assessment in respect of the £25,000. Their Lordships rejected the company's contention that there had been no discovery. Viscount Simonds could see no reason 'for saying that a discovery of undercharge can only arise where a new fact has been discovered. The words are apt to include any case in which for any reason it newly appears that the taxpayer has been undercharged' ([1962] A.C. 782 at 794).

Whatever the type of assessment, the general rule laid down in TMA s. 34(1) is that it must be made 'not later than six years after the end of the chargeable period to which the assessment relates', which means that an assessment for, say, 1967–68 must be made no later than 5 April 1974. Where, however, there has been "fraud or wilful default" TMA s. 36 authorizes assessments at any time, provided they reach back no further than 1936–37, for the purpose of recovering any loss of tax attributable to the fraud or wilful default. There is also a complicated procedure set out in TMA ss. 37 and 39 for extending the general time limit in cases of "neglect". Before he can use s. 36, 37, or 39, an Inspector must satisfy a General or Special Commissioner that there are reasonable grounds for believing that tax has been lost to the fisc by fraud, wilful default, or neglect. In giving leave the Commissioner is not required to give the taxpayer an opportunity to be heard: *Pearlberg* v. *Varty* [1972] 2 A.E.R. 6. Apart from these sections, a diversity of other provisions allow out-of-time assessments in special circumstances. Conversely, in several situations the time limit is cut down. In particular, assessments on the personal representatives of a deceased person in respect of income or gains arising before the date of death must be made no later than the end of the third year of assessment after that in which the death occurred (TMA s. 40(1)).

In the converse case of an excessive assessment by reason of "some error or mistake" in the taxpayer's return, he is given what looks like a corresponding right by TMA s. 33 to make a claim to the Board for relief no later than six years after the end of the chargeable period to which the assessment relates. The Board is bound to inquire into the matter and give such relief as is reasonable and just. If they refuse his claim, the taxpayer may give written notice of appeal to the Special Commissioners within thirty days. From them the usual right of appeal lies to the Courts of law under TMA s. 56. In practice s. 33 is a cardboard castle sheltering very few claims. For two reasons. One is that the Board can give no relief where the return was made 'in accordance with the practice generally prevailing at the time when the return was made' (s. 33 (2) proviso). The other, shades of *Catch 22*, is that the right of appeal offered in one hand by s. 56 is effectively withdrawn by the other in so far as it is restricted under s. 33(4) to 'a point of law arising in connection with the computation of profits'. Almost invariably, of course, the error or mistake is one of fact. More solid, though less ambitious, is TMA s. 32, which requires the Board to remit the overcharge in cases where the taxpayer has been assessed twice in respect of the same receipt.

'Income tax returns,' Herman Wouk has written, 'are the most imaginative fiction being written today.' If that is so, it is a comfort to know that the Revenue are far from helpless. Where they find that a taxpayer has failed to disclose taxable income or claimed allowances or reliefs to which he was not entitled, they may decide to treat his as a "back duty" case (for a lively example, *see Rose* v. *Humbles* [1972] 1 W.L.R. 33). Modest sums are dealt with by the Inspector, large amounts by the Inquiry Branch of the Inland Revenue.

Criminal prosecution is rare: in 1971–72 the Revenue instituted only 195 prosecutions, including 2 assaults on Revenue officers, of which there were 14 acquittals. Civil penalties are much more often involved, especially TMA s. 95, under which a person who negligently or fraudulently delivers an incorrect return is liable to a maximum penalty of £50 plus an amount equal to the tax lost if through negligence and twice the tax lost in the case of fraud. There is also a maximum penalty of £500 under TMA s. 99 for knowingly assisting in the making of an incorrect tax return. Overdue tax bears interest at the rate of 4% from the date when it first fell due (TMA ss. 88, 89). In the year ended 31 March 1972 the Revenue raised £13,281,870 in respect of under-assessments, of which £4,300,445 represented penalties and £2,332,069 of the amount of penalties represented interest.

The Commissioners sometimes mitigate or entirely remit a civil fine on penalty on the payment of interest, a practice which received judicial approval in *Att.-Gen.* v. *Johnstone* (1926) 10 T.C. 758. In minor cases the Inspector is

c

empowered to settle the case. He normally invites the taxpayer and his adviser to his office to discuss a settlement. A settlement is reached in this way in all but about 1% of cases (for reasons explained at p. 29 below).

1.53 ACT THREE: COLLECTION

Once he has arrived at his assessment, the Inspector brings up the final curtain by transmitting to the appropriate Collector particulars of the sums to be collected. There are about 250 local collection offices, each in the charge of a Chief Collector, assisted as necessary by Collectors and other staff. Heading the collection service is the Accountant and Comptroller General, internally known as the "A and C G". On receipt of the particulars, the Collector is *ipso facto* authorized to make the collection. His first duty is laid down by TMA s. 60(1): 'Every collector shall, when the tax becomes due and payable, make demand of the respective sums given to him in charge to collect, from the persons charged therewith . . .' If the demand is complied with, the Collector must if requested issue a receipt. If not, he presses on to the tragic dénouement of the drama—recovery.

The Collector has a daunting array of remedies at his disposal. In England and Wales, provided he has made a demand, the Collector may distrain upon the taxpayer's property under TMA s. 61. The distress once levied must be kept by him for five days, at the expense of the person neglecting or refusing to pay, before it is sold. To the extent that the proceeds of sale exceed the sum due and costs they are paid over to the defaulter. Alternatively, the Collector may institute civil proceedings either in the High Court (if the sum to be recovered exceeds £750), in the County Court (if it is £750 or less), or even in the Magistrates' Court (if it is less than £50). There are corresponding provisions as to remedies for Scotland and Northern Ireland.

The Collector's task is greatly simplified by the system of deduction at source in which the person making the deduction acts in effect as the Revenue's collecting agent. The system applies to a wide range of payments, including emoluments paid to an employee, which are governed of course by PAYE.

Any income tax, capital gains tax, or corporation tax paid more than two months after the due date for payment bears interest at the rate of 6% from the due date up to the date of payment (TMA ss. 86, 89). (*Cf.* "back duty" interest p. 27 above.)

How small, of all that human hearts endure,
That part which judges' laws can cause or cure.

[With apologies to] *Dr Johnson.*

1.6 The slippery slope of fiscal litigation

A taxpayer unhappy with his assessment to income tax, capital gains tax, or corporation tax may appeal against it by notice in writing to the Inspector within thirty days. The notice must specify the grounds of appeal which in practice are usually recited in very general terms. Most appeals are settled by agreement: the reason is not so much the Inspectorate's exceptional pacifism as the common knowledge that the game of litigation is played with loaded dice. Apart from the one-sided rules, the power balance is uneven: the Revenue have access to the bottomless public purse and, since their prize is not merely the appellant's tax but that of all persons similarly placed, a much keener appetite for further litigation. The Commissioners have no power to make an award as to costs; but in the Court of Appeal and the House of Lords the general practice is to award costs to a successful appellant "here and below". Only in the strongest cases will the disputed tax saving seem to justify the risk of potential legal costs (although, in cases where the principle involved far outweighs the amount of tax at stake, the Revenue sometimes undertake—or are ordered by the Court—to pay both parties' costs of appeal).

The General and Special Commissioners are two discrete appellate bodies which enjoy parity of status. Within certain statutory limits the choice between them lies with the taxpayer. The General Commissioners are unpaid local laymen who sit in a quorum of two with jurisdiction over one of the 700 or so "divisions". They are appointed in England and Wales by the Lord Chancellor on the advice of local committees and in Scotland by the local authority for that division; and in turn themselves appoint a Clerk, usually a solicitor, to assist them in much the same way that the Clerk to a Magistrates' Court assists the lay justices. By contrast the Special Commissioners are full-time salaried civil servants appointed by the Treasury. They are usually barristers or solicitors with extensive experience of tax law gained either in practice or with the Inland Revenue. The recent practice has been for them to sit alone.

The choice is therefore essentially between local knowledge and technical expertise. An appeal to the heart would do better before the General Commissioners, an appeal to the head before the Special Commissioners. In Northern Ireland, where there are no General Commissioners, the choice lies between the County Court—the judge sitting alone and in private—and the Special Commissioners.

The Clerk notifies both appellant and Inspector of the time and place of the hearing. The Revenue are usually represented by the Inspector, sometimes in difficult cases by someone from their Solicitor's Office, rarely by counsel. The taxpayer is free to conduct his own case or, if he prefers, to be represented by his accountant, solicitor, or barrister. If the case is likely to reach the Courts of law he should brief counsel from the outset. Where the taxpayer cannot attend in person, the Commissioners may allow him to be represented by an agent.

The hearing itself is informal. There are no pleadings or rules of procedure. One evidential norm pervades the proceedings—it is for the taxpayer to discharge the assessment, not for the Crown to affirm it. The Commissioners have power to summon witnesses to be examined under oath and to require any party to the proceedings other than the Revenue to deliver up relevant information or documents, which any officer of the Board may inspect and take copies of. They may also allow a ground of appeal to be argued which was not specified in the original notice of appeal if satisfied that the omission was not wilful or unreasonable. Where the issue is factual the parties will call evidence in the usual way, where legal the parties often settle between them a statement of agreed facts to be read and handed to the Commissioners. TMA s. 54 allow the parties to settle an appeal: any agreement as to the tax due operates as a formal determination of the appeal by the Commissioners at the time when the agreement was made. The taxpayer is given thirty days in which to repudiate the agreement if he has second thoughts. TA s. 54 provided us with a postscript to the decision in *Cenlon Finance Co. Ltd* v. *Ellwood,* which was discussed earlier at p. 26. The additional assessment in that case was held bad because the correspondence between the company's accountants and the original Inspector spelled out an agreement within s. 54. Curiously enough, apart from s. 54, there is no procedural machinery for withdrawing an appeal from the Commissioners once it has been set in motion.

The Commissioners are not bound to follow their own previous decisions. They may confirm, reduce, or increase the assessment. Once embodied in a formal order, their determination is final and can be altered only by order of the Court. Where the Commissioners are less than unanimous the majority decision prevails or, where only two sit, that of the senior Commissioner.

Further appeals lie to the Courts of law. 'Immediately after the determination of an appeal by the Commissioners,' states the tax code, 'the appellant or the Inspector or other officer of the Board, if dissatisfied with the determination as being erroneous in point of law, may declare his dissatisfaction to the Commissioners who heard the appeal' (TMA s. 56(1)) and 'may, within thirty days after the determination, by notice in writing addressed to the Clerk to the Commissioners, require the Commissioners to state and sign a case for the opinion of the High Court thereon' (ibid. s. 56(2)).

● Immediate notice of dissatisfaction was held in *R. v. H.M. Inspector of Taxes, ex parte Clarke* [1972] 1 A.E.R. 545 to be a directory and not a mandatory requirement, so that if the Commissioners decide to state a case in the absence of any, or any immediate, expression of dissatisfaction the Court has no right to prevent them.

The appeal must be on a point of law: the Commissioners are final arbiters of fact. Like all basic conceptions, however, fact and law have blurred edges; and at one time judicial formulations served if anything merely to broaden the penumbra of uncertainty surrounding their borderline. There was no dispute as to the Commissioners' exclusive right to determine the "primary" facts—whether so-and-so was born in the UK, whether or when such-and-such happened, etc—but almost invariably the determination required them to draw inferences from those primary facts. It was in characterizing these inferences that the judges tended to Babel. The reign of confusion came to an end in 1955 with a careful explication of principle by Lord Radcliffe in *Edwards* v. *Bairstow and Harrison*:

> 'When the Case comes before the court, it is its duty to examine the determination having regard to its knowledge of the relevant law. If the Case contains anything *ex facie* which is bad law and which bears on the determination, it is, obviously, erroneous in point of law. But, without any such misconception appearing *ex facie*, it may be that the facts found are such that no person acting judicially and properly instructed as to the relevant law could have come to the determination under appeal. In those circumstances, too, the court must intervene. It has no option but to assume that there has been some misconception of the law . . . I do not think that it much matters whether this state of affairs is described as one in which there is no evidence to support the determination, or as one in which the evidence is inconsistent with, and contradictory of, the determination, or as one in which the true and only reasonable conclusion contradicts the determination. Rightly understood, each phrase propounds the same test' ([1956] A.C. 14 at 35).

In England and Wales the appeal comes before the Revenue Judge in the Chancery Division. He may consent to an agreement to dismiss the appeal but not, if Megarry J.'s decision in *Slaney* v. *Kean* [1970] Ch. 243 is correct, to an agreement to allow it. From the Revenue Judge appeal lies to the Court of Appeal. Alternatively an appeal may now be taken on a point of law of general public importance direct to the House of Lords under the Administration of Justice Act 1969 ss. 12–16. The system of revenue appeals is less elaborate in Scotland and Northern Ireland, as indicated by the diagram opposite.

The ordinary rules of precedent apply to tax cases. Decisions of the House of Lords bind the inferior Courts in all three jurisdictions but decisions of the inferior Courts of one jurisdiction are of merely persuasive authority in the Courts of the others. Tax cases are reported in the official *Law Reports* and also in several special series, in particular the Board of Inland Revenue's *Reports of Tax Cases* (cited at "T.C.") and the admirable new series called *Simon's Tax Cases* (cited as "S.T.C."). The Courts appear to regard the *Law Reports* as more authoritative: *see* [1923] A.C. 74 at 78–9 and [1970] 1 W.L.R. 1400.

● A similar system of local tribunals has been established to deal with VAT appeals under the direction of the President of VAT Tribunals, Mr K. Suenson-Taylor QC. Each tribunal comprises a chairman sitting either alone or with one or two other members. The chairman has a casting vote. The chairmen are selected from one of the three panels of chairmen covering each of the three UK jurisdictions. Each panel includes at least one full-time paid chairman and one such chairman on each panel is given the title of Vice-President of VAT Tribunals. The President may himself sit as a chairman if he wishes. Tribunal members are similarly selected from one of the three panels of members. Further appeals lie on points of law to the Queen's Bench Divisional Court, the Court of Appeal and the House of Lords.

Laws are spider webs that catch little flies, but cannot hold big ones. *Honoré de Balzac.*

1.7 Interpretation of tax statutes: real rules and paper rules

Awareness is growing that construing statutory provisions is a creative, not a mechanical function. The settled rules are few; most of these are open-ended, some even contradictory. The author proposes in this division (1.7) to summarize the expressed legal norms before attempting an examination of the judiciary's value bias, i.e. its political and ethical assumptions. The latter, he believes, represents the more revealing line of inquiry.

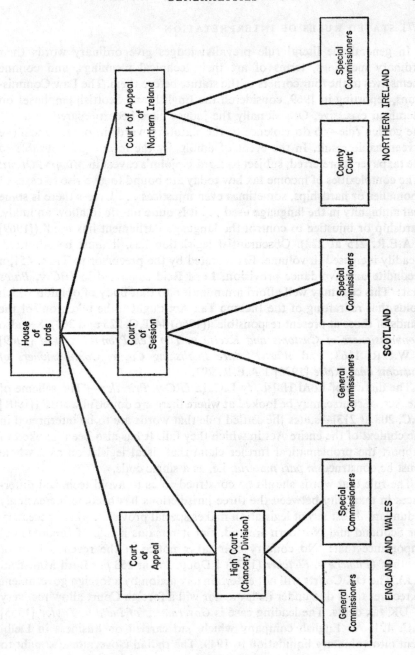

The system of revenue appeals

1.71 STATED RULES OF INTERPRETATION

In general the literal rule prevails: judges give ordinary words their ordinary meanings, terms of art their technical meanings, and confine themselves to the four corners of the statute before them. The Law Commissions, reporting in 1969, considered the English and Scottish emphases on literalism excessive. Occasionally the judges have been prepared to apply the golden rule—to do violence to the statutory words in order to achieve a reasonable result. In the event of ambiguity the meaning favourable to the taxpayer is preferred, subject to Lord Upjohn's caveat in *Mapp* v. *Oram*: 'The complexities of income tax law today are bound to give rise to cases of anomalies or hardships, sometimes even injustices . . . Unless there is some real ambiguity in the language used . . . it is quite unsafe to allow anomaly, hardship or injustice to control the language Parliament has used' ([1969] 3 A.E.R. 215 at 222). Obscurantist legislation has, it must be admitted, steadily increased in volume. Exasperated by the precursor to TA s. 451, a recondite anti-avoidance provision, Lord Reid suggested in *IRC* v. *Bates* that: 'This case may well afford ammunition to that body of opinion which holds that redrafting of the Income Tax Act ought to be taken out of the hands of those at present responsible' ((1966) 44 T.C. 225 and 263). See also *Commissioners of Customs and Excise* v. *Top Ten Promotions Ltd* [1969] 1 W.L.R. 1163; and *Warwickshire Publishing Co.* v. *Commissioners of Customs and Excise* [1970] 1 A.E.R. 291.

The dictum of Lord Halsbury L.C. in *IRC* v. *Priestley*—'The scheme of the Act, of course, may be looked at where there are doubtful words' ([1901] A.C. 208 at 213)—states the settled rule that words are to be interpreted in the context of the entire Act in which they fall. It has also been invoked to support the problematical further claim that fiscal legislation as a whole must be construed *in pari materia*, i.e. as a single code.

The rule that words should be construed so as to avoid technical differences in taxability between the three jurisdictions has become increasingly redundant. Most recent legislation makes special provision where necessary for Scotland and Northern Ireland. But it remains a rule of fundamental importance that: 'No country ever takes notice of the revenue laws of another' (*Planché* v. *Fletcher* (1779) 1 Doug. 251 at 253 *per* Lord Mansfield C.J.). The UK Courts will not entertain any action by a foreign government to recover taxes due under its laws, nor will a foreign Court allow recovery of UK tax debts. The leading case is *Government of India* v. *Taylor* [1955] A.C. 491. An English company which had carried on business in Delhi went into voluntary liquidation in 1949. The Indian Government sought to prove in the liquidation for tax alleged to be due from the company. Taylor, the liquidator, rejected the claim. The Government's appeals to the UK courts were firmly and unanimously dismissed by Vaisey J., the Court of Appeal, and the Lords.

In a statute introducing some new charge to tax, the provisions which impose the tax—the "charging" sections—are usually separated from those in which the rules for computing and collecting it are specified—the "machinery" sections. It is said that the Courts will not construe a machinery provision so as to defeat the charge: see, for example, *IRC* v. *Longmans Green & Co. Ltd* (1932) 17 T.C. 272 at 282. Where the efficacy of a charging provision is in doubt, however, the absence of machinery may be a material factor: see *Colquhoun* v. *Brooks* (1889) 14 App. Cas. 493 at 506.

Two final points. The usual presumptions apply to tax legislation, as does the rule that they yield to clear contrary language: a good illustration is the cheeky appeal in *Cheney* v. *Conn* [1968] 1 A.E.R. 779. Any attempt to recover tax paid in virtue of an interpretation of the law which is later seen to be incorrect will be frustrated by the general principle barring recoupment of payments made under mistake of law.

1.72 TAX AVOIDANCE: PLAYING WITH FIRE?

The judges' value bias is highlighted when they find themselves confronted with persons who coyly resist the unwelcome attentions of the Revenue. Resistance is of two kinds. The one, tax evasion, involves illegality and the judges have always abhorred it; but the other, tax avoidance, is, to borrow Professor Wheatcroft's aphorism, 'the art of dodging tax without actually breaking the law' ([1955] 18 M.L.R. 209), and has elicited widely discrepant responses from the bench.

The traditional approach, distilled from the literal rule, was formalistic. 'As I understand the principle of all fiscal legislation,' declared Lord Cairns in *Partington* v. *Att.-Gen.*, 'it is this: If the person sought to be taxed comes within the letter of the law he must be taxed, however great the hardship may appear to the judicial mind to be. On the other hand, if the Crown, seeking to recover the tax, cannot bring the subject within the letter of the law, the subject is free, however apparently within the spirit of the law the case might otherwise appear to be' ((1869) L.R. 4 H.L. 100 at 122). Rowlatt J., a masterly Revenue Judge, gave this approach its classic expression: 'In a taxing Act one has to look merely at what is clearly said. There is no room for any intendment. There is no equity about a tax. There is no presumption as to a tax. Nothing is to be read in, nothing is to be implied. One can only look fairly at the language used' (*Cape Brandy Syndicate* v. *IRC* [1921] 1 K.B. 64 at 71). One of the underlying assumptions was laid bare by Lord Clyde L.P. in *Ayrshire Pullman Motor Services* v. *IRC*: 'No man in this country is under the smallest obligation, moral or other, so to arrange his legal relations to his business or to his property as to enable the Inland Revenue to put the largest possible shovel into his stores' ((1929) 14 T.C. 754 at 763).

Understandably the advent of war caused judicial sympathies to shift dramatically from taxpayer to fisc. In 1941 Lord Greene M.R. issued a stern warning to would-be avoiders: 'For years a battle of manœuvre has been waged between the legislature and those who are minded to throw the burden of taxation off their own shoulders on to those of their fellow subjects. In that battle the legislature has often been worsted by the skill, determination and resourcefulness of its opponents of whom the present appellant has not been the least successful. It would not shock us in the least to find that the legislature has determined to put an end to the struggle by imposing the severest of penalties. It scarcely lies in the mouth of the taxpayer who plays with fire to complain of burnt fingers' (*Lord Howard de Walden* v. *IRC* [1942] 1 K.B. 389 at 397). Patriotism demanded a new morality: avoiders, explained Viscount Simon L.C. in *Latilla* v. *IRC*, may be 'within their legal rights, but that is no reason why their efforts, or those of the professional gentlemen who assist them in the matter, should be regarded as a commendable exercise of ingenuity or as a discharge of the duties of good citizenship' ([1943] A.C. 377 at 381).

After the war the pendulum swung back sharply. '[T]he nineteen-fifties were marked by a positive boom in the tax-avoidance industry. Dividends were "stripped", bonds were "washed" and a whole host of other avoidance transactions, of varying degrees of complexity, were carried out' (M. C. Flesch [1968] C.L.P. 215 at 223). The next turning point was perhaps *Griffiths* v. *J. P. Harrison* (*Watford*) *Ltd* [1963] A.C. 1. Though their Lordships in that case upheld a dividend-stripping operation, it was a bare majority decision and our greatest living judge, Lord Denning, delivered a portentous dissent in which he spoke of the avoiders with curled lip as 'prospectors digging for wealth in the subterranean passages of the Revenue, searching for tax repayments' (ibid. at 22).

Since then the avoider has been viewed with increasing antipathy. Lord Denning appears to have assumed his predecessor's mantle in a crusade against avoidance that owes more to moral fervour than to reason. For instance, in the Court of Appeal in *Commissioners of Customs and Excise* v. *Top Ten Promotions Ltd* he emoted: 'The people who ran these three companies were playing with fire. It scarcely lies in their mouths to complain of burnt fingers. No sympathy need be wasted on them' ([1969] 3 A.E.R. 39 at 68). An extraordinary reaction, one might think, in a case in which £10 million was involved and the relevant provision so widely and so ineptly drafted that on appeal two members of the House of Lords felt inclined to hold it meaningless. Fellow crusaders seem to display the same disregard for cool rational appraisal. Stamp J., for example, felt able in *Re Weston's Settlements* to distinguish 'a cheap exercise in tax avoidance' from 'a legitimate avoidance of liability to taxation' ([1968] 1 A.E.R. 720 at 725).

1.73 A DEMARCATION DISPUTE: WHOSE JOB IS IT TO FILL GAPS?

Lord Denning's crusade is made more effective by his resort to two heterodoxies. The first is well known. He has stubbornly refused to dispense with the heresy he professed—with characteristic boldness and clarity—in *Seaford Court Estates Ltd* v. *Asher*: 'When a defect appears a judge cannot simply fold his hands and blame the draftsman. He must set to work on the constructive task of finding the intention of Parliament, and he must do this not only from the language of the statute, but also from a consideration of the special conditions which gave rise to it and of the mischief which it was passed to remedy ... A judge should ask himself the question how, if the makers of the Act had themselves come across this ruck in the texture of it, they would have straightened it out? He must then do as they would have done. A judge must not alter the material of which the Act is woven, but he can and should iron out the creases' ([1940] 2 A.E.R. 155 at 164). He reiterated these views a few years later in the Court of Appeal in *Magor and St Mellons R.D.C.* v. *Newport Corporation* (1951), only to be sternly taken to task on appeal by a unanimous House of Lords. Lord Simonds described the Denning approach as 'a naked usurpation of the legislative function' ([1952] A.C. 189 at 191). 'If a gap is disclosed,' he insisted, 'the remedy lies in an amending Act' (ibid.). Unabashed, Lord Denning has returned to ironing out creases, straightening rucks, and filling gaps in a number of recent cases. He has been an equally resolute proponent of the second heterodoxy.

1.74 THE DOCTRINE OF "THE SUBSTANCE": NOT METAPHYSICS BUT ETHICS

Recurrent judicial dicta in the early cases were widely misinterpreted as suggesting that in revenue matters the substance of a transaction prevailed over its legal form. In *IRC* v. *The Duke of Westminster* (1935) the Duke had executed a series of seven-year deeds of covenant in favour of his employees under which the covenantees received the same amounts they would respectively have received as wages or salary, on the understanding that no employee would claim for his wages or salary whilst receiving payment under his deed. The rationale of the scheme was to mitigate the Duke's liability to surtax: the covenanted payments would rank as annual payments within Case III of Schedule D and as such could be deducted from the Duke's total income for surtax purposes. Their Lordships rejected the Revenue contention that the payments were in substance remuneration for services rendered to the Duke. 'This supposed doctrine . . .', said Lord Tomlin, 'seems to rest for its support upon a misunderstanding of language used in some earlier cases. The sooner this misunderstanding is dispelled, and the supposed doctrine given its quietus, the better it will be for all concerned' ([1936] A.C. 1 at 19).

It has often been mistakenly inferred that the Duke of Westminster's case destroyed the doctrine of "the substance" altogether. The better view seems to be that it merely refuted the broad suggestion which heads the preceding paragraph. A number of settled rules collectively constitute the modern version of the doctrine. One is that descriptions attached to a transaction by the parties to it are not decisive of its true nature: *see Secretary of State in Council of India* v. *Scoble* [1903] A.C. 299. A second is that rights and liabilities created by "sham" transactions are to be utterly disregarded: a case in point is *Johnson* v. *Jewitt*, in which a flagrant attempt to create an artificial tax loss was rejected by the Court of Appeal as 'a cheap exercise in fiscal conjuring and book-keeping phantasy' ((1961) 40 T.C. 231 at 253, *per* Donovan L.J.). A third is that, while rights and liabilities created by *genuine* transactions cannot be disregarded, the surrounding circumstances may help in determining what those rights and liabilities are: *see IRC* v. *Horrocks* (1968) 44 T.C. 645; and *Sargaison* v. *Roberts* (1969) 45 T.C. 612.

Lord Denning has recently attempted in effect to resurrect the doctrine of "the substance" in its broad form. In 1962 he refused in a dissenting judgment in *Morgan* v. *IRC* to acknowledge the validity of a "trust-grafting" operation. 'What does this come to?' he rhetorized. 'It means that, in order to avoid estate duty, the lawyer turns magician . . . It makes me rub my eyes. I cannot believe it is true. Those near me acclaim the feat. But I do not . . . Pull the covering aside and you will see it as it really is' ([1963] Ch. 438 at 458). A few years later in *Re Kirkwood* his Lordship refused also to uphold a deed of variation executed by a beneficiary under trusts with the object of saving estate duty on the death of his mother: 'By this sleight of hand, he has avoided estate duty on one-quarter of a million pounds. It is too good to be true. So good that I do not believe it is true' ([1965] Ch. 286 at 316). Russell L.J. concurred in the result but preferred to let sleeping doctrines lie: 'It is not right to label something a "device" and then strain to see that it fails' (ibid. at 327). The same contrast of approach is apparent between Lord Denning's judgment in *Littlewoods Mail Order Stores Ltd* v. *McGregor* (1969) 45 T.C. 519 at 536 and that of Buckley J. in *Fundfarms Developments Ltd.* v. *Parsons* (1969) 45 T.C. 707 at 721.

If Lord Denning is out of step, it has to be conceded that he is not the only one. In 1964 Harman L.J. caused a stir when he declared that: 'Accountants are the witch-doctors of the modern world and willing to turn their hands to any kind of magic.' In 1967 that learned judge sat in the Court of Appeal to unravel the complicated arrangement in *Campbell* v. *IRC* (*see* p. 143–4 below) whereby the directors and shareholders of a tutorial business hoped to minimize their liability to tax. He began his judgement by asserting that '[t]here are occasions, even in revenue cases, when what one comes to look for is substance and not form' ([1967]) Ch. 651 at 669), proceeded to describe the arrangement as a 'plan which smells a little of the lamp' (ibid. at 669), and concluded: 'It is a splendid scheme . . . almost too good to be true. In law quite too good to be true. It won't do' (ibid. at 670).

Before evaluating the crusade, a quick look at the other battle front.

1.75 PARLIAMENTARY STYLES IN ANTI-AVOIDANCE LEGISLATION

The tradition of literalism has given rise year by year to what Lord Morton once called a "game of chess" ([1954] A.C. at 468) between Parliament and taxpayers' advisers. Parliament imposes a charge, the advisers find ways to avoid it; Parliament enacts specific anti-avoidance legislation, the advisers devise more elaborate avoidance techniques; and so it goes on. It becomes tempting to widen the scope of anti-avoidance measures—with only one shot a year, a shotgun seems more useful than a rifle. In 1960 Mr Amory succumbed to this temptation and introduced the three widest anti-avoidance provisions in our code, including the notorious F.A. 1960 s. 28 (now TA s. 460) designed to nullify any tax advantage obtained in consequence of a transaction in securities. They have not worked satisfactorily. The danger of a shotgun is that it may hit innocent bystanders as well as its intended victims. S. 28, for example, was designed to cover artificial transactions but has worked injustice by disrupting the *bona fide* as well.

Some countries, Australia, Canada, and South Africa among them, have delivered checkmate in the form of legislation against *any* scheme designed primarily to secure tax advantage. Their experiences have not, it seems, been altogether salutary. The Radcliffe Commission felt that abandonment of our present system of detailed legislative control in favour of some general statement of principle would only cause harmful confusion; and their view seems to have been vindicated empirically.

1.76 CONCLUSION

Lord Denning is renowned for his dissenting opinions; he once told a group of students that he preferred sitting as Master of the Rolls than as a Law Lord because 'decisions in the Court of Appeal are two against one, not four against one'. His views, if initially rejected, have the disturbing habit of incubating for a period and then emerging as acceptable, eventually as settled, doctrine. He is a delight to some, an exasperation to others. The author of this book is one of his admirers, but nevertheless feels strongly that Lord Denning's crusade against the avoider is ill-conceived. For once his Lordship has neither his heart nor his head in the right place. The crusade should be seen as it really is: an attempt to undermine the fundamental principle of our constitution—Parliamentary supremacy. It is for Parliament to levy tax, for Parliament to reduce or abolish it, for Parliament to set up machinery for its assessment and collection. Equally it is for Parliamet to wage the battle against avoidance. The judges' duty is to see that the rules of battle are observed on both sides, not to hand to one side weapons it had the power but chose not to use itself. Lord Normand saw this clearly in 1959 when he warned: 'Tax avoidance is an evil, but it would be the beginning of much greater evils if the courts were to overstretch the language of the statute in order to subject to taxation people of whom they disapproved' (*Vestey's Executors* v. *IRC* (1949) 31 T.C. 1 at 90). Lord Hailsham L.C. was making the same point when, in 1972, he denied the judges' right 'to form first a judgment on the fairness of an Act of Parliament and then to amend or supplement it with new provisions so as to make it conform to that judgment' (*Pearlberg* v. *Varty* [1972] 2 A.E.R. 6 at 11).

1.8 Residence and domicile

A resident of the UK is liable to income tax on his income from every source, home and abroad, while a non-resident is liable only on income arising from a source within the UK. A person resident here but domiciled abroad is charged on a "remittance" basis, not on the usual "arising" basis, which

" 'An individual is resident and ordinarily resident in the United Kingdom if he is living in the ordinary course of his life, or for an extended period; also though normally he lives here, if he is abroad for occasional residence only; or if he visits the United Kingdom, year by year, even though his main home is abroad' . . . who on earth wrote this, Harold Pinter?' "

means that he pays tax on income arising abroad only to the extent that it is remitted to the UK. It follows that a non-resident is not liable to UK tax on income arising abroad.

Capital gains tax is charged on a person "resident *or* ordinarily resident" in the UK on the disposal of assets, wherever located. A person resident or ordinarily resident here but domiciled abroad is chargeable on gains from disposals of foreign assets only when, and to the extent that, those gains are received in the UK. A non-resident is liable only on the disposal of assets situated in the UK which have been used for the purposes of a trade carried on by him in this country through a branch or agency.

A company resident in the UK is liable to corporation tax on its total profits, both income and capital gains, wherever these arise. A company not resident in the UK is not chargeable to corporation tax unless it carries on a trade in the UK through a branch or agency. If it does, the charge is limited to (*a*) income accruing to the branch or agency, and (*b*) gains realized on the disposal of assets in the UK.

Clearly "residence", "ordinary residence", and "domicile" are core concepts. Yet nowhere are they defined in the tax legislation. The only statutory indications as to their meanings are TA ss. 49–51 (individuals), 153 (partnerships), 482 (companies), and F.A. 1965 ss. 25(1) (trusts) and 24(6) (personal representatives) which are of limited scope.

TA s. 49 provides that a British subject or citizen of the Irish Republic who has been ordinarily resident in the UK does not lose his status as a resident merely by leaving the UK for the purpose of occasional residence abroad. (On the meaning of "occasional residence" it is instructive to contrast *Levene* v. *IRC* [1928] A.C. 217 with *IRC* v. *Combe* (1932) 17 T.C. 405.) TA s. 50 requires the question of the residence of any person working full-time abroad to be decided without regard to any place of abode maintained in the UK for his use, provided that two conditions are satisfied:

(1) all his duties must be peformed outside the UK; and
(2) any duties performed in the UK must be merely incidental to the performance of other duties outside the UK.

Thus in *Robson* v. *Dixon* [1972] 1 W.L.R. 1493 a KLM pilot who maintained a house in the UK for his wife and children as well as a flat in Amsterdam was held resident in the UK despite only thirty-eight landings in the UK over six years. The landings, Pennycuick V-C held, were not merely incidental to his other duties. (At one time having a place of abode here was the decisive factor: *Re Young* (1875) 1 T.C. 57 and *Rogers* v. *IRC* (1879) 1 T.C. 225.) TA s. 51 lays down both (*a*) the rule that a visitor is to be regarded as resident for any tax year if he has spent during that year a total of six months or more in the UK, and (*b*) its corollary that he is not to be regarded as resident for any year in which he has spent less than six months here. A visitor is someone who is in the UK for some temporary purpose only and who has no intention of taking up residence here.

● TA s. 482(7) contains the important basic rule governing the residence of companies: 'A body corporate shall be deemed . . . to be resident or not to be resident in the United Kingdom according as the central management and control of its trade or business is or is not exercised in the United Kingdom.' S. 482 as a whole is designed to make it unlawful for a UK company to become non-resident or to transfer any part of its trade or business to a non-resident company without the prior consent of the Treasury. The section imposes heavy criminal penalties on any person, individual or corporate, who fails to comply.

TA s. 153 extends the same criterion to partnerships. By sub-s. (1), where a trade or business is carried on by a partnership and the control and management is situated abroad, the partnership is deemed to be resident abroad, even though some of the partners may be resident in the UK and some of the trading operations carried on here. TA s. 155(6) qualifies this rule where one of the partners is a company resident in the UK. It provides that, *as regards that company*, the partnership is deemed to be resident in the UK.

Under F.A. 1965 s. 25(1), which unfortunately is limited to capital gains tax, the trustees of a settlement are to be treated as a single and continuing body of persons which is resident and ordinarily resident in the UK unless (i) the general administration of the trusts is ordinarily carried on outside the UK and (ii) a majority of the trustees are neither resident nor ordinarily resident in the UK. F.A. 1965 s. 24(6), also limited to capital gains tax, provides that personal representatives should be treated as a single continuous body of persons having the deceased's residence or ordinary residence, and domicile at the date of death.

The decided cases contribute little to fill the yawning statutory silences. The entailment of *IRC* v. *Lysaght* [1928] A.C. 234, in which the House of Lords decided that "residence" and "ordinary residence" are questions of fact, is that the residence cases must be treated as illustrations rather than precedents except for the few in which the Commissioners were reversed on appeal. Moreover, there are no reported cases at all on such important questions as the residence of unincorporated associations, of trustees, and of personal representatives.

Although some judges have felt unable to differentiate ordinary residence from residence, the Act does trade on some kind of distinction between the two concepts. The better view seems to be that ordinary residence is the narrower concept, i.e. it is a sub-set of residence. In *Levene* v. *IRC* Lord Warrington defined "ordinarily resident" as meaning 'according to the way in which a man's life is usually ordered' ([1928] A.C. 217 at 232) and in *Lysaght* Viscount Sumner thought that 'the converse to "ordinarily" is "extraordinarily" and that part of the regular order of a man's life, adopted voluntarily and for settled purposes, is not "extraordinarily"' ([1928] A.C. at 243). The concept of ordinary residence therefore implies an element of continuity absent from that of residence.

From the scanty statutory and judicial materials available, the Revenue have extrapolated a more or less coherent code of practice with regard to residence and ordinary residence. This is a summary of it:

(1) A visitor to the UK is resident for any tax year in which his visits total six months or more; and is both resident and ordinarily resident when his visits have become habitual and substantial. Visits are regarded as substantial if they average at least three months a year and as habitual when they have continued for at least four years.

(2) A person who maintains a place of abode in the UK is resident for any tax year in which he sets foot in the UK, however short his stay; and is again both resident and ordinarily resident when the visits become habitual and substantial.

(3) A person resident and ordinarily resident in the UK who goes abroad for

less than one complete tax year continues to be both resident and ordinarily resident in the UK. Where the period of his absence abroad is greater than one but less than three years, he is resident for any year in which he sets foot in the UK and ordinarily resident throughout. Where the period is greater than three years, he is treated thereafter as a visitor, i.e. he goes back to square (1) above.

(4) Residence or ordinary residence are normally determined for an entire tax year. As an extra-statutory concession, however, the Revenue compute tax for the year in which residence is taken up not by reference to the entire year but only that part during which residence had been taken up. A similar concession is applied to the year of departure.

Space permits only a brief thumbnail sketch of the concept of domicile. For an adequate account reference should be made to the standard works on private international law such as *Cheshire* or *Dicey and Morris*. A person's domicile is the country in which he has or is deemed to have his permanent home. Every person must have one. No one can have more than one. Each legal jurisdiction has its own concept of domicile. It makes sense, therefore, to talk, say, of a Scottish domicile, but not of a British or UK domicile. Everyone has a "domicile of origin": a legitimate child whose father is living at the time of his birth takes that of his father, an illegitimate or posthumous child that of his mother. After attaining the age of majority, now eighteen, a person may acquire a "domicile of choice" by residing in a country other than that of his previous domicile with the intention of doing so permanently. Similarly he may abandon the domicile of choice by residing outside that country with the intention not to return; on abandonment the domicile of origin, which has meanwhile merely been in abeyance, *ipso facto* revives. For certain persons, including infants, married women, and mental patients, a "domicile of dependency" is fixed by operation of law. The domicile of a legitimate infant follows that of his father, the domicile of an illegitimate or posthumous infant that of his mother. A woman, even if an infant, acquires the domicile of her husband on marriage. During the marriage her domicile follows his, after it she retains her former husband's domicile until she acquires a domicile of choice.

2

Income Tax

But to say that there is an objection to income tax is only to say that this tax is a tax; for the ingenuity of the human mind never did and never will devise a tax to which there are not objections more than plausible and which would be absolutely convincing and irresistible if taxation were not a necessity. *Robert Lowe, Chancellor of the Exchequer*, 1869.

2.1 Conceptual framework of income taxation

2.11 THE SCHEDULAR SYSTEM AND ITS IMPLICATIONS

Although income tax 'is one tax, not a collection of taxes essentially distinct' (*L.C.C.* v. *Att.-Gen.* [1901] A.C. 26 at 35 *per* Lord Macnaghten), the cardinal feature of our system of income taxation is that: 'The Income Tax Acts nowhere define "income" any more than they define "capital"; they describe sources of income and prescribe methods of computing income, but what constitutes income they discreetly refrain from saying' (*Van den Berghs Ltd* v. *Clark* [1935] A.C. 431 at 438 *per* Lord Macmillan).

The sources are classified into Schedules as follows:

Schedule A: annual profits or gains arising from ownership of land in the UK;

Schedule B: income from the occupation of woodlands in the UK managed on a commercial basis and with a view to the realization of profits;

Schedule C: profits arising from public revenue dividends payable in the UK or from UK public revenue dividends payable in the Republic of Ireland (i.e. income from "gilt-edged securities");

Schedule D: annual profits or gains from any kind of property, chargeable under:

Case I: profits of a trade,

Case II: profits of a profession or vocation,

Case III: interest, annuities, or other annual payments, and certain other forms of "pure income",

Case IV: income from foreign securities not charged under Schedule C,

Case V: income from foreign possessions, or

Case VI: annual profits or gains not falling under any other Case or Schedule;

Schedule E: emoluments of any office or employment, chargeable under one or more of three Cases, of which Cases II and III involve a foreign element; pensions; etc; and
Schedule F: dividends and other distributions of a company resident in the UK.

One consequence of this schismatic definition of income is that each item of income has one and only one proper place in the Schedular scheme of things. It is, Viscount Simonds once declared, 'fundamental and well settled law that the Schedules to the Income Tax Acts are mutually exclusive, and that the specific Schedules . . . and the rules which respectively regulate them, afford a complete code for each class of income' (*Mitchell and Edon* v. *Ross* [1962] A.C. 813 at 832). The sequitur is crucial: the Revenue have no right to assess under one Schedule a receipt belonging to another. In particular, their attempts to bring escapees from the other Schedules within the capacious terms of Schedule D have been given short shrift by the Courts. For instance, in the days when Schedule A was a charge on the annual value of land—a notional figure which tended to become unrealistic—the Revenue sought in *Fry* v. *Salisbury House Estate Ltd* [1930] A.C. 432 to assess the landlord of an office block under Schedule A up to its annual value and under Schedule D to the extent that rents exceeded the annual value. The House of Lords held the Schedule A assessment exhaustive. "Excess rents" were later brought into charge in F.A. 1940 but the principle of the decision is unaffected. Similarly in *Glanely* v. *Wightman* [1933] A.C. 618 their Lordships decided that fees paid to the owner of a stud farm for allowing a stallion to service visiting mares were chargeable solely under Schedule B. In *Mitchell and Edon* v. *Ross* [1962] A.C. 813 GPs (Schedule D Case II) who also held part-time appointments under the Health Service (Schedule E) were refused their claim to have expenses incurred in the course of the part-time appointments deducted from their Schedule D earnings. (We will see that the rules governing deductibility of expenditure are more lenient under Schedule D than under Schedule E: *cf.* 2.23 § 7 and 2.31 § 3 below.)

While they may not choose between Schedules, the Revenue do have a right to selection where an assessment falls to be made under more than one Case of the same Schedule. Thus in *Liverpool etc Insurance Co.* v. *Bennett* [1913] A.C. 610 an assessment under Case 1 rather than Case IV of Schedule D on investment interest arising abroad was upheld. This decision is difficult to reconcile with *Westminster Bank etc Ltd* v. *National Bank of Greece* [1969] 3 A.E.R. 504, in which the Court of Appeal held that certain payments came within Case IV and did not come within Case III of Schedule

D, even though they were annual payments. Their decision was upheld, on a different point, by the House of Lords ([1971] A.C. 945). The Revenue's purported right to choose between Cases may provide a partial explanation for the Courts' reluctance to extend Case VI beyond a very narrow compass.

The Schedules, then, are mutually exclusive. They are also comprehensive. Any item emanating from a non-Schedular source is outside the definition of income for tax purposes and therefore escapes income tax. This is tax law's equivalent of the criminal law doctrine of *nulla poena sine lege*. The chief beneficiaries of the doctrine of Schedular comprehensiveness are gifts and windfalls. An example is *Dickinson* v. *Abel* [1969] 1 A.E.R. 484, which concerned a payment of £10,000 made to the taxpayer by the purchasers of a farm after he had suggested to the owners that they accept the purchasers' offer of £100,000. He had been under no obligation to make the suggestion, nor had the owners been obliged to accept it. Pennycuick J. therefore held the payment untaxable. For another narrow escape see *Walker* v. *Carnaby Harrower, Barnham & Pykett* [1970] 1 W.L.R. 276.

Newcomers to the Wonderland world of tax logic may need an incubation period before the *ah-ha!* experience makes it seem obvious that a taxpayer's income during a year of assessment, as the man in the street understands it, bears no necessary relation to his total income for that year as computed for tax purposes. We have seen that income is artificially restricted for tax purposes to items falling within one of the Schedules. This aspect of the discrepancy between lay and legal conceptions of income is well illustrated by *Mapp* v. *Oram*, considered at pp. 52–3 below. There are other aspects, equally significant. One is that the sources each have different computational rules. Another is the curious arrangement whereby assessments under some of the Schedules or Cases are made on an entirely different basis than the others. Schedules A, B, C, E, and F, as well as Case VI of Schedule D are on a "current year" or "actual" basis, which means that income from those sources is measured by reference to actual receipts during the year of assessment in question. Cases I to V of Schedule D, on the other hand, are on a "preceding year" basis according to which assessments are made by reference to the actual receipts of some previous period. Under Cases I and II the previous period is the taxpayer's accounting period ending in the preceding year of assessment, while under Cases III, IV, and V it is the preceding year of assessment itself. A further complication is the "remittance" basis according to which income under Case IV or V is sometimes chargeable only to the extent that it is received in the UK. Let us jump in at the deep end with an example.

Example 1

Owen U. Plenty is a London antique dealer (Schedule D Case I) resident here but domiciled in the United States. His accounts, made up for calendar years, disclose profits of £5,000 for 1971 and £20,000 for 1972. While abroad, Owen leases his London flat (Schedule A): in 1971–72 he received rent of £200 and in 1972–73 £600. While in London, he leases his Boston house (Schedule D Case V), the rent cheques being paid alternately into his bank accounts in Boston and London; cheques paid into his London account totalled £400 in 1971–72 and £700 in 1972–73.

For tax purposes Owen's total income for 1972–73 is £6,000, computed as follows:

    Schedule A £600 (actual basis)
    Schedule D Case I £5,000 (preceding year basis)
    Schedule D Case V £400 (preceding year and remittance bases)

To the layman or tax tyro who objects that Owen's real income in 1972–73 was probably well in excess of £20,000, an adequate rejoinder might be, in the words of Lewis Carroll's Tweedledee: 'if it was so, it might be; and if it were so, it would be: but as it isn't, it ain't. That's logic.'

2.12 THE SOURCE DOCTRINE

The assertion should now make sense that even income falling squarely within one or other of the Schedules may escape taxation if its source no longer exists. This doctrine's most notable achievement was to immunize the post-cessation receipts of a trade, profession, or vocation. It provided the Bar with a *de facto* retirement benefits scheme. Barristers are paid in arrears and were therefore once able to retire after a frenzy of activity with substantial tax-free fees yet to accrue. On appointment to the Bench, successful QCs were cushioned against the drop in earnings. (Nicholson recounts the story that, just after the War, an unctuous solicitor remarked to Holmes KC's clerk: 'I suppose we shall see him on the Bench soon.' 'I don't pretend that things are all they might be,' was the grim reply, 'but they are not that bad yet!' (*Esprit de Law* Wolfe Publishing Ltd 1973 p. 57)). Authors and actors also benefited. In *Stainer's Executors* v. *Purchase* (1951) (reported at [1962] A.C. 280) and in *Carson* v. *Cheyney's Executor* [1959] A.C. 412 the House of Lords held that the respective executors of Leslie Howard, the actor, and of Peter Cheyney, the "whodunit" writer, were not assessable on payments received by them under the terms of contracts made by the actor and writer with film companies and publishers respectively. (A measure of the Revenue's resentment of the source doctrine is the manner in which they doggedly fought and lost *Cheyney's case* from Commissioners through to Lords in the face of clear, contrary authority—a flagrant abuse of the public pursestrings.) In *Hume* v. *Asquith* [1969] 1 A.E.R. 868 James Barrie had bequeathed certain rights in his books and plays to Lady Asquith, who had subsequently assigned the royalties in two of the plays to her son. Penny-cuick J., allowing the source doctrine to run its logical course, held him entitled to receive the royalties free of tax.

This avenue of escape was imperfectly cut off by provisions in F.A. 1960, which were supplemented in F.A. 1968. The legislation on post-cessation receipts has now been consolidated in TA ss. 143–51, considered at 2.26 below.

The source doctrine also shielded from taxability "golden handshakes" paid to employees on termination of their contracts of service. These too were (partly) brought into charge by F.A. 1960 in a complicated set of provisions now contained in TA ss. 187, 188, and Schedule 8, which are considered at 2.43 below.

2.13 UNIFIED TAX: THE NEW SYSTEM OF PERSONAL DIRECT TAXATION

Before 1973–74 an individual was liable to both income tax and surtax. His assessment to income tax was made locally by the Inspector, any assessment to surtax centrally by the Surtax Office. For income tax purposes, every individual was entitled to personal reliefs which removed from taxability a slice (or the whole) of his "total income". Any remaining income was subjected to tax at the "standard rate" of 38·75%. However, a relief on earned income of two-ninths up to £4,005 and 15% thereafter reduced the effective rate on earnings to 30·14% (seven-ninths of 38·75%) up to £4,005 and 32·94% thereafter. An individual whose income exceeded a much higher threshold (£3,000 after deducting reliefs, expenses, etc) was liable also to surtax, for which a second computation was necessary since "total income" and the set of reliefs for surtax purposes differed to some extent from their income tax counterparts. The rates of surtax increased with each successive band of income above the threshold.

With effect from 6 April 1973 F.A. 1971 replaced this dual structure with a single progressive income tax called "unified tax", or, sometimes, "unitax". "Surtax", "earned income relief", and "standard rate" have all disappeared and their respective places taken by "higher rates of tax", "investment income surcharge", and "basic rate". These and the other more detailed changes are largely of form and not substance. However, they have made possible a considerable saving of Revenue staff. All income tax payers are now dealt with by the Inspectors. The Surtax Office has been made redundant.

Unified tax is charged at the basic rate of 30% on an individual's total income up to £5,000. Thereafter it is charged at higher rates which progress with each successive upward slice as follows:

£5,001 to £6,000	40%
£6,001 to £7,000	45%
£7,001 to £8,000	50%
£8,001 to £10,000	55%
£10,001 to £12,000	60%
£12,001 to £15,000	65%
£15,001 to £20,000	70%
£20,000 upwards	75%

The principle of differentiation between earned and unearned income has been retained in the form of a surcharge of 15% on investment income in excess of £2,000. Under unified tax there is therefore a top marginal rate of 90% on investment incomes over £20,000. "Investment income" is unhelpfully defined as 'any income other than earned income' (F.A. 1971 s. 32(3)). "Earned income" is defined in TA s. 530 to include an individual's remuneration from any office or employment he holds, and any pension or compensation for loss of office; and to include also any income charged under Schedules A, B or D which is "immediately derived" by him from any trade, profession, or vocation carried on by him either as an individual or as an *acting* partner (not, it seems, *qua* trustee or sleeping partner). For judicial elucidation *see FS Securities Ltd* v. *IRC* [1965] A.C. 631; *Bucks* v. *Bowers* [1970] 2 A.E.R. 202 (the effect of which has been reversed for unified tax by F.A. 1971 s. 32(4)) *Peay* v. *Newton* [1971] 2 A.E.R. 172; and *Pegler* v. *Abell* [1973] S.T.C. 23.

The new concept of "excess liability" has been introduced as shorthand for the difference between the tax that *is* payable—applying basic rate, the higher rates, and investment income surcharge—and the tax that *would have been* payable had the entire income been charged solely at the basic rate of 30%.

2.14 PERSONAL RELIEFS: TA SS. 5–27 AS AMENDED BY F.A. 1971 SS. 33 AND 34, F.A. 1972 S. 65, AND F.A. 1973 S. 12

Though the system of personal reliefs has been left substantially intact, unified tax presented the opportunity for some spring cleaning. Four reliefs —earned income relief, old age relief, small income relief, and the deduction for excess travelling expenses due to war dislocation—have been discarded (F.A. 1971 ss. 32(2), 33(1)). Reliefs are still available only if claimed (TA s. 5) but the method of granting them has been simplified. Previously they were given formally in terms of tax. ('The claimant shall be entitled . . .', ran the statutory formula, 'to a deduction from the amount with which he is chargeable to equal income tax at the standard rate on £x'.) Now they are given simply as deductions of specified amounts from total income (F.A. 1971 s. 33(2)). The change from standard rate to basic rate necessitated a general increase of nine-sevenths (roughly 38·75/30) in order to maintain the same level of exemption. In place of two overlapping sets of reliefs, one for income tax, another for surtax, there is now one. With one exception, all reliefs are now deducted from total income and any remaining income charged at both the basic and the higher rates in a single operation. The exception is life assurance relief, which was formerly a relief against income tax only and which in effect continues unaltered (*see* § 8 below).

The rule remains unchanged that the personal reliefs are available only to individuals resident in the UK during the relevant year of assessment (TA s. 27(1)). An individual is entitled to full personal reliefs in the year in which he arrives in the UK to take up permanent residence here or in which he leaves the UK to settle permanently abroad. Certain classes of non-resident are entitled to a proportion of personal reliefs dependent upon the ratio their income chargeable to UK tax bears to their world-wide income (TA s. 27(2)).

The personal reliefs currently available are these (*see also* Table, p. 55):

§ 1 Personal relief: TA s. 8 (1)

● A married man whose wife is living with him or who wholly maintains her throughout the year of assessment is entitled to deduct £775 from his total income (TA s. 8(1)(*a*)). Any other man is entitled to deduct £595 (TA s. 8(1)(*b*)). A married man whose maintenance payments are made under a court order or enforceable agreement is entitled to the lower relief only— these payments are made under deduction of tax and are deductible as charges on income (TA s. 8(1)(*a*)(ii)) (*see* p. 56 below). In the year of marriage a man is entitled to the higher relief only for the part of the year during which he was married. This works out as £595 plus £15 (one-twelfth of (£775 − £595)) for each complete month of marriage, working back from the end of the year on 5 April, as well as for the month of marriage (TA s. 8 (3)). A man who married on, say, 20 February 1974 would be entitled to a deduction of £625 (£595 plus £30).

§ 2 Wife's earned income relief: TA s. 8(2)

A married man living with his wife is also entitled, if she has earned income to a deduction of the amount of her earnings up to a maximum of £595. These are calculated, for purposes of this relief, as excluding (a) any pension or other payments received in respect of her husband's past services, (b) family allowances, and (c) any National Insurance benefits not payable by virtue of her own insurance.

§ 3 Child relief: TA ss. 10, 11

Any person who shows either (a) that there is a child of his living at any time within the year, or (b) that he has the custody of and maintains someone else's child at his own expense, may claim one of the following deductions:

   (i) £200 if the child is under 11,
   (ii) £235 if the child is between 11 and 16, and
   (iii) £265 if the child is over 16 (TA s. 10(1), (3)).

The age limits are calculated as at the beginning of the relevant year of assessment. "Child" is defined for this purpose so as to exclude an illegitimate child unless legitimated *per subsequents matrimonium* (TA s. 10(1)).

A person claiming (iii) must further prove that the child is receiving full-time instruction at an educational establishment or is undergoing a full-time course of training for any trade, profession, or vocation for a period of at least two years (TA s. 10(2)(b), (4)). In *Heaslip* v. *Hasemer* (1927) 13 T.C. 212 Rowlatt J. refused relief in respect of a girl of nineteen who was having music lessons four times a week at her teacher's private home; while in *Barry* v. *Hughes* [1973] S.T.C. 103 Pennycuick V-C refused the claim of a taxpayer whose son attended full-time at an intensive training unit for the mentally subnormal on the ground that ' "education" denotes training of the mind, in contradistinction to training in manual skills' (ibid. at 109).

The deduction for a child entitled in his or her own right to an income exceeding £115 (excluding scholarships, grants, and the like) must be reduced £ for £ by the excess over £115 (TA s. 10(5)). It therefore cannot be claimed where the child's income is £380 or more. In *Mapp* v. *Oram* [1970] A.C. 362 the House of Lords held that "income" in this context means income chargeable to UK tax and therefore did not include money earned and spent by a modern languages undergraduate at St Andrews while working for ten weeks as a teacher in a French *lycée*.

If two or more persons are entitled to child relief in respect of the same child, the relief must be apportioned as they agree or, failing that, in proportion to the provision respectively made by them for the child's maintenance and education during the year of assessment (TA s. 11(1), (3)).

§ 4 Dependent relative relief: TA s. 16

Any person who supports his mother or mother-in-law while she is widowed or divorced or separated from her husband, may claim a deduction of £100. The same deduction is allowed for supporting any relative of his or of his wife's who is incapable of maintaining himself or herself by reason of old age or infirmity (TA s. 16(1)). In either case the deduction is increased to £145 where the claimant is a woman other than a married woman living with her husband (TA s. 16(2)). Relief tapers off once the relative's income exceeds the basic retirement pension by more than £100: the deduction is diminished £ for £ by any excess of the relative's total income over the basic retirement pension plus £100 (TA s. 16(1) as amended by F.A. 1973 s. 12(2)(*a*)).

§ 5 Reliefs in respect of a housekeeper, a person in charge of a child, and a daughter's services: TA ss. 12, 13, 17 respectively

A widower or widow who has a female relative of his or hers or of the deceased spouse living with him or her as housekeeper is entitled to a deduction of £100. If no such relative is willing or able to do so, some other female person may be employed as resident housekeeper without losing the relief. It is not available, however, where the housekeeper is a married woman living with her husband if he has claimed married relief.

Alternatively, any unmarried person may claim to deduct £100 if he or she has a female relative living in so as to look after any brother or sister of the unmarried person. The claimant must show (*a*) if the relative is his or her mother, that she is widowed or separated from her husband, (*b*) that the relative is maintained at the claimant's expense, and (*c*) that the brother or sister qualifies for child relief.

A person compelled by old age or infirmity to depend upon the services of a daughter who lives with and is maintained by him is entitled to a deduction of £55.

§ 6 Additional child relief for widows and others: TA s. 14

Any widower, widow, or other person, who (1) is entitled to child relief in respect of a child residing with him or her, but (2) is not entitled to the higher personal relief, may claim an additional deduction of £130. The same relief is also available to a married man if throughout the year his wife was totally incapacitated by physical or mental infirmity.

§ 7 Relief for blind persons: TA s. 18

A man is entitled to a deduction of £130 if he or his wife living with him are registered blind persons throughout the year. If both husband and wife are registered blind persons throughout the year, the deduction is increased to £260. The deductions are proportionately reduced if the person was blind for part only of the year; and are also reduced by the amounts of any tax-free disability payments.

§ 8 Life assurance relief: TA ss. 19–21

Before 1973–74 life assurance relief was available for income tax only. The relief was either two-fifths of the total premiums if they exceeded £25, or, if they did not, the lesser of (a) the amount of the premiums, and (b) £10. Under unified tax virtually the same result has been achieved by granting as a deduction from the total tax liability a relief of either one half of basic rate tax on premiums exceeding £20 or, if they do not, full basic rate tax on the lesser of (a) the amount of the premiums, and (b) £10 (TA s. 19(1)).

The effect has been to replace an income tax relief of $15\frac{1}{2}\%$ on premiums over £25 by a unified tax relief of 15% on premiums over £20. (Premiums of £100 were previously relieved as to £40 (two-fifths), a tax saving at 38·75% of £15·50. Now premiums of £100 are relieved by granting a direct tax saving of £15.)

An extensive range of conditions must be satisfied before relief can be claimed. The following are a selection:

(1) The premiums must have been paid by the claimant under an insurance policy or deferred annuity contract (TA s. 19(2)).

(2) The policy or contract must have been made after 22 June 1916 (TA s. 19(2)(a)) by the claimant (TA s. 19(2)(c)); on his own or his wife's life (TA s. 19(2)(b)) and either he or his wife must be paying the premiums (TA s. 19(7)).

(3) If taken out after 19 March 1968 the policy must be a "qualifying" policy. The qualifying conditions, laid down in TA Schedule 1 Pt 1, require inter alia that the policy run with a fairly even spread of premiums for a minimum period of ten years (or earlier death of the assured) and that the capital sum payable on death be at least 75% of the total premiums. The requirement of qualification is an anti-avoidance expedient designed to ensure that the life assurance aspect of a policy is not outweighed by its endowment component.

(4) The amount on which relief is claimed may not exceed 7% of the capital sum payable on death (excluding bonuses) (TA s. 21(2)) nor may it exceed one-sixth of the claimant's total income (TA s. 21(1)).

There are special rules contained in TA ss. 20 and 21 for policies taken out on or before 22 June 1916.

§ 9 Family allowance "clawback": TA s. 24

When family allowances were raised by 50p a week in 1968, the Government were forced to resort to the administrative absurdity of "clawback" in order to restrict the benefit to the lower income groups. Every taxpayer receiving the increased family allowance had £42 deducted from his aggregate entitlement of personal reliefs for each child in respect of whom the allowances were payable (TA s. 24(1)). Under unified tax, the deduction has been increased to £60 (F.A. 1971 s. 33(4)(*b*), (*c*)).

The family allowance is currently £46·80 for two children—the eldest child is disregarded—and £52 for each additional child. The cut-off point beyond which it would be wise for a taxpayer to disclaim family allowances is therefore reached where his marginal rate is 45% or above (with two children) or 50% or above (with three or more children). (The family allowance of £46·80 would be taxed in the sum of £21·06 (45% of £46·80) plus "clawback" of £27 (45% of £60), i.e. £48·06. The allowance for three children of £98·80 would be taxed in the sum of £49·40 (50% of £98·80) plus "clawback" of £60 (50% of £120).)

Table of Personal Reliefs 1973–74

Single person ⎫ Wife's earned income ⎭	£595
Married man	775
Child—under 11	200
11 to 16	235
over 16	265
Additional child relief	130
Dependent relative—single woman claimant	145
any other claimant	100
Housekeeper	100
Relative taking charge of younger brother or sister	100
Daughter's services	55
Blind person	130

§ 10 **Old age exemption: TA s. 7 as amended by F.A. 1973 s. 12(1)**

A claimant is entitled to exemption from income tax if he proves:

(1) that at any time within the year of assessment either he or his wife living with him was aged sixty-five or upwards; and

(2) either (*a*) that his total income for that year does not exceed £700; or
(*b*) that he would be entitled to the higher personal relief and his total income does not exceed £1,000.

Marginal relief is available where the claimant is not entitled to the exemption because his total income for the year exceeds £700 or £1,000, as the case may be.

2.15 GENERAL CONCEPTUAL SCHEMA

Each of the taxes has a conceptual schema. For income tax it is this. An individual's income from each source must be computed according to the rules applicable to that source and the resultant amounts aggregated. Where income is liable to direct assessment, e.g. trading income under Schedule D Case I, the amount to be included in the computation is simply the sum chargeable under the rules applicable to that source. If, however, the individual has also received income which has suffered basic rate tax by deduction in the hands of the payer/s, e.g. annual payments under Schedule D Case III, he must bring into computation the "grossed-up" equivalent of the sum actually received. Thus the payee of an annual payment who receives £70 must include £100, not £70, in his total income.

From the aggregate figure comprising:

(1) income liable to direct assessment; and

(2) the grossed-up amounts of any payments *received* under deduction of tax,

certain deductions may be made, which are known as "charges on income". The grossed-up amounts of any payments *made* under deduction of tax are the typical charge on income but, exceptionally, certain items are deductible as charges even though paid without deduction, namely (*a*) certain types of interest payment, (*b*) small maintenance payments, (*c*) premiums paid under approved retirement annuity contracts, (*d*) contributions to approved superannuation funds, and (*e*) certain trading losses.

The figure that remains is the individual's "total income". From it he may claim to deduct any personal reliefs to which he may be entitled. Any remaining income—the individual's "taxable income"—is subjected to tax at the basic and higher rates and to the investment income surcharge, as appropriate.

The code in effect stipulates the order in which deductions should be made. F.A. 1971 s. 34(2) proclaims the generous general rule that: 'Any deductions allowable in computing a person's total income or to be made from a person's total income shall be treated as reducing income of different descriptions in the order which will result in the greatest reduction of his liability to income tax.' Statutory exceptions have left the rule only a wee bit more substantial than the Cheshire cat's smile. In the very next breath, the draftsman tells us that the personal reliefs are available only after all the other deductions have been made (F.A. 1971 s. 34(3)). Since excess personal reliefs cannot be carried forward from year to year, the taxpayer with insufficient income to cover his complement of personal reliefs simply loses their full benefit. We are then informed that the personal reliefs must be set first against earned income, next against the slice of investment income which is exempt from the surcharge, and finally against income liable to the surcharge (F.A. 1971 s. 34(4)). Another important exception is TA s. 168(4) (*see* p. 93 below). Beware the Greeks bearing gifts!

2.16 EXEMPTIONS

The exemptions are mostly contained in TA Pt XIII as amended. One set attaches to income, another to persons.

Exempt income includes:

(1) Various kinds of interest—on National Savings Certificates, on Tax Reserve Certificates, on damages for personal injuries. Also, from 1973–74 the first £40 of interest—which may be claimed separately by husband and wife—on deposits in (*a*) the National Savings Bank, other than investment deposits, or (*b*) a trustee savings bank (TA s. 414(1) as amended by F.A. 1973 s. 13).

(2) Interest and dividends paid by a building society which has entered into arrangements with the Revenue under TA s. 343 (but the grossed-up equivalents must be included in the recipient's total income if he is subject to excess liability because this exemption applies for basic rate purposes only).

(3) Terminal bonuses payable under any certified contractual savings scheme, e.g. "Save As You Earn".

(4) Scholarships, grants, and other educational endowments.

(5) Certain social security benefits, including unemployment benefit, sickness benefit, maternity benefit and grant, death grant, attendance allowance, and family income supplement.

(6) Compensation paid for Nazi persecution.

The Crown is liable to tax only if statute expressly so provides. Foreign sovereigns are altogether exempt; and some measure of exemption attaches to the political, diplomatic, and consular representatives of foreign states, to UN officials, and to visiting forces. Approved charities are exempted on income applied solely for charitable purposes arising from (*a*) lands, etc, in their occupation or ownership, (*b*) trades carried on mainly by the beneficiaries of the charity or by the charity itself in the course of executing its charitable function, and (*c*) interest, annuities, dividends, etc. There are circumstances in which trade unions, friendly societies, mutual associations, agricultural societies, scientific research associations, hospitals, churches, universities, public schools, and the British Museum may also claim exemption.

2.17 SPECIMEN COMPUTATION

O. B. Lax is a married man who, in 1973–74, has a son aged nine and a daughter aged fourteen. He is the managing director of Shiftless Removals Ltd at a salary of £6,000 per annum. His wife works part-time at Crocks End Hospital. During 1973–74 she earned £805. Over the years he has built up a portfolio of shares, from which he receives dividends totalling £2,100 in 1973–74. He receives too an annual payment of £140. Several years ago the Hapless, Hopeless & Helpless Building Society gave him the mortgage which enabled him to buy his house. In 1973–74 he paid the Society £600 in mortgage interest. On the other hand, he has a deposit account with the same Society which yielded interest in 1973-74 of £280. He has a qualifying policy on his own life in favour of his wife, on which he pays premiums of £10 per month.

The computation of O. B. Lax's liability to tax for 1973–74 is as follows:

	£	£
Salary		6,000
Wife's earnings*		805
Dividend received**	2,100	
plus tax credit	900	3,000
Annual payments	140	
plus basic rate tax deducted at source	60	200
Building society interest received	280	
plus notional tax at basic rate	120	400
		10,405
Deduct building society interest paid		600
Total income		9,805

Less personal relief	775	
wife's earned income relief	595	
child relief in respect of son	200	
child relief in respect of daughter	235	1,805
		8,000

Tax payable:	
Basic rate	
5,000 @ 30%	1,500
Higher rates	
1,000 @ 40%	400
1,000 @ 45%	450
1,000 @ 50%	500
Investment income surcharge	
1,000*** @ 15%	150
	3,000
Less life assurance relief	
120 @ 15% (half the basic rate)	18
Total tax liability****	2,982

Less tax deducted at source (actually or notionally)

(*a*) tax credit in respect of dividends	900	
(*b*) tax deducted from annual payments	60	
(*c*) notional tax on building society interest	120	1,080
Tax payable by PAYE and by direct assessment		1,902

* A wife's income, as we shall see in 2.06 below, is assessed and charged on her husband unless an election is made either for separate assessment or for separate taxation. In the absence of any such election, a wife's income is deemed to be her husband's.

** We shall discover in Chapter 4 of this book that under the imputation system of corporation tax a dividend declared by a company confers a tax credit on the recipient shareholder equivalent to basic rate tax on the grossed-up amount of that dividend. Thus a dividend of £70 confers on the shareholders a tax credit of £30. Here O. B. Lax has received a dividend of £2,100 and is entitled to a tax credit of £900 (30% of £3,000).

*** The amount of taxable income and the amount of investment income have to be computed separately. Here the amount of investment income is arrived at as follows:

		£
Dividend received		3,000
Annual payment		200
Building society interest received		400
		3,600
Less building society interest paid	600	
exempt slice	2,000	2,600
Investment income liable to surcharge		£1,000

Notice that building society interest paid is deductible in each computation.

**** This marks the completion of the first stage of our computation—directed to determining the total tax liability. In the second stage we need to subtract from the figure of total liability any amounts of tax suffered by deduction at source so as to yield the amount of tax to be collected by direct assessment or under the PAYE system.

D

2.18 DUE DATE FOR PAYMENT

Before 1973–74 income tax directly assessed on the taxpayer for a year of assessment was usually due on 1 January of that year (TA s. 4(1)). By way of exception, income tax charged under Schedule D Case I or II was payable in two instalments, the first on 1 January in the year of assessment, the second on the following 1 July (TA s. 4(2)). Certain types of income were taxed by deduction at source, e.g. emoluments under the PAYE system and annuities under the TA ss. 52 and 53 procedures; but deduction extended only to income tax. Surtax was always directly assessed and, as a deferred instalment of income tax, fell due on 1 January *following* the year of assessment for which it had been assessed (TA s. 4(3)). In the event of any assessment being made later than the due date, tax fell due the day after the making of the assessment.

The advent of unified tax meant the possibility of overlapping liabilities for the 1972–73 surtaxpayer. Under the unified system basic rate tax *and* excess liability for a year of assessment fall due, as a general rule, on 1 January in that year. Moreover, PAYE and the two-instalment plan for Schedule D Case I or II profits have both been extended to cover the higher rates as well as basic rate. Where the recipient of income, e.g. an annuity, from which tax has been deducted at the basic rate, is liable to the higher rates or to the surcharge, the additional tax falls due on 6 July following the year for which it is assessed or, if this should be later, thirty days after notice of assessment.

The former surtaxpayer would therefore have found himself on 6 April 1973 in the unfortunate position of having to meet both his surtax liability for 1972–73 and a large part of his unified tax liability for 1973–74 on 1 January 1974. He would also have been faced with the prospect of a sudden increase in his PAYE deductions. After heated Parliamentary debate—no surprise, the cynical might say, considering the number of surtaxpayers in the Commons—F.A. 1971 s. 24 allowed 1972–73 surtax liabilities to be met in three instalments, on 1 January 1974, 1975, and 1976. Deferment is not permissible of any surtax referable to income which has borne tax by deduction, s. 24(1), nor where the amount to be deferred is less than £100, s. 24(4).

2.19 POSTSCRIPT: THE PROPOSED TAX-CREDIT SYSTEM

In his 1972 Budget Speech Mr Barber outlined a scheme, devised by his special adviser on taxation, Sir Arthur Cockfield, for bringing together parts of the personal taxation and social security systems. The lynch-pin is the idea that each individual should receive a tax credit in lieu of (*a*) his main personal reliefs, and (*b*) his family allowances. The Green Paper of October 1972 assumes for illustrative purposes that the weekly credits would be £4 for a single person, £6 for a married man, and £2 for a child. Every person within the scheme would be sent a notice of his tax-credit entitlement. He would give it to his employer or, if not in employment, would make it available to the Department of Health and Social Security or the Department of Employment. The employer or other payer would then deduct tax at the basic rate from the emoluments, pension, or other benefit, as the case may be. If tax deduction exceeded credit, the payer would retain the balance. If not, the payer would make up the discrepancy.

The present cumulative PAYE would be replaced by a non-cumulative system whereby deductions would be made above the credit threshold and additional payments below it. New ways are to be found for giving effect to certain deductions which in their present form would not fit conveniently into the new tax-credit system, namely life assurance relief, relief for interest payments, and Schedule E expenses.

The main advantages claimed for the new system are that it would be simpler to administer; that it would therefore enable an eventual saving of 10,000 to 15,000 staff; that it would be easier for ordinary people to understand; that it would reduce reliance on means-tested benefits; and that it would enable the benefit of tax allowances to accrue not only to taxpayers but also to those who have insufficient income to pay tax or who, being old or ill or unemployed or the like, have no taxable income. Certainly it should help towards removing the notorious "poverty trap" whereby the extra £ in wages which brings the low earner within the tax net is subjected to a "poverty surtax" in that it loses for him such means-tested benefits as family income supplement. However, the cost of introducing the scheme is estimated at £1,300 million; and its success as a social measure will depend entirely on the precise level at which the credits are pitched.

2.2 The trader

Schedule D charges to tax the "annual profits or gains" arising or accruing from any trade (Case I) or from any profession or vocation (Case II (TA s. 108)). "Annual" in this context is one of those Humpty Dumpty words. Alice would probably have thought that it implied some element of recurrence. In the looking-glass world of tax law it simply means "of an income or revenue nature", as opposed to capital.

2.21 MONKEYS, ELEPHANTS, AND TRADES: THE PROBLEM OF
DEFINITION

The side-note to TA s. 526, "definitions", was also clearly not intended for the linguistic purist: ' "trade" ', s. 526(5) informs us, 'includes every trade, manufacture, adventure or concern in the nature of trade'. Rarely can thirteen statutory words have given rise to such extensive litigation; and rarely can such copious judicial exposition have given so little help in doubtful cases. It follows from the decision in *Edwards* v. *Bairstow and Harrison* [1956] A.C. 14 (*see* p. 31 above), in which the Commissioners' inference of trade or no trade was characterized as one of fact, that only a case in which the Commissioners were reversed involves any proposition of law.

"Trade", it seems, is like the proverbial elephant: 'We can recognize a "trade" when we see it . . .' said Lord Denning in *Griffiths* v. *Harrison*. 'But we are hard pressed to define it' ([1963] A.C. 1 at 20). The difficulty had been noticed in the Court below: 'Is a monkey a "human being",' Donovan L.J. had provoked Lord Denning to inquire, 'or an animal "in the nature of a human being" ?' (ibid.). The nub of the problem is that there is no single defining characteristic: trade is 'a compound fact made up of a variety of incidents' ((1882) 2 Q.B. at 416 *per* Jessel M.R.). Let us then look at some of these "incidents", starting with the six chosen by the Radcliffe Commission in 1954, which they called "the badges of trade".

§ 1 **The subject-matter of the realization**

Frequently decisive. Some kinds of property, especially in large quantities, are obviously intended neither for personal enjoyment nor as long-term investments. Even isolated dealings in them may fall within Case I. Thus in *Martin* v. *Lowry* [1927] A.C. 312 their Lordships affirmed a finding of trade in respect of the once-off disposal over several months of nearly 45 million yards of surplus aircraft linen by a wholesale agricultural machinery merchant, as did the Court of Session in *Rutledge* v. *IRC* (1929) 14 T.C. 490 in respect of the sale in one lot of a million rolls of toilet paper by a moneylender. In *Edwards* v. *Bairstow and Harrison* [1956] A.C. 14 (*see* p. 31 above) the House of Lords reversed a finding of no trade on the purchase and resale of a spinning plant though neither purchaser had previously dealt in machinery, while in *Wisdom* v. *Chamberlain* [1969] 1 A.E.R. 332 the Court of Appeal restored a finding of trade in respect of the purchase of £200,000 worth of silver bullion as a hedge against inflation and its resale at a profit of some £48,000 by the comedian Norman Wisdom. *See also Lowe* v. *Ashmore* [1971] Ch. 545.

In all these cases, and in several others, some importance was attached—more perhaps by taxpayers' counsel than by the Courts—to the fact that the transaction fell outside the scope of the taxpayer's usual trade or occupation.

● The other side of this "badge", to coin the phrase, is that certain forms of property are normally acquired by way of investment. Land is sometimes assigned to this category but is really equivocal. Contrast, for example, *IRC* v. *Reinhold* (1953) 34 T.C. 389 (investment) with *Stepnell Properties Ltd* v. *Eames* [1966] T.R. 347 (trade); and *Stepnell* v. *Eames* with *Fundfarms Developments Ltd* v. *Parsons* [1969] 3 A.E.R. 1161 (no trade). Most remarkable of all is Megarry J.'s frightening decision in *Ransom* v. *Higgs* [1972] 2 A.E.R. 817. The gist of a complicated series of transactions was this: land controlled by H was sold to a partnership at a considerable undervalue. One of the partners, H's wife, transferred her share to trustees on discretionary trusts for the benefit *inter alia* of H's family. The trustees later sold the partnership share to a company unconnected with H for its true market value of £170,000. H was assessed to tax on this sum. The learned judge upheld the assessment—'the categories of trading are not closed, nor is there any reason why there should not be a trade without a name' (ibid. at 848) —on the basis that H had initiated and controlled the various transactions even if he had not himself been a party to the transactions and had not received, or been entitled to, a penny of the £170,000. One learned writer's comment on the decision is apposite: 'although it would seem that tax avoidance itself is not yet a trade we may well be moving that way' (R.S. Nock [1972] B.T.R. at 186).

§ 2 The length of period of ownership

Relatively inconsequential.

§ 3 The frequency or number of similar transactions by the same person

Once a person has engaged in a number of similar transactions, the sheer fact of repetition might bring them collectively within Case I, even when each, discretely considered, might not have been a trading activity. *See Pickford* v. *Quirke* (1927) 13 T.C. 251; *Leach* v. *Pogson* (1962) 40 T.C. 585; and the unusual case of *Burdge* v. *Pyne* (1969) 45 T.C. 320 (club proprietor's personal card-playing profits held to be within Case I).

§ 4 Supplementary work on the property realized

Where work is done to make the property more marketable or steps are taken to find purchasers the Courts are certainly more inclined to support or insist upon an inference of trade. Thus in *Martin* v. *Lowry* [1927] A.C. 312 (*see* p. 62 above) their Lordships were impressed by the fact that the taxpayer had rented an office, set up a large and skilled organization, and advertised extensively. *See also IRC* v. *Livingston* (1926) 11 T.C. 538.

§ 5 The circumstances that were responsible for the realization

Usually insignificant.

§ 6 Motive

● On the one hand, transactions carried out with the intention to make a profit are not invariably trading ventures: *see* for example, *IRC* v. *Reinhold* (1953) 34 T.C. 389. On the other, as Lord Coleridge C.J. said in *IRC* v. *The Incorporated Council of Law Reporting* (1888) 22 Q.B.D. 279 at 293, 'it is not essential to the carrying on of a trade that the persons engaged in it should make, or desire to make, a profit by it'. On that basis, the Council, though non-profit-making, were held to be trading. A graphic illustration of Lord Coleridge's dictum is *Ransom* v. *Higgs* [1972] 2 A.E.R. 817 (*see* p. 63 above).

Motive has none the less sometimes been an important factor. In particular the Courts have used it as their compass in charting an uneasy course between genuine share transactions within Case I such as in *Griffiths* v. *Harrison* [1963] A.C. 1) and artificial devices designed to secure some fiscal advantage (as in *Bishop* v. *Finsbury Securities Ltd* [1966] 3 A.E.R. 105; *F.A. & A.B. Ltd* v. *Lupton* [1972] A.C. 634; and *Thomson* v. *Gurneville Securities* [1972] A.C. 661.

§ 7 Mutual trading

The refund of surplus contributions to a common fund in the case of mutual associations such as mutual insurance companies, co-operative societies, or members' clubs, does not constitute trading. However, as Lord Macmillan once said, 'there must be complete identity between the contributors and the participators' ((1932) 16 T.C. 430 at 448). For the sake of completeness he might have added "at any one point in time" since the doctrine applies notwithstanding fluctuations in an association's membership. Of course a mutual association is chargeable on the profits of any trade with outsiders. As to the borderline between mutuality and trading, *see Fletcher* v. *Income Tax Commissioner* [1972] A.C. 414.

§ 8 Profits realized after discontinuing a trade

Disposals of trading stock after discontinuance are not themselves by way of trade. However, it has sometimes proved difficult to differentiate disposals *in the course of* discontinuing, which are not Case I matters (e.g. *Cohan's Executors* v. *IRC* (1924) 12 T.C. 602; *IRC* v. *Old Bushmills Distillery Co. Ltd* (1928) 12 T.C. 1148; *IRC* v. *Nelson* (1938) 22 T.C. 716), from disposals *in order* to discontinue (e.g. *J. & R. O'Kane & Co.* v. *IRC* (1922) 12 T.C. 303), which remain chargeable as part of the trade. *See* further, pp. 74–5 below.

§ 9 Statutory trades

Three special provisions bring certain kinds of income from land within Case I. The first is TA s. 110(1), which declares that: 'All farming and market gardening in the United Kingdom shall be treated as the carrying on of a trade.' The second, TA s. 110(3), provides that: 'The occupation of land in the United Kingdom for any purpose other than farming or market gardening shall, if the land is managed on a commercial basis and with a view to the realization of profits, be treated as the carrying on of a trade.' Finally, TA s. 112 charges under Case I the profits of gains arising out of and in the case of certain specified concerns, including:

   (i) mines and quarries,
  (ii) ironworks, gasworks, salt springs, and waterworks,
 (iii) canals and docks,
  (iv) fishings,
   (v) rights of markets and fairs, tolls, bridges and ferries,
  (vi) railways, and
 (vii) other concerns similar to these.

2.22 THE MEANING OF "PROFESSION" AND "VOCATION"

Neither expression is defined in the tax legislation. Invariably cited is the ungrammatical dictum of Scrutton L.J.: 'A "profession" . . . involves the idea of an occupation requiring either purely intellectual skill, or of any manual skill controlled, as in painting and sculpture or surgery, by the intellectual skill of the operator' ([1919] 1 K.B. at 656). The Courts have held that a headmaster, an actress, an optician, and a journalist were each carrying on a profession, but that a photographer, a stockbroker, a film producer, and a dance band leader were not. In *Graham* v. *Green* [1925] 2 K.B. 37 Rowlatt J. discharged a Case II assessment made on a person whose sole occupation was betting on horses: and in an Excess Profits Duty case (as to EPD *see* p. 16 above) it was held that a company could not exercise a profession.

"Vocation" was said by Denman J. to be 'a word of wide significance, meaning the way in which a man passes his life' ((1886) 18 Q.B.D. 276).

Authors are the archetypes, though the term has been held to include a bookmaker, land agent, a jockey, and a playwright—not, however, our friend the film producer.

2.23 THE COMPUTATION OF PROFITS OF A TRADE, PROFESSION, OR VOCATION

Hereafter in division 2.2 "trade" and its derivatives will be used as shorthand for "trade, profession, or vocation" and their derivatives unless otherwise stated.

§ 1 The basis period rules

As we discovered earlier (*see* pp. 47–8 above) Cases I and II are normally chargeable on a "preceding year" basis (TA s. 115(1)). More precisely, the basis period for trading profits in a given year of assessment is normally the trader's accounting period ending in the preceding year of assessment (TA s. 115(2)(*a*)). A trader is of course free to make up accounts for whatever periods he likes. If he chooses to make up his accounts regularly for periods of one year (as is usual), each accounting period will be used as the basis period for the following year of assessment. If not, the Board have the right to decide what period of twelve months ending in the preceding year of assessment shall be the basis period (TA s. 115(2)(*b*)). No appeal lies against the Board's exercise of this right: *IRC* v. *Helical Bar Ltd* [1972] A.C. 773.

Since the preceding year basis cannot apply in the opening years of a trade, special rules, now contained in TA ss. 116–18, have had to be formulated.

In the first year of assessment profits are assessed on an actual basis (TA s. 116(1)). The basis period runs from the date of commencement to the following 5 April. Where the trader makes up his first account to 5 April, his taxable profit will be the profit disclosed by that account. If he makes up his first account to a date beyond the following 5 April, the profit disclosed by the account is apportioned on a time basis. Thus if the accounts of a trade commenced on 1 January were made up to the following 31 December, disclosing profits of £1,200, the taxable profit in its first year of assessment would be £300 ($\frac{3}{12} \times$ £1,200). Where the account is made up to a date earlier than 5 April, the taxable profit will be the profit disclosed by the first account plus an apportioned part of the profit disclosed by the second.

In the second year of assessment the basis period extends for one year from the date of commencement (TA s. 116(2)). If the first account is not made up for a period of exactly one year, the profits of one or more accounting periods will have to be apportioned in the manner explained in the preceding paragraph.

In the third year of assessment the assessment moves onto the normal preceding year basis (TA s. 115(1)).

The trader has a right, exercisable by notice in writing to his Inspector within seven years of the end of the second year of assessment, to elect under TA s. 117(2) that *both* the second and third years should be on an actual basis, i.e. on the profits to 5 April in each of the first three years of assessment; and the further right under the proviso to TA s. 117(2) to revoke this election by another notice within the same time limit.

These rules enable a canny trader, by keeping early profits low and choosing his first accounting period carefully, to effect considerable tax savings. If early profits are high, an election will probably be beneficial.

The special rules for the closing years of a trade, contained in TA s. 118, are to some extent compensatory. The assessment for the year in which the trade was discontinued is on an actual basis. The basis period extends back from the date of discontinuance to the preceding 6 April (TA s. 118(1)(*a*)). Assessments for the penultimate and pre-penultimate years of assessment will already have been made on a preceding year basis. They are re-calculated on an actual basis: if the *aggregate* of taxable profits in those two years on an actual basis exceeds the *aggregate* of the two assessments already made, an additional assessment may be raised on the excess (TA s. 118(1)(*b*)). If not, the assessments already made must stand. Where necessary, the profits disclosed by the trader's accounts are time-apportioned. In the event of conflict the discontinuance rules prevail over the commencement rules (TA s. 118(1)).

§ 2 Commencement, cessation, and succession

The life span of a trade extends from the time when it is "set up and commenced" to the time when it is "permanently discontinued"; and these are obviously pivotal issues.

Whether and, if so, when a trade has commenced or ceased are questions of fact. The Courts have had particular difficulty in deciding whether a new branch or activity constituted an extension of the existing trade or the commencement of a new one (e.g. *Cannon Industries Ltd* v. *Edwards* [1966] 1 A.E.R. 456) and in evaluating the significance of a temporary cessation in trading activities (e.g. *Ingram & Son Ltd* v. *Callaghan* [1969] 1 A.E.R. 433).

A change in the persons carrying on a trade operates by virtue of TA s. 154(1) as the cessation of one trade and the commencement of another, provided that there has been a succession to the old trade. The proviso is not actually stated in the section, but it appeared in its predecessors and is generally thought to have survived omission. In practical terms TA s. 154(1) means that a person carrying on a pre-existing trade who has succeeded to another trade will be treated as having two trades, his pre-existing trade assessed on the same basis as before and a new trade to be assessed on a commencement basis. Had he not succeeded to the other trade, the trader would have been treated as merely enlarging his existing trade.

What then is a succession? 'The test . . . appears to be whether the profit-making apparatus of the former trader has been transferred to and continued by the successor in an identifiable form' (*Whiteman and Wheatcroft* 6–10). Thus there will be a succession where the whole of a trade is taken over as a going concern but not where the assets only are acquired. Two contrasting cases illustrative of this distinction are *Laycock* v. *Freeman, Hardy & Willis Ltd* [1939] 2 K.B. 1 and *Briton Ferry Steel Co. Ltd* v. *Barry* [1940] 1 K.B. 463.

There are four exceptions to TA s. 154(1):

(*a*) Where one or more persons continue to carry on the trade, e.g. after a change in the members of a partnership, an election may be made under TA s. 154(2) that the trade be treated as continuing. The election must be by notice sent to the Inspector within two years of the change and signed by all the persons engaged in carrying on the trade before the change and all those so engaged after it.

(*b*) Where the change is in the trustees or personal representatives carrying on a trade in those capacities (TA s. 154(7)).

(*c*) Where a partnership consists of a company and individuals and there is no change in the individual partners (TA s. 155(3)(*b*)).

(*d*) Where a sole trader dies and his spouse, who was living with him, continues to carry on the trade (extra-statutory concession no. A8).

There was formerly a further exception under F.A. 1954 s. 17 (company reconstructions). This section has now been superseded for corporation tax purposes by TA s. 252, considered later at pp. 270–1.

§ 3 The "cash" or "earnings" basis

The taxable profit (or loss) of a trade is the net result of trading operations during the appropriate basis period, placing taxable receipts on one side of the account and allowable expenditure on the other. The Revenue and the Courts generally sanction accounts made up in accordance with ordinary principles of commercial accountancy, unless the accounting practice contravenes some legal norm: *see Patrick* v. *Broadstone Mills Ltd* [1954] 1 W.L.R. 158 and *Southern Railway of Peru Ltd* v. *Owen* [1957] A.C. 334. But it is for the Courts and not for accountants, however expert, to decide whether methods in dispute represent sound accounting practice: *see*

Heather v. *P-E Consulting Group* [1972] 3 W.L.R. 833, in which the Court of Appeal denied that *Odeon Associated Theatres* v. *Jones* [1972] 2 W.L.R. 331 had upgraded the evidence of accountants.

The accountant's essential concern is to obtain an accurate picture of trading over the accounting period. In the simplest cases, street vendors for instance, this can be obtained merely by deducting payments actually made from payments actually received. This "cash basis" is the method normally adopted for barristers and authors. In most cases, however, additional complexities obtain. The trader carries stock-in-trade and has work in progress at the beginning and end of the accounting period; and he both gives and receives credit. The crude cash basis has therefore usually to yield to the more refined "earnings basis", which takes these complexities into account in the manner outlined in the succeeding paragraphs. 'From the standpoint of strict accountancy practice,' ventured Lord Cooper L.P. in *Rankine* v. *IRC*, 'I have no doubt that the earnings basis is always the theoretically ideal method' though he hastened to add that 'in the case of some familiar vocations' the cash basis was the 'commonsense practical expedient' ((1951) 32 T.C. 520 at 527).

Rankine v. *IRC* established that the Revenue, having made an assessment on one basis, cannot later raise an additional assessment for the same year on the other basis. There is however nothing to prevent them changing the basis of assessment from one year of assessment to the next: *see Wetton, Page & Co.* v. *Attwooll* [1963] 1 W.L.R. 114.

Until 1968 a trader was able to cause profits to fall out of computation by changing from a cash to an earnings basis. F. A. 1968, in a provision now contained in TA s. 144(2), closed this loophole by charging sums escaping in this way under Case VI. The legislation omitted to provide corresponding relief against double taxation in the event of the converse change of basis—another case of heads the Revenue win, tails the taxpayer loses.

§ 4 Credits and debits

The trader on an earnings basis must bring sums into account as trading receipts as and when he becomes entitled to them, even if actual payment is to take place later. However, '[m]oney must not be taken as being, so to speak, in hand until all the conditions to earn it have been fulfilled' ((1946) 27 T.C. at 185 *per* Lord Greene M.R.). Thus the work must have been done, or the goods delivered, which entitle the trader to a payment before he can enter it in his accounts as a credit item. Conversely, he must bring debit items into account as and when they fall due, regardless of when payment is to be made.

Where a payment due to the trader is to be delayed for some time, it may be brought into account at an appropriately discounted value, as in *Absalom* v. *Talbot* [1944] A.C. 204, though their Lordships in that case were not agreed as to the proper method of arriving at the correct discount. If the amount eventually received is more than the discounted figure brought into account, the excess must be related back to the earlier period by reopening the earlier account: *see Severne* v. *Dadswell* [1954] 3 A.E.R. 243. Much the same factual result ensues where a trader incurs a debt which he enters in his accounts as a debit item but which in a later year is released. In *British Mexican Petroleum Co.* v. *Jackson* (1932) 16 T.C. 570 the House of Lords came to the remarkable conclusion that the earlier account could not be reopened because the liability in it had been correctly stated; and, moreover, that the release of the debt could not be regarded as a trading receipt of the later year. The effect of this decision was reversed as from 1960–61 by what is now TA s. 136, which constitutes a released debt a trading receipt of the period in which the release was effected.

A similar juridical problem has arisen in cases concerning unclaimed balances. In *Morley* v. *Tattersall* (1938) 22 T.C. 51 the famous bloodstock auctioneers received sums from purchasers for which they were liable to account to their clients, the vendors. Sums remaining uncollected were eventually transferred to the credit of the individual partners. The Court of Appeal held that they were not trading receipts. By contrast, in *Elson* v. *Prices' Tailors* (1962) 40 T.C. 671 customers ordering made-to-measure garments were asked to leave "deposits" which were returned if the garments proved unsatisfactory. Unclaimed deposits were transferred to an "unclaimed deposits account". Ungoed-Thomas J. held the deposits to be trading receipts of the year in which they were paid by the customers. The point of distinction seems to be that in the former case the sums *when received* were clients' money while in the latter the deposits on receipt became the tailors' property. As Greene M. R. said in the *Tattersall* case: 'The quality and nature of a receipt for income tax purposes is fixed once and for all when it is received' (ibid. at 65). *Cf.* the unsatisfactory decision in *Jay's the Jewellers Ltd* v. *IRC* (1947) 29 T.C. 274.

There is in theory no fiscal restraint on a trader's freedom to buy and sell his stock at whatever price he wishes. Thus in *Julius Bendit Ltd* v. *IRC* (1945) 27 T.C. 44 and in *Craddock* v. *Zevo Finance Co. Ltd* (1946) 27 T.C. 267 companies had bought stock at artificially low and artificially high prices respectively. In the former case the company, in the latter the Revenue, were not allowed to substitute market values for the actual buying prices. 'To put the matter in its simplest form,' said Viscount Simon in the *Zevo* case,' the profit or loss to a trader in dealing with his stock-in-trade is arrived at for income tax purposes by comparing what his stock in fact cost him with what he in fact realized on resale. It is unsound to substitute alleged market values for what it in fact cost him' (ibid. at 287).

TA s. 485 is an important exception to this principle. It applies where any property is sold between "associated persons", a term which denotes that the buyer is a body of persons over whom the seller has control, or vice versa, or that both the buyer and the seller are bodies of persons controlled by some other person. Where the sale is at an undervalue the seller must be treated as having made the sale at the price which the property would have fetched had the transaction taken place between independent persons dealing at arm's length (s.-s. (1)); and where the sale is at an overvalue the buyer must be treated likewise (s.-s. (2)). Though the section is extended by sub-section (6) to transactions other than sales, its scope is greatly curtailed by its exclusion from transactions in which the buyer (under s.-s. (1)) or the seller (under s.-s. (2)) is resident and carrying on a trade in the UK and the price of the property is taken into account in computing the profits or losses of his trade.

Sharkey v. *Wernher* [1956] A.C. 58 strikes a more curious point of departure from the principles underlying Viscount Simon's dictum. In that case Lady Zia Wernher had transferred five horses from her stud farm (a trade) to her racing stables (a hobby). The question at issue concerned the proper figure to appear in the stud farm accounts: was it cost or was it market value? (One wonders as to the outcome had Lady Zia's counsel pressed the bolder contention that no figure at all should have appeared, since no profit had been realized.) The Commissioners and four of the judges preferred cost, the other four judges market value, but the latter included a majority of the House of Lords. The Revenue quickly put *Sharkey* v. *Wernher* to work as an all-purpose harvester of unreaped profits. In *Petrotim Securities Ltd* v. *Ayres* [1964] 1 A.E.R. 269 a company dealing in shares, Petrotim, sold investments to its parent company, Ridge, for less than a quarter of their market value, and later sold War Loan to Blackheath, another Ridge subsidiary, for less than a tenth of the price at which Petrotim had bought the stock four days earlier. The Revenue successfully contended that the sale to Ridge was not a trading transaction and that, on the principle of *Sharkey* v. *Wernher*, market value should be substituted for the agreed sale price; and that neither the purchase nor the sale of War Loan were trading transactions and the relative figures should therefore be eliminated from the computation of Petrotim's tax liability. *Sharkey* v. *Wernher*, said Lord Denning, 'is not confined to cases where a person is a "self-supplier". It applies to any case where a trader may, for no reason, choose to give things away or throw them into the sea' (ibid. at 273). Followed in *Skinner* v. *Berry Head Lands Ltd* [1971] 1 A.E.R. 222.

The Revenue suffered a significant reverse in *Mason* v. *Innes* [1967] Ch. 1079. Hammond Innes, the author, had assigned the copyright in *The Doomed Oasis*, worth £15,425, to his father as a gift. The Court of Appeal held the gift untaxable (though today capital gains tax liability would attach to it). In the words once again of Lord Denning: 'The proposition in *Sharkey* v. *Wernher* does not apply to professional men. It is confined to the case of traders who keep stock-in-trade and whose accounts are, or should be, kept on an earnings basis' (ibid. at 1090). It remains undecided whether a professional man on an earnings basis falls within the principle of *Sharkey* v. *Wernher*. Intuitively, one would think not. It seems a little incongruous that the accountant who fills in his own tax return, or the solicitor who draws up his own will, should account to the Revenue for the market value of the professional expertise involved.

● The ramifications of *Sharkey* v. *Wernher* have yet to be fully explored. In particular, it will be interesting to discover, whether a purchaser (in *Petrotim's case*, Ridge or Blackheath) can invoke the principle against the Revenue. The true principle, it is submitted, is that market value is to be substituted where the price is not merely artificial but utterly derisory or absurd. Only on this basis can the *Petrotim* case be reconciled with the *Julius Bendit* and *Zevo Finance* cases (*see* pp. 70–1 above) or with the line of authority on which *Griffiths* v. *Harrison* [1963] A.C. 1 was based. In *Jacgilden (Weston Hall) Ltd* v. *Castle* [1969] 3 A.E.R. 1110, R contracted to buy an hotel for £72,000. The original intention was to put the property into the J company, of which he and his wife were the sole shareholders, with a view to demolishing the hotel and erecting flats; but he changed his mind and, on completion, when the hotel's market value was £150,000, directed the vendors to convey it to the J company. Plowman J. held that the proper amount to be debited in the J company's accounts in respect of the acquisition of the hotel was £72,000; he applied the *Zevo Finance* case and distinguished *Sharkey* v. *Wernher* on the basis that there was no question 'of the contract . . . having been an illusory or colourable or fraudulent transaction' (ibid. at 1121).

A measure of convergent validity is provided for the principle in *Sharkey* v. *Wernher* by the established rule that payments made in money's worth rather than money must be brought into account at market value. Thus when a gold-mining concession had been sold by one company to another for fully paid shares, the House of Lords held in *Gold Coast Selection*

Trust Ltd v. *Humphrey* [1948] A.C. 459 that the selling company should be treated as having acquired the shares at market value, but since such a large block of shares would depress the market, that the case should be remitted to the Commissioners for them to make the correct valuation. On the other hand, their Lordships held in *Varty* v. *British South Africa Co.* [1966] A.C. 381 that no taxable receipt had accrued to a company which had been granted an *option* to purchase shares and which in due course had exercised the option.

§ 5 Stock-in-trade and work in progress

The earnings basis attempts to reflect any fluctuations in trading stock and work in progress over the accounting period. Standard accountancy practice is to notionally sell stock and work in progress at the beginning and end of each accounting period. As Viscount Simonds once explained: 'Stock-in-trade and work in progress are brought into account because, fictitiously, but as a matter of plain common sense, they are treated as a receipt of the year's trading' ([1961] 2 A.E.R. at 171).

Where stock has fallen in value during the accounting period, the trader is allowed, though he has suffered no real loss (yet), to artificially depress his tax bill by bringing stock into account at the end of the period at market value. What is more, *IRC* v. *Cock, Russell & Co. Ltd* [1949] 2 A.E.R. 889 sanctioned the practice of picking and choosing, i.e. valuing items that have gone up in value at cost and those that have depreciated at market value. Whether work in progress can be brought in at market value and, if so, how this would be ascertained, are moot points.

The cost of stock normally means the cost of its acquisition, allowing nothing for maintenance. In a situation in which quantities of stock have been bought at different times and then drawn on more or less indiscriminately to be used or sold, it may be impossible to work out the price at which existing stock-in-hand was bought. In the case of perishables, accountants invariably make the assumption of "F.I.F.O." (first-in-first-out), i.e. that the stock first used or sold was the stock first bought. However, non-perishables may be problematical. In the *Anaconda case* [1965] A.C. 85 a company which purchased vast quantities of metals for manufacture into sheets, rods, and tubes decided in 1947, in the wake of the sharp post-War rise in metal prices, to change from F.I.F.O. to L.I.F.O. (last-in-first-out). The Privy Council advised that, while L.I.F.O. was a perfectly acceptable method in appropriate circumstances, F.I.F.O. was the only accurate method in the instant case.

The market value of stock is the best price obtainable in the market in which the trader actually sells. Thus for a retail trader it means the retail, not the wholesale, price: *see B.S.C. Footwear Ltd* v. *Ridgway* [1971] 2 W.L.R. 1313.

Where the builder or developer of an estate grants leases of the various plots of land, reserving a ground rent, each freehold reversion is an item of trading stock which must therefore be brought into successive accounts at the lower of cost or market value. There is a special formula for valuing the freehold reversions in this type of situation, called the "Emery formula" because first applied by the Commissioners in *Emery & Sons* v. *IRC* [1937] A.C. 91 (though their determination was overruled by the House of Lords], or the "Macnaghten formula" after the learned judge who once described it as a "simple" rule of three sum: 'As A, the premiums, plus B, the selling value of the ground rents, is to B, so is C, the total expenses of the builder, to D, the cost of the ground rents or reversions' ((1944) 26 T.C. 119 at 124).

All nine judges hearing *Duple Motor Bodies Ltd* v. *Ostime* (1961) 39 T.C. 537 were able to agree that the cost of work in progress is a matter of accounting practice rather than law. In that case a company had since 1924 been using the "direct cost" method, according to which only materials and labour are taken into account. Assessments on the company for 1951–52 to 1953–54 were made by the "on-cost" method, which includes in addition a proportion of indirect expenditure, such as general factory or office over-heads. The Courts held that the case stated revealed nothing that could justify compelling the company to change its practice. The Commissioners were roundly taken to task for expressing their preference for the on-cost method ('I cannot very well tell them that their own opinions are irrelevant . . . that their case is inconsistent in itself and ought to be redrafted from top to bottom; that would not be polite . . .' (ibid. at 554 *per* Vaisey J.)).

TA ss. 137 and 138 drain of avoidance potential the doctrine that the disposal of stock after discontinuance is not trading (*see* 2.21 § 8 above). S. 137 applies only to trades. It requires that at discontinuance trading stock and work in progress be valued at the amount realizable on sale in the open market (TA s. 137(1)(*b*)). However, there is an important saving: where the stock or work in progress is sold to a UK trader or intending trader who would be entitled to treat the cost as a deductible expense, the actual consideration can be entered in the final account (s. 137(1)(*a*)). An interesting case in point is *Moore* v. *Mackenzie* [1972] 2 A.E.R. 549. A company (X) dealing in land wished to discontinue and had the opportunity to sell at full value its remaining stock (a block of flats), then worth much more than the book value, to an association (Z). In one hectic afternoon, Y (a company dealing in land and shares) bought the shares in X at their net asset value, then its assets at book value. There was then a board meeting of X at which it was resolved to discontinue. Finally, Y sold the block of flats to Z at market value. From Y's viewpoint the gain on the flats was almost balanced by the fall in value of the shares in X, treated as trading stock in Y's books. The Revenue invoked *Petrotim* and *Sharkey* v. *Wernher* in submitting that market value should be substituted in X's books for the actual sale price to Y. However, X succeeded in persuading Megarry J. that TA s. 137(1)(*a*) prevented any such substitution. S. 137(1), the learned judge pointed out, applies to 'any trading stock belonging to the trade at the discontinuance' and 'I have heard nothing to shake me from my belief, primitive though it may be, that "at" means "at" ' (ibid. at 560). It is tempting to infer that the transactions in *Petrotim* would have succeeded had they been arranged to coincide with a discontinuance. Whether or not *Moore* v. *Mackenzie* provides us with 'a new-found fiscal causeway'—in Megarry J.'s phrase (ibid. at 560)—remains to be seen. S. 138 applies a similar rule to work in progress on the discontinuance of a profession or vocation. It differs from s. 137 in that (*a*) it does not extend to stock, and (*b*) it does not make a valuation mandatory, merely prescribes the method of making the valuation if it should be undertaken. It follows from (*b*) that accounts rendered on a cash basis are unaffected by s. 138, since valuation of work in progress is not necessary for cash-based accounts. Neither section applies to a discontinuance brought about by the death of a sole trader or person carrying on a profession or vocation. Death has not come to be regarded (yet) as an avoidance technique.

§ 6 Capital and income: how to tell night from day or red from orange

We have seen how, as a matter of accounting, a trader's credits and debits arise. The next step is to colour in the outline by showing which are the receipts and disbursements that respectively qualify as credits and debits. Before moving to the specific, a general point must be elaborated, namely that receipts and expenditure of a capital nature have no place in a Case I or II computation. Telling capital from income is by no means always an easy matter.

Receipts

In the leading case of *Van den Berghs Ltd* v. *Clark* [1935] A.C. 431 Lord Macmillan summarized the position admirably: 'In general the distinction is well recognized and easily applied, but from time to time cases arise where an item lies on the borderline and the task of assigning it to income or capital becomes one of much refinement . . . While each case is found to turn upon its own facts, and no infallible criterion emerges, nevertheless the decisions are useful as illustrations and as affording indications of the kind of considerations which may relevantly be borne in mind in approaching the problem' (ibid. at 438–9). That case arose when Van den Berghs, the margarine manufacturers, were a separate company and Jurgens, a Dutch company, their principal rival. The two companies had entered into agreements to share profits and losses from 1908 through to the end of 1940. Disputes then arose and complicated negotiations were settled by rescinding the old agreements in favour of a fresh one under which the Dutch company paid the English company £450,000 "as damages". The House of Lords held this sum an untaxable capital receipt, applying a test which in compensation cases has almost become the "infallible criterion" Lord Macmillan referred to: does the receipt relate to the permanent profit-making apparatus of the business? If so, it is capital: *see*, for example, *Chibbett* v. *Robinson & Sons Ltd* (1924) 9 T.C. 48 and *Barr, Crombie & Co. Ltd* v. *IRC* (1945) 26 T.C. 406. If not, it is income: *see Short Bros.* v. *IRC* (1927) 12 T.C. 955; *Kelsall Parsons & Co.* v. *IRC* (1938) 21 T.C. 608; *London & Thames Haven Oil Wharves Ltd* v. *Attwooll* (1966) 43 T.C. 491; and *John Mills Productions Ltd* v. *Mathias* (1967) 44 T.C. 441. In *London & Thames Haven etc* v. *Attwooll* Diplock L.J. stated the governing principle in these words: 'Where, pursuant to a legal right, a trader receives from another person compensation for the trader's failure to receive a sum of money . . ., the compensation is to be treated for income tax purposes in the same way as that sum of money would have been treated if it had been received instead of the compensation' (loc. cit. at 515).

A similar problem arises where compensation is received, not for the trader's failure to receive a sum of money, but for the sterilization of an asset. Even though the amount of compensation may in this type of situation be calculated on the basis of lost profits, it will constitute a capital receipt if the degree of sterilization represents a substantial emasculation of the profit-making structure of the trade. Thus in *Glenboig Union Fireclay Co. Ltd* v. *IRC* (1922) 12 T.C. 427 a railway company exercised its statutory powers to require the fireclay under its railway to remain unworked and paid more than £15,000 in compensation to the lessees of the fireclay fields. The House of Lords held this sum a capital receipt. On the other side of the line falls *Burmah Steamship Co.* v. *IRC* (1931) 16 T.C. 67.

An alternative rationale for the *Glenboig* decision, that the receipt was not a profit *of the trade*, found favour in several other cases. Thus in *Higgs* v. *Olivier* [1952] Ch. 311, Sir Laurence Olivier escaped taxation on a payment of £15,000 for agreeing with a film company not to act in, produce, or direct a film for any other company for a period of eighteen months. Similarly, in *Walker* v. *Carnaby Harrower, Barham & Pykett* [1970] 1 A.E.R. 502 a solatium for loss of office paid to a firm of accountants was held untaxable.

A second judicial touchstone in distinguishing capital and income is borrowed from economics: sums derived from "fixed" capital are capital receipts while those from "circulating" capital are on revenue account. In a case relating to expenditure, Lord Haldane said of this test: 'My lords, it is not necessary to draw an exact line of demarcation between fixed and circulating capital. Since Adam Smith drew the distinction . . ., a distinction which has since become classical, economists have never been able to define much more precisely what the line of demarcation is. Adam Smith described fixed capital as what the owner turns to profit by keeping in his own possession, circulating capital as what he makes profit of by parting with it and letting it change masters' ([1921] 2 A.C. 13 at 19–20). A good illustration of the application of this test is *Davies* v. *The Shell Co. of China* (1951) 32 T.C. 133. Shell required its Chinese agents to provide it with deposits, usually in Chinese dollars, which it held in the form of sterling. Sino-Japanese hostilities brought about the eventual devaluation of the Chinese dollar, with the result that the sums repayable to the agents were much less in aggregate value than the sums held by Shell. This exchange profit was held to be of a capital nature since the deposits had been used as fixed capital.

The test was also central to an important series of cases concerning "know-how". Receipts from sales of "know-how" were held capital in *Moriarty* v. *Evans Medical Supplies Ltd* [1957] 3 A.E.R. 718, in which an English company manufacturing pharmaceuticals entered into an agreement with the Burmese Government to provide the "know-how" which would enable the Government to manufacture similar products for itself in consideration of a lump sum payment of £100,000, and in *Wolf Electric Tools Ltd* v. *Wilson* [1969] 2 A.E.R. 724, which concerned a similar arrangement whereby another English company contracted to supply an Indian company with the "know-how" necessary for the establishment of a factory to make electric tools in return for shares in the Indian company. The opposite result was reached in *Rolls-Royce Ltd* v. *Jeffrey* [1962] 1 A.E.R. 801, where Rolls-Royce had made a number of agreements with foreign governments and companies for the supply of (*a*) "know-how" as to the construction of engines, and (*b*) licences to manufacture them, in consideration of lump sums and also, in some cases, annual technical liaison fees; in *Musker* v. *English Electric Co. Ltd* (1964) 41 T.C. 556, in which "know-how" relating to marine turbines and aircraft had been supplied to various companies at the request of the British Government for lump sum payments; and in *Coalite &*

Chemical Products Ltd v. *Treeby* [1971] T.R. 425, in which secret processes and information were supplied by a company for payments totalling £68,000 to a consortium engaged in developing a project in East Germany.

A provision in F.A. 1968, now contained in TA s. 386, sought to codify the law along the lines of the decided cases. "Know-how" is defined by s.-s. (7) as 'any industrial information and techniques likely to assist in the manufacture or processing of goods or materials, or in the working of a mine, oil-well [etc] . . ., or in the carrying out of any agricultural, forestry or fishing operations.' The section may be summarized as follows: (1) Where a trader disposes of "know-how" used in his trade, and continues his trade after the disposal, the amount or value of any disposal consideration received by him must be treated as a trading receipt.

(2) Where he disposes of the trade itself (or part of it) together with "know-how" used in the trade, any disposal consideration received by him must be treated, *vis-à-vis* both the vendor and the purchaser, as a payment for goodwill (i.e. as capital) unless both the vendor and the purchaser jointly elect otherwise within two years of the disposal.

(3) Where a sale of "know-how" takes place between "associated persons" (*see* p. 71 above), any consideration must be treated *vis-à-vis* both parties as a payment for goodwill.

(4) Where, in connection with any disposal of "know-how", a person gives an undertaking which might restrict his or another's activities, any consideration for the undertaking must be treated as additional consideration for the "know-how".

(5) Any consideration for the disposal of "know-how" not otherwise chargeable falls within Case VI of Schedule D.

Expenditure

There have been many more borderline cases on expenditure than on receipts. 'Indeed,' ventured Lord Greene M.R., 'in many cases it is almost true to say that the spin of a coin would decide the matter almost as satisfactorily as an attempt to find reasons' ([1938] 2 K.B. at 498). A survey of the cases reveals that this is by no means an unduly pessimistic appraisal. It is fortunate therefore that the present Master of the Rolls has shown the fly the way out of the fly-bottle. After describing the borderline between capital and revenue expenditure as 'a blurred and undefined area in which anyone can get lost', he commented: 'It is like the border between day and night, or between red and orange. Everyone can tell the difference except in the marginal cases, and then everyone is in doubt'; and concluded with the advice that: 'the only safe rule is to go by precedent. . . . [S]earch through the cases and see whether the instant problem has come up before. If so, go by it. If not, go by the nearest you can find' (*Heather* v. *P-E Consulting Group* [1972] 3 W.L.R. 833 at 837).

The dictum of Viscount Cave L.C.—to the effect that expenditure is capital which 'is made, not once and for all, but with a view to bringing into existence an asset or an advantage for the enduring benefit of a trade' (*British Insulated & Helsby Cables* v. *Atherton* [1926] A.C. 205 at 213)—has frequently commended itself to the judges, perhaps less often in reaching conclusions than to justify conclusions already reached. Thus in *Commissioner of Taxes* v. *Nchanga Consolidated Copper Mines Ltd* [1964] A.C. 948 the Anglo-American group of copper mines, comprising Bancroft, Nchanga, and Rhokana, instituted a scheme whereby Bancroft would cease production for a year and Nchanga and Rhokana would make compensatory payments to Bancroft. The Privy Council advised that the right to have Bancroft out of production for a year was not a sufficiently "enduring" benefit to constitute the payments capital. Similarly in *Heather* v. *P-E Consulting Group* [1972] 3 W.L.R. 833 a trust fund was set up by a deed in which a subsidiary company covenanted to pay annually to the trustees 10% of its gross profits. The trustees were to use the fund to purchase shares in the holding company. The payments were to cease when the trust had acquired 40% of the shares in the holding company. The dual objects were (1) to remove the possibility of outsiders obtaining control, and (2) since the trustees had power to transfer shares at a fair value to any employees wishing to buy them, to provide senior staff with an incentive. The Court of Appeal held the payments revenue (but leave has been given to appeal to the House of Lords). See also *IRC* v. *Carron Co* (1968) 45 T.C. 18; and *Sargent* v. *Eayrs* [1973] S.T.C. 50.

Another helpful dictum, though not often cited, is that of Lord Sands: 'Broadly speaking, outlay is deemed to be capital when it is made for the initiation of a business, for the extension of a business, or for a substantial replacement of equipment' ((1927) 13 T.C. at 14). In *Anglo-Persian Oil Co. Ltd* v. *Dale* (1931) 16 T.C. 253 Rowlatt J. at first instance, but with the approval of Romer L.J. in the Court of Appeal, ingeniously married Viscount Cave's dictum with the fixed/circulating capital test by interpreting "enduring" to mean "enduring in the way that fixed capital endures", with the result that an expenditure on circulating capital would not be made to acquire an enduring asset.

§ 7 Deductible expenditure

PUNCH

"Is this deductible?"

The basic rule governing expenditure, now TA s. 519(1), is one of the finer specimens of fiscal logic: 'In arriving at the amount of profit or gains for tax purposes . . .,' it declares, 'no other deductions shall be made than such as are expressly enumerated in the Tax Acts. . . .' Yet originally no deductions whatever were enumerated and even now there are very few. Furthermore, there is an impressively long list of *dis*allowances. *Mirabile dictu* we are able to make sense of the provision by turning it on its head. The negative disallowances are interpreted as bearing the implication that their positive counterparts are deductible; and, besides, the very concept of a trading profit is taken to mean the *excess* of a receipt over any expenditure incurred in earning that receipt. Accordingly, in the words of Jenkins L.J., 'It has long been well settled that the effect of these provisions as to deductions is that the balance of the profits and gains of a trade must be ascertained in accordance with the ordinary principles of commercial trading, by deducting from the gross receipts all expenditure properly deductible from them on those principles, save in so far as any amount so deducted falls within any of the statutory prohibitions' ((1954) 35 T.C. at 393).

As a general rule a trader is entitled to deduct any payments he considers commercially expedient. Thus in *Morgan* v. *Tate & Lyle Ltd* [1955] A.C. 21 their Lordships held the sugar refiners entitled to deduct expenditure on a campaign to avert the threat of nationalization. What is more, expenditure may be deducted in the year in which it is incurred even though the profits to be derived from it are to accrue in later years: *see Vallambrosa Rubber Co. Ltd* v. *Farmer* (1910) 5 T.C. 529. On the other hand, only expenses incurred *in earning* profits are deductible. Those representing the application of profits *once earned* are not: *see*, for instance, *Racecourse Betting Control Board* v. *Young* (1959) 38 T.C. 426. For this reason UK direct taxes and foreign income taxes are not deductible while UK indirect taxes and national insurance payments apparently are. Strictly speaking, any expenses in computing taxable profits or in disputing liability ought not to be deductible since, as Lord Simonds once put it, the trader's 'profit is no more affected by the exigibility of tax than is a man's temperature altered by the purchase of a thermometer, even though he starts by haggling about the price of it' ([1948] A.C. at 527). However, accountants' fees are the subject of a Revenue concession.

The main statutory disallowances are these:

(1) 'any disbursements or expenses, not being money wholly and exclusively laid out or expended for the purposes of the trade, profession or vocation' (TA s. 130(*a*))

"For the purposes of the trade" was construed by Lord Davey in *Strong & Co.* v. *Woodifield* [1906] A.C. 448, discussed at p. 85 below, to mean "for the purpose of earning the profits". His embellishment is not regarded as an improvement on the statutory formulation.

● Another troublesome part of s. 130(*a*) is the phrase "wholly and exclusively". The meaning of these three words is a matter of some consequence since they appear in a number of provisions of the Taxes Acts and, in particular, in the basic rules governing expenditure under Schedule E and capital gains tax respectively. Several years ago one might confidently have asserted that the phrase ruled out duality of purpose in the sense that money expended partly for a trading and partly for a non-trading purpose was disallowed. There is certainly no shortage of authority for this assertion.

There are, for example, two decisions of Pennycuick J. refusing the claims, firstly, of the sole partner in a Lancashire firm of solicitors who visited America with his wife with a view to attending law conferences in Washington and Ottawa and having a holiday at the same time (*Bowden* v. *Russell & Russell* [1965] 2 A.E.R. 258) and, secondly, of a part-time guitarist who underwent an operation to graft a tendon on to the little finger of his left hand (*Prince* v. *Mapp* [1970] 1 A.E.R. 519). Similarly Plowman J. held in *Murgatroyd* v. *Evans-Jackson* [1967] 1 W.L.R. 423, which concerned a trade-mark agent who had ruptured a disc and had opted for a nursing home rather than a Health Service hospital so as to be able to use the telephone and confer with his staff and clients, that the claim for 60% of the total expenditure was bound to fail since it tacitly admitted an element of duality. For a look at some of the other deduction claims which fell at the duality hurdle, *see Norman* v. *Golder* [1945] 1 A.E.R. 352 (p. 83 below), followed in *Knight* v. *Parry* [1973] S.T.C. 56, and *Ransom* v. *Higgs* [1973] S.T.C. 330.

Bowden v. Russell is consistent with the contrary decision in *Edwards* v. *Warmsley, Henshall & Co.* [1968] 1 A.E.R. 1968, in which Cross J. allowed a firm of accountants to deduct expenditure incurred in sending one of the partners—who had been instructed to go—to a congress of accountants in New York. On the other hand, *Prince* v. *Mapp* and *Murgatroyd* v. *Evans-Jackson* are not easy to reconcile with *Copeman* v. *Flood* [1941] 1 K.B. 202. In that case a daughter aged seventeen and a son aged twenty-four were credited in the accounts of a family business with sums of £2,600 each as remuneration, of which they had drawn only £70 and £277 respectively. Lawrence J. remitted the case to the Commissioners to determine what proportion of those sums of £2,600 were wholly and exclusively for trading purposes.

● There are several recent cases in which the duality argument has been undermined by the judges with more subtle constructs than Lawrence J.'s rather dubious expedient of apportionment. The need for intervention arose out of a number of harsh decisions on travel expenses, both under Schedule E and under Cases I and II of Schedule D. For example, in *Newsom* v. *Robertson* [1952] 2 A.E.R. 728 a barrister was disallowed his expenditure in travelling between his chambers in Lincoln's Inn and his home in the country, even though he did much of his work at home. (There is, incidentally, a Reader's Digest ending to the case: according to Mr Newsom's son, one of the author's students, the attendant publicity brought Mr Newsom a sudden shower of briefs.) It is instructive to compare *Newsom's case* with *Horton* v. *Young* (1971) 47 T.C. 60, in which a self-employed bricklayer was held entitled to deduct his expenses of travelling to building sites up to fifty-five miles from his home on the ground that, since he negotiated all his contracts at home (by 'phone), his home constituted his base of operations. He was therefore travelling, not from home to work, but merely from one place of work to another. The same argument had commended itself to the House of Lords in a Schedule E case—*Owen* v. *Pook* [1970] A.C. 244—and later found favour with Pennycuick V-C in another Schedule E case—*Taylor* v. *Provan* [1972] 1 W.L.R. 1459. Moreover the Courts have found other ways round the duality argument, which was rejected in both *Elwood* v. *Utitz* (1965) 42 T.C. 482 (Schedule E) and *IRC* v. *Richards' Executors* [1971] 1 W.L.R. 571 (capital gains tax). It will be interesting to see where the Courts' new liberal approach will lead us. (We will be taking a closer look at the Schedule E and capital gains tax cases later: *see* pp. 113–14 and 207 below.)

We realize of course that duality is only relevant where one is a trading and the other a non-trading purpose. It has never been doubted that a trader is entitled to deduct money expended for more than one purpose where both or all are trading purposes. Thus in *Heather* v. *P-E Consulting Group* [1972] 3 W.L.R. 833, the facts of which are set out at p. 79 above, the Court further held that the payments were deductible under s. 130(*a*).

Generally payments to or for the benefit of employees are deductible within s. 130(*a*). Thus in *Smith* v. *The Incorporated Council of Law Reporting* [1914] 3 K.B. 674 Scrutton J. upheld the deductibility of a retirement gratuity paid by the Council to one of its reporters. Even payments to get rid of troublesome employees, as in *Mitchell* v. *Noble Ltd* [1927] 1 K.B. 719, have been allowed. But a take-over situation is more equivocal: *see Snook* v. *Blasdale* (1952) 33 T.C. 244 and in particular the comments of Donovan J. at 251. And, for a claim refused, *see Bamford* v. *A.T.A. Advertising Ltd* [1972] 3 A.E.R. 535 (p. 85 below).

(2) 'any disbursements or expenses of maintenance of the parties, their families or establishments, or any sums expended for any other domestic or private purposes distinct from the purposes of the trade, profession or vocation' (TA s. 130(*b*))

In *Norman* v. *Golder* [1945] 1. A.E.R. 352 expenses incurred during a shorthand writer's illness, allegedly due to unfavourable working conditions, were disallowed under both s. 130(*a*) and (*b*). Similarly *Murgatroyd* v. *Evans-Jackson* and *Prince* v. *Mapp* involved unsuccessful alternative claims under this head (for the facts of those cases, *see* p. 82 above).

On the other hand Professor Emil Korner scored a notable success in persuading the House of Lords in *IRC* v. *Korner* [1969] 1 A.E.R. 679 that *all* the expenditure he had incurred in maintaining his hobby farm was deductible despite the finding that nine-tenths of it was for domestic or private purposes. This decision was quickly reversed by statute.

(3) Expenditure on business premises and equipment

Several of the statutory disallowances may conveniently be grouped under this heading. The effect of TA s. 130(c) is to allow a trader to deduct rent in respect of business premises. Rates and premiums to insure the premises against fire, flood, etc are also deductible.

In *Hinton* v. *Maden & Ireland Ltd* [1959] 3 A.E.R. 356 their Lordships interpreted s. 130(d) as implying that the cost of replacing "implements, utensils or articles" used for trading purposes is deductible. This "renewals" basis, as it has come to be called, applies only to replacements; it does not apply to the original cost of acquiring the articles or to the cost of any later additions: *see* the interesting case of *Abbott* v. *Albion Greyhounds* [1945] 1 A.E.R. 308. Revenue practice is to allow the cost of replacing assets which have a short life, such as an hotelier's cutlery, either to be deducted as the replacements fall to be made or, in some cases, to be written off over two or three years. In practice traders prefer, where possible, to claim capital allowances rather than the renewals basis.

The combined effect of s. 130(a) and (d) is to permit a deduction for the cost of repairing business premises but not of improving or replacing them. This distinction between repair and renewal seems to depend more than anything upon the physical extent of the business premises: contrast *O'Grady* v. *Bullcroft Main Collieries Ltd* (1932) 17 T.C. 93, in which the cost of removing an old chimney and replacing it with a new one was not allowed, with *Jones* v. *IRC* (1951) 32 T.C. 513, in which it was. *See also Conn* v. *Robins Bros Ltd* (1966) 43 T.C. 266.

According to the Law Shipping rule, derived from *Law Shipping Co. Ltd* v. *IRC* (1923) 12 T.C. 621, repairs to premises acquired in a dilapidated condition are not deductible because in a sense they represent part of the capital cost of the premises. The Law Shipping Company had bought an old ship, had sailed her for six months, and had then, to obtain a Lloyd's certificate, been obliged to spend £50,000 on repairs. The Court of Session held that only £12,000 of the £50,000 was deductible, since only this part was attributable to the period of the company's ownership. This decision must now be considered in the light of the Court of Appeal judgments in *Odeon Associated Theatres Ltd* v. *Jones* [1972] 2 W.L.R. 331, from which it appears that the question whether expenditure attributable to wear and tear incurred before a change of ownership should be regarded as revenue or capital must depend upon the facts of each case; and that accountants are the persons best placed to suggest an answer. The Regal Cinema, Marble Arch, had been purchased in 1945 in a state of disrepair for £240,000. Between 1947 and 1954 large sums had been spent on additions (charged to capital) and on repairs (partly charged to revenue). It was agreed that about £8,000 of the money spent on repairs was attributable to the period before purchase. The Court of Appeal held, distinguishing the *Law Shipping case*, that this sum had been properly charged to revenue and was therefore deductible. There are several points of distinction: in the *Law Shipping case* the price of the ship was less than it would have been but for her disrepair, the ship could not have earned profits until repaired, the repairs represented a much greater proportion of the price (40% compared with 3·3%), and there was no accountancy evidence in favour of charging the repairs against revenue. We must await future decisions for guidance as to the relative significance of these *differentiae*. (For one authoritative opinion, *see* [1972] B.T.R. at 53 (G.S.A.W.).)

(4) 'any loss not connected with or arising out of the trade, profession or vocation' (TA s. 130(*e*))

In *Strong & Co.* v. *Woodifield* [1906] A.C. 448 a customer sleeping in an inn owned by a brewery company was injured by the fall of a chimney owing to negligence on the part of the company's servants. In due course he recovered damages and costs from the company. Their Lordships held the sum non-deductible. By the same token Brightman J. refused in *Bamford* v. *A.T.A. Advertising Ltd* [1972] 3 A.E.R. 535 to allow the respondent company to deduct a sum of £15,000 misappropriated by one of the directors and written off in the books of the company as a bad debt: 'The loss is not, as in the case of the dishonest shop assistant, an incident of the company's trading activities. It arises altogether outside such activities' (ibid. at 544).

(5) 'any debts, except bad debts proved to be such, and doubtful debts to the extent that they are respectively estimated to be bad' (TA s.130(*i*))

Where a debt thought to be good has been entered in the trader's accounts as a debit item but turns out in a later year to be bad or doubtful, it seems that a deduction may be made in the later year: *see* the remarks of Viscount Simon L.C. in *Absalom* v. *Talbot* [1944] A.C. 204 at 213, concurred in by Lords Atkin and Porter, and followed in *Bristow* v. *Dickinson Ltd* [1946] K.B. 321.

(6) Miscellaneous

TA ss. 130 (f) and 519(2) disallow capital expenditure, s. 130(k) disallows 'any sum recoverable under an insurance or contract of indemnity', ss. 130(1) and 519(1)(b) disallow any annual payments made out of profits or gains brought into charge to tax (see 2.5 below), and s. 130(n) disallows 'any royalty or other sum paid in respect of the user of a patent'.

(7) Business entertainment expenditure

In two remarkably lenient decisions, both Roxburgh J. and a unanimous Court of Appeal in *Bentleys, Stokes & Lowless* v. *Beeson* [1952] 2 A.E.R. 82 reversed the Commissioners and held a firm of solicitors entitled to deduct their expenses in entertaining clients within the predecessor to TA s. 130(a). In 1965 the Labour Government took the opportunity to remove what had become a fertile source of discontent by means of a set of provisions now contained in TA s. 411, the drafting of which leaves something to be desired. The general rule is that business entertainment expenditure is no longer deductible (s.-s. (1)(a)) unless 'of a kind and on a scale which is reasonable having regard to all the circumstances' and incurred by a UK trader or member of his staff on entertaining an overseas customer (s.-s. (2)). Gifts fall within the general prohibition with the exception of any gift incorporating a conspicuous advertisement for the donor, being an article (a) which is not food, drink, tobacco, or a token or voucher exchangeable for goods, and (b) the cost of which to the donor, taken together with the cost to him of any other such articles given by him to that person in the same year, does not exceed £2 (s.-s. (8), as amended by F.A. 1971 s. 27).

There is one important exception. The prohibition does not, s.-s. (9) tells us, extend to expenses incurred in 'the provision by any person of anything which it is his trade to provide, and which is provided by him in the ordinary course of that trade for payment or, with the object of advertising to the public generally, gratuitously'. In *Associated Newspapers Ltd.* v. *Fleming* [1970] 3 W.L.R. 809 a newspaper company persuaded Megarry J. that it was entitled to deduct £67,143 spent in providing hospitality for informants and contributors who supplied material for its papers, on the ground that persuading informants and others to provide news was part of the company's trade within s.-s. (9). No sooner had the learned judge driven this coach and horses through s. 411, the Court of Appeal and a unanimous House of Lords showed them the way back again in reversing Megarry J.'s decision: the company's trade was to provide newspapers and news, not entertainment or hospitality. However, it must be added that Lord Denning in the Court of Appeal described s.-s. (9) as 'very obscure' and Lord Reid in the House of Lords suggested at one point that it was 'so obscure that no meaning can be given to it'. 'Draftsmen as well as Homer can nod,' Lord Reid suggested, 'and Parliament is so accustomed to obscure drafting in Finance Bills that no one may have noticed the defects in this subsection. *See* [1971] 3 W.L.R. 551 and [1972] 2 W.L.R. 1273.

§ 8 The presentation of accounts to the Revenue

A trader will normally have annual accounts prepared on a commercial basis. These will include a profit and loss account (in the case of a trade, the equivalent for a non-profit-making body being an income and expenditure account) and a balance sheet. In practice the trader will submit also a computation showing whatever adjustments to the accounts are necessary to bring them into conformity with the Income Tax Acts. Thus to the profit for that accounting period as disclosed by the accounts he will add:

(*a*) any non-deductible expenses that are charged in the accounts, as well as

(*b*) any trading profits not already included, and will deduct:

(*a*) any items featuring in the accounts which are not chargeable under Case I or II of Schedule D, either by reason of some exemption or because they properly fall within some other Case or Schedule,

(*b*) any deductible expenses not already charged (a rarity in practice), and

(*c*) any capital allowances for that period.

The adjusted profit will usually form the basis for negotiation with the Inspector.

2.24 CAPITAL ALLOWANCES

In principle a trader is not entitled to any deduction for capital expenditure (*see* pp. 75, 78–9, and 86 above) or for the depreciation of capital assets (*Coltness Iron Co.* v. *Black* (1881) 6 App. Cas. 315). As stated earlier (p. 18 above), however, a system of capital allowances was instituted at the end of the War in an attempt to encourage reinvestment. It can hardly be accounted a success: in 1970 this country invested only 15% of her national income, compared with an average figure of 19% for the Common Market and 28% for Japan. A parallel system of "investment allowances" was introduced in 1954, proved unsatisfactory, and was discarded in 1966 in favour of a system of "investment grants". These were cash incentives administered by the Board of Trade outside the tax system, though they were taken into account in calculating the amount of any capital allowances. The rates of investment grants and the range of qualifying assets were increased where the assets were used in "development areas". Grants ceased to be payable in respect of expenditure incurred after 26 October 1970, but by 1972 Mr Barber had changed his mind and decided to reintroduce investment grants, though he could not bring himself to mouth the phrase and preferred in his Budget Speech to refer to "investment allowances". These new cash incentives, officially known as "regional development grants", are completely disregarded in calculating capital allowances. They are given for expenditure after 21 March 1972 on industrial buildings and plant or machinery, and are confined to the development areas.

Turning now to capital allowances, we might first of all remind ourselves that the governing legislation is to be found in the Capital Allowances Act 1968, as amended by F.A.s 1971–73 (except in relation to patent rights and "know-how", which are governed by TA ss. 378–88). Capital allowances are available in respect of eight types of capital expenditure. They take the form of:

(i) "first-year" or "initial" allowances to cover the cost of acquisition or construction;
(ii) "writing-down" allowances to cover depreciation; and
(iii) "balancing" allowances (or charges) to adjust the position when assets which have qualified for allowances under (i) and/or (ii) are sold.

They are available both to individuals (including employees who use plant or machinery in the performance of their duties) and to companies.

There is space for just a cursory look at each of the types of expenditure that attract capital allowances.

§ 1 Plant or machinery

This category includes furniture, fittings, office equipment, motor vehicles, and even such esoteric artifacts as movable office partitioning (*Jarrold* v. *John Good & Sons* [1963] 1 A.E.R. 141) and knives and lasts used by the thousand in the manufacture of shoes (*Hinton* v. *Maden & Ireland Ltd* [1959] 3 A.E.R. 356).

Expenditure incurred before 27 October 1970 attracted an "initial" allowance at varying rates up to 30%. This was replaced by a "first-year" allowance of 60%, increased with effect from 20 July 1971 to 80%, and again with effect from 22 March 1972 to 100%—free depreciation.

Before 27 October 1970 there were also various rates of writing-down allowances, available for the first as well as for subsequent years. Since that date, writing-down allowances have not been available in the year of outlay. Instead they have been given at the rate of 25% in the second and subsequent years against the balance which remains after each item of plant or machinery has been "pooled" at its original cost less any allowances already given. Where the trader has claimed the full 100% first-year allowance for an asset, there will of course be no writing-down allowances available for that asset. He may sometimes prefer, however, not to claim the first-year allowance at all, or to claim only part of it, so as to obtain a more even spread of allowances.

When any item is sold that was acquired before 27 October 1970, the sale proceeds must be compared with the written-down value of that item, i.e. its cost less any allowances already given for it. Any deficit will be covered by a balancing allowance, any excess by a balancing charge. Where the item was acquired after 26 October 1970, however, the sale proceeds must be compared with the "pool" balance, i.e. the aggregate written-down values of *all* the trader's plant or machinery. Any excess is subjected to a balancing charge, but there is no balancing allowance in the event of a deficit, the sale proceeds merely reducing the "pool" balance. A balancing allowance now normally arises only in the event of a cessation so as to enable the discontinuing trader to reap the benefit of any unrelieved capital expenditure.

● The allowances cover both new and second-hand plant or machinery. Moreover, they are available in full to the trader who acquires plant or machinery after 26 October 1970 on hire-purchase as soon as it is brought into use in the trade, though only in respect of the capital component of the hire-purchase price, i.e. the "principal sum" or "cash price". The interest component, i.e. the "finance charge", is deductible from the profits of the trade in any year in which instalments are paid. The allowances are available also to a trader who purchases plant or machinery and lets it in the course of his trade; but where he lets it otherwise than in the course of his trade, the letting must be treated as a separate trade and any plant or machinery on lease separately "pooled". Private motor vehicles used in a trade do not qualify for any first-year allowance; but a writing-down allowance of 25% is available in the first and succeeding years up to a maximum in any one year of £1,000. Cars costing more than £4,000 must be separately "pooled".

§ 2 Industrial buildings and structures

Allowances are available for expenditure on the *construction* of industrial buildings and structures. The rate of initial allowance was 15% before 6 April 1970, 30% between 6 April 1970 and 21 March 1972 (40% in a development area), and since 22 March 1972 has been 40% throughout the country. Each year, including the first, a writing-down allowance of 4% of the original cost is given (2% if the expenditure was incurred before 6 November 1962). When the building or structure is sold, the sale proceeds must be compared with the balance which remains after any allowances obtained have been subtracted from the original cost. Any excess will be assessed as a balancing charge, any deficit relieved by a balancing allowance.

§ 3 Agricultural or forestry buildings

The owner or tenant of farm or commercial forestry land may claim a writing-down allowance of 10% of the cost of constructing farmhouses, farm or forestry buildings, cottages, fences, etc for each of the first ten years of his ownership, starting with the year of outlay. In order to exclude any element of personal benefit, the allowance in the case of a farmhouse is calculated on one-third of the cost of construction, or the appropriate smaller fraction where the house's amenities are out of proportion to the farm.

§ 4 Scientific research

The cost of research for the benefit of a trade is wholly allowed in the year of outlay.

§ 5 Patent rights

The trader who purchases a patent for use in his trade is entitled to a writing-down allowance of one-seventeenth of the expenditure for each of seventeen years starting with the year of purchase. When the patent is sold, a balancing charge or allowance is made to cover any excess or deficit, as the case may be, of the sale proceeds relative to the original cost less allowances.

§ 6 "Know-how"

A trader is also entitled to a writing-down allowance of one-sixth of any payments made after 19 March 1968 to obtain "know-how" for use in his trade for each of six consecutive years, starting with the year of outlay.

§ 7 Mines, oil wells, and other mineral deposits of a wasting nature

There are three classes of expenditure, each with its own set of allowances. The details can be found (for those who need them) in the Capital Allowances Act 1968 ss. 51–66 and Schedules 5 and 6.

§ 8 Dredging

The rules are substantially similar to those relating to industrial buildings and structures.

2.25 TRADING LOSSES: TA SS. 168–75

Losses are computed in precisely the same way as profits (TA ss. 168(7), 171(1)). A loss arises when, in any accounting period, deductible expenditure happens to exceed chargeable income. There are three main ways in which a loss can be used. In general the trader is free to choose whichever proves most beneficial. He may also treat certain items—in particular, capital allowances—as though they were losses. A loss accruing to a partnership is apportioned between the partners according to their respective shares of the putative profits for that year of assessment. Each partner is then free to deal with his share of the loss as he thinks fit.

§ 1 Set-off against general income in the same and following year: TA s. 168

● 'Where any person sustains a loss in any trade, profession, employment or vocation carried on by him either solely or in partnership, he may, by notice in writing given within two years after the year of assessment, make a claim for relief from income tax on an amount of his income equal to the amount of the loss' (s. 168(1)). The relief is available against his other income of the same year or, if that income proves insufficient, against his other income of the next succeeding year of assessment, provided that the trade, etc is still being carried on then (s. 168(2)).

Whereas profits are computed on a preceding year basis, a loss is treated as arising in the year of assessment in which it is incurred, i.e. on an actual basis. The effect of s. 168 is therefore to make a trading loss disclosed in the accounts of one period available against profits, if any, disclosed in the previous accounts. An example should make this easier to grasp.

Example 2

E. B. Smart, a well-known tax accountant, makes up his accounts for periods corresponding to years of assessments. They disclose the following amounts:

1970–71	profits of £4,000
1971–72	profits of £7,000
1972–73	loss of £12,000

E

| 1973–74 | profits of | £6,000 |
| 1974–75 | profits of | £8,000 |

His only other source of income is a large house, which he lets to tenants, receiving rents annually totalling £2,400.

If Smart were to make no claim for loss relief, the amounts on which he would be assessed are:

	Schedule A	Schedule D Case II
1971–72	£2,400	£4,000
1972–73	£2,400	£7,000
1973–74	£2,400	nil
1974–75	£2,400	£6,000
1975–76	£2,400	£8,000

At any time before 6 April 1975 Smart may claim relief under s. 168, in which case his Case II assessment for 1972–73 will be reduced to nil, leaving £5,000 unrelieved, which may be set against his Schedule A income for 1972–73, reducing the Schedule A assessment for 1972–73 to nil. The £2,600 still unrelieved may then be set against Schedule A income for 1973–74. In this way all but £200 of the loss would be relieved by a claim under s. 168.

This is all very well if the trader chooses accounting periods which correspond to tax years. If he does not, the loss arising in an accounting period should, strictly speaking, be apportioned on a time basis between the two years of assessment across which the accounting period lies. The effect would be that the forward portion of the loss would be offset against profits of the previous accounting period while the backward portion would be offset against profits of the previous accounting period but one. While the Revenue insist on this method in the opening years or final year of a trade, in the other years they normally allow a loss to be treated as a loss of the year of assessment in which the accounting period ends.

Let us now assume that E. B. Smart makes up his accounts for calendar years rather than years of assessment and that they disclose the following amounts:

| 1970 | profits of | £4,000 |
| 1971 | profits of | £7,000 |

1972	loss of £12,000
1973	profits of £6,000
1974	profits of £8,000

Revenue practice under s. 168 is to shift the accounting periods along, so to speak. E. B. Smart would, assuming no claim for loss relief, be assessed on the same amounts as before (*see* p. 92 above). The strictly correct method is to apportion the loss as to £3,000 to 1971–72 and as to £9,000 to 1972–73; the £3,000 would then be offset under s. 168(1) against the £4,000 earned in 1970 so as to reduce Smart's Case II assessment for 1971–72 to £1,000, while the £9,000 would be set against the £7,000 earned in 1971 so as to produce a nil assessment for 1972–73 under Case II, leaving £2,000 unrelieved to be offset against Schedule A income for 1972–73 so as to reduce the amount on which Smart's Schedule A assessment for that year is made to £400.

Where income available for set-off is both earned and unearned, the loss must be set first against income of the corresponding class, earned or unearned as the case may be, then against income of the other class, then against his or her spouse's corresponding income, and finally against the spouse's other income (s. 168(4)).

A claim made under s. 168 may require that the amount of any capital allowances available for the year of assessment be taken into account so as to create or augment the loss (TA s. 169(1)).

A provision contained in F.A. 1960, now TA s. 170, purports to prohibit set-off of a loss incurred in any trade not shown to be carried on on a commercial basis and with a view to the realization of profits. Despite its wide terms, the provision applies only to farming and market gardening, and to commercial woodlands of which the occupier has elected for Schedule D. The intention was to prevent hobby farmers and their ilk from operating at a loss and setting off that loss against general income. S. 170 is dismally ineffectual: the hobby farmer who states that his *intention* had been to make a profit, even admitting that the odds were stacked against him, is not deprived of the benefit of s. 168. It was therefore supplemented in F.A. 1967 by the predecessor to TA s. 180, which provides that a loss incurred in farming or market gardening may not be offset against general income if a loss was incurred in that trade in each of the five preceding years of assessment. S. 180 is not a great deal more effective than s. 170: the hobby farmer need not worry about s. 180 for the first five years of trading, and even after that retains his right to claim relief if he can bring himself within s. 180(3), i.e. if he can show that a competent farmer or market gardener carrying on the trade would not reasonably have expected profits until after the end of the year next following the five years of loss.

§2 Carry-forward indefinitely against income of the same trade: TA s. 171

Under s. 171(1) a loss may be carried forward and set against profits *of the same trade* in subsequent years of assessment. As to what constitutes the same trade, *see Gordon & Blair v. IRC* (1962) 40 T.C. 358. By s. 171(2) the loss must be relieved in the first subsequent year, then the next, and so on. S. 171(3), which applies only to Case I of Schedule D, enables a dealer in securities to treat any interest or dividends on investments, which would have ranked as trading receipts but for the fact that they had already suffered tax by deduction, as though they were trading profits for purposes of carry-forward relief. Thus if trading profits do not fully absorb a loss carried forward, the loss may be set against income taxed at source.

The loss must be suffered by the same person except in two situations. The first is where a change in partners brings about a discontinuance: any continuing partner may carry forward his share of any loss accruing before the change against profits arising after it (TA s. 171(4)). The second is where an individual carrying on a business, either solely or in partnership, sells it to a company: the individual may set any loss incurred before sale against profits derived from the company after it, provided that (*a*) the consideration consisted solely or mainly in the allotment of shares of the company to the vendor(s); (*b*) he has retained the beneficial interest in his shares throughout the relevant year of assessment; and (*c*) the company carried on the business throughout that year (TA s. 172).

S. 171 may be resorted to either in addition or as an alternative to the other relieving provisions. Of course only the unused part of any loss partially relieved under some other provision may be carried forward: *see IRC* v. *Scott Adamson* (1932) 17 T.C. 679, followed in *Westward Television Ltd* v. *Hart* [1968] 3 A.E.R. 91. The usual practice is to claim under s. 168 so as to obtain the greatest possible immediate relief and then under s. 171 so as to relieve any unused part of the loss against future trading income. Thus, to return to Example 2 (*see* pp. 91–2 above), E. B. Smart would probably in practice claim relief under s. 171 in addition to s. 168, with the result that the £200 remaining unrelieved under s. 168 would be offset against his Case II earnings for 1974–75 of £6,000. If he were to claim s. 171 relief as an alternative to s. 168, his Case II assessments would be on the following amounts:

1971–72	£4,000
1972–73	£7,000

1973–74	nil
1974–75	nil
1975–76	£2,000

while his Schedule A assessments would be unaffected.

§3 Carry-back for three years of a terminal loss: TA s. 174

By s. 174(1), where a trade is permanently discontinued and any person then carrying it on, either solely or in partnership, has sustained in it a "terminal loss", he may claim to offset the loss against any chargeable profits for the three years of assessment preceding that in which the discontinuance occurs. S. 174(2) provides that relief must be given for later before earlier years. S. 174(3) corresponds to s. 171(3), which is set out at p. 94 above.

A terminal loss is the actual loss sustained in the twelve months immediately preceding the date of discontinuance (as reduced by the amount of any capital allowances given for that period). Unless the trade was discontinued at the end of an accounting period, the terminal loss will usually be ascertained by time-apportioning the ultimate and penultimate accounts.

2.26 POST-CESSATION RECEIPTS: TA SS. 143–51

We will recall (from pp. 48–9 above) the statement that before F.A. 1960, post-cessation receipts escaped taxation. That statement is only partly true. A more complete version of the truth is this. Post-cessation receipts formerly escaped tax if the accounts of the person discontinuing were kept on a cash basis; but where his accounts were prepared on an earnings basis, items not included in the final account slipped the tax net only if the Revenue were unable to reopen that account, e.g. because out of time or because the item was not of the nature of a trade debt. (As to the reopening of accounts, *see* p. 70 above.)

F.A. 1960 s. 32, now replaced mainly by TA s. 143, attempts to bring post-cessation receipts within charge under Case VI of Schedule D. This provision distinguishes the situation in which the accounts of the trade were prepared on an earnings basis from that in which the accounts were on a "conventional" basis, defined as any method other than the full-blown earnings basis, e.g. the cash basis. Certain sums are expressly exempted from the charge, namely:

(i) sums received beneficially by or on behalf of a non-resident which represent income arising directly or indirectly outside the UK (s. 143(3)(*a*));

(ii) a lump sum paid to the personal representatives of the author of a literary, dramatic, musical, or artistic work as consideration for an assignment of copyright in that work (s. 143(3)(*b*)); and

(iii) sums realized by the transfer of trading stock belonging to a trade, or work in progress belonging to a profession, at the discontinuance (s. 143(3)(*c*));

(iv) sums transferred, on a change in the persons carrying on a trade in respect of which there has been no election for continuance, to the persons carrying on the trade after the change (TA ss. 146, 147(2)).

Subject to these exceptions, s. 143(2) tells us that the charge applies:
(*a*) where the profits of the trade were computed on an earnings basis, to *all* post-cessation receipts in so far as their value was not brought into account in computing the profits of the trade; and
(*b*) where the profits were computed on a conventional basis, only those post-cessation receipts which, had the profits been computed on an earnings basis, would not have been brought into account either because (i) the date on which they became due, or (ii) the date on which the amount due was ascertained, fell after the discontinuance. S. 143 does not, strictly interpreted, catch barristers (whose post-cessation fees would not be omitted from an earnings-based account for either of the two specified reasons), nor authors on royalties outstanding at the date of discontinuance.

F.A. 1968 s. 18, now replaced mainly by TA s. 144, therefore seeks to close up some of the gaps in the earlier provision. S. 144 applies only where the profits of the trade were computed on a conventional basis. It imposed a charge, also under Case VI, on any sums arising from the trade which were not brought into account in computing profits up to the time of discontinuing and which are not chargeable under some other provision, e.g. s. 143 (s. 144(1)). Three of the four exceptions from the charge under s. 143, namely (i), (ii), and (iv) of those listed at pp. 95–6 above, are exceptions also from s. 144 (ss. 144(1)(*b*), 147(2)).

Relief from s. 144 is available under TA s. 150 for any individual born before 6 April 1917 who was engaged in carrying on the trade on 18 March 1968. The amount chargeable under s. 144 is reduced, if the individual was aged 65 or older on 18 March 1968, by fifteen twentieths, if he was 64 on that date by fourteen twentieths, and so on, until an individual aged 51 on that date has the amount on which he would otherwise be charged under s. 144 reduced by one twentieth only and an individual aged 50 on that date receives no relief at all.

A final point. No restriction is placed, either by s. 143 or by s. 144, on the person who may be charged. The inference is that *any* person in receipt of a chargeable sum, e.g. the ex-trader's personal representatives, will be liable under Case VI in respect of that sum.

2.3 The partner

2.31 THE EXISTENCE OF A PARTNERSHIP

It has on occasions proved difficult to determine whether a partnership exists: *see*, for example, *Pratt* v. *Strick* (1932) 17 T.C. 459. Positive *indicia* include the execution of a partnership agreement, the registration of a business name, the existence of profit-sharing arrangements, etc. However, none of these by itself is conclusive. Thus a partnership agreement will constitute a partnership only if put into effect: *Dickenson* v. *Gross* (1927) 11 T.C. 614. Conversely, an agreement which states that it does not constitute a partnership may be held to have done so: *Fenston* v. *Johnstone* (1940) 23 T.C. 29.

Difficulties have also arisen as to the period for which a partnership existed. For example in *Ayrshire Pullman etc* v. *IRC* (1929) 14 T.C. 754 the taxpayer had acquired a motor-bus in January 1926 for his son-in-law to drive for hire under an agreement. The son-in-law withdrew and initially one of the taxpayer's own sons, and later four of his other children as well, continued the business, without any definite agreement. In October 1927 a contract of "co-partnership" was drawn up between the father and his five children expressed to date back to January 1926. The Court of Session held that the partnership existed only from October 1927; prior to that the father had been sole owner of the business. For a similar decision, see *Waddington* v. *O'Callaghan* (1931) 16 T.C. 187.

2.32 TAXABILITY OF THE PARTNERSHIP AND OF THE PARTNERS

In English law a partnership is not a separate legal entity. In Scots law it is. In effect the Taxes Acts—for once taking a lead from North of the border—accord to a partnership a separate identity. The basic rule, contained in TA s. 152, is that where a trade or profession is carried on by two or more persons jointly the assessment of their profits to income tax under Case I or II of Schedule D must be made in the partnership name separately from any other assessment for which any of them is personally liable. However, as Lord Denning put it in a case we will shortly be discussing, 'the liability of partners to pay tax is the joint liability of all the partners, and not the several liability of each' (*Harrison* v. *Willis Bros* (1965) 43 T.C. 60 at 73): see *Income Tax Commissioners for the City of London* v. *Gibbs* [1942] A.C. 402. The partnership return must be made by the precedent acting partner (TMA s. 9(1)), or where there is no partner resident in the UK, by the firm's agent, manager, or factor in the UK (ibid. s. 9(2)).

The operation of s. 152 where one partner has died fell to be considered in *Harrison* v. *Willis Bros* (1965) 43 T.C. 60. Two brothers, H. H. and W. H. Willis, traded as dairymen from 1941–42 to 1947–48. H. H. died in 1957. In March 1962 additional assessments were raised on the firm to recover tax alleged to have been lost owing to the fraud, wilful default, or neglect of the partners. The Court of Appeal held that, although normally an assessment on a partnership cannot be made more than three years after one of the partners has died, the additional assessments were valid in so far as they had been raised on the partnership and imposed liability on W. H. Willis. When a partner dies, stated the Court, assessments should still be made in the partnership name notwithstanding that liability devolves upon the remaining partners or, if all the partners have died, on the personal representatives of the last surviving partner. (The case is also notable for Lord Denning's declaration, shortly after the passage quoted in the preceding paragraph, that: 'The partnership firm is not an entity for taxing purposes or any other purposes. Its name is simply a convenient way of describing the persons who constitute the firm' (ibid. at 73).)

● When the statutory income of the partnership has been determined, using the normal rules of computation applicable to individuals, it must be split between the partners according to their respective shares in the profits for the tax year in question. These shares are not necessarily the same as they were for the year in which the profits actually arose. Suppose that Hyrem, Firem & Co., a firm of employment agents comprising three partners, make profits of £10,000 in the year to 31 January 1972 at which time their profit-sharing ratio is 40 : 30 : 30. The partnership assessment for 1972–73 (on a preceding year basis) will be £10,000. If their profit-sharing ratio changed to 80 : 10 : 10 on 1 March 1972, the partners will each be assessed for 1972–73 on £8,000, £1,000, and £1,000 respectively. Clearly the rules are capable of producing some strange results: and the confusion may be further confounded by a change of partners.

Where a partner is partly remunerated by way of salary, the salary is not normally assessed under Schedule E but is included in his share of the partnership income assessable under Case I or II of Schedule D. Similarly interest on capital contributed by a partner is not an annual payment and the partner is therefore credited with the full amount of that interest and assessed on it under Case I or II of Schedule D.

TA s. 26 preserves the right of partners to claim the personal reliefs. A partner's income is deemed to be the share to which he is entitled during the year to which the claim relates in the partnership profits (ibid. proviso). Since 1957, the Revenue have accepted the recommendation of the Royal Commission (Cmd para 513) that a partnership's annual payments made under deduction of tax should be treated as paid out of any unearned income of the partnership and then out of unearned income of the individual partners, to the extent of their respective shares, and only finally out of earned income of the partnership itself. In practice, each of the partners makes an individual return claiming the appropriate reliefs and the total of those reliefs is then taken into account by the Revenue in making the partnership assessment.

2.33 LOSSES

These are dealt with at p. 91 above.

2.34 CHANGES OF PARTNERS

The provisions of TA s. 154(1) and (2), considered above at pp. 67–8 *et seq.*, are of particular importance to a partnership, since any change in partners—whether by way of reduction, substitution, or addition—will operate by virtue of s. 154(1) as a discontinuance of the old firm and commencement of a new one, unless all the partners both before and after the change elect for continuance under s. 154(2).

2.35 COMPANY PARTNERSHIPS

There are special rules, contained in TA s. 155, governing partnerships of which one or more of the members is a company. In effect the corporation tax liability of the company is kept distinct from the income tax liabilities of the individual partners. *See also* summary at pp. 290–1 below.

2.4 The employee

Schedule E is a charge to tax on:

(1) the emoluments of any office or employment;
(2) golden handshakes;
(3) pensions and retirement benefits;
(4) periodical payments granted out of the House of Commons' Members Fund, i.e. our MP's pension fund (TA s. 211(4)); and
(5) social security benefits other than sickness benefit, unemployment benefit, attendance allowance, maternity benefit, and death grant (TA s. 219).

(1) and (2) are dealt with in this division (2.41 and 2.43 respectively). (3) is dealt with in division 2.5. Neither (4) nor (5) merit further consideration.

2.41 EMOLUMENTS OF AN OFFICE OR EMPLOYMENT

Schedule E is charged by TA s. 181(1) under one or more of three Cases, the extent of chargeability under each depending primarily on the place where the duties are performed. A person domiciled outside the UK and employed by a foreign employer is liable only under Case III; if resident in the UK he is liable on a remittance basis, if not he escapes taxability. Where, however, a person is either domiciled in the UK or, if domiciled elsewhere, is employed by a UK employer, the permutations are more complex, as indicated in the table below (taken from *Simon* C4.103):

	SERVICES PERFORMED			
	Wholly in UK	*Partly in UK*	*Partly abroad*	*Wholly abroad*
Non-resident	All (Case II)	That part (Case II)	None	None
Resident but not ordinarily resident	All (Case II)	That part (Case II)	Remittances (Case III)	Remittances (Case III)
Resident and ordinarily resident	All (Case I)	All (Case I)	All (Case I)	Remittances (Case III)

Three basic questions fall to be considered:

§1 What is an "office" or "employment"?

Under Addington's Act Schedule E was confined to *public* offices or employments, other employments falling within Schedule D (*see* p. 14 above). F.A. 1922 transferred Schedule D emoluments to Schedule E and F.A. 1956 deleted "public" from the charging words of Schedule E and "employment" from those of Schedule D. Since then Schedule E has charged the emoluments of *any* office or employment.

Rowlatt J. once defined an "office" as 'a subsisting, permanent, substantive position, which had an existence independent of the person who filled it, and which went on and was filled in succession by successive holders' ([1920] 3 K.B. at 274); and, though the learned judge's decision was reversed on appeal to the Lords, his definition was cited with approval by Lord Atkinson (*see* [1922] A.C. at 15). The word has been held to include:

(*a*) The director of a company which is resident in the UK, whether public or private, and regardless of where he resides or the extent of his involvement in the company: *McMillan* v. *Guest* [1942] A.C. 561.

(*b*) A trustee or executor: *Dale* v. *IRC* [1954] A.C. 11. Despite this decision, Revenue practice is to assess remuneration of an ordinary trustee or executor under Schedule D Case III and of a professional trustee or executor under Schedule D Case II.

(*c*) The part-time Health Service appointments of medical specialists: *Mitchell and Edon* v. *Ross* [1962] A.C. 814 (a case we came across at p. 46 above).

(*d*) Auditors: *Ellis* v. *Lucas* [1967] Ch. 858; *Walker* v. *Carnaby Harrower, Barham & Pykett* [1970] 1 W.L.R. 276.

(*e*) Registrarships of companies held by a firm of advocates (the Scots equivalent of solicitors): *IRC* v. *Brander & Cruickshank* [1971] 1 A.E.R. 36.

(*f*) The appointment as local land charges registrar held by a clerk to a local council: *Ministry of Housing and Local Government* v. *Sharp* [1969] 3 A.E.R. 225 at 223 and [1970] 1 A.E.R. at 1022–3.

● "Employment" is a wider concept than "office", though 'it means something analogous to an office and which is conveniently amenable to the scheme of taxation which is applied to offices' ([1931] 2 K.B. at 634 *per* Rowlatt J.). Of course the important line of division is between offices or employments on the one hand (Schedule E) and professions or vocations on the other (Schedule D Case II). This division is largely coincident with the distinction between a contract of service and a contract for services (respectively), of which the determining criterion is the degree of control exercisable by one contracting party over the other. In _Davies_ v. _Braithwaite_ [1931] 2 K.B. 628 an actress, under separate contracts, had appeared on stage, in films, and in radio plays, as well as making records. Rowlatt J. held that all her engagements were part of one profession carried on by her. On the other hand there have been cases in which the taxpayer has been held to carry on a profession and one or more employments simultaneously. For example, in _Blackburn_ v. _Close Bros Ltd_ (1960) 39 T.C. 164 it was common ground that merchant bankers who received allowances and fees for performing managerial and secretarial services for companies were assessable under Schedule D Case I in respect of their ordinary trading profits and under Schedule E in respect of the allowances and fees. More recently in _Fall_ v. _Hitchen_ [1973] S.T.C. 66 a ballet dancer was engaged by Sadler's Wells under a standard contract for a minimum period and thereafter until determination by a fortnight's notice on either side. He was to work full time during specified hours for a regular salary and was to undertake no other engagements without consent. Pennycuick V-C held that there existed a contract of service, from which it followed that the taxpayer's salary arose from an 'employment' within Schedule E. He had therefore been correctly assessed under that Schedule. _See also Household_ v. _Grimshaw_ [1953] 2 A.E.R. 12 and the cases mentioned in paras (_c_), (_e_), and (_f_) at p. 101 above.

§2 What are "emoluments"?

The expression "emoluments" includes 'all salaries, fees, wages, perquisites and profits whatsoever' (TA s. 183(1)). It is settled law, however, that to rank as emoluments payments must be (i) in money or a form convertible into money, and (ii) _derived from_ an office or employment.

(i) Benefits in kind

'I do not deny,' said Lord Halsbury L.C. in the leading case, 'that if substantial things of money value were capable of being turned into money they might . . . represent money's worth and be therefore taxable' (_Tennant_ v. _Smith_ [1892] A.C. 150 at 156). Thus in principle benefits in kind are taxable only to the extent that they may be converted into money. However, a number of exceptions to the principle have been admitted. Moreover, the concept of convertibility has itself become increasingly attenuated. The result is that today few benefits in kind are excluded from taxation. It is interesting to see this process working itself out in decided cases. In _Weight_ v. _Salmon_ (1935) 19 T.C. 174 the directors of a company allowed the managing director, in addition to his salary, the privilege of applying for unissued shares in the company at par. Their Lordships held him assessable on the difference between par and market values of the shares taken up. The same conclusion was reached in *Ede* v. *Wilson and Cornwall* [1945] 1 A.E.R. 367 despite a stipulation that the shares should not be transferred without the directors' permission. In *Heaton* v. *Bell* [1970] A.C. 728 an employee joined his company's car loan scheme on terms *inter alia* that he would permit no one else to use the car, that he would forgo part of his wages, and that either party could resile from the agreement on giving fourteen days' notice. The House of Lords held (i) (Lord Reid dissenting) that the true agreement was that his wages were to remain unchanged, so that joining the scheme made no difference to the employee's taxability; and (ii) (Lords Hodson and Upjohn dissenting) that even assuming the agreement had been for a lower weekly wage, use of the car was itself a taxable perquisite since the employee would become entitled to a higher monetary wage on surrendering it.

(1) *Accommodation*

An employee whose contract of employment requires him to reside on the premises in order to perform his duties is said to be in "representative" occupation and is not assessable on the value of his occupation. Thus in *Tennant* v. *Smith* [1892] A.C. 150 an agent for a bank occupied the bank house both as caretaker and in order to conduct bank business after hours. Their Lordships declined to include the yearly value of his occupation in the agent's total income. For many years the crucial determinant in this decision was thought to be the fact that the agent had no power to sublet, since this rendered the benefit non-convertible. *IRC* v. *Miller* [1930] A.C. 222 exposed this as a misconception. The test is simply whether the occupation is "representative" or "beneficial".

One or two statutory provisions are worth mentioning. TA s. 185(1) imposes a charge under Schedule E on any person who occupies premises by reason of his own or his spouse's office or employment, the extent of the charge being the annual value of the premises less any rent paid. Where the rent was originally an economic one, s. 185(1) does not apply unless the landlord was entitled at some stage to obtain a higher rent, whether by terminating the tenancy or otherwise, in which case the employee is chargeable from that time on the amount forgone. Where the premises are provided by a local authority, the occupier can escape s. 185(1) by showing that his terms of occupation are no more favourable than those of persons similarly placed (s. 185(3)).

Full-time clergymen or ministers who occupy residences from which they perform their duties are treated by TA s. 194 as representative occupiers. Moreover, they are entitled to deduct, whether under Schedule E or any other Schedule, up to one-quarter of their rent and other outgoings.

(2) *Satisfying an employee's liabilities*

Where an employer himself satisfies a liability incurred by one of his employees towards some third person, the payment ranks as a taxable emolument. (The employee will not necessarily pay tax on it; if incurred in performing his duties, the employee's liability might be deductible: *see* p. 111 below.) The measure of taxability is normally the cost *to the employer* of satisfying the liability. Where, however, the employer buys something which he gives to the employee, it is the value of the benefit *to the employee*. Thus in *Wilkins* v. *Rogerson* [1961] Ch. 133 a company decided to give some of its staff a Christmas present of clothes to the value of £15. One of the company's employees chose a suit costing £14·75. The Court of Appeal held him chargeable on £5 only—the suit's second-hand value.

The principle contained in the opening sentence of the preceding paragraph has brought into taxability as emoluments a wide variety of payments, of which these are a sample:

(1) Payments by an employer towards the outgoings of an employee's house: *Nicholl* v. *Austin* (1935) 19 T.C. 531.

(2) A cash allowance to cover rent: *Robinson* v. *Corry* [1934] 1 K.B. 240.

(3) A clothes allowance: *Ferguson* v. *Noble* (1919) 7 T.C. 176 (though the Court of Session acknowledged (ibid. at 180) that clothing or a uniform supplied by an employer for his employee to wear on duty only and to remain the employer's property could not be included in the employee's taxable emoluments).

(4) Payments by an employer of his employee's tax. An agreement to pay a salary of £x free of tax is valid, but the employee's emoluments are then £x plus the amount of tax borne by his employer: *Hartland* v. *Diggines* [1926] A.C. 289; *Jaworski* v. *Institution of Polish Engineers* [1951] 1 K.B. 768. The Companies Act 1948 s. 189 prohibits payment of tax-free remuneration to directors; the words "free of tax" or their equivalent are to be disregarded.

(3) *Share option schemes and share incentive schemes*

In *Abbott* v. *Philbin* [1961] A.C. 352 the directors of a company resolved that company executives be granted non-transferable options, at a price of £1 per 100 shares, to purchase ordinary shares in the company at 68/6

(£3·42½) per share (the quoted mid-price on the date of the directors' resolution). The taxpayer applied for an option to purchase 2,000 shares, enclosing £20, and in due course exercised the option in respect of 250 shares when the price had risen to 82/– per share. He was assessed on the amount of his gain. By a bare majority the House of Lords held the assessment bad: the option was itself a taxable emolument *when granted*, notwithstanding that it was then of indeterminate value, so that no Schedule E liability arose at the time of its exercise. The majority reasoned, somewhat fancifully, that the taxpayer could have converted his option by arranging with a third party that he would exercise the option and transfer the shares to him. A much more convincing analysis is to be found in the powerful dissenting judgment of Lord Denning, based on the wholly plausible assertion that: 'A bird in the hand is taxable, but a bird in the bush is not' (ibid. at 384).

Share option schemes mushroomed in the favourable climate of *Abbott* v. *Philbin*, until the Labour Government effectively put an end to them by instituting the minority view of Lords Denning and Keith in a provision of F.A. 1966, now TA s. 186. That section provides that a person who realizes a gain by (*a*) the exercise, (*b*) the assignment, or (*c*) the release of a right to acquire shares obtained by him as a director or employee of any company, is chargeable under Schedule E on the gain. No liability arises on the grant of an option. In the case of (*a*) the gain is the difference between the market price at the time of exercising the option and the aggregate consideration given by him for the grant of the right and for the shares themselves; and in the case of (*b*) or (*c*) the difference between the consideration for the assignment or release and the consideration given by him for the grant of the right.

The result was that share option schemes were displaced by a variety of share incentive schemes. The usual type involved the company lending money to trustees to enable them to subscribe for or purchase shares. The employee bought the shares from the trustees, paying for them by instalments with interest. Any gains were liable only to capital gains tax.

In the conviction that the 1966 legislation had been altogether too drastic and that share option schemes have a valuable rôle to play in stimulating management enterprise, the present Conservative Government recently enacted provisions whereby:

(1) share option schemes approved by the Revenue as meeting prescribed conditions are exempted from TA s. 186 (F.A. 1972 s. 78 and Schedule 12);
(2) the gains from unapproved share incentive schemes are brought into charge under Schedule E (ibid. s. 79(4) and (7)); and

(3) similar conditions are prescribed for the approval of share incentive schemes (ibid. Schedule 12).

The Share Option and Share Incentive Schemes Regulations 1972, governing applications for approval under F.A. 1972 Schedule 12, came into force on 25 August 1972.

Certain conditions applicable to both types of scheme are set out in Part II of Schedule 12, these among them:

(i) The scheme must be adopted by a resolution of the ordinary shareholders (ibid. para 1).

(ii) Rights under the scheme must not be exercisable more than ten years after the shareholders' resolution (ibid.).

(iii) The shares must either be quoted on a recognized Stock Exchange or be in a company which is not under the control of another company (ibid. para 3).

(iv) The number of shares comprised in a scheme must not exceed 10% of the company's ordinary share capital if its ordinary capital is £2 million or less, or 5% if its ordinary capital is more than £2 million (ibid. para 5).

In addition, under both types of scheme there is a sophisticated form of means-testing whereby the rights obtained by a participant in a year of assessment are restricted to four times the amount of his "relevant emoluments" for that or the preceding year of assessment (whichever is the greater) (ibid. paras 1–3 of Parts III and IV).

Other conditions are laid down by Part III of Schedule 12 for share option schemes only. For example, the rights must be exercisable not more than seven years after being granted (ibid. para 4). Yet others, contained in Part IV, apply only to share incentive schemes. The overall impression is one of complexity and a measure of unnecessary rigidity.

Share incentive schemes are defined as those in which a person acquires shares or an interest in shares *qua* director or employee of a company rather than by public offer (F.A. 1972 s. 79(1)). S. 79 contains two Schedule E charges on the profits or gains of unapproved share incentive schemes. The first—contained in s. 79(4)–(6)—is a charge on the (unrealized) increase in market value of the shares or interest in shares between the acquisition date and the earliest of the following times:

(*a*) seven years from the acquisition date;

(*b*) the time when the acquirer ceases to have any beneficial interest in the shares (where the acquirer loses part only of his beneficial interest, the charge is proportionately reduced); and

(c) in the case of those who acquired shares, as opposed to an interest in shares, the time when the shares cease to be subject to any special restrictions.

The charge arises in the year of assessment in which the earliest of those times falls. The second charge under Schedule E—contained in s. 79(7)—attaches to any benefit received by a participant in a share incentive scheme not made available to shareholders outside the scheme: it arises in the year of receipt.

Thus share option and share incentive schemes have to a large extent been assimilated. The general rule is that profits or gains arising from unapproved schemes are chargeable under Schedule E, those from approved schemes to capital gains tax only. By way of exception, s. 78(2) provides that if a participant in an approved share option scheme has to pay less both for the option and for the shares than the market value of those shares at the time of grant, he is chargeable on the deficit under Schedule E in the year of obtaining the option: he may later exercise the option without incurring further liability and on the first subsequent disposal of those shares, the deficit already assessed under Schedule E may be included as allowable expenditure in computing liability to capital gains tax.

(4) *The Norman conquest: F.A. 1973 amendments to the régime governing share incentive schemes*

● In November 1972 Mr Charles Norman, an expert on share schemes, devised for Schreiber Industries, a share incentive scheme linked to Save As You Earn and available to all workers, the beauty of which was that the participants were placed in a "heads we win, tails we don't lose" situation. In his 1973 Budget Mr Barber adopted Mr Norman's scheme. The Budget proposals have now been translated into Schedule 8 of the 1973 Act. F.A. 1973 s. 19 provides that F.A. 1972 s. 79 and Schedule 12 are to take effect subject to the amendments contained in Schedule 8. What follows is a summary of some of those amendments.

Part II of Schedule 8 deals with savings-related share incentive schemes, defined as 'any share incentive scheme under which employees pay for part of the shares or interests acquired by them under the scheme, or repay a loan made to them for the purpose of the acquisition, out of repayments made to them under a certified contractual savings scheme', e.g. SAYE. Part II proceeds to make a number of amendments to the code of approval contained in Schedule 12, including the following:

  (i) every full-time employee of the company must be entitled to participate in the scheme to a reasonable extent if he is not less than eighteen years old and has been a full-time employee of that company for a continuous period of not less than two years (para 10);

(ii) the Schedule 12 restrictions on the number of shares to be comprised in the scheme (*see* p. 106 above) are to be disregarded (para 11);

(iii) the acquisition of shares under the scheme by any person must be so limited that:

    (*a*) not less than 95% of the consideration either is payable after the acquisition or is paid out of a loan which is repayable after the acquisition; and

    (*b*) the part of the consideration payable after the acquisition or out of the loan, as the case may be, must not exceed the repayment due to that person under the certified contractual savings scheme out of which it is payable (para 13);

(iv) the minimum acquisition cost must not be less than 70% of the market value of the shares at the time of their acquisition (para 14);

(v) the scheme must be linked to an adequate certified contractual savings scheme in respect of each participant (para 17);

(vi) every participant must have the right—and this is where "heads we win, tails we don't lose" comes in—at the time payment of the deferred part of the consideration or repayment of the loan is due, to discharge his obligation by surrendering the shares (para 18); and

(vii) an employee must not, while participating in a savings-related share incentive scheme, participate also in any approved share incentive or share option scheme (para 19).

(5) *Tax-free fringe benefits*

Items which do not rank as emoluments are a variety of non-convertible benefits such as board and lodging, working clothes, meals, outings, private health insurance benefits, and the like. Cash payments towards any of these benefits are of course taxable, though by Revenue concession luncheon vouchers are tax free up to 15p per working day provided that, if restricted, they are available to lower-paid staff. Moreover, in the case of employees earning £2,000 a year or more and directors, whatever their earnings, there are special rules by which even some of these non-convertible benefits are brought into charge as emoluments (*see* 2.42 below).

(ii) Gifts and voluntary payments

● The requirement that emoluments must *derive from* the office or employment has operated to exclude payments of a voluntary nature. For this reason voluntary payments made to an employee on termination of his office or employment or on variation of its terms (known as "golden hand-shakes") formerly escaped taxation. In *Cowan* v. *Seymour* [1920] 1 K.B. 500, C had acted as secretary of a company without pay for nearly five years until the company was voluntarily wound up; he was then appointed liquidator and acted as such, again without pay; at the final general meeting the shareholders voted him a payment. In *Chibbett* v. *Robinson & Sons* (1924) 9 T.C. 48 a firm of ship-managers employed by a steamship company which went into voluntary liquidation was given £50,000 worth of 5% War Bonds as "compensation for loss of office". In *Stedeford* v. *Beloe* [1932] A.C. 388 a retiring headmaster was granted a pension out of school funds. These payments were all held to fall outside the scope of Schedule E: they were not remuneration but "testimonials" or "tributes" in appreciation of past services. Since 1960, however, these "golden handshakes" have partly been brought into charge by provisions we will be considering in division 2.43 below.

There has been a surprising volume of litigation to determine whether the proceeds of benefit matches are remunerative or testimonial. In *Seymour* v. *Reed* [1927] A.C. 554 the proceeds of a benefit match for a cricketer were invested together with certain public subscriptions. He received the income and, when the investments were realized, a lump sum as well. The House of Lords held the payments to be gifts. On the other hand, in *Davis* v. *Harrison* (1927) 11 T.C. 707 Rowlatt J. held that accrued benefit money paid to a footballer on transfer pursuant to an agreement between player and club in accordance with the rules of the Football League, constituted remuneration; and the Court of Appeal reached the same conclusion in *Moorhouse* v. *Dooland* [1955] Ch. 284 in respect of collections made on behalf of a crick-eter, it being one of his terms of employment that the club would make collections for any meritorious performance.

Inducement fees pose the same problem. In *Jarrold* v. *Boustead* [1964] 3 A.E.R. 76 the Court of Appeal held that lump sum signing-on fees paid to three Rugby League players were not advance remuneration but induce-ments to relinquish amateur status. Similarly in *Pritchard* v. *Arundale* [1972] Ch. 229 an accountant was given shares in a company as an inducement to give up his practice and become managing director of the company for seven years. Megarry J. held that the payment was not an emolument *from* the employment. By contrast, in *Riley* v. *Coghlan* [1968] 1 A.E.R. 314 a Rugby League player was paid £100 on signing the professional forms and £400 on taking up residence in York. If for reasons other than football injury he should prove unable to serve the club throughout the contract period, a proportionate part of the £500 was to be repaid. Ungoed-Thomas

J. held the sums to be part of his remuneration. Similarly, in *Holland* v. *Geoghegan* [1972] 3 A.E.R. 333, the London Borough of Lambeth induced refuse collectors who had gone on strike to return to work by offering them *inter alia* £450 as compensation for loss of "totting" rights, i.e. their right to extract salvageable materials from the refuse and sell them. One of the men appealed against his Schedule E assessment on the £450. Foster J. dismissed his appeal: the £450 was received by the taxpayer as a form of substituted remuneration for his former totting rights.

In *Beak* v. *Robson* [1943] A.C. 352 their Lordships occupy no more than one page of the Law Reports in coming to the important decision that payments in respect of restrictive covenants preventing an employee competing with his employer either during or after the employee's period of service are not taxable emoluments. Far from being derived from an office or employment, they arise from agreeing *not* to engage in a type of employment. *See also Hose* v. *Warwick* (1946) 27 T.C. 459 and *Higgs* v. *Olivier* [1952] Ch. 311 (pp. 76–7 above). The decision in *Beak* v. *Robson* was nullified so far as surtax was concerned by a provision (now TA s. 34) that for surtax purposes the payment should be treated as a net amount from which standard rate tax had already been deducted. The grossed-up amount was therefore included in the taxpayer's total income for surtax purposes. In effect this result is preserved for 1973–74 under the unified system: the payment is treated as received after deduction of tax at the basic rate, but no assessment is made on the taxpayer for income tax at the basic rate, nor can he make a repayment claim for tax notionally deducted. The deduction is treated as made out of profits or gains not brought into charge to tax, i.e. under the s. 53 procedure. (F.A. 1971 s. 36 and Schedule 6 para 15: as to the s. 53 procedure, *see* pp. 129 and 131 *et seq.* below.)

In *Hochstrasser* v. *Mayes* [1960] A.C. 376 an employee was given an interest-free loan under his company's housing scheme. The House of Lords held the payment untaxable. The employment was the *causa sine qua non* but not the *causa causans* of the loan. The Crown's contention that every payment to an employee as such should be included in his taxable profits was emphatically rejected. Lord Denning's short judgment is worth reading: a definition of "profits", he said, would be a pearl of great price: the Crown's was cultivated and not real: on close scrutiny it was found to be studded with ambiguities and defaced by exceptions. *Cf. Clayton* v. *Gothorp* [1971] 2 A.E.R. 1311.

The principle that voluntary payments attributable to the recipient's personal qualities are outside the ambit of Schedule E does not protect:
(*a*) Easter offerings: *Blakiston* v. *Cooper* [1909] A.C. 104 (Easter offerings

[margin note: only chargeable at higher rates.]

to vicar of East Grinstead held taxable by aptly-named Bray J. in a decision later affirmed by the House of Lords).

(b) Tips: *Calvert* v. *Wainwright* [1947] K.B. 526 (taxi-driver's tips); *Wright* v. *Boyce* [1958] 2 A.E.R. 703 (huntsman's customary cash collection at Christmas from persons connected with the hunt).

(c) Bonuses: *Radcliffe* v. *Holt* (1927) 11 T.C. 621 (£1,000 free of income tax voted to the company chairman by shareholders informed of a rise in profits); *Denny* v. *Reed* (1933) 18 T.C. 254 (bonuses given to employees of a firm of stockbrokers); *Weston* v. *Hearn* [1943] 2 A.E.R. 421 (£250 and 67 National Savings Certificates presented to W and C respectively on completing twenty-five years' service with a firm of bankers). *Cf. Ball* v. *Johnson* [1971] T.R. 147 (£130 awarded to a bank clerk, in accordance with the bank's usual practice, for passing the Institute of Bankers exams held untaxable by Plowman J.); *Moore* v. *Griffiths* [1972] 1 W.L.R. 1024 (£1,000 paid by the Football Association to each member of England's victorious 1966 World Cup squad held an accolade rather than remuneration).

§ 3 What expenditure is deductible?

The basic rule, widely criticized for its narrowness—'undoubtedly its most striking characteristic', Lord Blanesburgh once said of it, 'is its jealously restricted phraseology' ([1926] A.C. at 7)— is laid down by TA s. 189(1): 'If the holder of an office or employment is necessarily obliged to incur and defray out of the emoluments thereof the expenses of travelling in the performance of the duties of the office or employment, or of keeping and maintaining a horse to enable him to perform the same, or otherwise to expend money wholly, exclusively and necessarily in the performance of the said duties, there may be deducted from the emoluments to be assessed the expenses so necessarily incurred and defrayed.' At first blush the provision appears to lay down three conditions for the deductibility of expenditure:

(a) the taxpayer must be "necessarily obliged" to incur the expenditure;
(b) the expenditure must be incurred "in the performance of the duties"; and
(c) the expenditure must be "wholly, exclusively and necessarily" so incurred.

A closer look reveals, however, that s. 189(1) draws a distinction between travelling and non-travelling expenditure: while conditions (a) and (b) must be satisfied by travelling and non-travelling expenditure alike, condition (c) applies to non-travelling expenditure only. (Occasionally judges fail to take this point: *see*, for example, the slips of Lord Blanesburgh in [1926] A.C. at 9 and of Pennycuick J. in [1965] 2 A.E.R. at 366 (though his

Lordship, by then Pennycuick V-C, later corrected himself in [1972] 1 W.L.R. at 1462).)

Let us take a look at the conditions for deductibility, first for non-travelling and then for travelling expenditure.

(1) Non-travelling expenditure

(a) "necessarily obliged"

● The text of necessity is objective. Thus in *Roskams* v. *Bennett* (1950) 32 T.C. 129 a district manager of the Prudential had defective eyesight and found it difficult to travel. He therefore did some of his business at home. Danckwerts J. refused his claim to deduct a fifth of the outgoings of his house as business expenditure. Again, in *Brown* v. *Bullock* (1961) 40 T.C. 1 it was virtually a condition of appointment that the manager of the Pall Mall branch of a bank should join a club. Though already a member of the RAC, the appointee joined the Devonshire, the bank paying half the RAC and the full Devonshire subscription. The Court of Appeal refused these sums as deductions. Donovan L.J. made the rather dubious suggestion that: 'The test is not whether the employer imposes the expense, but whether the duties do, in the sense that, irrespective of what the employer may prescribe, the duties cannot be performed without incurring the particular outlay' (ibid. at 10). The logic of his Lordship's statement is what Orwell might have called "doubleplusungood", since, within the broad confines of the contract of service, it is the employer himself who defines his employee's specific duties. *Brown* v. *Bullock* was distinguished in *Elwood* v. *Utitz* (1965) 42 T.C. 482, a case we will return to at p. 113 below. Truer to the spirit of s. 189(1) is *Owen* v. *Burden* [1972] 1 A.E.R. 356: the county surveyor for Denbighshire was engaged in preparing a scheme for the construction of a by-pass. Without obtaining special leave or the authority of his county council, he attended a world road conference in Tokyo in the hope of obtaining an independent first-class opinion on the merits of his scheme. The Court of Appeal held that his expenses of attending the conference were not necessarily incurred in the performance of his duties.

(b) "in the performance of the duties"

For this reason subscriptions and fees to professional and learned societies were formerly not strictly deductible (*Simpson* v. *Tate* [1925] 2 K.B. 214), though in practice they were allowed where membership was a condition of employment. Since 1958, the formal position has been governed by what is now TA s. 192, under which fees and subscriptions are allowed if they are payable as a condition of employment and if performance of the duties of the office or employment is directly affected by them.

Similarly, commission paid to an employment agency is not incurred by the employee in performing his duties: *Shortt* v. *McIlgorm* [1945] 1 A.E.R. 391. Nor can a laboratory assistant required to attend evening classes deduct the cost of his textbooks or travel (*Blackwell* v. *Mills* [1945] 2 A.E.R. 655) or a solicitors' articled clerk his Law Society exam fees (*Lupton* v. *Potts* [1969] 3 A.E.R. 1083).

(c) *"wholly, exclusively and necessarily"*

The words "wholly" and "exclusively" have been examined in the context of Schedule D Cases I and II (*see* pp. 81–3 above). In *Lucas* v. *Cattell* [1972] T.R. 83 telephone installation and rental charges incurred by a clerk to an Executive Council of the NHS who needed to be contacted out of hours on urgent NHS matters were held not "exclusively" incurred in performing the duties of his office. The word "necessarily" makes the expenditure rule much more stringent under Schedule E than under Schedule D. It has brought about the downfall of many a promising claim. One among the legion of casualties is *Nolder* v. *Walters* (1930) 15 T.C. 380, in which Rowlatt J. held that a pilot's expenses of installing a telephone, keeping a motor car, special flying clothes, books, and instruments, and undergoing medical tests were all unnecessarily incurred.

(2) Travelling expenses

In *Ricketts* v. *Colquhoun* [1926] A.C. 1 a barrister living and practising in London held the Recordership of Portsmouth. He claimed to deduct his expenses in travelling there, his Portsmouth hotel bills, and the cost of carriage of his tin box to and from the Court. Their Lordships refused his claim as failing to satisfy both of conditions (*a*) and (*b*) above. Similarly in *Marsden* v. *IRC* [1965] 2 A.E.R. 364, a case of the biter bit, a Revenue investigator was required to travel throughout Lancashire. His claim to deduct the difference between what it cost him to travel in his own car and the official mileage rates was refused in its entirety, though Pennycuick J. implied that in appropriate circumstances claims of this kind might be allowed.

● Recently judges have baulked at the stringency of these rules. A more liberal approach was apparent as early as 1965 in *Elwood* v. *Utitz* (1965) 42 T.C. 482, a case which we omitted to consider in its proper place at p. 112 above. The taxpayer, as managing director of a company operating in Northern Ireland, was obliged to visit London from time to time and stay at first-class accommodation. To save money, he joined two London clubs. His claim to deduct the subscriptions was upheld by the Court of Appeal of

N. Ireland. Significantly, Lord MacDermott C.J. invoked (ibid. at 495) the untypical precedent of *Bowden* v. *Russell & Russell* (*see* p. 82 above). *Bowden* v. *Russell & Russell* and *Elwood* v. *Utitz* paved the way for *Owen* v. *Pook* [1970] A.C. 244. Dr Owen was in general practice at Fishguard but held part-time appointments at a hospital in Haverfordwest, fifteen miles away. His travel expenses were not payable for a single journey in excess of ten miles, so that he had to meet the cost of the additional five miles himself. The Commissioners allowed his claim to deduct this sum: his duties began when the hospital phoned, so that his journey to the hospital was made in the course of performing his duties. A minority of the Court of Appeal (Lord Denning M.R.) and a majority of the House of Lords (Lords Donovan and Pearson dissenting) upheld the Commissioners' decision. Lord Pearce suggested that *Ricketts* v. *Colquhoun* should be considered afresh by the House. *Owen* v. *Pook* in turn gave way to *Taylor* v. *Provan* [1972] 1 W.L.R. 1459. In *Taylor* v. *Provan* [1972] 1 W.L.R. 1459 T, who was resident in Canada and not resident in the UK, held directorships in an English brewery group. His special assignment, to expand the group, was to be performed so far as possible from his residence abroad. He did his planning wherever he happened to be. He spent an average of between 100 and 150 days a year in Canada, 50 to 85 in the UK, and the remainder in the Bahamas. The English group gave him no remuneration but paid his air fares between Canada or the Bahamas and the UK. Pennycuick V-C held that the travelling expenses were necessarily incurred in the performance of the duties of office because 'the only legitimate conclusion is that in the performance of the duties of his office as a director of the company Mr Taylor had two places of work, one in Canada coupled with the Bahamas and one in the United Kingdom' (ibid. at 1469).

All these decisions, alongside *Horton* v. *Young* (1971) 47 T.C. 60 (Schedule D Case I) and *IRC* v. *Richards' Executors* [1971] 1 W.L.R. 571 (capital gains tax), have created a climate of liberality in which the efficacy of some of the older decisions must be regarded as doubtful.

Directors' travel expenses are the subject of an extra-statutory concession: a director who gives his services without fee to a company not managed with a view to dividends, such as a club, is not assessed on any travelling expenses paid to him.

The prohibition of entertainment expenditure applies also to Schedule E (s. 411(1)(*b*)). However, a little *caveat*—the Schedule E taxpayer is excluded from the exceptions to that prohibition contained in s. 411(2) and (9) (*see* pp. 86–7 above). Here we are tracing an exclusion from exceptions to a prohibition of a deduction!

2.42 EXPENSES AND BENEFITS IN KIND OF DIRECTORS AND HIGHLY-PAID EMPLOYEES

In derogation of the principles in 2.41, provisions were introduced in 1948 (now TA ss. 195–203) which, regardless of convertibility, bring into charge as emoluments expenses allowances and benefits in kind paid to directors, whatever they earn, or to employees earning £2,000 a year or more. Every year employers are required to complete form P11D in respect of every such director or employee in receipt of an expenses allowance or benefit in kind. Employers with a large number of highly-paid employees are able to negotiate with the Revenue an increased earnings limit of £2,500 and thereby reduce their paper work.

The benefits in kind brought into charge are specified in s. 196(1) as 'the provision . . . of living or other accommodation, of entertainment, of domestic or other services or of other benefits or facilities of whatsoever nature'. Expressly excluded are:

(a) accommodation, supplies, or services in the business premises used by the director or employee solely in performing his duties (s. 196(2));
(b) living accommodation occupied by an employee in a representative capacity or provided in accordance with a trade practice which has prevailed since at least 30 July 1928 (s. 196(3));
(c) canteen meals (s. 196(4));
(d) retirement benefits (s. 196(5)); and
(e) assets which remain the employer's own property (s. 197(1)), i.e. payments or benefits for the exclusive benefit of the employer.

Where the employer's expense partly provides the employee with a benefit within s. 196(1) and is partly for the employer's exclusive benefit, the expense must be apportioned (s. 196(6)).

Expenses allowances or benefits in kind charged under these provisions may be deductible under TA s. 189 or 192. An Inspector satisfied that a taxable payment or benefit will be balanced by a corresponding deduction is therefore empowered under s. 199 to make a "dispensation", i.e. to notify the employer that the provisions are not to apply to the payments or benefits in question. S. 199 operates only where a company furnishes the Inspector with a statement of the circumstances. The other sections apply not merely to corporate employers but also to unincorporated associations and individuals carrying on a trade, profession, or vocation, though not to charities or non-trading bodies.

"Director" is given an extended definition by ss. 198(1) and 203(1). The limit of £2,000 a year for employees must be calculated by including payments or benefits to which ss. 195–203 apply. The provisions do not apply to any employment at a school or other educational establishment (s. 198(5)).

Turning to such case law as there is on these provisions, the Revenue appear to have enjoyed a procession of successes. In *Doyle* v. *Davison* (1961) 40 T.C. 140 the managing director of a company lived in a house owned by the company. Sums paid by the company for repairs were held assessable under s. 196(1); that the employer received some incidental benefit was immaterial. Similarly in *McKie* v. *Warner* [1961] 3 A.E.R. 348 the taxpayer on appointment as export sales supervisor was required to live in London. His company rented a flat for him at £500 a year, for which he paid the company £150 a year. Assessments on the remaining £350 a year were upheld, notwithstanding that his duties included entertaining foreign buyers and that a room was available at the flat for their use. (*Quaere* whether the taxpayer could have claimed an apportionment under s. 196(6): *see* [1969] 3 A.E.R. at 568). In *Butter* v. *Bennett* [1962] 3 A.E.R. 204 the manager of a mill was required to live in a company house at his own expense. The Court of Appeal held him assessable on payments made by the company to meet the costs of coal, electricity, and the services of a gardener; s. 196(3) only excluded expenses of providing accommodation and maintaining it in a habitable state, as opposed to expenses of inhabiting the accommodation. In *Rendell* v. *Went* [1964] 2 A.E.R. 464 a company car, with R at the wheel, unaccountably left the road and killed a pedestrian. R's services being virtually indispensable, the company spent £641 on securing his acquittal. The House of Lords upheld an assessment on R which included the £641 as a benefit: an expense was not the less advantageous to the director or employee because it suited the employer to make it. Moreover, there would be no apportionment under s. 196(6) since no part of the money could be identified as not providing a benefit to R.

However, the Revenue suffered an important reverse in *Luke* v. *IRC* [1963] A.C. 557. The managing director of a large public company bought a house in Ayrshire at the company's suggestion. Later he advertised it for sale, but the company chairman suggested that the company buy the house and rent it to him, and he agreed. During the tenancy the company spent £950 on owner's rates, feu duties, insurance, and repairs. The House of Lords held that this sum should not be included in the managing director's emoluments either (Lords Jenkins and Guest dissenting) under s. 195(1) (because the expense conferred on him no benefit beyond his pre-existing legal rights) or (Lord Jenkins dissenting) by reason of s. 197(1) (because the expense bought for the company, in place of a defective house, premises of a very different character).

The lenience of this decision has to some extent been tempered by *Westcott* v. *Bryan* [1969] 2 Ch. 324, in which a similar fact pattern arose. *Luke* v. *IRC* was distinguished by Pennycuick J. as 'a binding authority on repairs for which a tenant would not ordinarily be responsible' (ibid. at 706): expenditure on maintenance for which a tenant would ordinarily be responsible did not come within s. 197(1). The learned judge further held that, where a company established living accommodation for common enjoyment by a director or highly-paid employee and others, the total expense required apportionment under s. 196(6) regardless of any spatial or temporal division; and that no precise formula could be applied for effecting the apportionment, though regard should be had to the need to keep the accommodation in a state of availability. The Court of Appeal affirmed his decision.

Where an employer's expenditure on providing living accommodation is chargeable on a director or employee both under TA s. 185(1) (*see* p. 103 above) and under TA s. 196(1), the amount chargeable under s. 196 is reduced by the amount chargeable under s. 185 (s. 196(1) proviso).

2.43 GOLDEN HANDSHAKES

A payment on termination of an office or employment or on variation of its terms is taxable as deferred remuneration if made pursuant to some prior arrangement, in the contract of service or otherwise: *see Henry* v. *Foster* (1932) 16 T.C. 605 and *Dale* v. *De Soissons* [1950] 2 A.E.R. 460. (In the latter Evershed M.R. described the line between success and failure in these cases as 'a little wobbly' (ibid. at 461.) Similarly a payment in consideration of an agreement not to resign (*Cameron* v. *Prendergast* [1940] A.C. 549) or to serve at a reduced salary (*Tilley* v. *Wales* (p. 118 below)) is treated as advance remuneration, though a payment in consideration of a restrictive covenant not to compete with the employer escapes tax at the basic rate (*see* p. 110 above).

These principles remain good law. However, provisions were enacted in F.A. 1960 with a view to removing the immunity formerly enjoyed:

(1) by payments made *voluntarily* on termination of an office or employment or in variation of its terms (*see* pp. 108–9 above);

(2) by damages for wrongful dismissal: *Du Cros* v. *Ryall* (1935) 19 T.C. 444 (action for wrongful dismissal compromised on terms which included payment by a company to its former general manager of £57,250 as "agreed damages": Finlay J. held the entire payment capital);

(3) by compensation for loss of office: *Hunter* v. *Dewhurst* (1932) 16 T.C. 605 (£10,000 paid to a company director to compensate him for loss of the chairmanship held untaxable); and

(4) by payments in commutation of pension rights: *Tilley* v. *Wales* [1943] A.C. 386 (the inventor of a secret chemical process agreed to a reduction in salary and released the company employing him from its obligation to pay him a pension in consideration of £40,000 payable by two equal instalments: their Lordships held the portion of the payment in commutation of pension capital, the rest chargeable under Schedule E).

The provisions, now contained in TA ss. 187, 188, and Schedule 8, extend also to redundancy payments and to the compensation for unfair dismissal provided for in the Industrial Relations Act. S. 187 imposes a charge under Schedule E on the holder or past holder of an office or employment (hereafter mnemonically referred to as "Mr Hophoe") on all payments not otherwise chargeable to tax which are made:

(1) (*a*) to Mr Hophoe, or
   (*b*) on his behalf or to his order, or
   (*c*) to his personal representative(s), or
   (*d*) to any spouse, relative, or dependant of his,

(2) by Mr Hophoe's employer or by any other person (so that a present from Mr Hophoe's aunt because he has been dismissed would, literally, be caught, *sed quaere*: G.S.A.W. [1961] B.T.R. at 23),

(3) (*a*) in connection with the termination of an office or employment or any change in its functions or emoluments, or
   (*b*) in commutation of annual or periodical payments.

The payments may be made in money or in kind; and are treated as earned income received on the date of termination, change, or commutation, as the case may be. The payer must give particulars to the Inspector within thirty days of the end of the year of assessment in which the payment is made.

S. 188 exempts certain payments from the charge under s. 187:

(1) Any payment not exceeding £5,000. Thus in *IRC* v. *Brander & Cruickshank* [1971] 1 A.E.R. 36 the House of Lords held a payment of £2,500 in compensation for loss of office exempt. Where a payment exceeds £5,000, only the excess is chargeable. Payments made in respect of the same office or employment or by the same or associated employers in respect of different offices or employments, must be aggregated.

(2) Payments made in connection with the termination of an office or employment by reason of the death, injury, or disability of Mr Hophoe.

(3) Payments within TA s. 34 (*see* p. 110 above).

(4) Payments under unapproved retirement benefits schemes taxable under TA s. 220 or under approved Top Hat schemes authorized by TA s. 221(1) and (2) or by F.A. 1970 s. 24(1).
(5) Terminal payments to HM Forces.
(6) Payments under certain overseas government superannuation schemes.
(7) Payments made when Mr Hophoe is not domiciled in the UK and his employer is not resident here.
(8) Payments of compensation for loss of office the duties of which were performed outside the UK.
(9) Payments other than compensation for loss of office where Mr Hophoe's service included substantial periods of foreign service.

In computing the amount of the charge under s. 187 it is necessary to distinguish payments of compensation for loss of office from any other payments. With a compensation payment the chargeable amount is arrived at simply by subtracting £5,000 from the payment. With any other payment the chargeable amount is arrived at by subtracting from the payment not only £5,000 but also:

(i) the excess over £5,000 (if any) of Mr Hophoe's "standard capital super-annuation benefit" (hereafter "s.c.s.b."); and
(ii) a *pro rata* deduction corresponding to the proportion Mr Hophoe's foreign service bears to his entire service in point of time.

The s.c.s.b. is determined in accordance with the formula:

$$\text{s.c.s.b.} = \left(\frac{AE}{20} \times N\right) - L,$$

where AE = average emoluments over Mr Hophoe's last three years' service,
$\quad N$ = the number of his complete years of service, and
$\quad L$ = any non-taxable lump sum received or receivable by him under an approved retirement benefits scheme authorized by TA s. 221(1) and (2) or by F.A. 1970 s. 24(1).

It will be recalled (from p. 118 above) that payments within s. 187 are treated as income of one year of assessment. Schedule 8 paras 7–11 therefore give Mr Hophoe a complicated form of relief known as "top slicing", the effect of which is to enable him to notionally spread the payment over a number of years as though it were the top slice of his earned income in each year. In the case of a compensation payment the period is the number of years of unexpired service, in the case of other payments six years.

2.44 "GOURLEY" AND THE GOLDEN HANDSHAKE PROVISIONS: AN
UNHOLY ALLIANCE

It was once the settled rule that in assessing damages for personal injuries
the Court was not concerned with the plaintiff's liability to tax on the sum
awarded: see *Billingham* v. *Hughes* [1949] 1 K.B. 643. This gave rise to the
anomaly that a plaintiff received a tax-free sum to compensate him for an
amount which, had it accrued as earnings in the ordinary course of events,
would have been greatly reduced by taxation. The House of Lords therefore
reversed this settled rule in *B.T.C.* v. *Gourley* [1956] A.C. 185, re-asserting
the principle that damages are intended to compensate the plaintiff, not to
punish the defendant. Their Lordships held that a civil engineer gravely
injured in a railway accident was entitled, not to the gross sum of £37,720
representing his loss of earnings, actual and prospective, but to the net sum
of £6,695 he would actually have received after the ravages of income tax
and surtax.

Their Lordships had unwittingly opened a Pandora's box. *Gourley* was
predicated upon two assumptions: one, that the earnings for the loss of
which the damages constituted compensation would have been subject to
tax, the second that the damages awarded were themselves immune from
tax. When F.A. 1960 brought damages for wrongful dismissal partly into
charge difficult problems arose. For instance, did *Gourley* apply to the
exempt slice of £5,000? In *Parsons* v. *B.N.M. Laboratories Ltd* [1964] 1 Q.B.
95 a chemist obtained interlocutory judgment for damages for wrongful
dismissal to be assessed by a master. Master Jacob found his lost earnings
to be £1,200 and the tax that would have been paid on that sum £320; but
declined to deduct the £320 on the ground that *Gourley* did not apply to
golden handshakes *at all* now that they were taxable. The Court of Appeal
(Sellers L.J. dissenting) preferred to apply *Gourley* and deduct the
£320.

What, though, if the damages exceeded £5,000? Master Jacob had gone
to one extreme in rejecting *Gourley* altogether. In *Stewart* v. *Glentaggart*
1963 S.C. 300 Lord Hunter had gone to the other, applying *Gourley* not
merely to the tax on the lost earnings but also to the tax on the damages
themselves. Starting with the amount of the award (£x), Lord Hunter had
subtracted tax that would have been paid on the lost earnings (£y) and
had then grossed up the resultant sum £(x − y) by adding back the tax that
would have been paid on an award of £(x − y). In *Parsons* Harman L.J.
admitted that Lord Hunter's was the "logical conclusion" and Pearson L.J.
that it appeared to produce "perfect justice", but both rejected it, suggesting

obiter that *Gourley* did not apply at all where the compensation exceeded £5,000.

These dicta were not followed in *Bold* v. *Brough, Nicholson & Hall Ltd* [1964] 1 W.L.R. 201. The managing director of a company with a contract of service for ten years was summarily dismissed. He claimed *inter alia* £26,312 loss of earnings. Phillimore J. compromised between the perfect justice of Lord Hunter's method and the practicality of Harman and Pearson L.JJ.'s method, holding that *Gourley* applied to the first £5,000 of the award but not to any excess over £5,000. The learned judge made his award on the footing that the total lost earnings were £5,000 spread evenly over the remainder of the ten-year period of the service agreement, calculated the tax that would have been paid on the £5,000 in those circumstances, and subtracted that amount of tax from the gross award payable without regard for tax.

Gourley does not of course apply only to a Schedule E taxpayer claiming damages for wrongful dismissal. Indeed the engineer in *Gourley* itself was a Schedule D taxpayer claiming damages for personal injuries. The rule has been applied to claims for defamation (*Lewis* v. *Daily Telegraph* [1964] A.C. 234), under the Fatal Accidents Acts in respect of injuries that resulted in death (*Zinovieff* v. *B.T.C.* (discussed in Kemp & Kemp *The Quantum of Damages in Fatal Injury Claims* 1962 2nd ed. p. 132)) and *Taylor* v. *O'Connor* [1971] A.C. 115) even to an award of removal expenses on a compulsory purchase (*Rosenberg* v. *Manchester Corporation*, a Lands Tribunal decision noted in [1972] B.T.R. at 69). On the other hand, the rule is not usually followed in commercial cases (*see*, for example, *Herring* v. *B.T.C.* [1958] T.R. 401) and it is doubtful whether *Gourley* applies to damages for loss of pension rights consequent on a wrongful dismissal; though applied in *Re Houghton Main Colliery Co. Ltd* [1956] 3 A.E.R. 300 *Gourley* was not even mentioned in that regard in *Beach* v. *Reed Corrugated Cases* [1956] 2 A.E.R. 652 or in *Bold* v. *Brough etc* [1964] 1 W.L.R. 201 (*see* paragraph above).

It is interesting to see that in *Ontario* v. *Jennings* [1966] the Supreme Court of Canada rejected the principle of *Gourley*. The single judgment delivered by Judson J. contains a number of cogent arguments against *Gourley*, of which these are two:

(i) It is irrelevant what the plaintiff would have done with his earnings— tax is a charge on income after it is received and should no more be taken into account than rent, rates, mortgage payments, etc.

(ii) Future tax liability is an imponderable—the plaintiff might be promoted, he might marry a wife with an income, he might move to a country where taxation is lower, his liability might depend on his attention to tax planning (though Pitcher J. took account of tax planning in *Beach* v. *Reed etc* [1956] 2 A.E.R. 652).

2.45 ASSESSMENT AND COLLECTION

Since 1944 income tax (but not surtax) has been collected under a cumulative system of deduction at source—the PAYE system—except where inconvenient (e.g. casual employments) or impracticable (e.g. employer resident abroad). From 6 April 1973 PAYE has extended to the higher rates of tax as well as the basic rate. An employer is supplied with the code of each of his employees and with tables to enable him to make the correct cumulative deduction. The code is based on personal reliefs and is made up of a number and a letter. The letter does not affect the deduction: "L" signifies that the employee has been given the single person's allowance, "H" the married man's allowance. Thus a married man with a child of twelve, entitled to the married man's allowance of £775 and child relief of £335 (totalling £1,010), would be given the code 101 H. If the employee notifies his tax office of an objection to disclosure of L or H, the Inspector will replace it with "T". Equally, if the employee's circumstances change during the tax year, he should notify the Inspector, who will adjust his code without waiting for the end of the year.

The employer is notified of an employee's code by a card (P9 if he is paid weekly, P11 if monthly or at longer intervals), on which the employer must enter details of emoluments and deductions. Pending receipt of a P9 or P11, the employer must make up an emergency card. When an employee leaves, the employer must prepare, by reference to the deduction card, a P45 certificate, of which Parts 2 and 3 are carbon copies of Part 1. Entries include the name and address of the employee, the date of his leaving, his code, the last entries on his deduction card, and the name and address of his new employer (if known). Part 1 is sent to the Inspector, Parts 2 and 3 handed to the employee for production to his new employer (or, on permanent cessation of all employment, to the Inspector). The new employer enters in the space provided in Part 3 the nature of the work, the date it commenced, and the employee's address; and prepares a deduction card from the particulars on the P45, sending Part 3 on to the employee's new tax office. If the employee objects to disclosure to the new employer of his previous emoluments he may send Parts 2 and 3 of his P45 to the Inspector. (An employer is not required to complete an emergency card or a P45 where the emoluments are less than £8 per week or £34·50 a month, since these sums would normally be covered by personal reliefs.)

Within fourteen days of each tax month the employer must send in a remittance card (P30) detailing his deductions and any refunds that month. He is liable for sums he should have deducted, unless the error was made in good faith, in which case the Inspector will recover the under-deduction directly from the employee. An employer can only recover under-deductions by deduction from subsequent emoluments of that year. He cannot recover it by Court action as money paid under a mistake of fact or as money had and received or as money belonging in equity to the employer: *Bernard & Shaw Ltd* v. *Shaw* [1951] 2 A.E.R. 267.

Within fourteen days of the end of each tax year the employer must return to the Collector details of emoluments, deductions, etc, in respect of each employee. In practice the employer simply sends in all his deduction cards. He must make a further return on P11D of any expenses and benefits in kind given to directors and highly-paid employees and must give each employee a P60 certificate showing *inter alia* total emoluments and deductions.

General advice and assistance on PAYE matters can be obtained by the public at local inquiry offices, which are plentiful in the London area but thin on the ground elsewhere.

2·5 The pensioner

2.51 SOME BACKGROUND INFORMATION

State pensions exist alongside occupational schemes provided by employers. Where the employees meet part of its cost an occupational scheme is said to be "contributory", if not "non-contributory". Since 1948 the State pension has been financed under the national insurance scheme. At first flat-rate contributions secured flat-rate benefits. Later a measure of earnings-relation was introduced, with graduated contributions and a correspondingly higher level of benefits. Flat-rate contributions are collected either by stamped cards or by direct payment, graduated contributions through PAYE. Employees may be "contracted out" of the State system, in which case they continue to pay the basic national insurance rate but are relieved of paying graduated contributions.

The number of pensioners having doubled between 1948 and 1972, the essential injustice of flat-rate contribution was manifest. The Social Security

F

Act 1973 therefore enacts a new system by which, with effect from April 1975, a uniform scale of earnings-related contributions, collected via PAYE is to finance two pensions—a basic State pension at a flat rate and also a State reserve pension. The reserve scheme is to be entirely separate from the State basic scheme: it is to be a funded scheme run on the lines of an occupational pension by an independent Board of Management. Reserve pensions will be assessed by reference to the contributions paid on behalf of each contributor; and will be enhanced periodically by "bonuses". Employers with occupational schemes that satisfy certain minimum requirements will be able to obtain complete exemption from the State reserve scheme in respect of employees covered by their schemes. It will be one of the functions of the Occupational Pensions Board to be established under the Act to accord "recognition" to occupational schemes of the required standard.

2.52 THE TAX TREATMENT OF PENSIONS

A pension paid by or on behalf of a person outside the UK is chargeable as a foreign possession under Schedule D Case V. Virtually all other pensions are chargeable as earned income under Schedule E: the charging provisions are in a formidable state of disarray but seem comprehensive enough (see TA ss. 181(1) Schedule E paras 2–4, 182(1), 208(3), 220, F.A. 1970 s. 23 and Schedule 5 Part II para 1, and F.A. 1971 Schedule 3 para 9). The only major doubt surrounds annuities payable under retirement benefit schemes, which fall within both (i) Schedule E, and (ii) Schedule D Case III. Revenue practice is to treat them as within Schedule E if legally exigible and payable by business concerns or in connection with employments, otherwise as within Case III. (See also McMann v. Shaw [1972] 3 A.E.R. 732.)

Turning from taxability to deductibility, the position with regard to State pensions is that an employee is entitled to deduct neither national insurance nor graduated contributions, while his employer is entitled to deduct his (the employer's) contributions. Similarly, in the case of occupational schemes, the employer is entitled to deduct from his profits both the ordinary annual contributions (Morgan Crucible Co. v. IRC [1932] 2 K.B. 185) and the pensions themselves, even where voluntary (Smith v. Incorporated Council of Law Reporting [1914] 3 K.B. 674). He faces only two major difficulties:

(i) a pension incommensurate with the nature of the employment might fall foul of TA s. 130(a) (pp. 81–3 above); and

(ii) an initial payment by an employer constitutive of a pension fund may rank as a capital disbursement, as in *British Insulated & Helsby Cables Ltd* v. *Atherton* [1926] A.C. 205.

On the other hand, as with State pensions, so with occupational schemes the employee fares less well. Not only are his ordinary annual contributions not normally deductible, the employee has to contend with a formidable provision originally enacted in F.A. 1947, now contained in TA s. 220, and due to be replaced, as we shall see in the succeeding paragraphs, at some time before 6 April 1980 by F.A. 1970 s. 23. TA s. 220 and F.A. 1970 s. 23 provide that where, pursuant to a retirement benefits scheme, an employer pays a sum for the provision of relevant benefits for any of his employees, the sum paid, if not otherwise chargeable to income tax as income of the employee, is deemed for all the purposes of the Income Tax Acts to be an emolument of that employee.

"Retirement benefits scheme" is widely defined as 'a scheme for the provision of benefits consisting of or including relevant benefits' other than the State scheme (F.A. 1970 s. 25(1)). This definition embraces not only the usual methods by which employers provide retirement benefits for their employees (e.g. by setting up and contributing to their own fund, by contributing to an established fund, or by paying premiums to an insurance company in return for retirement benefits) but also any other means of providing them, e.g. service agreements. "Relevant benefits" are also widely defined to include all payments on death or retirement, or in anticipation of retirement, or in connection with any change in the nature of the employee's service (TA s. 224(1), F.A. 1970 s. 26(1)). The provision does not, however, apply to statutory schemes, to schemes set up by foreign governments for the benefit of their employees, or to employees working abroad and liable to UK tax, if at all, only under Schedule E Case III (TA s. 221, F.A. 1970 s. 24(1)).

2.53 REVENUE APPROVAL

Nor, more significantly, does the provision apply to approved schemes. The code of approval currently in force is to be found in TA ss. 220–5, but any scheme coming into being after 5 April 1973 or any existing scheme subjected to substantial alteration after that date must conform to a new code of approval set out in F.A. 1970 ss. 19–26 and Schedule 5. As from 6 April 1980 all schemes will have to conform to the new code. Revenue approval is the employee's escape route from Schedule E taxability on his retirement benefits.

The basic conditions of approval (under the new code) are laid down by F.A. 1970 s. 19(2):

(a) the scheme must be 'bona fide established for the sole purpose of providing relevant benefits in respect of service as an employee . . . payable to, or to the widow, children or dependants or personal representatives of the employee';

(b) it must be 'recognised by the employer and employees to whom it relates, and . . . every employee who is, or has a right to be, a member of the scheme' must have been 'given written particulars of the essential features of the scheme which concern him';

(c) there must be a UK resident 'responsible for the discharge of all duties imposed on the administrator of the scheme';

(d) the employer must contribute;

(e) the scheme must be 'established in connection with some trade or undertaking carried on in the United Kingdom by a person resident in the United Kingdom';

(f) where the employer is a director controlled company (one in which the directors own or control over 50% of the ordinary shares), the scheme must not include any controlling director (one who owns or controls over 5% of the ordinary shares); and

(g) in no circumstances are any employee's contributions to be repaid.

The Board are bound to approve any scheme which satisfies also the further requirements contained in F.A. 1970 s. 19(2A):

(a) that the benefit for an employee be a pension on retirement between the ages of 60 and 70 (if a man) or 55 and 70 (if a woman), not exceeding in amount one-sixtieth of the employee's final remuneration for each year of service up to a maximum of forty;

(b) that any benefit for his widow be a pension not exceeding two-thirds of his;

(c) that no other benefits be payable under the scheme; and

(d) that the pension be incapable of surrender, commutation, or assignment, except to allow an employee on retirement to commute his pension for a lump sum not exceeding three-eightieths of his final remuneration for each year of service up to a maximum of forty.

Under F.A. 1970 s. 20 the Board have a discretion to approve a scheme notwithstanding that it does not satisfy one or more of these prescribed conditions.

The advantages of an approved scheme are that the employer's contributions are not included in his employees' emoluments, and that both employer and employees are entitled to deduct their contributions. Even more favourable treatment is available for any retirement benefits provision which qualifies under F.A. 1970 s. 21 as an "exempt approved scheme", defined in s. 21(1) simply as 'any approved scheme which is shown to the satisfaction of the Board to be established under irrevocable trusts' (e.g. where an employer has set up his own pension fund). An exempt approved fund pays no tax on either the income or the gains accruing from its investments.

2.54 RETIREMENT ANNUITIES

Only in F.A 1956 were provisions introduced—now contained in TA ss. 226–9, as extended by F.A. 1971 s. 20 and Schedule 2—with a view to assisting those unable or not allowed to participate in approved schemes— partners, controlling directors, the self-employed, those not in pensionable employment, *et alia*.

Assistance comes in the form of a relief from income tax (and formerly also surtax) for any individual with "relevant earnings" under Case I or II of Schedule D or under Schedule E who pays a "qualifying premium", which means 'a premium or other consideration under an annuity contract for the time being approved by the Board' (TA s. 226(1)). A number of conditions for approval are specified, e.g. the annuity must not commence beyond the age of 70 or (normally) before 60, or provide for a greater annual payment to the widow or widower than to the individual, but the Board again have a discretion to approve contracts which do not satisfy them. An annuity contract is eligible for approval if:

(a) its main object is to provide for a life annuity for an individual;
(b) its main object is to provide for a life annuity for an individual's spouse or dependant(s); or
(c) its sole object is to provide for a lump sum on the death of an individual before he reaches the age of 70 payable to his personal representatives.

Relief is restricted in amount. The maximum of allowable premiums in any year for contracts within (a) in the preceding paragraph is the lower of £1,500 or 15% of "net relevant earnings" (income from trades, etc, and from non-pensionable employments less certain deductions, such as trading losses, capital allowances, expenses, etc.). The limits are increased for older taxpayers: they are £1,600 or 16% for those born in 1914 or 1915, £1,700 or 17% for those born in 1912 or 1913, £1,800 or 18% for those born in 1910 or 1911, £1,900 or 19% for those born in 1908 or 1909, and £2,000 or 20%

for those born in 1907 or earlier. The maxima for contracts within (b) or (c) are £500 or 5%.

Relief is normally given by way of set-off of contributions against earned income in the year in which they are paid. There is provision for carry-forward of unused relief in excess of the percentage, but not the monetary, limits.

A measure of commutation was allowed for the first time in 1971. The annuity contract may provide for a lump sum in commutation of the annuity payments, provided that it does not exceed three times the annual annuity payments remaining. Since retirement annuity payments are taxable as earned income while the lump sum is tax free, maximum commutation would usually be advisable. Indeed the lump sum could then be used to purchase a fresh annuity, which would be received partly free of tax.

2.6 The investor

2.61 THE TAXATION OF PURE INCOME

This division is concerned broadly speaking with investment income from property other than land, or, to put it more grandly, with the fiscal effects in the UK of funded capitalism. The closest generic description is "pure income", the epithet signifying that no deduction is permitted for the cost of acquiring the income and that no expenditure is needed to maintain it. Most pure income is collected by deduction at source, some by direct assessment. Moreover the different types of pure income are confusingly sprawled across a number of charging provisions. This table is intended to clarify the situation:

Type of payment	Nature of charge
(1) public revenue dividends	deduction and assessment under Schedule C
(2) interest (a) yearly	(usually) deduction and assessment under TA s. 54; (otherwise) direct assessment under Case III of Schedule D
(b) non-yearly	direct assessment under Case III of Schedule D
(3) annuities or other annual payments	(usually) deduction and assessment under TA s. 52 or 53; (otherwise) direct assessment under Case III of Schedule D
(4) patent royalties and payments treated by TA ss. 156 and 157 in the same way as patent royalties	(usually) deduction and assessment under TA s. 52 or 53; (occasionally) direct assessment under Case I or II of Schedule D; (exceptionally) direct assessment under Case VI

From the payer's point of view it is important to distinguish the situation in which a payment is made entirely out of taxable profits, when he is allowed to retain the tax deducted as an offset against the tax to be paid in respect of his profits—"the s. 52 procedure"—from that in which the payment is not so made and he must therefore account for the deduction to the Revenue—"the s. 53 procedure". Under the s. 52 procedure the Revenue stand to lose no tax if the payer fails to make the deduction, since they have recourse to the profits out of which the payment was made; whereas under the s. 53 procedure the Revenue are vulnerable. Deduction under s. 52 is therefore permissive; deduction and payment over under s. 53 are mandatory.

Deduction should be seen as a zero sum game for adjusting basic rate liability as between payer, payee, and the Revenue. To give an example, if Ernie Nuff were to make an annual payment of £1,000 out of his assessable income of £1,100 to his brother Justin Nuff, he would be entitled to deduct and retain £300. If Ernie's assessable income, on the other hand, were only £900, he would be bound to deduct £300 and account for £30 of it to the Revenue. For purposes of their basic rate computations, the payment is, in effect, entirely ignored (unless there is a failure to make the correct, or any, deduction), while in computing their liability to the higher rates and to the surcharge Ernie is entitled to deduct, and Justin must include, the gross amount of the payment, in this example £1,000. If Justin is not liable to tax, or is liable at less than the basic rate, he may make a repayment claim.

2.62 SCHEDULE C

TA s. 94 and Schedule 5 apply the s. 53 procedure to Schedule C income, defined in TA s. 93 as:

(1) public revenue dividends payable in the UK;
(2) UK public revenue dividends payable in the Republic of Ireland;
(3) public revenue dividends paid to a banker or other person in the UK in respect of coupons received from or on behalf of any other person; and
(4) the proceeds of sale or other realization of coupons for overseas public revenue dividends.

Deduction is made under (1) by the person entrusted with payment, under (2) by the Bank of England, under (3) by the banker or other person in receipt of the coupons, and under (4) by the banker or other person paying over the proceeds.

Where a person entitled to public revenue dividends payable in the UK exercises an option to have the dividends paid abroad, they are charged not under Schedule C but under Schedule D Case V. Where a government, public institution, or company discharges a liability to pay interest on a debt by issuing "funding bonds" to the creditor, the issue is treated by virtue of TA s. 417(1) as if it were a payment of interest equal to the value of the bonds at the time of their issue; the redemption of the bonds is disregarded for tax purposes, and any excess on redemption over the value of the bonds at issue escapes tax.

2.63 THE TAX TREATMENT OF INTEREST: A POLITICAL HOT POTATO

Ss. 52 and 53 applied to any 'interest, annuity or other annual payment' until F.A. 1969 removed interest from their clutches. Interest is now payable in full, unless it falls within TA s. 54. S. 54 subjects to the s. 53 procedure any payments of yearly interest, whether out of taxable profits or otherwise, made:

(a) by a company or local authority on its own account and not in a fiduciary or representative capacity;
(b) by or on behalf of a partnership of which a company is a member; or
(c) by any person to any other person whose usual place of abode is outside the UK.

Deduction is not required of:

(i) non-yearly ("short") interest, i.e. interest incapable of continuing for more than a year (s. 54(1));
(ii) interest payable in the UK on a bank loan (s. 54(2)); or
(iii) share or loan interest payable by an industrial or provident society to a person whose usual place of abode is within the UK (TA s. 340(2)).

Before 6 April 1969 interest was deductible from total income for income tax and surtax purposes. In F.A. 1969 the Labour Government disallowed interest as a deduction except for interest on loans for certain "qualifying purposes", namely:

(i) the purchase or improvement of land in the UK or Republic of Ireland;

(ii) the purchase of plant or machinery for use in a partnership or in an office or employment;

(iii) the payment of estate duty; and

(iv) the acquisition of an interest in a close company or partnership.

With an equal air of satisfaction, the Conservatives restored interest relief in F.A. 1972. S. 75(1) of that Act provides that a person who, on or after 6 April 1972, pays either (a) annual interest chargeable under Case III of Schedule D; or (b) interest payable in the UK on an advance from a UK bank, stockbroker, or discount-house, may claim to deduct it from or set it off against his income for the year of assessment in which the payment is made. Relief is not available for any excess of interest over a reasonable commercial rate (s. 75(2)). Moreover, the first £35 of interest does not qualify for relief unless it ranks as "protected interest" (s. 75(3)), defined in Schedule 9 to mean interest, other than bank overdraft interest, on loans for (i) and (ii) above. It is a moot point whether interest paid by personal representatives for (iii) above is deductible in full: Homer may have nodded in confining the £35 exclusion to interest paid *by an individual*. Of course interest has always been deductible if it qualified as allowable business expenditure under the "wholly and exclusively" rule (*see* pp. 81–3 above) and nothing in the 1969 or 1972 Act purported to affect this.

The 1972 changes will rarely benefit the lower rate taxpayer, while the higher rate taxpayer is in a position to take advantage of all sorts of ingenious schemes involving borrowing linked to life assurance. The Labour Party are pledged to repeal the 1972 interest provisions.

2.64 THE SS. 52 AND 53 PROCEDURES

Section 52	Section 53
(1) Applies to certain payments made wholly out of profits or gains brought into charge to tax, namely: (a) annuities or other annual payments not being interest (s. 52(1)); and (b) patent royalties and payments treated by TA ss. 156 and 157 in the same way as patent royalties (s. 52(2)).	Applies to the same payments as in (a) and (b) in the column opposite where they are not made or wholly made out of profits or gains brought into charge to tax (s. 53(1)). Also applies to a number of other payments irrespective of whether payable out of taxed profits or not, namely: (c) yearly interest within TA s. 54 (*see* p. 130 above); (d) payments by public offices and departments of the Crown (TA s. 56); (e) rents etc chargeable under Schedule A or Schedule D Case VI paid directly

Section 52	Section 53
	to a person whose usual place of abode is abroad (TA ss. 89(1), (2));
	(*f*) capital sums paid for the purchase of patent rights (TA s. 380(2)(*b*): *see* p. 146 below);
	(*g*) copyright royalties where the copyright owner's usual place of abode is abroad (TA s. 391(1)); and
	(*h*) payments within TA s. 209(2), 473(1) proviso, or 477.
(2) Payer entitled but not bound to deduct tax.	Payer bound to deduct tax.
(3) Payer retains any deduction.	Payer must account for the deduction to the Revenue to the extent that it is not paid out of taxable income.
(4) Deduction is at the basic rate for the year in which the payment is *due*.	Deduction is at the basic rate for the year in which the payment is *made*.

A number of questions fall to be considered:

§ 1 Which section applies?

Only if the payment falls within s. 52 will the payer be entitled to retain the tax deducted. S. 52 applies to sums "payable *wholly* out of profits or gains brought into charge to tax", s. 53 to other payments, whether made by individuals out of insufficient profits or out of capital or by companies. The expression "profits or gains brought into charge" was interpreted in *Att.-Gen.* v. *Metropolitan Water Board* [1928] 1 K.B. 833 to mean the figure of assessment of those profits or gains after they have been assessed and charged for that year. In *Allchin* v. *Corporation of South Shields* (1943) 25 T.C. 445 the reasoning in that case was criticized by the House of Lords (except for Lord Romer, who preferred to express no opinion on it), though its result was approved. 'To give an illustration,' explained Viscount Simon L.C., 'if in a given year [an annual payment of] £900 . . . is paid away [by a person chargeable under Case I or II of Schedule D] out of profits or gains and in that year the actual profits or gains of the payer are £1,000, while in the previous year they were £800, can the [payment] be regarded as wholly paid out of profits or gains brought into charge? . . . The "profits or gains brought into charge" must, in my view, mean the actual profits of the years calculated with such deductions, additions, or allowances as the Income Tax law prescribes—the £1,000 in my illustration' (ibid. at 461). As Lord Macmillan pointed out, the difficulty with the phrase arises out of the draftsman's failure to appreciate that a real payment cannot be made out of notional profits: 'Bluntly,' he added, 'I do not think that a logical solution is possible of an illogical problem' (ibid. at 464).

The proper approach is therefore to compare the aggregate of a taxpayer's annual payments in a particular year of assessment with his assessable income for that year. If the annual payments are less, s. 52 applies to all of them, if more s. 52 applies only to payments of a lesser aggregate amount than the figure of assessable income, the remaining payments falling within s. 53. Profits or gains brought into charge in previous years cannot be carried forward: *Luipaard's Vlei Estate and Gold Mining Co. Ltd* v. *IRC* [1930] 1 K.B. 593.

When a person makes a payment from which he had a right or duty to deduct tax, that payment may have the effect of reducing his total income below the level of his aggregate entitlement of personal reliefs. TA s. 25(1), as substituted by F.A. 1971 s. 53(5), provides that, in such a case, the payer should be deprived of his personal reliefs (other than those given for higher rate purposes) to the extent of the encroachment.

"Payable" in ss. 52 and 53 means "properly chargeable against" (*Att.-Gen.* v. *Metropolitan Water Board* [1928] 1 K.B. 833 at 851 *per* Lawrence L.J.): see *Sugden* v. *Leeds Corporation* [1914] A.C. 483; *Allchin* v. *Corporation of South Shields* (1943) 25 T.C. 445; *Postlethwaite* v. *IRC* (1963) 41 T.C. 224. Careful accountancy is called for. Where a taxpayer's accounts charge a payment otherwise than against taxed profits, he may be estopped from asserting that it was wholly paid out of taxed profits. Thus in *Corporation of Birmingham* v. *IRC* [1930] A.C. 307 the Corporation's Housing Scheme Account over several years included deductions in respect of the full amount of interest payments, which the Corporation had in fact made under deduction of tax, the idea being to maximize the Exchequer subsidy. The House of Lords held the deductions in full in the Account tantamount to an admission that the interest had not been paid out of taxed profits; and the Corporation could not now set up the contrary.

Similarly, where a payment has been charged to capital the payer must account to the Revenue under s. 53 even if he has taxable profits out of which the payment *might* have been made. This principle, which stems from *Central London Railway Co.* v. *IRC* [1937] A.C. 77, was applied in two recent cases, *B. W. Nobes & Co. Ltd* v. *IRC* [1966] 1 A.E.R. 30 and *Chancery Lane Safe Deposit & Offices Co. Ltd* v. *IRC* [1966] A.C. 85. In the first, company A covenanted to pay company B certain sums each year from 1958 to 1968 in consideration of shares in company B. In each of those years company A had sufficient profits to cover the covenanted payments, but not both the payments and its dividends. In company A's accounts the annual payments were charged to capital account, the dividends out of current profits. In the second case the appellant company borrowed £650,000 by way of mortgage in order to rebuild premises destroyed by fire. Apart from one year, for which the company accepted s. 53 liability, there were sufficient profits in all the relevant years to cover both the interest payments and dividends. In the company's accounts a proportion of the mortgage interest was charged to capital. In both cases, the House of Lords held that the covenanted payments and mortgage interest respectively fell to be treated under the s. 53 rather than the s. 52 procedure.

The principle cannot be invoked by the Revenue in the absence of a positive decision to charge payments to capital account: see *Hume* v. *Asquith* [1969] 1 A.E.R. 868.

§ 2 What is a payment?

The right to deduct under s. 52 and the duty to do so under s. 53 arise "on making the payment". What constitutes a payment is usually a matter of commercial practice. Making a credit entry in a book of account would therefore be one way of making a payment. Difficult cases do of course arise. For example, in *Stocker* v. *IRC* (1919) 7 T.C. 304 the appropriation by each brother in a family partnership of 6% of his share of partnership income to a reserve fund to meet possible capital losses was held an "annual payment". In relation to interest, what constitutes payment has been said to be 'one of the most troublesome questions' ([1944] 1 A.E.R. at 427 *per* Lord Greene M.R.). Two decisions of the House of Lords have made the question what constitutes a payment of interest much less troublesome, and provisions in F.A. 1969 (discussed in 2.63 above) have made it much less important than it formerly was. The two cases are *Paton* v. *IRC* [1938] A.C. 341 (F borrowed £250,000 from a bank; *held* bank's action in debiting his account half-yearly with the interest due did not constitute a payment from F to the bank) and *IRC* v. *Oswald* [1945] A.C. 360 (B thrice mortgaged her reversionary interest under a settlement to secure sums of £2,300, £500, and £300 respectively, on terms *inter alia* that interest not paid within twenty-one days might, at the option of the mortgagee, be capitalized and added to the principal sums; arrears of interest having twice been capitalized in accordance with this provision, *held* neither constituted a payment).

§ 3 How do ss. 52 and 53 apply to payments in advance and in arrears?

A payment in advance of any legal obligation is treated as voluntary unless, say, a sum due monthly is paid annually in advance, in which case

Revenue practice is to regard it as fulfilling the obligation. It is not clear how far the Revenue are prepared to extend this practice.

Payment in arrears is problematical. Two solutions are possible where a payment due in year 1 is made, say, in year 3. One thing is common to both—the extra-statutory concession (no. 20) requiring the payer to account for the *excess* of the deduction over any chargeable profits of year 1 out of which the payment might have been made. The first solution (*see Simon* A3.411, *Whiteman & Wheatcroft* 3–49 fn. 14) is that the question which section applies depends upon the payer's circumstances in the year of payment: if he has a sufficiency of chargeable profits in year 3, s. 52 applies, if not, s. 53. If s. 52 applies, tax is deductible at the rate obtaining in year 1 and the payment ranks in the hands of the payee as income of year 1: see TA s. 528(3) and *Re Sebright* [1944] Ch. 287; *cf. Leigh* v. *IRC* [1928] 1 K.B. 73. If s. 53 applies, the Revenue concession together with s. 53(2) limit the payer's accountability to the Revenue to the excess of the deduction over the higher of the two figures of chargeable profits in years 1 and 3. The second solution (*see Pinson* 5–20) is that the question which section applies depends upon the level of the payer's chargeable profits in year 1. If they are sufficient to cover the payment, s. 52 applies, if not, s. 53, though if there are sufficient profits to cover the payment in year 3, the payer is in view of s. 53(2) under no obligation to account to the Revenue. If there is also not a sufficiency of profits in year 3, accountability is limited to the excess of the deduction over the higher figure of chargeable profits in years 1 and 3. The first solution, it is submitted, is preferable in so far as it minimizes the need to refer back to earlier tax returns, but in view of the Revenue concession the adoption of one solution rather than the other will rarely affect the extent of the payer's liability.

§ 4 Who is the payer?

An assessment under s. 53 may be made on a person "by or through whom" a payment is made. A firm of solicitors instructed to pay advance royalties to Sacha Guitry, the French playwright, were held in *Rye and Eyre* v. *IRC* [1935] A.C. 274 to be within this description. They were therefore liable for the tax which they ought to have deducted on making the payment. Similarly, in *Howells* v. *IRC* [1939] 2 K.B. 597 a solicitor in the habit of lending money to one of his clients, a builder, received the proceeds of sale of the completed properties and deducted the net amount of arrears of interest due to him as mortgagee before paying the proceeds of sale over to his client. He was held liable for tax on the interest: in paying the interest *qua* solicitor to himself *qua* mortgagee he ought to have deducted tax and accounted for it to the Revenue under s. 53. *See also Aeolian Co. Ltd* v. *IRC* [1936] 2 A.E.R. 219.

§ 5 What if the payer under-deducts?

Where tax is not deducted, or is under-deducted, from a payment to which s. 52 applies, the Revenue are unaffected, since they will recover tax in respect of the payment from the profits out of which it was made. In effect the payer will simply have made a tax-free gift to the payee of the amount under-deducted. On the other hand, where the payment falls within s. 53, the Revenue may recover the under-deduction by direct assessment under s. 53. Alternatively, they may assess the payee under the appropriate Case or Schedule: *see Glamorgan Q.S.* v. *Wilson* [1910] 1 K.B. 725, *Grosvenor Place Estates Ltd* v. *Roberts* [1961] 1 Ch. 148.

Neither under s. 52 nor under s. 53 does the payer incur a penalty for failure to deduct (even though a person who refuses to *allow* a deduction authorized by the Taxes Acts is liable to a penalty of £50 under TMA s. 106). However, failure to deduct is regarded *prima facie* as a mistake of law. The payer is therefore not entitled to recover amounts overpaid from the payee either by Court action or by compensatory over-deduction from later payments (*Re Hatch* [1919] 1 Ch. 351), unless (*a*) the mistake is shown to be one of fact, as in *Turvey* v. *Dentons* [1953] 1 Q.B. 218, (*b*) an annual payment is made in instalments, in which case under-deductions from earlier instalments may be recovered from the later: *see Taylor* v. *Taylor* [1938] 1 K.B. 320, or (*c*) the failure is made by trustees making payments in the course of administering an estate, a situation to which the mistake of law doctrine has no application: *Re Musgrave* [1916] 2 Ch. 417. There is also a statutory exception: where under-deductions are due to an increase in the basic rate of tax, TA s. 521 provides that they may be recovered in the next payment after the Act, or, if there is none, as a debt.

The payer usually furnishes the payee with a statement on form R185—he is bound to do so under TA s. 55 if the payee so requests in writing—showing the gross amount of the payment, the amount deducted, and the net amount paid. Where the payee is not given a certificate it may be difficult to say whether the sum received is the gross or net amount of the payment: compare *Hemsworth* v. *Hemsworth* [1946] K.B. 431 with *Stokes* v. *Bennett* [1953] Ch. 566.

2.65 TAX-FREE ANNUITIES

TA s. 106(2) vitiates any agreement for the payment of interest, rent, or other annual payment in full without allowing any deduction authorized by the Taxes Acts. Its effect is to vitiate not the entire agreement but merely the provision relating to payment in full: *Booth* v. *Booth* [1922] 1 K.B. 66; *cf. Whiteside* v. *Whiteside* [1950] Ch. 65. The conventional formula for payment of a net sum despite s. 106 (2) is "such a sum as after deduction of income tax therefrom at the basic rate for the time being in force will leave £x". Where the formula has been used and the payee makes a repayment claim, he is not accountable to the payer for any tax repaid: *Re Jones* [1933] Ch. 842: on the other hand, he is not entitled to an indemnity from the payer against any excess liability or investment income surcharge to which the payment might subject him: *Re Bates* [1925] Ch. 157.

S. 106(2) applies only to agreements, including deeds of covenant. Provisions for tax-free annual payments in wills, though effective, should be used advisedly. For one thing, they are construed as requiring the trustees of the will to indemnify the annuitants against the higher rates and surcharge as well as against basic rate tax: *Re Reckitt* [1932] 2 Ch. 144. Thus a tax-free payment of £x costs the estate, so to speak, £x "grossed up" to include basic rate, higher rates, and any surcharge payable by the annuitant. Furthermore, the residuary estate is entitled, under the rule in *Re Pettit* [1922] 2 Ch. 765, to the proportion of any repayment made to the annuitant that the annuity bears to his total income. According to *Re Kingcome* [1936] Ch. 566 the annuitant is a trustee of the statutory right to recover tax overpaid and can therefore be compelled by the trustees to sign an application form claiming repayment.

Neither s. 106(2) nor the rule in *Re Pettit* apply to court orders. A court order for a tax-free annual payment requires the payer to pay the specified sum in full, unless the order requires payment of the sum "less tax", in which case the payer may or must deduct tax from the specified sum under s. 52 or s. 53 respectively.

Following an unreserved judgment of Scrutton J. in *Blount* v. *Blount* [1916] 1 K.B. 230 as to the meaning of the expression "free of tax", it came to be thought that in a voluntary settlement or will or court order that expression meant what it said but in an agreement or deed it fell foul of s. 106(2). In *Ferguson* v. *IRC* [1968] 1 A.E.R. 1025 the House of Lords, aware that '[f]ew questions of construction are more encumbered by more and conflicting streams of authority than this one' resolved to 'join the stream into a comprehensible single flowing river' (ibid. at 1032 *per* Lord Upjohn). A husband working in Malaya had agreed to pay his wife in Scotland £35 monthly "free of income tax". The Inspector sought to assess the wife under Case III of Schedule D on the footing that s. 106(2) applied and there had therefore been a failure to deduct tax from a payment within s. 53. Their Lordships discharged the assessment, overruling *Blount* v. *Blount* and declaring the anomalous distinction referred to earlier erroneous. In each case the crucial question was whether the parties intended the payments to be made in full or as net amounts after deduction.

A partial mirror image of s. 106(2) is to be found in TA s. 425, whereby any provision for the payment as a net amount of a stated quantum of any interest payable without deduction of tax, e.g. short interest (*see* p. 130 above), is to be construed as requiring payment of the stated quantum as a gross amount.

2.66 SCHEDULE D CASE III

TA s. 109 contains a charge to tax under Schedule D Case III in respect of:

(*a*) any interest of money, whether yearly or otherwise, or any annuity, or other annual payment, wherever payable, but excluding any payment chargeable under Schedule A;

(*b*) all discounts; and

(*c*) income from public revenue securities not chargeable under Schedule C.

A miscellany of other statutory provisions extends the scope of Case III so as to encompass also:

    (i) small maintenance payments (TA s. 65(3));

    (ii) interest on certain UK government securities (TA ss. 93 para 5 and 101(1));

    (iii) rents from one of the statutory trades listed in TA s. 112(2) (*see* p. 65 above) rendered in produce of the concern (TA s. 156(2));

    (iv) wayleave rents (*see* p. 159 below) not exceeding £2·50 (TA s. 157(3));

    (v) certain income of overseas life insurance companies (TA s. 316(1));

    (vi) savings bank interest in excess of the exempt £40 (TA s. 339(2));

    (vii) share or loan interest paid by a registered industrial and provident society other than to a person whose usual place of abode is abroad (TA s. 340(3));

    (viii) borrowings secured by policies of life assurance (TA s. 405(1)); and

    (ix) dividends on shares in a common investment fund set up to provide for the investment of funds in court (TA s. 143(1)).

It can be seen that: 'Case III is, within its ambit, a sweeping-up Case; it only applies to those special types of income where, for one reason or another, tax is not deducted under ss. 52 and 53 or assessed under some other Case or Schedule' (*British Tax Encyclopaedia* 1–310 to release 32).

§ 1 The basis of assessment

A Case III assessment is normally based on income arising in the preceding year of assessment (TA s. 119). In the case of non-traders, income does not arise until it is received: *Whitworth Park Coal Co. Ltd* v. *IRC* [1961] A.C. 31 'because until then it is not part of their income' (ibid. at 63 *per* Viscount Simonds). *See also Dewar* v. *IRC* [1935] 2 K.B. 351.

There are special rules governing fresh (TA s. 120) and ceasing (TA s. 121) sources of income, which may be summarized as follows:

Year of assessment	Basis period
1 (in which source first arose)	Date when income arose to following 5 April.
2	Where income first arose on 6 April, first year of assessment: otherwise, second year of assessment.
Final (in which source ceased)	Date when source ceased back to preceding 6 April.
Penultimate	Preceding year. (Additional assessment if actual basis produces a greater yield.)

The taxpayer has a right to elect that his first assessment on a preceding year basis (usually for the third year of assessment) be made on an actual basis instead. The Revenue do not in practice always apply these rules, for example where a taxpayer with one bank deposit makes another deposit with a different bank, or where a taxpayer with several bank deposit accounts closes one of them. The crucial determinant seems to be the relative size of the source. *See*, for example, *Hart* v. *Sangster* (1956) 37 T.C. 231 (deposit of £2 million into existing deposit account of £20,496 held the creation of a new Case III source).

§ 2 The meaning of "interest"

"Interest" is not defined in the Taxes Acts. Rowlatt J. was close to the mark when he described it succinctly as 'payment by time for the use of money' (15 T.C. at 379), Lord Wright a shade too restrictive with 'a payment which becomes due because the creditor has not had his money at the due date' (28 T.C. at 189).

By common practice a creditor often requires of the debtor a premium on redemption over and above any interest payable. Whether such a receipt ranks as capital or as additional interest was held in *Lomax* v. *Peter Dixon & Son Ltd* [1943] K.B. 671 to be a question of fact: where a commercial rate of interest is charged, there is no presumption that a premium is in the nature of interest, where no interest is payable there is. In *Riches* v. *Westminster Bank Ltd* [1947] A.C. 390 a long-standing controversy was laid to rest when all eight judges held that interest awarded by the Court or under an arbitration was "interest of money" chargeable under Case III. In *Westminster Bank etc Ltd* v. *National Bank of Greece S.A.* (1970) 46 T.C. 472 the appellant bank contended that payments of interest by a guarantor on behalf of the principal debtor were "interest" within Case III. Lord Denning M.R. in the Court of Appeal accepted this contention (ibid. at 485), but it was abandoned before the House of Lords, who were unable to deal with it and left the question open (ibid. at 494). However, Lord Hailsham L.C. did say *obiter* that Lord Denning's view would have been attractive but for the reasoning in *IRC* v. *Holder* [1932] A.C. 624, a case which he (Lord Hailsham) thought might deserve fresh consideration. In that case, Romer L.J. in the Court of Appeal and Lord Thankerton in the House of Lords preferred the view that a guarantor pays not interest but a debt due under his guarantee. Faced with these two conflicting views, Megarry J. plumped in *Re Hawkins decd* [1972] 3 W.L.R. 265 for that of Lord Denning *et al*. In that case F. Ltd had, by a promissory note, promised to pay by instalments to the order of P. Ltd at a bank in America a certain sum expressed in dollars plus interest. On failure to pay any instalment the entire unpaid principal and interest to date were to fall immediately due. The deceased had signed a guarantee endorsed on the note. Megarry J. held *inter alia* that interest payments due from the deceased's estate on the guarantee retained their nature as interest, especially since in the instant case what the deceased had guaranteed was not liabilities generally but "the principal and interest" on the note as and when due.

§ 3 The meaning of "annuity or other annual payment"

The word "annuity" is not confined to a purchased life annuity: *Ceylon Commissioner of Inland Revenue* v. *Rajaratnam* [1971] T.R. 451. We need not examine more closely what annuities are, since they are unquestionably a species of annual payment.

The crucial question is: what is an annual payment? A passage from

Jenkins L.J.'s lengthy judgment in *IRC* v. *Whitworth Park Coal Co. Ltd* (1959) 38 T.C. 531 provides a convenient set of pegs to hang the cases on:

'(i) To come within [Case III] as an "other annual payment" in question must be *ejusdem generis* with the specific instances given in the shape of interest of money and annuities . . . '

In *Earl Howe* v. *IRC* [1919] 2 K.B. 336, the Court of Appeal held that premiums on life assurance policies were not annual payments deductible from total income for super-tax purposes. Nor, decided Hamilton J. in *Hill* v. *Gregory* [1912] 2 K.B. 61, was rent. Similarly, post-cessation receipts of a trade etc formerly escaped the clutches of Case III as well as of Cases I and II of Schedule D (*see* the cases at pp. 48–9 above).

'(ii) The payment in question must fall to be made under some binding legal obligation as distinct from being a mere voluntary payment . . .'

This requirement is culled from the charging words of Case III in TA s. 109(2). Gifts are certainly excluded. With other payments, it is immaterial how the legal obligation arises, whether under a contract (*Peter's Executors* v. *IRC* (1941) 24 T.C. 45: husband held by Court of Appeal entitled to deduct from his total income for surtax purposes payments under a verbal separation agreement with his wife), a will (*Dealler* v. *Bruce* (1934) 19 T.C. 1: a bank held shares on trust to pay an annuity out of the income to Mrs S, with power to sell or mortgage the shares in order to secure the annuity, not exercisable while her brother B paid the annuity himself: B's payments held annual payments deductible from his total income), a trust (*Lindus and Hortin* v. *IRC* (1933) 17 T.C. 442; *Cunard's Trustees* v. *IRC* (1946) 27 T.C. 122: payments by trustees out of capital in exercise of their absolute discretion held taxable income in the hands of the recipient *cestuis que trust: see also Drummond* v. *Collins* [1915] A.C. 1011, or a statute (the *Whitworth Park* case itself (1959) 38 T.C. 531: "interim income" received by coal mining companies under the Coal Industry Acts 1946 and 1949 on nationalization of the coal industry pending payment of full compensation held annual payments).

If *Watkins* v. *IRC* [1939] 2 K.B. 420 was correctly decided the payment must also constitute income in the payee's hands. In that case Lawrence J. held a husband's payments to maintain his wife in a mental home were non-deductible because not taxable income in her hands.

'(iii) The fact that the obligation to pay is imposed by an Order of the Court and does not arise by virtue of a contract does not exclude the payment . . .'

See, for example, *Stokes* v. *Bennett* [1953] Ch. 566.

'(iv) The payment in question must possess the essential quality of recurrence implied by the description "annual" . . .'

● In *Moss' Empires Ltd* v. *IRC* [1937] A.C. 785 the appellant company guaranteed a fixed preferential dividend of 7½% for each of the first five financial years of Dominion Theatre Ltd; and was called upon to make payments under the guarantee in each of those years. The House of Lords held them annual payments. "Annual", said Lord Maugham, implies 'the quality of being recurrent or being capable of recurrence' (ibid. at 795) so that, in Lord Macmillan's words, '[t]he fact that the payments were contingent and variable in amount does not affect the character of the payments as annual payments' (ibid. at 793). This latter dictum was cited with approval by Lord Denning M.R. in *Westminster Bank etc Ltd* v. *National Bank of Greece S.A.* (pp. 46–7 and 140 above) where, with the support of Sachs L.J., he suggested that, even if his view that the payments ranked as "interest of money" were incorrect, they qualified as "annual payments".

Weekly or monthly payments therefore constitute "annual payments" if capable of continuing for longer than a year: *see*, for example, *Taylor* v. *Taylor* [1938] 1 K.B. 320.

'(v) The payment in question must be in the nature of a "pure income" profit in the hands of the recipient . . .'

This doctrine was applied in *Earl Howe* v. *IRC* [1919] 2 K.B. 336 (p. 141 above) though the phrase "pure income profit" derives from Greene M.R.'s judgment in *Re Hanbury* (1939) 38 T.C. 588. In *Barclays Bank Ltd* v. *Naylor* [1961] Ch. 7 Cross J. held that covenanted payments made by ICI Ltd to trustees for the education of children of its overseas employees were annual payments notwithstanding any incidental benefit to ICI Ltd of obtaining better employees by offering attractive conditions of service. On the other hand in *IRC* v. *National Book League* [1957] Ch. 488 the League, a charity, was refused its repayment claim in respect of membership subscriptions paid net by deed of covenant. 'Looking at the substance and reality of the matter,' Lord Evershed M.R. asked, 'can it be said that those who entered into these covenants have paid the sums covenanted without conditions or counter-stipulations' (ibid. at 503). Here the subscriptions entitled members to substantial benefits including restaurant and club facilities at the League's headquarters in the West End; and therefore failed to qualify as annual payments. In *Campbell* v. *IRC* [1970] A.C. 77 a director and the secretary of a tutorial company set up an educational trust, of which they were to be the first trustees, secured the company's execution of a seven-year deed of covenant in favour of the trust in respect of 80% of the company's profits, and proceeded to don their trustees' hats to claim repayment of the tax deducted from the covenanted payments. The House of Lords held that the payments were deprived of their character as income in the hands of the trustees by the clear understanding—a binding arrangement enforceable in law—that the trustees would use them to purchase the business of the company. They approved the result but not the reasoning of the *Book League* case. In the wake of *Campbell* it is submitted that payments represent pure income profit only if the recipient is entitled to no deduction for the cost of their acquisition or maintenance over and above any deductions to which he would otherwise be entitled. Thus if X covenanted to pay a theatre £50 a year for a seat at any performance during the year he might care to attend, the payment would *not* be an annual payment (notwithstanding that no conditions or counter-stipulations are attached) because it might cost the theatre something to maintain X's payment, namely the price of a ticket that might have been sold to someone else at every full house X attends. If, on the other hand, X were to agree only to take seats which would not otherwise be used, his payment might be an annual payment.

Clearly a payment will lack the quality of pure income profit if it is a trading receipt in the hands of the payee. Thus in *British Commonwealth International Newsfilm Agency Ltd* v. *Mahany* [1963] 1 A.E.R. 88 the Rank Organisation and the BBC, which had set up the appellant company, each covenanted for seven years to pay one half the amount of its annual trading deficit. The company's claim for tax deducted from payments under these covenants was refused since it received them as trading profits. *Cf. IRC* v. *City of London* [1953] 1 A.E.R. 1075.

Annual payments must be of an income and not a capital nature

This additional characteristic, assumed but not stated in Jenkins L.J.'s exposition, derives from the phrase "annual profits or gains" in the charging words of Schedule D in TA s. 108 (*see* p. 61 above). Here as elsewhere, the distinction between income and capital has necessitated a great deal of hair-splitting.

Where a person voluntarily covenants to make a series of payments, the form of covenant is generally decisive: see, for example, *Postlethwaite* v. *IRC* (1963) 41 T.C. 224 (income). Where, however, the payments are made in discharge of a pre-existing obligation, they will, in the absence of special circumstances, take on the nature of the obligation. Thus in *IRC* v. *Mallaby-Deeley* [1938] 4 A.E.R. 818 covenanted payments in discharge of an obligation to finance a literary work were held capital. A similar result had been arrived at in *Dott* v. *Brown* [1936] 1 A.E.R. 543.

Where the payments are made as the price of an asset or for some other consideration, the Courts have regarded them as:

(a) instalments of capital: *see Campbell* v. *IRC* [1970] A.C. 77 (*see* p. 143 above); *IRC* v. *Ramsay* (1935) 20 T.C. 79;

(b) annual payments within Case III: *Chadwick* v. *Pearl Life Assurance Co.* [1905] 2 K.B. 507; *IRC* v. *Hogarth* (1940) 23 T.C. 491; or

(c) partly capital and partly income: *Vestey* v. *IRC* [1962] Ch. 861 (V sold shares worth £2 million to a company for £5½ million, expressed to be without interest and payable by 125 annual instalments of £44,000: Cross J. held, following the House of Lords decision in *Secretary of State in Council of India* v. *Scoble* [1903] A.C. 299, that every payment, other than the first, should be dissected into a capital and an income component); *cf. IRC* v. *Land Securities Investment Trust Ltd* [1969] 2 A.E.R. 430 (a company purhcased the reversions on various leases and sub-leases it held of a landlord, in consideration of rentcharges, each payable for ten years, totalling £96,000 a year, which sum the company sought to deduct: Cross J. at first instance favoured dissection, the higher Courts thought neither *Scoble* nor *Vestey* in point and held the entire sum non-deductible; but before the House of Lords the Crown were prepared to allow a deduction for the "interest content" and the case was therefore remitted to the Commissioners).

The form of the transaction was thought to be the decisive criterion in assigning payments to one or other of these three categories: *see*, for example, 20 T.C. at 98 *per* Romer L.J. In the light of *Vestey* it seems that *all* the surrounding circumstances may be taken into account. It would certainly be difficult to accommodate *Littlewoods Mail Order Stores Ltd* v. *McGregor* [1969] 3 A.E.R. 855 within the earlier view.

§ 4 Purchased life annuities

Where an annuity is purchased for a fixed term, each annual payment is treated as part capital and part interest in the hands of the annuitant: *see*, for example, *Perrin* v. *Dickson* [1930] 1 K.B. 107. Other purchased annuities were treated entirely as income in the hands of the recipient until a provision of F.A. 1956, now TA s. 230, required each instalment of any "purchased life annuity" to be dissected and only the income component subjected to tax. The capital component of each instalment is arrived at by dividing the total consideration given for the annuity by the annuitant's expectation of life at the date when the annuity begins to accrue (or, alternatively, by working through the more convoluted statutory version of the formula). In practice, the division between income and capital is normally agreed between the annuity company and the Revenue; the company then deducts tax at the basic rate from the income element of each instalment, unless the annuitant obtains authority under the "DX-DR procedure" for deduction at a lesser or no rate.

S. 230 does not apply to annuities which:

(a) would, apart from the section, be treated as having a capital element (e.g. fixed term annuities);

(b) are paid for by premiums which qualify for life assurance relief under TA s. 19 or 20 or for retirement annuity relief under TA s. 277;

(c) are purchased in pursuance of a direction in a will or to provide for an annuity which is payable under a will or settlement out of the income of property disposed of by the will or settlement; or

(d) are purchased under a sponsored superannuation scheme or retirement annuity or in recognition of another's services (or past services) in any office or employment.

§ 5 Discounts

In the context of Case III, the term "discount", undefined in the Taxes Acts, means the amount deducted from the face value of a bill of exchange or promissory note by a bank or discount house when advancing payment before the due date. The charge under Case III extends to the entire difference between the price paid and the sum realized by the purchaser, whether by selling or converting before maturity or by holding until maturity: *Brown* v. *National Provident Institution* [1921] 2 A.C. 222. Profits from discounts are assessable in the year in which they are received: ibid. at 232. Each transaction is treated as a separate source of income and no set-off is allowed for losses.

2.67 PATENT ROYALTIES AND PAYMENTS TREATED AS SUCH

The ss. 52 and 53 procedures apply also to:

(a) any royalty or other sum paid in respect of the user of a patent, or

(b) any rent, royalty or other payment which, by TA s. 156 or 157 (mining etc rents and royalties: *see* 2.77 below), is declared to be subject to deduction at source as if it were a royalty or other sum paid in respect of the user of a patent. Where any such payment is made without deduction, the payee is assessable, presumably under Case VI.

The ss. 52 and 53 procedures do not of course apply to payments which are of a capital nature. In this area the line between income and capital is so gossamer fine as sometimes to be undetectable to the non-judicial eye. The leading case, in which Greene M.R. was tempted to try coin-spinning as an alternative to reasoning (*see* p. 78 above), is *IRC* v. *British Salmson Aero Engines Ltd* [1938] 2 K.B. 482, in which the Court of Appeal held that a lump sum payment for an exclusive licence to use a foreign patent was capital, though payable in three instalments. (Followed in *Murray* v. *ICI Ltd* [1967] Ch. 1038). On the other hand, in *Rustproof Metal Window Co. Ltd* v. *IRC* [1947] 2 A.E.R. 454 a lump sum payment for a non-exclusive licence was held income.

In *Constantinesco* v. *Rex* (1927) 11 T.C. 730 the House of Lords held that lump sum payments by the British and American Governments for past user of patents were not capital receipts and fell within s. 53. TA s. 384 now provides that the recipient of any royalty or other sum paid in respect of past user of patent may, in computing his income tax or corporation tax liability, notionally spread the payments backwards in equal instalments over a period of six years or, if the past user was for less than six complete years, over the lesser number of complete years of past user.

On the other hand, lump sum payments received for the sale of patent rights are taxed as income by virtue of TA s. 380. By s.-s. (1) a UK resident vendor of patent rights is chargeable under Case VI and may elect to spread the capital sum over six years but the purchaser is required to deduct tax from it under the s. 53 procedure. This requirement is something of a paper tiger where the purchaser is resident abroad.

2.7 The landlord

2.71 SCHEDULE A: THE OLD AND THE NEW

Income from land has always primarily been chargeable under Schedule A, but F.A. 1963 so transformed the Schedule that it is necessary to differentiate the "old" Schedule A from the "new". The old Schedule A was a charge on the ownership of land capable of occupation. The assessment was based on the land's "net annual value", a figure arrived at by deducting from its "gross annual value" a statutory repairs allowance. Gross annual values were supposed to represent letting values in the open market with the landlords liable for repairs and the tenants for rates, but intended quinquennial valuations were not kept up and annual values tended consequently to become unrealistic. The statutory repairs allowance was normally a fixed fraction of gross annual value. The Revenue's attempt to assess rents under Schedule D to the extent that they exceeded annual values failed, as we learned at p. 46 above, in *Fry* v. *Salisbury House Estate Ltd* [1930] A.C. 432 but was sanctioned by F.A. 1940. The old Schedule A, unlike the new, charged owner-occupiers as well as landlords and was more limited in scope in so far as rents under long leases were not within Schedule A but ranked as annual payments chargeable under Schedule D Case VI and as such were deductible from total income for surtax purposes, a boon for the wealthy. Tenants were entitled to deduct Schedule A tax borne by them on behalf of their landlords from their payments of rent.

F.A. 1963 replaced Schedule A with a new Case of Schedule D Case VIII, and put the charge on its new basis, which was retained when F.A. 1969 rechristened it Schedule A, thereby depriving the Revenue of their right to assess the taxpayer under Case I rather than Case VIII (*see* pp. 46–7 above). Thus Schedule A was on one basis up to and including 1962–63 and on another from 1964–65, 1963–64 being partly on one and partly on t'other basis.

2.72 AMBIT OF THE NEW SCHEDULE A

Like Gaul Schedule A is divided into three parts: TA s. 67(1) imposes the charge on 'annual profits or gains' to which 'a person becomes entitled' in respect of:

(a) rents under leases of land in the UK;
(b) rentcharges (or their Scottish equivalent) and any such other annual payments; and
(c) other receipts from the ownership either of land or of any incorporated hereditament (or its Scottish equivalent).

A convenient generic description of these three types of income is "rents etc".

A number of points arise out of the terms of this charging provision. The familiar phrase "annual profits or gains" puts capital receipts beyond the reach of Schedule A (*see* p. 61 above). The word "entitled" indicates that the charge arises on receivability, regardless of receipt, contrary to the normal rule. However, amounts receivable but not actually received may be taken out of account under TA s. 87(1) if the taxpayer is able to prove either (a) where the non-receipt is attributable to default by his tenant, that he has taken reasonable steps to enforce payment, or (b) that he waived payment without consideration and reasonably in order to avoid hardship. TA s. 87(2) extends this relief to premiums and similar payments chargeable under TA ss. 80–2 (see 2.74 below). If an amount relieved under this provision is subsequently received, the taxpayer or his personal representatives must inform the Inspector in writing of its receipt within six months. The receipt is then related back to the year of receivability, even if more than six years earlier. "Rent" in TA s. 67(1) is not defined. It is given a special extended meaning for purposes of the deductions rules, discussed at 2.75 below, and presumably bears its normal unextended meaning in other context. "Lease" includes an agreement for a lease and any form of tenancy, even a tenancy at will; but excludes a mortgage and, semble, an option to take a grant or lease.

The apparently wide sweep of s. 67(1)(c), broader than its predecessor in F.A. 1963, is confirmed by the cases. In Lowe v. J. W. Ashmore [1971] Ch. 545 Megarry J. held that receipts from the sale over a period of two years of pieces of turf were profits of the trade of farming chargeable under Case I of Schedule D, but alternatively that they fell within Schedule A (then Case VIII) under s. 67(1)(c) on the basis that the buyer had acquired a profit à prendre. On the other hand, the Court of Appeal in Bennion v. Roper [1970] T.R. 309 held that rents from a lease of 100 acres of pasture and 110 acres of arable land fell solely within Schedule A, either as being within s. 67(1)(a) or, even if the agreement were construed as a mere licence to graze the pasture and to grow crops upon the arable land, within s. 67(1)(c). Although the literal terms of s. 67(1)(c) may well take in payments for mere licences, as in the case of cinemas, racecourses, car parks, and the like, it is submitted that these are more properly regarded as trading receipts.

Schedule A does not include:

(a) income from land outside the UK (s. 67(1) para 1);
(b) yearly interest (ibid. para 3);
(c) profits or gains of a person himself using land for one of the statutory trades specified in TA s. 112(2) (mines, quarries, and other concerns: see p. 65 above) (ibid.).
(d) rents or royalties indirectly in respect of any s. 112(2) trade carried on by another (chargeable under TA s. 156: see 2.77 below) (ibid.).

(e) wayleave rents in respect of electric wires or cables (chargeable under TA s. 157: *see* 2.27 below) (ibid.).

(f) rents under a lease which includes the use of furniture (ibid. para 4).

Both before and since F.A. 1963, the component of rent under a furnished letting attributable to the use of furniture has been assessable under Case VI of Schedule D. TA s. 67(1) para 4 provides that the rent itself is to be charged also under Case VI, unless the landlord elects that he does not wish the provision to apply, in which case the rent will be charged under Schedule A whilst payment for the use of the furniture continues to be charged under Case VI. The election must be made by notice in writing to the Inspector within two years after the end of the chargeable period (TA s. 67(2)). The landlord of furnished premises will make the election if the Schedule A provisions with regard to expenditure and losses would be more favourable than those governing Case VI. In practice Inspectors often allow the land-lord of a furnished letting a deduction for depreciation on furnishings in the form of an annual percentage, usually 10% of the gross rents receivable.

2.73 ASSESSMENT AND COLLECTION

Schedule A is assessed on a current year basis. Thus liability cannot be accurately determined until the end of the year of assessment. Tax is generally payable, however, on 1 January during the year. The problem is solved by TA s. 69(2), which requires that Schedule A assessments be made on the assumption that all relevant amounts are the same as for the last preceding year, subject to adjustment at the end of the current year. There is a proviso to s. 69(2): if the taxpayer delivers to the Inspector before 1 January a written statement showing that he has ceased to possess a Schedule A source of income since the beginning of the preceding year of assessment, and if the Inspector is satisfied as to the correctness of the statement, then the assessment will be proportionately reduced.

Another administrative problem dealt with by the Act is the situation where the owner of land, who does not himself occupy it, defaults in paying Schedule A tax. TA s. 70(1) empowers the Revenue to recover the tax due from the defaulter's lessees or agents. The Collector starts the ball rolling by serving notice on any derivative lessee of the person in default requiring the lessee to pay the tax due within a specified time. The amount demanded must not exceed the sum payable by that lessee within the specified period either to the person in default or to another derivative lessee. The lessee in receipt of the notice is in turn allowed to deduct any sum paid to the Revenue from any subsequent payments he may be required to make either to the person in default or to another derivative lessee. In the latter case the superior derivative lessee will have suffered, by deduction, tax due from the person in default; and that person is entitled therefore to recover any amounts lost by deducting them in turn from payments to be made by him over the next twelve months to the person in default and, if these prove insufficient to absorb the loss, he may then recover the amount unabsorbed from the Revenue.

The Collector is similarly empowered by TA s. 70(2) to recover *any* unpaid Schedule A tax charged on a defaulter ("the principal") from any person ("the agent") in receipt of payments arising out of land on behalf of the defaulter. The agent is required to pay over any sums in his hands at the date of the notice as well as any future sums he receives on behalf of the principal until the tax due has been fully paid. Each failure to comply with these requirements on the part of the agent incurs a penalty of £50 (ibid. proviso).

Tenants who make payments, whether in the UK or elsewhere, directly to persons whose usual place of abode is outside the UK, are required to deduct tax and account for it to the Revenue under the s. 53 procedure (TA s. 89(1)). This applies also to tenants of furnished lettings, whether their payments of rent are chargeable under Schedule A or under Case VI (TA s. 89 (1)(*a*), (2)). A tenant would therefore be well advised to have inserted in the lease a covenant by the landlord that he, the tenant, should be notified in the event of the landlord deciding to settle abroad.

2.74 LEASE PREMIUMS: TA SS. 80–5

§ 1 General outline

Payments of a capital nature on the granting of a lease formerly escaped taxation. This immunity could not survive the advent of a tax on actual, as opposed to notional, receipts from land because lessors would otherwise have avoided the new charge by the simple expedient of taking low rents and correspondingly large premiums. F.A. 1963 therefore brought lease premiums into charge, initially (in 1963–64) under Case VI, subsequently (1964–65 and subsequent years) as additional rent chargeable on the landlord under Schedule A. The supervening capital gains tax legislation contrives, without resort to double taxation, to leave these provisions untouched while imposing a parallel liability to capital gains tax in the manner explained at pp. 213–14 below.

§ 2 The meaning of "premium"

Let us define our terms before discussing the charge itself. "Premium" includes any like sum, whether payable to the immediate or a superior landlord or to a person connected with either of them (within the meaning of TA s. 533, as to which *see* pp. 179–80 below) (TA s. 90(1), as extended by F.A. 1972 s. 81(3), (6)). Any sum (other than rent) paid on or in connection with the granting of a tenancy is presumed to have been paid by way of premium except in so far as other sufficient consideration is shown to have been given (TA s. 90(2)). A number of items are taxed as if they were premiums, namely:

(a) where the lease requires the tenant to carry out work on the premises, the consequent increase in value of the landlord's interest immediately after the commencement of the lease (s. 80(2));

(b) sums payable in lieu of rent, or as consideration for surrender of the lease (s. 80(3)); and

(c) sums payable by the tenant, otherwise than by way of rent, as consideration for the variation or waiver of any of the terms of a lease (s. 80(4)).

The meaning of s. 80(4)—or, rather, of its predecessor in F.A. 1963—was considered by the House of Lords in *Banning* v. *Wright* [1972] 1 W.L.R. 972. B was the tenant of two shops under a seven-year lease which gave him an option to renew for a further seven years if the rent was duly paid and the covenants observed. He sublet the shops and the lessor, on discovering this, commenced proceedings for re-entry and forfeiture. Negotiations were eventually settled by the tenant agreeing to pay to the lessor the sum of £3,000, of which £1,750 was to secure that B retained his option to renew. Their Lordships held (Lord Morris of Borth-y-Gest dissenting) that the £1,750 was payable for a variation or waiver of the terms of the lease within s. 80(4). 'When a contract is broken,' observed Lord Hailsham L.C., 'the injured party in condoning the fault may be said either to waive the breach, or to waive the term in relation to the breach. What in each case he waives is the right to rely on the term for the purposes of enforcing his remedy to the breach. I cannot construe "waiver" as only applicable to the total abandonment of any term in the lease both as regards ascertained and past breaches and as regards unascertained or future breaches' (ibid. at 980).

§ 3 **The duration of leases**

The duration of a lease is determined according to the following rules, now contained in TA s. 84 as amended by F.A. 1972 s. 81(2), (5), (6):

(*a*) where it is unlikely for any reason that the lease will continue to the date of expiry, its term is treated as extending to the date on which, judging by circumstances prevalent at the time when the lease was granted, it is likely to end (TA s. 84(1)(*b*);

(*b*) where the lease provides for its extension by notice given by the tenant, account may be taken of any circumstances making it likely that the lease will be so extended (TA s. 84(1)(*c*)); and

(*c*) where the tenant, or a person connected with him, is or may become entitled to a further lease or the grant of a further lease (whenever commencing) of the same premises or of premises including the whole or part of the same premises, the term of the lease may be treated as not expiring before the term of the further lease (TA s. 84(1)(*d*), added to counter avoidance by F.A. 1972 s. 81(2)(*b*), (6)).

Where an Inspector has reason to believe that a person (other than a solicitor acting for a client) has information relevant to the ascertainment of the duration of a lease, he may by notice in writing require that person to disclose the information in his possession (TA s. 84(3A), inserted by F.A. 1972 s. 81(5)).

§ 4 **The charge**

If from the application of the rules outlined in the preceding paragraphs there emerges a landlord who has (1) granted a lease of a certain duration, say *T*, not exceeding 50 years, and (2) received a premium of a certain amount, say £*P*, then he is treated as becoming entitled when the lease was granted to a notional rent of

$$£\left[P - \left(\frac{P}{50} \times (T - 1)\right)\right]$$

in addition to any actual rent; or, in the statutory words, 'to the amount of the premium reduced by one-fiftieth of that amount for each complete period of twelve months (other than the first) comprised in the duration of the lease' (TA s. 80(1)). Thus a landlord taking a premium of £1,000 on granting an eleven-year lease would be chargeable under Schedule A at the time of grant on £800 (£1,000 — £200).

Where the premium is payable to a person other than the landlord, the same computation is made, but the person is charged on the resultant amount under Case VI rather than Schedule A (TA s. 80(5)).

§ 5 Top slicing relief

It would be rather drastic if a lessor were to be taxed on a premium in a single year only. TA Schedule 3 therefore entitles an *individual* to a complicated form of relief known as "top slicing", the object of which is to spread "the chargeable sum" over the duration of the lease ("the relevant period") in such a way that the landlord is taxed in each year of the duration of the lease on one year's proportion of the chargeable sum ("the yearly equivalent") on the assumption that it forms the top slice of his income. If the chargeable sum were £3,000 and the relevant period ten years, the yearly equivalent would be £300. Any allowable deductions must be set against rents before being applied towards the reduction of the yearly equivalent.

§ 6 Premiums payable by instalments

Top slicing relief is not available where the premium is payable by instalments. A widespread avoidance scheme involved the lessor taking the consideration over, say, ninety-nine years with a large part payable in the last year, thereby deferring income tax virtually to the point of extinction. TA s. 80(6) (as substituted by F.A. 1972 s. 81(1)) has put an end to this device by restricting the period of deferment to a maximum of eight years. A person to whom a premium, or sum taxed as a premium, is payable by instalments is required, if he wishes to postpone the charge at all, to satisfy the Board that he would otherwise suffer undue hardship. If he does so, the tax chargeable on the premium or other sum may be paid at his option by such instalments as the Board may allow over a period not exceeding eight years and ending not later than the time at which the last of the first-mentioned instalments is payable. (For capital gains tax *see* p. 204 below.)

§ 7 Relief for the sub-lessor

To avoid double taxation, relief is made available where the first charge under TA s. 80(1) arising on the grant at a premium of a lease not exceeding fifty years is followed by a second charge under TA s. 80(1) when the lessee grants a sub-lease or makes some other disposition of his interest. Under TA s. 83(1) and (4), the second charge must be reduced to

$$C_2 - \left(\frac{R_2}{R_1} \times C_1 \right)$$

where C_1 is the chargeable sum on the original grant, C_2 the chargeable sum on the second transaction, R_1 the relevant period for computing the charge on the first transaction (based on the duration of the original lease), and R_2 the relevant period for computing the charge on the second transaction (based on the duration of the sub-lease or other interest). The same reduction operates where there are third or subsequent sub-leases or other dispositions, the reduction on the third being by reference to the second, the reduction on the fourth by reference to the third, and so on.

§ 8 Avoidance

Two anti-avoidance measures are worth bearing in mind. The first, contained in TA s. 81, deals with leases not exceeding fifty years granted at an undervalue. The mischief at which s. 81 is aimed is this. S. 80(1) is a charge which operates on the *grant* of a lease but not on an *assignment*. It would therefore be a simple matter for L, wishing to grant a lease to A at a premium of £P, to avoid tax by granting the lease to a friend at a small premium of £p on the understanding that the friend would then assign the lease to A at a premium of £(P − p). The remedy prescribed by s. 81 for this mischief is the provision that, where a premium obtained on the grant of a lease is less than the premium obtainable at arm's length, "the amount forgone" may be recovered on subsequent assignments of the lease. Each assignor is chargeable under Case VI on a notional premium equal to the difference between the consideration he paid and the consideration he received until the amount forgone is fully recouped. The notional premiums may be reduced in accordance with the statutory formula; and each assignor is entitled to top slicing relief.

The second anti-avoidance measure is aimed at the mischief of L wrapping up an intended grant of a lease of T years at a premium of £P in the guise of a sale for a consideration of £(P + x) on the understanding that the land will be reconveyed, or leased back, after T years for £x. TA s. 82(1), (3) contains a two-pronged charge whereby, in cases where land is sold with a right to reconveyance or lease back, the vendor is taxed under Case VI on the notional premium representing respectively the excess, if any, of the original sale price over:

(1) the price on reconveyance, and

(2) the premium for the lease, if any, plus the value at the date of sale of the right to receive a conveyance of the reversion. This notional premium is reduced by the usual one-fiftieth for each complete year other than the first between the date of sale and the earliest possible date for reconveyance or lease back. These provisions apply also where the reconveyance or lease back is not to the original vendor but to a person connected with him (as to which, see pp. 179–80 below). However, to protect the genuine sale and

lease back transaction (as to which *see* pp. 155–6 below), the proviso to s. 82(3) excludes the charge under s. 82 where the lease is granted and begins to run within a month of the sale.

2.75 DEDUCTIONS: TA SS. 71–7

What is sauce for the Revenue goose, gobbling up Schedule A tax immediately any taxpayer "becomes entitled" to Schedule A receipts, is not sauce for the taxpaying gander, who can deduct allowable expenditure only if actually paid. There are several other prohibitory norms, which may conveniently be discussed now before we move on to the code of deductions itself. Firstly, expenditure must be deducted first from Schedule A income for the current year of assessment and, if this should prove insufficient, from Schedule A income of successive subsequent years until exhausted (s. 77(1)). However, where his Schedule A income of a particular year of assessment does not absorb all his items of expenditure, the taxpayer has a right to choose which items are to be identified as carried forward (s. 77(2)). Secondly, no payment is deductible which has been or will be:

(*a*) balanced by insurance moneys,
(*b*) recovered from any other person (unless the payment recovered is itself chargeable under Schedule A), or
(*c*) made under deduction of tax (unless made by a company) (s. 77(3)).

Thirdly, expenditure cannot be deducted in a Schedule A computation which has been otherwise allowed as a deduction in computing the income of any person for tax purposes (s. 77(4)).

A final prohibition is directed against that long-established avoidance institution, the sale and lease back transaction. The appeal to tax planners of this type of transaction lies in its dual legal consequences: (1) the profit on sale (ideally to a charity or other exempt person) ranks as a capital receipt; and (2) the rent under the lease is deductible in computing the appropriate charge, usually as a trading expense. At one time it was possible to optimize the utility of the device by arranging for a high rent in the early years of the lease. TA s. 491 put an end to this by limiting the permissible deduction in a sale and lease back transaction to a "commercial rent" (s. 491(4)), defined in s. 491(8) as the rent negotiable in the open market at the time when the lease was created.

In the early seventies the practice grew up of businesses which occupied premises under a lease at a very old rent selling out to an institution and taking a lease back for which they would pay rent at the market value. They

G

would thus have received a capital sum and also, since the new rent would be deductible, tax relief on the rent. This practice has now been struck down by F.A. 1972 s. 80, which brings a fraction of the capital sum into charge, namely $(16 - n)/15$, where n is the term of the new lease expressed in years (s. 80(1), (3)). There are three pre-conditions: the original lease must have no more than fifty years to run, the lease back must be for a term not exceeding fifteen years, and the lessee must be entitled to tax relief on the rent he pays under the new lease. The fraction brought into charge is treated either as a receipt of the trade etc (if the lessee is entitled to tax relief on the rent under the new lease under Case I or II of Schedule D) or, in any other case, as a profit or gain chargeable under Case VI (s. 80(3)). If the lessee is an individual, he is entitled to top slicing relief (*see* p. 153 above) (s. 80(5)). Apart from this, the provisions of s. 80 apply to companies as well as individuals. They apply also to trusts.

The code of deductions is divisible into three categories, the first comprising expenditure deductible from rents, the second deductions from Schedule A receipts other than rents, and a third expenditure on sea walls.

§ 1 Deductions from rents: TA s. 72

The person entitled to rent under a lease ("the person chargeable") may, under s. 72(1), deduct payments in respect of:

(a) maintenance, repairs, insurance, or management,
(b) any services provided by him otherwise than by way of maintenance or repairs, being services which he was obliged to provide but in respect of which he received no separate consideration,
(c) rates or other charges on the occupier which the person chargeable was obliged to defray,
(d) any rent, rentcharge (or its Scots equivalent) or other periodical payment reserved in respect of, or charged on or issuing out of, land.

These are referred to hereafter as "the s. 72(1) deductions". The person chargeable may not deduct any payment of interest (ibid. proviso).

While expenditure on maintenance and repairs is deductible, expenditure on replacements and improvements is not (*see*, for a discussion of this distinction, p. 84 above).

Normally payments made by a landlord in respect of premises may only be deducted from rent payable in respect of those premises and must represent expenditure incurred during the currency of the lease or, in the case of a payment for maintenance or repairs, must be incurred by reason of dilapidation attributable to a period falling within the currency of the lease

(s. 72(2)). Moreover, if the person chargeable became the landlord after the lease began, the currency of the lease must be regarded as excluding the period before he became landlord (ibid. proviso). There are detailed provisions in s. 72(3), (5), and (7) which, by way of exception to the general rule contained in s. 72(2), enable a lessor who grants successive leases at a full rent to carry forward any unused allowable expenditure. The idea is that a lessor's right to carry forward expenditure should be lost only if he allows a period of owner-occupation or a letting at less than a full rent to supervene. S. 72(4) allows a lessor who has granted a lease of premises at a full rent to deduct payments in respect of those premises from rent of another lease at a full rent granted by the same lessor in respect of different premises, provided that this other lease is not a tenant's repairing lease. S. 72(6) is a singularly inept provision purporting to enable the landlord of a block of flats or offices to deduct any expenditure on maintaining the common parts (e.g. the stairs and landings) againt rents from his various tenants. Not so much nodding as nodding off, its Homeric draftsman omitted to provide any machinery for apportioning the expenditure, a deficiency supplied, presumably, in practice by *ad hoc* negotiation between Inspector and taxpayer.

S. 73 gives the owner of land managed as one estate the right under certain circumstances to elect that the s. 72(1) deductions be set not merely against rents from the particular property on which the expenditure was incurred but against rents from the entire estate.

§ 2 Deductions from receipts other than rent: TA s. 74

A person entitled to a Schedule A receipt other than rent may deduct an item of expenditure only if it constitutes an "expense of the transaction" under which he became entitled to the receipt. Moreover, the payment must be in respect of:

(a) maintenance, repairs, insurance, or management of premises to which the receipt relates,

(b) any rent, rentcharge (or its Scots equivalent), or other periodical payment relating to those premises, or

(c) any other payment not being an expense of a capital nature.

Where the person entitled to possession of any land is in the practice of granting sporting rights over the land for payment, he would normally be entitled to the deductions outlined in the preceding paragraph. If in any year of assessment he does not grant the rights, however, he may nevertheless use expenditure which would normally have been deductible as if it were a deduction from rent to which he was entitled for that year (s. 75(1)). The rather curious result is that this expenditure becomes available against rents under leases, either in the same or subsequent years, whilst it cannot apparently be carried forward against future payments for the sporting rights.

§ 3 Expenditure on making sea walls: TA s. 76

'Where in any year of assessment the owner or tenant of any premises incurs expenditure in the making of any sea wall or other embankment necessary for the preservation or protection of the premises against the encroachment or overflowing of the sea or any tidal river, he shall be treated . . . as making in that year of assessment and in each of the succeeding twenty years of assessment a payment in relation to the premises preserved or protected by the embankment of an amount equal to a twenty-first part of the expenditure and incurred in respect of dilapidation attributable to the year' (s. 76(1)).

2.76 SCHEDULE B

At one time Schedule B could boast of having within its confines practically every species of occupier of land or buildings in the UK. Over the years, species after species has been removed to securer enclosures until, since 1963–64, only one has remained—the occupier of woodlands in the UK managed on a commercial basis and with a view to the realization of profits (s. 91 Schedule B para 1). Tax is charged on the occupier on the "assessable value" of his occupation (s. 92(1)), this being one-third of the annual value of the woodlands or a proportionate part if the chargeable period is less than a year, e.g. because the woodlands were occupied for part only of the tax year (s. 92(2)(a)). Annual value is ascertained on the assumption that the land, instead of being woodlands, is let in its natural and unimproved state (s. 92(2)(b)). It is immaterial whether or not woodlands are in fact occupied at the time of assessment, since any person having the use of woodlands is deemed to be the occupier (s. 92(3)).

Since 1915 the occupier of commercial woodlands has been given the right, now contained in TA s. 111, to elect for assessment under Schedule D rather then Schedule B (s. 111(1)). An election does not mean that the occupation of woodlands is deemed to be a trade, merely that any income from the occupation of woodlands is deemed to be trading income. The election must be made by notice in writing to the Inspector not later than two years after the chargeable period to which it relates (s. 111(2)). Thereafter it has effect for all future chargeable periods for which the person making it continues to occupy the woodlands (ibid.). An election extends to all commercial woodlands on the same estate (s. 111(3)) with the exception of newly planted or replanted woodlands, which may be treated as a separate estate if the occupier so elects within ten years of the planting or replanting (s. 111(3) proviso).

The occupier of commercial woodlands, though he suffers tax on one-third of their annual value, cannot deduct any of his expenditure. Conversely, even if he makes large profits, tax will continue to be charged on the same notional amount. He will therefore normally find it beneficial to elect for Schedule D in the early years, principally so as to be able to claim loss relief and capital allowances, and then, when the mature trees are to be felled and marketed, to transfer the woodlands to a company. The line between occupying woodlands within Schedule B and trading in the produce of woodlands within Schedule D is explored in Megarry J.'s judgment in *Collins* v. *Fraser* (1969) 46 T.C. 143. Apart from the considerable estate duty concessions available to occupiers of woodlands, perhaps their greatest boon lies in the exemption from tax of afforestation grants. We seem somehow to have allowed a war-time concession based on necessity to become an utterly unwarranted fiscal bonanza.

2.77 MINING AND CABLE RENTS AND ROYALTIES: TA SS. 156 AND 157

TA s. 156 charges to tax by deduction:
(1) rent payable in respect of any land or easement used, occupied or enjoyed in connection with any of the "statutory trades" specified in TA s. 112(2) (mines, quarries, etc: *see* p. 65 above), and
(2) rent payable under a lease or other agreement which provides for the recoupment of the rent by way of reduction of royalties or payments of a similar nature in the event of the land or easement being so used, occupied, or enjoyed. The charge is under Schedule D and the deduction is made in accordance with the s. 52 or 53 machinery, as the case may be, as if the rent were a patent royalty. Where, however, the rent is rendered in produce of the concern, it is charged under Schedule D Case III.

TA s. 157 similarly charges by deduction:
(3) rent payable in respect of any easement enjoyed in the UK in connection with any electric, telegraphic or telephonic wire or cable, i.e. wayleave rentals. If the rent does not exceed £2·50 per year the payer may elect to make the payment without deduction, in which case the recipient is charged under Schedule D Case III. He is also liable under Case III if the payer fails to deduct and yet is not charged in accordance with the s. 53 procedure.

TA s. 156 must now be read in the light of F.A. 1970. By s. 29(1) of that Act, mineral royalties are treated as to half as income (liable, depending on whether the recipient is an individual or company, to income tax or corporation tax) and as to the remainder as capital (liable, as the case may be, to capital gains tax or corporation tax).

2.78 "ARTIFICIAL" TRANSACTIONS IN LAND: TA s. 488

Explicitly 'enacted to prevent the avoidance of tax by persons concerned with land or the development of land' (s. 488(1)), TA s. 488 is a notoriously widely drafted measure that undoubtedly in terms applies not merely to the "artificial" transactions at which it is aimed, if its small heading in the Act is anything to go by, but also to innumerable innocent dealings.

There are three requirements (s. 488(2)):

(1) either (a) land, or any property deriving its value from land, must have been acquired with the sole or main object of realizing a gain from disposing of the land, or
    (b) land must be held as trading stock, or
    (c) land must have been developed with the sole or main object of realizing a gain from disposing of the land when developed;
(2) a gain of a capital nature must have been obtained from the disposal of the land; and
(3) this gain must have been obtained
    either (a) by the person acquiring, holding or developing the land, or by any connected person, or
    (b) where any arrangement or scheme is effected as respects the land which enables a gain to be realized by any indirect method, or by any series of transactions, by any person who is a party to, or concerned in, the arrangement or scheme,
and whether obtained for himself or for any other person.

In connection with the first condition it is worth noting that 'property deriving its value from land' is defined to include any shareholding in a company deriving its value directly or indirectly from land (s. 488(2)(b) (ii)). A gain accruing to an individual on disposal of his principal private residence is exempt from the charge (s. 488(9)).

Where s. 488 applies, the whole of the gain must be treated as income of the person by whom it is realized chargeable under Case VI and deemed to arise at the time when the gain is realized (s. 488(3)).

A person who has obtained a gain from a disposal of land, or who expects to do so on a proposed disposal, may supply his Inspector with written particulars showing how the gain has arisen or would arise; and within thirty days of his receipt of these particulars the Inspector must notify him whether or not he is satisfied that the gain is not, or would not be, chargeable under s. 488 (s. 488(1)). If the Inspector gives that person a clearance the gain cannot be charged on him under s. 488 (s. 488(11)(b)).

● A widely-held view is that *Ransom* v. *Higgs* [1972] 2 A.E.R. 817, which we discussed at p. 63 above, renders s. 488 virtually unnecessary. The adjective used in that discussion to describe Megarry J.'s decision—"frightening"—will probably now seem less extreme.

2.79 LAND HOARDING

The Government have announced their intention to introduce legislation, as soon as Parliamentary time is available, with a view to penalizing, by a special land hoarding charge, any unjustifiable delay in developing land which is the subject of planning permission for housing. The charge will be levied for failure to complete the permitted development within a specified period appropriate to the land in question (usually four years from the grant of outline planning permission) and will be retroactive to Budget day 1973 (6 March). The rate of charge will be 30%—for each full year of delay but accruing on a daily basis—of the market value of the property as on the day immediately after planning permission was granted. The charge will be secured on the land and will be collected by the Inland Revenue.

The intention is to counter soaring land prices by making more land available for building. Critics have doubted that these are the optimal proposals for achieving that end. Some have roundly condemned the proposals as "political window-dressing"; and it is certainly difficult to see the charge in Mr Barber's terms as any sort of "curb on land speculation". It will be interesting to see how much the new charge raises in revenue.

2.8 The remittance man

2.81 FOREIGN INCOME: THE OVERVIEW

This division is concerned with foreign income, i.e. income which arises outside the UK. We will recall from p. 41 above that non-residents are not liable to income tax on income arising abroad. The assumption we must make, therefore, in the ensuing paragraphs, is that the taxpayer is resident in the UK.

Income arising from the public revenue of any foreign government or public institution is chargeable under Schedule C if it is payable in the UK. Foreign emoluments of an office or employment are taxed under Case III of Schedule E. Any other foreign income, e.g. income from property situated outside the UK, dividends from a non-resident company, income from a trust fund situated outside the UK, etc is assessable either under Case IV of Schedule D (securities) or under Case V (possessions).

2.82 SECURITIES AND POSSESSIONS ABROAD: BASES OF CHARGE

Case IV charges 'income arising from securities out of the United Kingdom, except such income as is charged under Schedule C' (TA s. 109 (2)). Case V charges 'income arising from possessions out of the United Kingdom, not being income consisting of emoluments of any office or employment' (ibid.).

As a general rule, 'income tax chargeable under Case IV or Case V of Schedule D shall be computed on the full amount of the income arising in the year preceding the year of assessment, whether the income has been or will be received in the United Kingdom or not' (TA s. 122(1)). In the case of income not received in the UK, the same deductions may be made as if it had been so received (TA s. 122(1)(a)). For example, in computing tax on rents arising abroad, the normal s. 72(1) deductions may be made; and, if any overseas taxes are paid in respect of the income for which no form of double tax relief is available, the overseas tax may be deducted. Moreover, a deduction may be made for any annual payment made out of the income to a non-resident (TA s. 122(1)(b)).

Thus Cases IV and V are normally charged on income *arising* in the preceding year of assessment. However, the arising basis does not apply to:

(a) any person who satisfies the Board that he is not domiciled in the UK, or that, being a British subject or a citizen of the Republic of Ireland, he is not ordinarily resident in the UK, or

(b) any income which is immediately derived by a person from the carrying on by him of any trade, profession, or vocation, either solely or in partnership, or

(c) any income which arises from a pension (TA s. 122(2)). In these three cases, tax is charged on the remittance basis, i.e. on sums *received* in the UK in the preceding year of assessment (TA s. 122(3)).

The question what qualifies as a remittance often gives rise to difficulty. The principle is that any form of applying foreign income so as to cause it to emerge in the UK as spendable resources ranks as a remittance: *Thomson* v. *Moyse* [1961] A.C. 967. Thus, there would be a remittance if foreign income is used to buy a car abroad which is imported into this country. Moreover, as Lord Denning said in *Thomson* v. *Moyse*, if a taxpayer pays his butcher in England with money from abroad it is regarded as here when the butcher gets it (ibid. at 1003). TA s. 122 (4)–(7) provide for a number of "constructive remittances" with a view to putting an end to the circumvention of the remittance rule by arrangements to borrow money here and repay the indebtedness abroad. Capital remitted to the UK is not liable to tax (*Kneen* v. *Martin* [1935] 1 K.B. 499) but the taxpayer should be careful to maintain separate bank accounts for income and capital, making remittances from the latter only, or he may have difficulty persuading the Revenue that the remittance was a capital sum. The Revenue do, however, allow a taxpayer intending to pay for his holiday abroad out of non-remitted income to receive travellers' cheques in the UK provided he refrains from cashing them here. (Also informative on the question of remittances are *Carter* v. *Sharon* (1936) 20 T.C. 229 and *Timpson's Executors* v. *Yerbury* [1936] 1 K.B. 645, which should be read together.)

2.83 SCOPE OF CASES IV AND V

The distinction between Cases IV and V is no longer of any significance. Neither "securities" nor "possession" is defined. In *Singer* v. *Williams* [1921] 1 A.C. 41 the House of Lords confirmed the narrowness of Case IV in holding that when "securities" is used in its normal sense 'some form of secured liability is postulated' (ibid. at 49 *per* Viscount Cave L.C.). Shares are therefore not securities within Case IV (*Gramophone & Typewriter Ltd* v. *Stanley* [1908] 2 K.B. 89), though personal guarantees (*Westminster Bank etc Ltd* v. *National Bank of Greece S.A.* [1971] A.C. 945; *see* pp. 46–7 above) and *a fortiori* debentures or mortgages are.

'The word "possessions",' observed Lord Macnaghten in *Colquhoun* v. *Brooks*, 'is not a technical word. It seems to me that it is the widest and most comprehensive word that could be used' ((1889) 14 App. Cas. 493 at 516). In that case B, resident in England, was the sleeping partner in a firm which carried on business in Australia. The House of Lords held that a trade, profession, or vocation wholly carried on abroad ranks as a foreign possession chargeable under Case V of Schedule D; and that B was therefore not chargeable on income arising from the business which had not been remitted to the UK. However, if any of the business activities are carried on in the UK, all the profits arise from a UK source and are therefore chargeable under Case

I or II of Schedule D, as the case may be: *see*, for example, *San Paulo* (*Brazilian*) *Ry Co.* v. *Carter* [1896] A.C. 31 (Case I) and *Davies* v. *Braithwaite* (1931) 18 T.C. 198 (Case II).

It becomes a matter of considerable importance to determine whether a trade is carried on wholly abroad. The case law is not altogether satisfactory. In *Ogilvie* v. *Kitton* (1909) 5 T.C. 338 the crucial determinant was held to be where the power of control, whether exercised or not, resided. *Cf. Mitchell* v. *Egyptian Hotels Ltd* [1915] A.C. 1022. In *Grainger & Sons* v. *Gough* [1896] A.C. 325 their Lordships relied on a distinction between trading *with* the UK and trading *within* the UK, a distinction which is easier to state than to apply, while in *Firestone Tyre & Rubber Co. Ltd* v. *Lewellin* (1957) 37 T.C. 111 the House preferred not to accede to the contention that the place where contracts of sale are made is the crucial issue.

The word "possessions" brings virtually every kind of property other than securities within the ambit of Case V, including:

(*a*) rents from land abroad: *Swedish Central Railway* v. *Thompson* [1925] A.C. 495;

(*b*) dividends from foreign stocks and shares, even when paid out of a capital source: *IRC* v. *Reid's Trustees* [1949] A.C. 361;

(*c*) interest on unsecured foreign loans: *Manton's Trustees* v. *Steele* (1927) 11 T.C. 549;

(*d*) a premium of an income nature on an unsecured foreign loan: *Howard de Walden* v. *Beck* (1940) 23 T.C. 384;

(*e*) income from a trust fund situated abroad: *Baker* v. *Archer-Shee* [1927] A.C. 844;

(*f*) an annuity paid to a UK resident under a deed of separation executed abroad: *Chamney* v. *Lewis* (1932) 17 T.C. 318.

Moreover TA s. 113(2) brings certain foreign pensions into charge under Case V. *See also* TA s. 405(1) (borrowings against life policies).

2.84 DOUBLE TAXATION RELIEF: TA SS. 497-518

Where a person resident in the UK is liable to foreign tax as well as UK income tax in respect of income arising abroad, he may be entitled to one of several forms of relief, namely:

(*a*) Treaty relief, i.e. relief under a double taxation convention

Under most double taxation treaties—nowadays our treaties conform closely to the OECD model—certain classes of income are made taxable in one of the countries only, e.g. that in which the taxpayer resides, while other classes of income are taxable in both countries but UK residents are allowed a credit for foreign tax paid against their UK tax liability.

(b) Unilateral relief

If there is no double taxation convention available, unilateral relief may be available enabling a UK resident to offset any foreign tax suffered against his UK income tax liability on the same income.

(c) Relief by deduction

If neither (a) nor (b) is available, the taxpayer is allowed a deduction for the foreign tax in computing his liability to UK income tax.

(d) Republic of Ireland relief

The taxpayer resident in the Republic of Ireland but not in the UK (or vice versa) is exempted from tax in the country in which he is not resident.

2.85 NORTH SEA OIL

The Finance Act 1973 contains provisions designed to bring into charge profits arising from the exploration and exploitation of the UK sector of the continental shelf. This objective is seen to have an ironic twist by those aware that the North Sea oil companies have yet to market the first barrel of oil derived from their operations there; indeed the Public Accounts Committee reported in March 1973 that nine major oil companies had accumulated £1,500 m worth of losses. This of course is the real point: the present system of taxation allows companies to offset losses on overseas operations against profits earned here—to such effect that a company the size of BP pays no UK tax although in 1972 37% of its profits were earned here—but the Government are not prepared to allow the £1,500 m worth of losses (two-thirds attributable to BP, a large slice of the remainder to Shell) to be offset against future North Sea profits. The solution to be adopted is the subject of discussions between the Department of Trade and Industry and the major oil companies. Merely wiping out the losses is regarded by the Revenue, who apparently intend no pun, as "too crude". The most likely solution is a complete overhaul of the posted price system rather than the barrelage tax suggested by the PAC. The negotiations are expected to be protracted.

● In the meantime the territorial jurisdiction of UK tax law has been extended to include the territorial sea (F.A. 1973 s. 38(1)), *inter alia* to bring into charge certain UK residents who would otherwise not be liable (ibid. s. 38(3)) and also to charge non-residents to UK tax on profits made on North Sea operations or through selling North Sea licences (ibid. s. 38(4)). These North Sea oil provisions are to take effect for purposes of income tax and capital gains tax from 1973–74 and for corporation tax from the financial year 1973 (ibid. s. 38(7)).

2.9 The sweeper up

2.91 RESTRICTIONS ON THE SCOPE OF CASE VI

This division is concerned with Case VI of Schedule D. Case VI is charged in sweeping terms on 'any annual profits or gains not falling under any other Case' or Schedule (TA s. 109(2)). Its operations has, however, been confined within a narrow compass. In effect, Case VI is limited in scope to certain "casual" profits escaping the other charging provisions and to those items, most of which we have already come across from time to time in this chapter of the book, which have been specifically assigned to Case VI.

The first restricting factor is the generally held view that "annual profits or gains" means simply profits of an income rather than a capital nature (*see*, for example, (1912) 6 T.C. at 38, [1923] 2 K.B. at 455 *per* Rowlatt J., where he interprets the phrase as meaning 'profits or gains in any one year or in any year as the succession of years comes round'). The second restricting factor is the requirement that profits or gains chargeable under Case VI be *ejusdem generis* with those falling within the other five Cases of Schedule D. A third factor is the principle that any profit from an isolated transaction of purchase and resale of property must be taxed, if at all, under Case I of Schedule D.

2.92 THE CASES

The leading case, illustrative of all three restrictions, is *Jones* v. *Leeming* [1930] A.C. 415. L was a member of a syndicate which acquired options over two rubber estates. These options were subsequently transferred to a company at a profit. The Commissioners found that the transaction was not a concern in the nature of trade. But was L's share of the profit assessable under Case VI? 'It seems to me,' said Lawrence L.J. in the Court of Appeal, 'that in the case of an isolated transaction of purchase and re-sale of property there is really no middle course open. It is either an adventure in the nature of trade, or else it is simply a case of sale and re-sale of property' ([1930] 1 K.B. at 301). The House of Lords affirmed the Court of Appeal's decision that L escaped tax under Case VI also: 'It is, to my mind . . .,' Lord Buckmaster summed up, 'purely an affair of capital' ([1930] A.C. at 420).

The appeal in *Jones* v. *Leeming* was founded upon an attempt to extend the decision in *Cooper* v. *Stubbs* [1925] 2 K.B. 753 to cover capital accretions. S was a partner in a firm of cotton brokers whose practice was to protect themselves against fluctuations in the market by buying cotton "futures". S engaged in private speculations in futures in which his firm had no interest. In the Court of Appeal Pollock M.R. held that these private speculations constituted a trade, while Warrington and Atkin L.JJ. preferred to uphold the Commissioners' finding of no trade and regard the transactions as assessable under Case VI.

The *ejusdem generis* principle preserves the immunity from taxability of gifts (*Turner* v. *Cuxon* (1888) 22 Q.B.D. 150, *Bloom* v. *Kinder* (1958) 38 T.C. 77), betting winnings (*Graham* v. *Green* [1925] 2 K.B. 37), and receipts by finding (*Ryall* v. *Hoare* [1923] 2 K.B. 447). On the other hand, a contract for services may constitute a taxable source within Case VI, the anomalous consequence being that an isolated transaction of a professional nature (which cannot fall within Case II because, unlike "trade", "profession or vocation" is not artificially extended) may give rise to liability under Case VI. In *Hobbs* v. *Hussey* [1942] 1 K.B. 491 a solicitor's clerk who contracted with *The People* newspaper to write his reminiscences was held liable to tax under Case VI on the payment he received, even though the contract involved the sale of his copyright in the articles. The same principle was applied in *Ryall* v. *Hoare* [1923] 2 K.B. 447, in *Norman* v. *Evans* (1964) 42 T.C. 188, in *Hale* v. *Shea* (1964) 42 T.C. 260. On the other side of the line fall cases like *Dickinson* v. *Abel* (1969) 45 T.C. 353 (p. 47 above).

2.93 BASIS OF COMPUTATION UNDER CASE VI

Income tax under Case VI is computed either on the full amount of the profits or gains arising in the year of assessment or according to an average of any period not exceeding one year that the case requires and the Inspector directs (TA s. 125(1)). No express provision is made for the deduction of expenses under Case VI but the cases appear to justify our falling back on the principle that "profits or gains" means the excess of receipts over expenses incurred in earning them (*see*, for instance, *IRC* v. *Forth Conservancy Board* [1929] A.C. 213). Moreover, had the intention been to exclude the possibility of deducting expenses, no provision would have been made for losses.

As it is, Case VI losses are dealt with by TA s. 176. The taxpayer who suffers a Case VI loss may claim, within six years after the year of assessment in question (s. 176 (4)), to offset the loss against Case VI income of the same or any subsequent year (s. 176(1)).

2.0 The left overs

2.01 TRUSTEES

● Trust income is normally assessed at the basic rate in the hands of the trustees. There are exceptions. Foreign income paid to a non-resident beneficiary without passing through the trustees' hands is not liable to tax, even if the trustees are resident here: *Singer* v. *Williams* [1921] A.C. 41. Trustees are not usually assessed on trust income which has been paid under their authority direct to a beneficiary. Moreover, trustees may be able to resist an assessment on the ground that the income in respect of which it was made accrues to a beneficiary, e.g. a company, in whose hands it is exempted from income tax: *Reid's Trustees* v. *IRC* (1929) 14 T.C. 512 at 525 *per* Lord Clyde, approved by Lord Hanworth M.R. in [1935] 2 K.B. at 463.

Trustees are assessed under the Case or Schedule appropriate to the source from which the income derives. Thus if they carry on a trade, trustees are assessed like any other trade under Schedule D Case I, except that a change of trustees does not effectuate a discontinuance under TA s. 154(1) (*see* p. 68 above). However, not being "individuals", trustees cannot claim any of the personal reliefs. Nor are they entitled to any deduction for expenses incurred in administering the trust. Even more significantly, they are not subject to excess liability either on their own account or on behalf of any beneficiary (see TMA s. 76(1)).

2.02 A BENEFICIARY UNDER A TRUST

A beneficiary is liable to tax both at the basic and any additional rate on trust income arising in any year of assessment, whether he receives the income in that year or not: *Baker* v. *Archer-Shee* [1927] A.C. 844. This principle is subject to two possible strictures. Firstly, the beneficiary must be entitled to the income as and when it arises: *IRC* v. *Abbey* (1938) 22 T.C. 211, a requirement which is not satisfied if his title to the income is liable to be divested: *Stanley* v. *IRC* (1944) 26 T.C. 12.

Secondly, income which takes the form of an annuity will be received under the s. 52 or s. 53 deduction procedure. This may be an issue of some importance. If paid out of taxed income, the annuity ranks as income of the beneficiary in the year when it fell due (s. 52), if not, e.g. because paid out of capital, it will rank as income of the year when paid (s. 53). *See Brodie's Will Trustees* v. *IRC* (1933) 17 T.C. 432, a case whose implications Mrs Dashwood might have had in mind in Jane Austen's *Sense and Sensibility* when she remarked that: 'An annuity is a very serious business.'

In computing his total income, a beneficiary may, for excess liability purposes, deduct any trustees' expenses payable out of trust income: *Macfarlane* v. *IRC* (1929) 14 T.C. 532. Where the expenses are paid out of taxed income, the deduction for excess liability purposes is grossed-up. Neither the trustees nor the beneficiary may claim any repayment of basic rate tax on the basis that the expenses were paid out of income which suffered tax in the hands of the trustees.

A beneficiary must also include in his total income:

(*a*) the grossed-up amounts of any sums applied for his benefit in accordance with the provisions of the trust instrument: *IRC* v. *Miller* [1930] A.C. 222;

(*b*) the grossed-up amounts of any sums applied for his maintenance or education: *Drummond* v. *Collins* [1915] A.C. 1011;

(*c*) payments made by trustees to the beneficiary in exercise of a discretion conferred on them by the trust instrument or by statute: *Lindus & Hortin* v. *IRC* (1933) 17 T.C. 442;

(*d*) any payments by trustees, whether out of income or capital, which are received by him as income, the determining criterion being either (i) whether, as a matter of construction, the trust instrument confers on the beneficiary a benefit of an income or one of a capital nature, or (ii) the terms of the relevant statutory provisions: *Brodie's Will Trustees* v. *IRC* (1933) 17 T.C. 432, *Cunard's Trustees* v. *IRC* (1945) 27 T.C. 122, *Morant Settlement Trustees* v. *IRC* (1948) 30 T.C. 147, *Lawson* v. *Rolfe* (1969) 46 T.C. 199.

● The question whether accumulating income forms part of the beneficiary's total income—entitling him to personal reliefs, if his income is small, or giving rise to excess liability, if it is large—depends upon whether he has a vested or a contingent interest in the income. Where he has a vested interest, the income forms part of his total income year by year as it accumulates. Where his interest is contingent, the accumulating income does not form part of his total income; and, moreover, even when ultimately the contingency occurs and the accumulations are paid over, the beneficiary receives them as capital. The distinction between a vested and a contingent interest is determined according to the general law and in particular s. 31 of the Trustee Act 1925 as amended by the Family Law Reform Act 1969.

2.03 THE SETTLOR: TA SS. 434–59

● TA ss. 434–59 are designed to counter the avoidance of tax by persons liable to high marginal rates of tax by various devices involving settlements, e.g. by settling income or income-bearing assets on persons, e.g. the settlor's children, who are subject to tax at much lower rates. The general approach of the legislation is to treat income caught by one of the provisions as if it were income of the settlor. The beneficiary's position is only affected to the extent that he normally loses his right to claim personal reliefs in respect of any such income.

● "Settlement" is widely defined for purposes of ss. 434 to 436 and 445 to 459 to include 'any trust, covenant, agreement or arrangement', while for purposes of ss. 437 to 444 the definition is extended yet further to cover 'a transfer of assets'. This definition clearly encompasses deeds of covenant and other income settlements as well as settlements of income-bearing assets, i.e. capital settlements. It has even been held to include an order of the Court requiring a husband to make payments to his wife in trust for their children (*Yates* v. *Starkey* [1951] Ch. 465).

The provisions are conveniently broken down in the Taxes Act under several heads. Under § 1, § 2, § 3, § 4(*a*), and § 5 below, trust income is deemed to be that of the settlor for *all* tax purposes, under § 6 for excess liability purposes only. The effect of the provisions relating to § 1, § 2, § 3, § 4(*a*), and §5 is to require that income deemed to be the settlor's be treated as the highest part of his income (ss. 435(3), 441(3), 449(5)); and, under each of those heads, with the notable exception of § 6 below, there are provisions whereby tax paid by the settlor may be recovered by him from the trustees or other person to whom the income was actually paid.

§ 1 Dispositions for periods which cannot exceed six years: TA ss. 434–6

Income which, by virtue of a disposition made by any person other than for valuable and sufficient consideration, is payable to or for the benefit of any other person for a period which cannot exceed six years, is deemed for income tax purposes to be income of that person, if living, by whom the disposition was made, and not to be the income of any other person (s. 434(1)).

A disposition falls outside s. 434 not only if made for a definite period of more than six years, e.g. a seven-year deed of covenant, but also if made for a period which may or may not exceed six years, e.g. a covenant for the covenantor's life. It is immaterial that, as things turn out, the payments in fact cease before six years have elapsed: *IRC* v. *Black* (1940) 23 T.C. 715. The *possibility* of lasting six years suffices. The six-year period runs between the respective due dates of the first and last payments under the disposition: *IRC* v. *St Luke's Hostel Trustees* (1930) 15 T.C. 682; *IRC* v. *Verdon-Roe* (1962) 40 T.C. 541.

Where the payments fluctuate in amount from year to year only the lowest common denominator, so to speak, escapes s. 434: *IRC* v. *Mallaby-Deeley* (1938) 23 T.C. 153. However, s. 434 may be entirely excluded by providing for the annual amounts to be determined according to a formula which remains constant in relation to each payment, e.g. a fixed percentage of the settlor's income: *D'Ambrumenil* v. *IRC* [1940] 1 K.B. 850.

§ 2 Settlements on children: TA ss. 437–44

Where, by virtue of a settlement and during the life of the settlor, income is paid to or for the benefit of a child of the settlor in any year of assessment, the income is treated for income tax purposes as income of the settlor for that year and not as income of any other person, provided that at the time of the payment the child was unmarried and below the age of eighteen (s. 437(1), as amended by F.A. 1971 s. 16(2)(*b*))—unless the aggregate amount paid does not exceed £5 (s. 437(3), as substituted by F.A. 1971 s. 16(2)(*d*)).

"Settlement" in this context includes even a transfer of assets to a child absolutely: *Thomas* v. *Marshall* [1953] A.C. 543.

S. 438 constitutes an important exception to s. 437. Income accumulated for the benefit of an infant unmarried child of the settlor is not treated as the settlor's income until paid out for the child's benefit. The accumulation settlement must, however, be "irrevocable" (s. 438(2)) within the very narrow definition accorded the term by s. 439. A settlement is not irrevocable which provides for:

(*a*) income or assets to be paid or applied for the benefit of the settlor or settlor's spouse in any circumstances whatsoever during the life of the settlor's child;

(*b*) its determination by the act or default of any person; or

(c) payment of a penalty by the settlor in the event of his failing to comply with any of its provisions (s. 439 (1)).

S. 438(2)(b) provides that any payments to or for the benefit of the settlor's child are deemed to be income except to the extent that all accumulated income has been exhausted. The idea of this provision is to remove the possibility of avoiding s. 437 by means of an arrangement whereby the trustees accumulate income, which *ipso facto* becomes capital, and then makes advances to a child of the settlor out of the accumulations. Indeed the only means available to the wealthy of providing for their infant unmarried without suffering adverse fiscal consequences is a capital settlement, i.e. a settlement of income-bearing assets, under which the income is accumulated.

§ 3 Revocable settlements: TA ss. 445–6

If and so long as the terms of a settlement are such that any person has a power of revocation, and in the event of the exercise of that power the settlor or his wife would cease to be liable to make annual payments, or would become beneficially entitled to capital or income of the settlement, the annual payments or the income arising under the settlement, as the case may be, are treated as income of the settlor for all income tax purposes (ss. 445(1), 446(1)).

The power must be contained in the settlement itself: *Wolfson* v. *IRC* (1949) 31 T.C. 141. Where the power cannot be exercised within six years from the time when the first of the annual payments is made, or from the time when the trust property first became comprised in the settlement, as the case may be, ss. 445(1) and 446(1) do not apply until the six years have elapsed (ss. 445(1), 446(1) provisos). *See* the saga of *Hood-Barrs* v. *IRC* (1960) 39 T.C. 209 and *IRC* v. *Hood-Barrs* (*No. 2*) (1962) 41 T.C. 339.

§ 4 Settlements where the income is undistributed: TA ss. 447, 450, 451

We have three provisions to consider under this head:

(a) Settlements where the settlor has retained an interest: TA s. 447

S. 447(1) provides that income arising under a settlement in any year of assessment is deemed to be the settlor's income to the extent to which it is undistributed, if and so long as he has an interest in the income or in any property comprised in the settlement. The circumstances in which income arising under a settlement is deemed not to have been distributed are elaborated in TA s. 455.

A settlor is deemed to have retained an interest if any benefit is reserved to the settlor or the settlor's spouse in any circumstances whatsoever (s.

447(2)). *See*, for example, *Muir* v. *IRC* [1966] 3 A.E.R. 38 and *IRC* v. *Wachtel* (1970) 46 T.C. 561. There are a number of exceptions to this principle. By the proviso to s. 447(2), the settlor is not deemed to have an interest in a settlement:

(a) if and so long as the settlement income or property cannot become payable or applicable to the settlor or the settlor's spouse except in the event of:

    (i) the bankruptcy of some person who is or may become beneficially entitled to that income or property;

    (ii) any assignment of or charge on that income or property being made or given by some such person;

    (iii) in the case of a marriage settlement, the death of both the parties to the marriage and of all or any of the children of the marriage; or

    (iv) the death under the age of twenty-five or some lower age of some person who would be beneficially entitled to that income or property on attaining that age; or

(b) if and so long as some person is alive and under the age of twenty-five during whose life that income or property cannot become payable or applicable to the settlor or the settlor's spouse except in the event of that person becoming bankrupt or assigning or charging his interest in that income or property.

From the tax planning angle the only safe course is for the settlement to exclude from all benefit the settlor or his spouse, except on failure of the trusts under the provisions of section 447, or if the entitlement to the benefit only accrues to the settlor's spouse after his (or her) death (*Vestey's Executors* v. *IRC* [1949] 1 A.E.R. 1108 (H.L.)) because the term "wife" does not include "widow" (*Harvey*, p. 110).

(b) Payments by a settlor to the trustees: TA s. 450

Where, by virtue of a settlement, the settlor or the settlor's spouse pays directly or indirectly in any year of assessment to the trustees any sums which would otherwise be deductible in computing his total income for that year, those sums are not allowed to the extent that they are covered by income which remains undistributed at the end of the year (s. 450(1), (5)). The purpose of this provision is to prevent income settlements being used to avoid excess liability; in the hands of the trustees the accumulations would become capital. *See IRC* v. *Pay* (1955) 36 T.C. 109.

(c) Payments of capital sums by the trustees to the settlor: TA s. 451

S. 451 provides that capital sums paid by trustees, or by any body corporate connected with the settlement, to the settlor or to the settlor's spouse should be treated as income of the settlor for that year, to the extent that there is "available" income; and that any excess should be carried forward and treated as the settlor's income of the following year to the extent that there is "available" income of the following year; and so on (s. 451(1), (4), (8)). Income is "available" which is undistributed income not deemed to be the settlor's income under some other provision (s. 451(2)). The object of this provision was explained by Lord Reid in *IRC* v. *Bates*: 'These provisions were first enacted in 1938. The mischief against which they were directed appears to have been that some taxpayers, intending to avoid paying surtax, transferred to trustees of settlements shares in companies controlled by them; they then borrowed money from the trustees, who used the dividends on these shares to make the loans. In that way the settlors got possession of the income from the shares which they had settled in the form of capital payments which did not attract surtax. And if the trustees were complacent the settlors might never repay these "loans" ' ((1966) 55 T.C. 255 at 259). Since *IRC* v. *De Vigier* [1964] 2 A.E.R. 907 and *Potts' Executors* v. *IRC* [1951] A.C. 443 only a settlor with a strong nerve or a weak head will venture to borrow money from his trustees.

§ 5 **Discretionary settlements: TA s. 448**

● If and so long as the terms of any settlement are such that any person has or may have a discretionary power, whether immediately or in the future, and whether with or without the consent of any person, to pay or apply to or for the benefit of the settlor or the settlor's spouse the whole or any part of the income or capital of the settlement, the income or property subject to the discretion is to be treated for all income tax purposes as the income of the settlor (s. 448(1)). The operation of this provision is suspended where the power cannot be exercised within six years (s. 448(2)).

§ 6 **Settlements of property from which the settlor is not wholly excluded: TA s. 457**

● Formerly seven-year deeds of covenant were an effective device for saving tax by the alienation of income from high to low marginal rate taxpayers. As a result of legislation in F.A. 1965 and F.A. 1966, deeds of covenant are nowadays effective only in securing basic rate relief. The governing provision in s. 457 requires that where income arising under a settlement made on or after 7 April 1965 is payable to or applicable for the benefit of any person other than the settlor, then the income is to be treated for excess liability purposes as income of the settlor and not as the income of any other person (s. 457(1)). This provision is expressed not to apply where the income derives from property of which the settlor has divested himself absolutely (s. 457(1)(d)), but deeds of covenant are alienations, not of property (i.e. capital), but of income; and therefore fall within the governing provision regardless of whether the settlor divested himself absolutely. The governing provision is also expressed not to apply to income which is treated as income of the settlor under one of the other provisions (s. 457(1)(e)), a point of some significance in view of the settlor's inability under s. 457 to recoup the tax from the trustees or beneficiary.

The several exceptions to s. 457(1) represent the only situations in which seven-year deeds of covenant continue to be an effective device for excess liability saving. The exceptional situations are where the income consists of annual payments:

(a) made for full consideration under a partnership agreement to or for the benefit of a retired partner or his widow or dependants (s. 457(1)(a));
(b) made for full consideration by the purchaser of the whole or part of a business to the vendor of his widow or dependants (s. 457(2));
(c) made by one party to a marriage by way of provision for the other divorced or separated spouse (s. 457(1)(c)).

2.04 PERSONAL REPRESENTATIVES

If a person chargeable to income tax dies, the executor or administrator of the deceased is liable for the tax chargeable on the deceased person up to the time of his death and may deduct the tax from the deceased's assets and effects (TMA s. 74(1)). Income which arises during the administration period is treated as income of the personal representatives in their representative capacity. Tax suffered by them either by deduction at source or by direct assessment at basic rate is deducted from the payments made to those entitled under the will or intestacy. Like trustees, personal representatives are not entitled to claim any personal reliefs.

2.05 BENEFICIARIES ENTITLED TO A SHARE OF THE ESTATE OF A DECEASED PERSON: TA SS. 426–33

● The general idea is that each beneficiary's share of the income is ascertained at the end of the administration period and then allocated to the tax years in which it arose. The beneficiaries then claim personal reliefs and/or pay excess liability accordingly. The administration period, s. 426(1) rather unhelpfully informs us, runs from the date of death to the completion of the administration of the estate. Unfortunately there is nothing to tell us when the completion of administration takes place. Nothing, it should be added, but s. 433(a), which is concerned with the application of ss. 426–33 to Scotland, and which suggests that the administration period is completed when the residue is ascertained. Thereafter the beneficiaries are taxed as beneficiaries under a trust in the manner described in 2.02 above. The point at which administration ends and a trust begins is a controversial issue among Chancery lawyers. In the realm of taxation it is significant because *inter alia* a residuary beneficiary is not (as a matter of general law, and apart from the statutory provisions considered in the succeeding paragraphs which derogate from the general law) liable to tax on income of an estate in the course of administration: *see*, for example, *Corbett* v. *IRC* [1938] 1 K.B. 567.

The ascertainment of the beneficiary's total income under ss. 426–33 depends upon whether he has an absolute or a limited interest in residue. A person has an absolute interest in the residue of the estate if and so long as any part of the capital of the residue would, if the residue had been ascertained, be properly payable to him or to another on his behalf (s. 432(2)). A person not having an absolute interest in residue is deemed to have a limited interest therein during any period where the income of any part of the residue for that period would, if the residue had been ascertained at the commencement of that period, be properly payable to him or to another on his behalf (s. 432(3)).

Where a beneficiary has an absolute interest, the idea is that only the income component of payments made to the beneficiary should enter into the computation of his total income. This is achieved by complicated rules, which may be summarized as follows. The first step is to ascertain the amount of the "residuary income" of the estate for each year or part of a year of assessment during which the administration continues. This is, roughly, the aggregate income arising to the estate less certain outgoings of a revenue nature. Sums which are paid, or assets which are transferred, to the beneficiary are deemed to be part of his total income up to the amount of the "residuary income", as and when the payments are made or the assets transferred. Adjustments are made if necessary on completion of the administration.

Where the beneficiary has a limited interest in residue, any sums paid or assets transferred to him or on his behalf are deemed to have been paid or transferred to him as income of the year of assessment in which they were paid or transferred. Any such sum or asset, at least where the estate is a UK estate, will normally be received by the beneficiary under deduction at basic rate. The amount or value must therefore be grossed-up on inclusion in his total income. The result will be only an approximation to his true liability, which cannot accurately be determined until the residue is ascertained. Therefore, on completion of the administration, sums or assets already paid or transferred are aggregated with sums or assets then due, the aggregate amount and value is spread over the administration period as if they accrued evenly day by day, and appropriate adjustments are made.

2.06 LEGATEES AND ANNUITANTS

In the exceptional case where a general legatee is entitled to interest, the interest ranks as income within Case III of Schedule D, unless the legatee declines to accept payment: *Dewar* v. *IRC* [1935] 2. K.B. 351.

Income arising under a will is payable from the date of death and is therefore included in the annuitant's total income from that date.

2.07 HUSBAND AND WIFE

The income tax rules governing husband and wife adhere strongly to the ethic of a traditional separation of rôles—man the provider, woman the home-builder. Under pressure of attack from the Women's Lib movement the rules have shown some signs of change; and a modicum of insight is sufficient basis for the prediction that over the next few years the assumptions on which this little corner of our system is based will undergo a radical overhaul. The basic rule—and, one might add, the basic assumption—is that the income of a married woman living with her husband is deemed to be his and not hers for purposes of assessment and collection (TA s. 37(1), (2)). A married woman not living with her husband is taxed on the same basis as a single woman.

The circumstances under which a married woman is to be regarded as living with her husband are delineated negatively in TA s. 42. A married woman, states s. 42(1), is assumed to be living with her husband unless either:

(*a*) they are separated under an order of a Court of competent jurisdiction; or

(*b*) in fact separated in such circumstances that the separation is likely to be permanent.

S. 42(2) adds that they are to be treated as coming within (b) above for any year of assessment in which:

(a) one is and one is not resident in the UK; or
(b) both are resident here but one is and one is not abroad throughout the year.

In the year of assessment in which a marriage takes place, income of the bride-to-be up to the date of the marriage is treated as income of a single woman and only her income as wife is aggregated with that of her husband. She is entitled to deduct the full single personal relief of £595 from her income up to the date of marriage; since, as from the date of marriage she (or, rather, her husband) becomes entitled also to the wife's earned income relief of £595, it might pay a couple to choose the date of their marriage carefully so as to use up both reliefs against the wife's income. Similarly when a wife dies her income up to the date of death is aggregated and her income after that falls into her estate (though her husband is entitled to a full year's reliefs as a married man). If the husband dies during the year of assessment, aggregation again applies only to income up to the date of death; thereafter the wife is treated as a *feme sole*.

To the basic rule stated at p. 177 above there are three exceptions. Firstly, the rule that partnership income is assessable jointly in the name of the firm is adhered to even where one of the partners is a married woman whether or not her husband is one of the other partners (s. 37(2) proviso). Secondly, either spouse may elect under T.A. s.38 to be separately *assessed*. The application must be made within six months before 6 July in any year of assessment except in the year of assessment in which the marriage took place, for which the application must be made before the *following* 6 July. The election remains in force until withdrawn. The notice of withdrawal for a particular year must be given within the period available that year for lodging applications. Where an election has been made the reliefs remain the same in amount, but are apportioned between husband and wife in accordance with T.A. s. 39. Separate assessment does not in any way affect the total amount of tax due from a married couple. Its effect is simply to reverse the rule that the burden of completing returns and satisfying tax assessments falls solely on the husband's shoulders while the benefit of any repayments or recoveries are likewise his alone. An election for separate assessment has none the less proved popular among married women as a demonstration of their financial independence and of the fact of their contribution to matrimonial expenditure.

The third exception is additional, and entirely unrelated to the second.

This exception represents an important encroachment on the assumption of masculine superiority. For 1972–73 and future years a married couple living together are given a right under F.A. 1971 s. 23 to make a joint election for separate taxation of the wife's earnings. The election must be made in the form and manner prescribed by the Board not earlier than six months before the beginning of the year of assessment for which it is made (6 October) and no later than six months after the end of that year (5 October) or such later time as the Board may in any particular case allow. It will continue for later years of assessment unless jointly revoked for a particular year of assessment no later than six months after the end of that year (5 October). For purposes of separate tax treatment the wife's earnings exclude (1) any pension or other payments in respect of the husband's past services; and (2) any family allowances. Each spouse is entitled to a full set of personal reliefs—each spouse is given the lower personal reliefs—except that child relief is given only to the husband. An election under F.A. 1971 s. 23 does not extend to the wife's investment income, which will continue to be treated as accruing to the husband not withstanding any such election. Where one or both of the spouses are dead the personal representatives may act in the joint election or revocation. Only if the wife's earned income is sufficient to push the couple into the higher rates is an election under s. 23 likely to prove financially advantageous.

Although in general infancy makes no difference to taxability, there was recently an attempt, now abrogated, to bring infants within the family unit of husband and wife. From 6 April 1969 to 5 April 1972, investment income of an infant who was neither married nor working regularly was treated as income of the parents. Aggregation does not apply to an infant's income arising on or after 6 April 1972 unless derived from a settlement created by one of his parents (*see* 2.03 § 2 above).

2.08 CONNECTED PERSONS: TA s. 533

The category of connected persons include the following for income tax and corporation tax purposes:

(1) an individual with his/her wife or husband;
(2) an individual with his relatives and with relatives of his/her wife or husband;
(3) a trustee with the settlor, with any person connected with the settlor, and with any company connected with the settlement under TA s. 454;
(4) a partner with any other partner and with the wife or husband or relative

of any other partner (except in relation to *bona fide* commercial transactions);

(5) a company with another company if both are controlled by the same person, or if one is controlled by one person and the other by persons connected with him or by him and persons connected with him;

(6) a company with any person who controls it, or who together with persons connected with him controls it; and

(7) any two or more persons acting together to control a company.

For purposes of this provision "company" is defined to include any body corporate or unincorporated association, but not a partnership; any unit trust scheme is treated as if it were a company and as if the rights of the unit holders were shares in the company; and "relative" means brother, sister, ancestor, or lineal descendant (s. 533(8)).

3

Capital Gains Tax

Capital gains tax takes in all
Who make disposals, big or small.
This minnow as conceived at birth
A whale will be of mighty girth.
Real gains or none it does not care:
Inflation is its staple fare.

3.1 General description of the tax

A new tax, called "capital gains tax", was introduced by F.A. 1965
s. 19(1), (3) as a charge on capital gains accruing in 1965–66 and subsequent
years of assessment on the disposal of assets. All forms of property are
assets. Most forms of transferring, or ceasing to own, or deriving sums
from, assets are disposals. "Year of assessment", in relation to capital
gains tax, bears the same meaning as in the Income Tax Acts, i.e. the fiscal
year running from 6 April in one calendar year to 5 April in the next
(F.A. 1965 s. 45(1)).

The tax was not intended to be retroactive. Although it is charged on
all disposals after 6 April 1965, regardless of when the assets disposed of
were acquired or created, there is an elaborate set of rules designed to
exclude from chargeability any part of the gain attributable to the period
up to 6 April 1965.

Capital gains which accrue to a company are charged not to capital
gains tax but to corporation tax; the company's income and capital gains
are calculated in accordance with the income tax and capital gains tax
rules respectively and are then aggregated to form its "profits" chargeable
to corporation tax. Thus companies pay tax at a uniform rate on both
income and capital gains.

Capital gains tax was not included in the 1970 consolidation. The basic
legislation contained in Part III and Schedules 6–10 of F.A. 1965 has been
successively amended by subsequent Finance Acts. In this chapter, unless
otherwise stated, references are to F.A. 1965.

3.2 Historical conspectus of capital gains taxation

The distinction between capital and income was once of crucial importance. Until 1962 it remained broadly true that only income receipts were taxable and that conversely only expenditure of an income nature could be taken into account in reducing tax liability. The exceptions were not widespread. In favour of the Revenue, certain capital receipts, e.g. from the sale of patent rights, had from time to time been treated as income so as to bring them within the charge to income tax; while, in favour of the taxpayer, capital allowances had been available for a limited range of capital expenditure since 1878.

The capital/income dichotomy undoubtedly produced capricious and undesirable effects. Capricious because, as we have seen, the borderline is so difficult to draw; and undesirable because taxpayers were encouraged to go in for speculative capital-yielding ventures or for elaborate devices by which anticipated income might be magically converted into tax-free gains. Inevitably, the wage and salary earner resented having the cards so blatantly stacked in favour of the wealthy.

3.21 1962: THE TORIES TEST THE WATER

F.A. 1962 contained the first scheme for the systematic taxation of capital gains. The Act created a new head of charge to income tax and surtax, called Case VII of Schedule D, in respect of capital gains realized, in the case of land, within three years of acquisition, and in the case of any other chargeable assets, within six months of acquisition. These short-term gains were to be treated as unearned income assessable on a current year basis and were to form part of the taxpayer's total income for income tax and surtax purposes. Case VII losses were to be deductible from Case VII gains of the same year and any excess of loss available for carry-forward and set-off against Case VII gains of later years.

Case VII was not a true capital gains tax, merely a new head of income tax. 'I have not . . . ,' said Selwyn Lloyd in his 1962 Budget Speech, 'come here today to propose a capital gains tax, but to suggest that what may loosely be called speculative gains should be subject to tax.' He went on to explain that his primary purpose in introducing the new charge was not to raise revenue, but rather 'to produce a feeling of broad equity of treatment between taxpayers. At present, it is pretty widely felt to be inequitable that those who supplement their income by speculative gains should escape tax on those gains. . . . It is on this account, and not mainly for yield, that I put forward this proposal.'

Nevertheless it was mainly on account of low yield that Case VII was abolished (F.A. 1971 s. 56(1)). The amounts produced were paltry by normal fiscal standards and it came as no surprise when Anthony Barber announced in his 1971 Speech that 'now that we have a general tax on capital gains, the additional yield from the higher charge on short-term gains, which is only about £1·5 million, is in my view too small to justify the complexities which result from having two sets of rules'. He might have added that the short-term tax had been expensive to collect, had been widely avoided and evaded, and had unduly restricted the dealing market in securities, since the ability to deal in sizable blocks of shares is enhanced by the presence of "speculators".

3.22 1965: LABOUR PLUNGES IN

The introduction of capital gains tax in F.A. 1965 was the occasion for a number of important amendments to Case VII. In particular, the time limits were unified: from 1956–66 Case VII applied to gains on *all* chargeable assets realized within twelve months. Mutual exclusivity of the two charges on capital gains was achieved by providing that, while a gain might be within the ambit of capital gains tax irrespective of the period between acquisition (or creation) and disposal, 'a gain accruing on a disposal . . . chargeable under Case VII of Schedule D shall not be a chargeable gain for the purposes of' capital gains tax (Schedule 6 para 3(1)). Thus gains accruing on disposals not chargeable under Case VII might be caught by capital gains tax even though the period between acquisition (or creation) and disposal was less than twelve months. Consequently, when Case VII was abolished for 1971–1972 and subsequent years of assessment, no special provision was necessary to extend capital gains tax to cover short-term gains. It was, however, specially provided that unrelieved Case VII losses could be carried forward against gains chargeable to capital gains tax arising in 1971–72 and subsequent years (Schedule 10 para 2).

The capital gains tax provisions of F.A. 1965 are an extraordinarily poor example of the draftsman's art. Produced in haste, often obscurely worded, they bristle with anomalies and inconsistencies. 'Few people pretend that they can understand the legislation sufficiently to advise with any confidence what it means on most of the problems involved; no one, not even the Revenue, can deny that there are innumerable problems of construction of the statutory language which will await decisions by the courts or clarifying legislation' (*Wheatcroft and Park* 0–07). Though greatly improved by the amending provisions, the capital gains tax legislation still leaves a great deal to be desired.

The new tax was intended primarily to promulgate a general feeling of 'equity and fair play' and to reinforce an incomes policy. Yield was again regarded as a secondary consideration; Mr Callaghan estimated that it would eventually build up to a figure of about £125 million a year. What he failed sufficiently to appreciate, or at any rate what he failed to disclose, was that as the years rolled by inflation would cause capital gains tax to take effect as a wealth tax snowballing along with an ever-increasing payload for the Revenue. To demonstrate this with an example, let us assume that the real value of an asset bought for £100 remains constant throughout the period of its ownership but that inflation occurs at a uniform rate of 5% a year. In 5 years' time the asset will be worth £127·60, in 10 years' time £162·90, and in 20 years' time £265·30. Since capital gains tax is (and always has been) normally payable at a flat rate of 30%, if the purchaser were to sell the asset at its market value after 5 years he would pay £8·30 in tax, if he were to sell it after 10 years he would pay £18·90, and if he were to sell it after 20 years £49·60, in respect of these purely inflationary gains. He would, in effect, have been subjected to a wealth tax at a rate of about 1% a year (since, on these figures, in the case of a sale after 5 years the tax payable represents 6·5% of the value of the asset at the date of sale, i.e. a little over 1% per year; after 10 years it represents 11·6%, again a little over 1% per year; and after 20 years it represents 18·7%, which is a little under 1% per year). The Revenue statistics appear to support this line of argument:

1966–67	£7·5 m
1967–68	£15·8 m
1968–69	£46·9 m
1969–70	£127·6 m
1970–71	£138·9 m
1971–72	£160 m
1972–73	£210 m
1973–74	£225 m (Budget estimate)

Moreover in *Secretan* v. *Hart* (1969) 45 T.C. 701 a taxpayer who had made a large profit on the sale in 1967 of shares bought between 1932 and 1944 appealed against his assessment to capital gains tax on the ground that the declining value of the pound ought to have been taken into account in making the assessment. Buckley J. sympathetically but firmly rejected this contention: 'If the intention had been that the effects of inflation were to be taken into account . . . there would clearly have been in the Act some explicit statement to that effect and some machinery provided for ascertaining the effect of inflation. . . . There is nothing anywhere in the Act of that kind' (ibid. at 706). The author is reminded of a sign he once saw in a Rhodesian bank: 'Inflation means that your money won't buy as much today as it did when you didn't have any.'

3.23 1967: A SHORT-LIVED BLITZ ON THE LAND SPECULATOR

In F.A. 1962 land was singled out for special treatment. F.A. 1965 placed land in the same position as other chargeable assets: if disposed of within twelve months of acquisition land was charged under Case VII, otherwise to capital gains tax. Continuing public concern over land speculation culminated in the Land Commission Act 1967, which imposed a "betterment levy" on land, including any buildings thereon, in Great Britain (i.e. excluding Northern Ireland, which continued to be governed by the normal capital gains tax rules). Betterment levy was a charge on the realization of the development value of land disposed of after 6 April 1967, whether this took the form of a sale (Case A), the grant of a lease (Case B), the commencement of a project of material development (Case C), or the receipt of compensation or other valuable consideration in respect of the land (Cases D, E, F). The rate was 40% of net development value.

The idea, broadly speaking, was that disposals of land, where the land had development value, should attract both capital gains tax and a betterment levy. The full value of land consisted of its "current use value" plus its "development value". "Current use value" was the value of the land on the assumption that planning permission for material development would not be granted; "development value" was the sale price (or market value) less either the cost of the land or eleven-tenths of the current use value. Capital gains tax covered increases in the current use value, betterment levy increases in development value.

The Land Commission (Dissolution) Act 1971 abolished betterment levy in respect of disposals after 22 July 1970. The full value of land disposed of since that date attracts capital gains tax (F.A. 1971 s. 55(2)), but a person who has paid a betterment levy under Case B, C, or F is entitled to capital gains tax relief for the amount paid in calculating the chargeable gain arising on a disposal of the land after 22 July 1970 (F.A. 1971 Schedule 9 para 5).

In summary, land has been charged:

(1) in the case of disposals (within three years of acquisition) between

6 April 1962 and 5 April 1965 inclusive, to income tax and surtax under Case VII of Schedule D;

(2) in the case of disposals (within one year of acquisition) between 6 April 1965 and 5 April 1967 inclusive, to Case VII;

(3) in the case of disposals (other than those chargeable under Case VII) between 6 April 1965 and 5 April 1967 inclusive, to capital gains tax;

(4) in the case of disposals (other than those chargeable under Case VII) between 6 April 1967 and 22 July 1970 inclusive, to capital gains tax in respect of increases in current use value;

(5) in the case of disposals between 6 April 1967 and 22 July 1970 inclusive, to betterment levy in respect of increases in development value (if the disposal was chargeable under Case VII (*see* (2) above) the betterment levy was allowed as a deduction in computing the gain); and

(6) in the case of disposals after 22 July 1970, to capital gains tax.

3.3 Principles of computation

A capital gains tax computation should be made in three stages. The first step is to ascertain whether certain pre-conditions are satisfied, because a capital gain is taxed, or a capital loss allowed, only if it results from (1) a disposal by (2) a chargeable person of (3) a chargeable asset. If all three prerequisites are satisfied, the second step is to apply the statutory rules for calculating the "*chargeable* gain" or "*allowable* loss" arising from the disposal in question. (The same rules apply for both.) Finally, after arriving at the chargeable gain or allowable loss for each disposal in the year of assessment in question, the totting up: all the allowable losses of that year must be aggregated and set against the total of chargeable gains. If the resultant sum is a net gain, then, after deducting unallowed losses from previous years, the gain is subjected to tax at the appropriate rate, normally 30%. In the event of a net loss, the loss may be carried forward indefinitely against gains of subsequent years. The idea is thus to compute the chargeable gain or allowable loss for each disposal in a particular year of assessment and then at the end of the year to total these amounts so as to arrive at the net chargeable gain or allowable loss for that year.

Tax is payable within three months of the end of the year of assessment or within thirty days after the assessment, whichever is the later (s. 20(6)).

3.31 THE FIRST PRE-CONDITION OF CHARGEABILITY: A DISPOSAL

"Disposal" is nowhere defined in the Act. In filling out the concept of a disposal the legislation draws on a wide catchment area that include its natural meaning (i.e. any way of changing an asset's ownership—sales, gifts, creating settlements, and the like) and various extensions to its natural meaning (e.g. various "deemed" disposals, such as when a beneficiary becomes absolutely entitled as against his trustee or when assets are appropriated to or from trading stock à la *Sharkey* v. *Wernher*, etc). Some special cases are discussed in the ensuing paragraphs.

To remove doubt it was provided in F.A. 1971 that, where an asset is disposed of and acquired under a contract, the time at which the disposal and acquisition is made is the time the contract is made (Schedule 10 para 10(1)), except that in the case of a conditional contract disposal and acquisition take place when the condition is satisfied (ibid. para 10(2)).

§ 1 Part disposals

"Disposal", s. 22(2)(*a*) informs us, includes a part disposal, whereupon we proceed to s. 22(2)(*b*) for the revelation that a part disposal occurs where an interest or right in or over an asset is created by the disposal as well as where it subsists before the disposal and, generally, where, on a person making a disposal, any description of property derived from the asset remains undisposed of.

§ 2 Capital sums derived from assets

There is also a disposal, declares s. 22(3), where any capital sum is derived from assets and in particular where any capital sum is received:

(*a*) as compensation for damage to, or for the loss, destruction, dissipation, depreciation, or risk of depreciation of, an asset;
(*b*) under an insurance policy covering damage to, or the loss or depreciation of, assets;
(*c*) for forfeiture or surrender of, or for refraining from exercising, rights; and
(*d*) as consideration for use or exploitation of assets.

In these cases disposal occurs at the time when the capital sum is received (s. 45(5)).

§ 3 (i) Transfers by way of security: (ii) disposals by a nominee or bare trustee: (iii) an insolvent's assets

The transfer of an asset or of an interest or right therein by way of security (e.g. when a house is mortgaged), and its retransfer on redemption of the security, involve no acquisition or disposal (s. 22(6)). A person entitled to an asset by way of security, such as a mortgagee, receiver, or manager, who deals with it for the purpose of enforcing or giving effect to the security, does so as nominee of the person entitled to the asset (s. 22(7)). This leads us back to s. 22(5), which lays down the rule that the acts of a nominee are to be treated as acts of the person for whom he is the nominee.

The same rule applies also to:

(a) the acts of a trustee for any person absolutely entitled as against him or who would be but for infancy or disability (s. 22(5)); and

(b) acts of a trustee or assignee in bankruptcy or under a deed of arrangement in relation to the assets of an insolvent (F.A. 1966 Schedule 10 para 10(1)).

A disposal by a nominee or bare trustee gives rise to a chargeable gain or allowable loss in the hands of the beneficiary, while tax in respect of any chargeable gain on a disposal by a trustee in bankruptcy etc is assessable on and recoverable from him. Transfers between a nominee/bare trustee/ trustee in bankruptcy/etc on the one hand and the beneficiary or insolvent, as the case may be, on the other, are disregarded for capital gains tax purposes. On the death of an insolvent, however, any assets then held by, or transferred to, the trustee in bankruptcy etc are deemed to have been acquired by him at their market value as if he were the insolvent's personal representative (F.A. 1966 Schedule 10 para 10(2)).

§ 4 Loss or destruction of an asset

The occasion of the entire loss, destruction, dissipation, or extinction of an asset constitutes a disposal by virtue of s. 23(3). If the Inspector is satisfied, on a claim by the owner of an asset, that its value has become negligible, the claimant is deemed to have sold and immediately re-acquired it for the value specified in the claim (s. 23(4)). For purposes of s. 23(3) and (4) a building or semi-permanent structure in the nature of a building may be regarded as an asset separate from the land on which it stands, but the owner of a building or structure which has been destroyed or become negligible in value is treated as if he had also sold and immediately re-acquired its site at market value (s. 23(5)).

§ 5 Life assurance policies and deferred annuity contracts

Payment of the sum assured by a life assurance policy, or of the first instalment of a deferred annuity, constitutes a disposal of the policy or contract, as does the surrender of the policy or contract (s. 28(3)). No chargeable gain can arise, however, if the person making the disposal is the original beneficial owner of the policy or contract, or acquired his interest in it otherwise than for valuable consideration (s. 28 (2)).

§ 6 Capital distributions by companies

Where a person receives or becomes entitled to receive in respect of shares in a company any capital distribution from the company (other than a new holding: as to which *see* pp. 216–17 below) he is treated as having disposed of an interest in the shares in consideration of that capital distribution (Schedule 7 para 3(1)). "Capital distribution" means any distribution in money or money's worth, including a distribution in the course of dissolving or winding up a company, other than on income distribution (ibid. para 3(4)). There is, however, no part disposal where the Inspector is satisfied that the distribution is small relative to the value of the shares in respect of which it is made, and so directs; but on a subsequent disposal of the shares the amount or value of the capital distribution must be deducted from any allowable expenditure (Schedule 7 para 3(2)). In practice the Revenue regard a capital distribution as small if it does not exceed 5% of the value of the shares.

§ 7 Debts

There is also a disposal, Schedule 7 para 11(2) tells us, when a debt is wholly or partly paid, to which para 11(1) adds the rider that no chargeable gain can accrue if the person making the disposal is the original creditor or his personal representative or legatee, unless the debt is a debt on a security. "Security" is defined in Schedule 7 para 5(3)(*b*) to include any loan stock issued by a government, public authority, or company, whether secured or unsecured.

§ 8 Options

The exercise or abandonment of an option by the person entitled to exercise it does not constitute a disposal by him (Schedule 7 para 14(3)), unless it is:

(*a*) an option to subscribe for shares, or
(*b*) an option to acquire assets with a view to their use in a trade carried on by the acquirer,

disposed of or abandoned on or after 20 April 1971 (F.A. 1971 s. 58(1), (2)). To come within (*a*) an option must normally be of a kind which is quoted on a recognized Stock Exchange and there dealt in in the same manner as shares (ibid. s. 58(4)).

§ 9 Transfers of value derived from assets

Schedule 7 para 15(1) constitutes the following transactions disposals, to the extent that they involve an element of gift:

(i) a person's exercise of his control over a company so that value (1) passes out of shares in or rights over the company owned or exercisable by him or by a person with whom he is connected and (2) passes into other shares in or rights over the company (ibid. para 15(2));

(ii) after an owner of land or other property has become the lessee of the property, any adjustment of the rights and liabilities under the lease which is as a whole favourable to the lessor (ibid. para 15(3)); and

(iii) the extinction or abrogation of any right or restriction to which an asset is subject by the person entitled to enforce it (ibid. para 15(4)).

The assets disposed of are, respectively, (i) the shares or rights out of which value passed, (ii) an interest in the property, and (iii) the right or restriction. (The disposal consideration is market value: *see* 3.34 § 2.)

3.32 THE SECOND PRE-CONDITION OF CHARGEABILITY: A CHARGEABLE PERSON

A person is liable to capital gains tax if he has chargeable gains in a year of assessment during any part of which he is resident in the UK or during which he is ordinarily resident here (s. 20(1)). Non-residents are liable only if they carry on a trade in the UK through a branch or agency, in which case the charge is limited to gains accruing on the disposal:

(*a*) of assets situated in the UK and used in or for the purposes of the trade at or before the time of the disposal, or

(*b*) of assets situated in the UK and used or held for the purposes of the branch or agency at or before that time, or assets acquired for use by or for the purposes of the branch or agency (s. 20(2)).

§ 1 The remittance basis

Individuals who are resident or ordinarily resident here but domiciled abroad are taxed on a remittance basis: their gains accruing from disposals of assets situated outside the UK are deemed to accrue if and when received in this country and their losses therefrom do not qualify as allowable losses (s. 20(7)). The situation of assets is determined according to the rules contained in s. 43(3): rights or interests in or over property are situated where the property is; a debt is situated in the UK if and only if the creditor is resident here, except that a judgment debt is situated where the judgment was recorded; shares or securities are situated where they are registered or, if entered in more than one register, where the principal register is kept, except those issued by a municipal or governmental authority, which are situated in the UK if and only if the owner is resident here; the goodwill of a trade or profession is situated where the trade or profession is carried on; patents, trade marks, and designs are situated where they are registered; copyright, franchises, rights, and licences to use any copyright material, patent, trade mark, or design are situated in the UK if they are exercisable here.

Under s. 40(1) a person charged or chargeable on a disposal of assets situated outside the UK may claim relief if he is in a position to show that he was unable to transfer the gains to the UK in the year of assessment in which they arose due to:

(a) the laws of the territory where the income arose,
(b) the executive action of its government, or
(c) the impossibility of obtaining foreign currency in that territory;

and *not* due to any want of reasonable endeavours on his part. Relief is given by postponing the charge to the year of assessment in which remittance becomes possible (s. 40(2)). The claim must be made within six years of the end of the year of assessment in which the gains arise (s. 40(3)) and may be made by the personal representative of a deceased person who would have been entitled to claim (s. 40(4)).

"Individual" in s. 20(7) (see preceding paragraph but one), and indeed for capital gains tax purposes generally, does not include a trustee or personal representative (Schedule 10 para 12(2)), so that the remittance basis does not apply to a trustee or personal representative. Nor does the rule contained in s. 43(2) that an individual in the UK for some temporary purpose only and not with a view to establishing residence here is liable on chargeable gains accruing in a year of assessment only if during that year he spent a total of more than six months in the UK.

§ 2 Trustees and personal representatives

Chargeable gains accruing to a settlement, or to the estate of a deceased person, may be assessed in the name of any one or more of the trustees of the settlement or personal representatives of the deceased (Schedule 10 para 12(1)) but the persons assessed must not include a non-resident unless all the trustees or personal representatives are named in the assessment.

The trustees of settled property are treated under s. 25(1) as being a single and continuing body of persons (distinct from the persons who may from time to time be the trustees). That body, continues s. 25(1), must be treated as being resident and ordinarily resident in the UK unless:

(a) the general administration of the trusts is ordinarily carried on outside the UK; and

(b) the trustees or a majority of them for the time being are neither resident nor ordinarily resident here.

A person carrying on the business of managing trusts is treated as not resident in the UK in relation to any trust managed by him if the whole of the settled property was provided by a person who was not domiciled or resident in the UK at the time of creating the settlement, if it is a settlement *inter vivos*, or, in the case of a testamentary disposition or intestacy, at the time of his death (s. 25(1) proviso).

Non-resident trusts are governed by s. 42, which applies only where:

(a) the trustees are non-residents; and

(b) the settlor, or one of the settlors, is domiciled and either resident or ordinarily resident in the UK or was so resident and domiciled when he made the settlement.

Any chargeable gain accruing to the trustees is apportioned under s. 42(2) to those beneficiaries who are domiciled and either resident or ordinarily resident in the UK. The apportionment must be made in a just and reasonable manner according to the respective values of the beneficiaries' interests. There are special rules for beneficiaries under a discretionary trust (s. 42(3)) and for settlement made before 6 April 1965 (s. 42 (4)). A loss made by a non-resident trust is not apportioned to its beneficiaries (s. 42(6)).

In relation to the estate of a deceased person, the personal representatives are treated as being a single and continuing body of persons (distinct from the persons who may from time to time be the personal representatives) and as having the deceased's residence or ordinary residence, and domicile at the date of death (s. 24(6)).

§ 3 **Husband and wife**

Chargeable gains accruing to a married woman in a year of assessment, or part of a year of assessment, during which she is living with her husband, are assessed and charged on the husband (Schedule 10 para 3(1)), unless an application for separate assessment is made by either husband or wife under

Schedule 10 para 3(2). An application for separate assessment to capital gains tax must be made before 6 July following the year of assessment for which it is to take effect; and applies for that and subsequent years of assessment until a notice of withdrawal is given. A notice of withdrawal must conform to the same time limit as indicated for an application for separate assessment. Any application or notice must be in the form prescribed by the Board (ibid. para 3(5)).

As to disposals between husband and wife, *see* pp. 199–200 below; and as to the alternative basis of charge, *see* 3.35 § 2 below.

§ 4 Partnerships

Chargeable gains accruing to two or more persons carrying on a trade or business in partnership are assessed and charged on them separately (s. 45(7)(*a*)). Any partnership dealings are treated as dealings by the partners and not by the firm as such (s. 45(7)(*b*)). The income tax rules in TA s. 153(1), (2) for determining the residence of a partnership (*see* p. 42 above) apply also to capital gains tax (s. 45(7)(*c*)).

§ 5 The donee of a gift

As we shall see (p. 196 below), a gift is a deemed disposal at market value under s. 22(4). Schedule 7 para 19 is designed to protect the Revenue in the event of a donor failing to meet his capital gains tax liability in respect of the gift. If, para 19(1) provides, tax is not paid by the donor within twelve months from the due date for payment, the donee may be assessed and charged in the name of the donor (or, if he has died, of his personal representatives). The assessment may not be raised more than two years after the due date of payment. The donee is entitled to recover any tax he pays from the donor or his personal representatives (ibid. para 19(2)). "Gift" in this context includes any transaction otherwise than by way of a bargain at arm's length made for less than full consideration (para. 19(4)).

§ 6 Connected persons

A number of special rules of computation apply to transactions between "connected persons". The definition of "connected persons" for capital gains tax purposes is tucked away in Schedule 7 para 21 and it is convenient to set it out at this stage, though its significance will only emerge later as and when, on our journey through the rules of computation (3.34 below), the special rules governing connected persons crop up. Para 21 connects:

(i) an individual with his relatives (i.e. brother, sister, ancestor, or lineal descendant);

(ii) a husband with his wife and her relatives, and vice versa;

(iii) the trustee of a settlement with the settlor, with any person connected with the settlor, and with any company deemed to be connected with the settlement under the provisions of TA s. 454(4) (i.e. if at any time in the year of assessment it is a close company, or only not a close company because not resident in the UK, and the participators then include the trustees or a beneficiary);

(iv) a partner with his other partners and with the husbands or wives or relatives of the other partners (except in relation to acquisition and disposals of partnership assets pursuant to *bona fide* commercial arrangements);

(v) a company with the person who controls it, either individually or together with other persons connected with him;

(vi) any two or more persons acting together to secure or exercise control of a company with one another and with any person acting on the directions of any one of them.

3.33 THE THIRD PRE-CONDITION OF CHARGEABILITY: A CHARGEABLE ASSET

The general rule, contained in s. 22(1), is that all forms of property are assets for capital gains tax purposes, whether situated in the UK or not, including:

(*a*) options, debts, and incorporeal property generally,

(*b*) any currency other than sterling, and

(*c*) any form of property created by the person disposing of it, or otherwise coming to be owned without being acquired.

Certain assets are the subject of special exemptions or reliefs, which are considered at 3.6 and 3.7 below.

3.34 THE COMPUTATION OF CHARGEABLE GAINS AND ALLOWABLE LOSSES

The normal rules of computation are contained in F.A. 1965 Schedule 6 Part I, as amended. Part II of the Schedule, as amended, makes special provision for assets held on 6 April 1965.

(A) THE NORMAL RULES OF COMPUTATION

The basic schema is straightforward. Taking the disposal consideration as a starting point, the next step is to deduct any "allowable expenditure".

The resulting sum is either the taxpayer's chargeable gain or his allowable loss.

A number of difficulties may, however, arise in applying the basic schema to particular circumstances. In the first place the actual disposal consideration must be replaced sometimes either by the market value of the assets disposed of or by the sum securing neither gain nor loss to the disponer (and, to add a minor point, there are complications where the consideration is payable by instalments). Secondly there is the problem of determining whether an expense qualifies as "allowable expenditure". Thirdly on a part disposal allowable expenditure may need to be apportioned between the part disposed of and the part retained. Fourthly capital allowances may have to be taken into account. Finally there are several situations which attract special rules.

These difficulties will now be considered. A small general point. Any apportionment acquired of any consideration on expenditure for purpose of a capital gains tax computation must be made by the Inspector in a just and reasonable manner, unless a method of apportionment is specifically provided for (Schedule 6 para 21(4)).

§ 1 Consideration for disposals or acquisitions

The consideration for the disposal and consequent acquisition of an asset will normally be the capital sum payable to the disponer.

An asset is normally treated as having been acquired or disposed of free of any right or interest by way of security subsisting at the time of acquisition or disposal (s. 22(8)). Where the asset is acquired subject to any such right or interest, the amount of the liability assumed by the acquirer forms part of the consideration for the acquisition and disposal, in addition to any other consideration (ibid.).

The consideration for an asset which is disposed of without being acquired (*see* 3.31 § 1 above) is the capital sum receivable in respect of the event giving rise to the disposal. A disposal of this kind is deemed to occur at the time when the capital sum is received (s. 45(5)).

On the disposal of an asset, any sum charged to income tax as income of the disponer or taken into account in computing his trading or other income for income tax purposes must be excluded from the disposal consideration (Schedule 6 para 2(1)), unless that sum is taken into account in the making of a balancing charge (ibid. para 2(2)). This does not preclude bringing into account the capitalized value of a right to income payments over a period, e.g. a rentcharge (ibid. para 2(3)).

§ 2 Market value

S. 22(4) specifies two situations in which a person's acquisition of an asset and the disposal of it to him are deemed to be for market value:

(1) Where he acquires the asset otherwise than by way of a bargain at arm's length. Two examples are given in the sub-section. The first is an acquisition by way of gift: the donor and the donee are treated as having respectively disposed of and acquired the asset at market value. (In *Turner* v. *Follett* [1973] S.T.C. 148 a taxpayer who had made a gift of shares to his children resisted his assessment to capital gains tax on their increase in value since 6 April 1965 on the basis that under F.A. 1965 a gift did not amount to a disposal. The Court of Appeal dismissed his remarkably brave appeal; although the Act nowhere defined a disposal, several provisions made it plain that a gift was a deemed disposal at market value.) The second is a distribution by a company to its shareholders. If, for instance, a company holding a block of shares in another company were to distribute those shares to its shareholders in proportion to their respective holdings, the distributing company would be treated as having disposed of and its shareholders as having acquired the shares for market value. A third example is appended by Schedule 7 para 17(1), (2), which provide that, where a person acquiring an asset and the person disposing of it are "connected", the acquisition and disposal constitute a transaction otherwise than by way of a bargain at arm's length. The consideration for any asset transferred between connected persons is therefore deemed to be market value, except in the case of husband and wife (*see* pp. 199–200 below). For the meaning of "connected persons", *see* pp. 193–4 above. A fourth example is where value derived from assets is transferred (Schedule 7 para 15(1): *see* p. 190 above). A fifth example is Schedule 7 para 11(3) which provides that, so far as both the debtor and creditor are concerned, where property (as opposed to money) is transferred in satisfaction of a debt, the consideration must not be treated as greater than the market value of that property at the date of transfer (*see*, as to debts, 3.31 § 7 above).

(2) Where he acquires the asset wholly or partly for a consideration that cannot be valued. Again the sub-section gives two examples: namely where the consideration represents (i) compensation for loss of office or employment or for reduction of emoluments, and (ii) services rendered or to be rendered.

Market value is invariably determined as at the date of disposal. S. 44(1) defines "market value" to mean 'the price which those assets might reasonably be expected to fetch on a sale in the open market', to which s. 44(2) adds the rule that no reduction can be made on the assumption that placing the assets on the market all at the same time might depress their value. These provisions are borrowed from the estate duty legislation, their counterparts being F.A. 1894 s. 7(5) and F. (1909–10) A. 1910 s. 60(2) respectively, which govern the ascertainment of the "principal value" of property passing on death for estate duty purposes. The case law on the meaning of open market value for estate duty purposes is now equally relevant to capital gains tax, just as the capital gains tax cases are now coming to cross-fertilize the estate duty provisions.

The open market price, according to Sankey J. in *Ellesmere* v. *IRC*, means 'the best possible price that is obtainable' ([1918] 2 K.B. at 740), a formulation approved by their Lordships in *Buccleugh* v. *IRC* [1967] 1 A.C. 506. A hypothetical sale must be postulated between a willing seller and a willing buyer (*Findlay's Trustees* v. *IRC* (1938) 22 A.T.C. 437 at 440), at which every possible purchaser is taken into account (*IRC* v. *Clay* [1914] 3 K.B. 466 at 474), including any person to whom the property is more valuable or desirable than it is to the general public (*Glass* v. *IRC* 1915 S.C. 449). Conversely any depreciation due to some personal quality of the disponer, for example in shares on the death of a managing director, must be taken into account.

Where the transfer of shares in a company is restricted—as in the case of a private company it must be (under the Companies Act 1948 s. 28(1)) and in the case of a public company it may be and often is—market value is determined on the assumption that the purchaser is to stand in the shoes of the former shareholder, holding the shares subject to the same restrictions: *IRC* v. *Crossman* [1937] A.C. 26. The effect of this rule is by no means always depreciatory: in the common situation in which the articles give the other shareholders or the directors rights of pre-emption, market value is likely to be much higher than the pre-emption price. In *Holt* v. *IRC* [1953] 2 A.E.R. 1499 Danckwerts J. suggested (at 1508–9) that the hypothetical purchaser of shares in a private company would be more prudent than the ordinary Stock Exchange investor and 'would seek to get the fullest possible information about the past history of the company, the particular trade in which it was engaged and the future prospects of the company'. The question of the hypothetical purchaser's state of knowledge has been clarified by *Lynall* v. *IRC* [1971] 3 W.L.R. 759. At the time of her death Mrs Lynall owned 28% of the shares of a private company. Private documents of the directors were in existence at the date of the death, indicating that a public flotation of part of the share capital was under consideration. The Court of Appeal, on the assumption that the private documents were admissible, valued the shares at £4·50 each. The House of Lords, reversing that decision, held that in the circumstances, since the board had come to no decision but were maintaining a cautious and uncommitted attitude, the confidential information ought not to be regarded as available to a hypothetical purchaser; and, accordingly, valued the shares at £3·50 each.

In relation to shares or securities listed in The Stock Exchange Daily Official List, s. 44(3) (as amended by F.A. 1973 s. 54(1) and Schedule 21 para 4) gives statutory force to those rules of valuation established by estate duty practice. Market value is the lower of two figures worked out from The Stock Exchange Daily Official List for the relevant date, namely:

(a) the figure one-quarter up from the lower of the two prices shown (i.e. the buying and selling prices); and

(b) the figure mid-way between the highest and lowest prices of recorded dealings.

The same rule is applied by Schedule 6 para 22(3)(a) to shares or securities quoted on The Stock Exchange which were held on 6 April 1965, except that "one-quarter up from" in (a) above is replaced by "mid-way between". The Council of The Stock Exchange have issued a booklet listing 6 April 1965 values.

If the London trading floor is closed on the relevant date market value is ascertained by reference to the latest previous date or earliest subsequent date on which it is open, whichever is the lower (s. 44(3) proviso (ii), as amended).

S. 44(3) is displaced in two situations:

(1) Where The Stock Exchange provides a more active market elsewhere than on the London trading floor (s. 44(3) proviso (i)). Presumably in this eventuality, falling back on s. 44(1) (see p. 196 above), market value is the selling price quoted on the more active trading floor.

(2) '[W]here in consequence of special circumstances prices so quoted are by themselves not a proper measure of market value' (s. 44(3)). The meaning of "special circumstances" arose for decision before the House of Lords in *Crabtree* v. *Hinchcliffe* [1971] 3 W.L.R. 821. From September 1964 Vickers Ltd had been negotiating to take over R. W. Crabtree & Sons Ltd. By 6 April 1965 the negotiations had reached an advanced stage and in August 1965 Vickers made a cash offer for the entire issued share capital of Crabtrees. The appellant, a substantial shareholder in Crabtrees, accepted the offer and was assessed to capital gains tax on the difference between the mid-market prices of his shares on 6 April 1965 and their sale price. He contended that the confidential negotiations constituted "special circum-

stances" within s. 44(3) since they pushed the real value of the shares on 6 April 1965 well above the quoted prices. Their Lordships unanimously rejected his contention. 'There must be many occasions,' Viscount Dilhorne observed, 'on which the directors of a company are in possession of information which if made public would affect the prices quoted on the London Stock Exchange . . . but the fact that directors have such information and the Stock Exchange has not, cannot ordinarily by itself amount, in my opinion, to "special circumstances". . . . For circumstances to be special they must be exceptional, abnormal or unusual' (ibid. at 842). 'If, however,' he added, 'it clearly was the duty of the directors to make public such information, and there was failure to do so . . . it might well be that that would amount to special circumstances' (ibid. at 842).

The market value of unit trusts is the holder's selling price, i.e. the lower of the two prices published on the relevant date, or, if none were published on that date, on the latest date before (s. 44(4)), except that 6 April 1965 values are the mid-market prices (Schedule 6 para 22(3)(b)).

If a person is given, or acquires from a connected person, by a series of transactions, two or more assets whose combined market value when considered together is more than their aggregate market value when considered separately (e.g. car registration plates MZH 1, MZH 2, MZH 3, MZH 4, and MZH 5; or a set of Chippendale chairs), their market value for capital gains tax purposes is taken to be the larger market value, apportioned rateably to each disposal (Schedule 7 para 16).

§ 3 No gain no loss

In three situations now to be discussed the consideration on a disposal is deemed to be the sum which results in there being neither gain nor loss to the disponer. The gain that would otherwise have accrued in the hands of the disponer does not escape tax altogether. The charge on that gain is merely postponed to a later disposal.

(a) Husband and wife

On a disposal between husband and wife living together, both are treated as if the asset in question were respectively disposed of and acquired for such consideration as would secure neither gain nor loss to the disposing spouse (Schedule 7 para 20(1)). When the asset is subsequently disposed of, the spouse making the subsequent disposal is treated as if the other's acquisition or creation of the asset had been his or her acquisition or creation of it (Schedule 6 para 30). Thus the gain in the hands of the spouse making the original disposal falls into computation on the subsequent disposal. Schedule 6 para 30 is particularly important where the spouse making the original disposal acquired or created the asset before 6 April 1965.

The "no gain no loss" rule does not apply in two situations. First, where until the disposal the asset formed part of the disposing spouse's trading stock, or where it was acquired as trading stock by the acquiring spouse, the disposal consideration is deemed to be market value (the tortuous statutory reasoning can be traced from Schedule 7 para 20(2)(*a*) through Schedule 7 para 21(2) and 17(2) to s. 22(4)). Second, where the disposal is by way of *donatio mortis causa*, the "no gain no loss" rule is displaced by the provision in F.A. 1971 Schedule 12 para 3 that no chargeable gain can accrue to a person making a disposal by way of *donatio mortis causa* (Schedule 7 para 20(2)(*b*), substituted by F.A. 1971 Schedule 12 para 5).

(*b*) "Roll-over" relief on the replacement of business assets

S. 33 enables a trader to claim "roll-over" relief where he disposes of assets used in his trade and applies the proceeds in purchasing replacements. Relief takes the form of treating:

(*a*) the consideration on disposal of the "old assets" as 'such amount as would secure that on the disposal neither a loss nor a gain accrues' (s. 33(1)(*a*)); and

(*b*) the acquisition consideration of the "new assets" as reduced by the excess of the actual disposal consideration over (*a*) (s. 33(1)(*b*)).

("New" and "old" in this context are not qualitative descriptions: relief may be available even though the assets are second-hand.)

The effect of "roll-over" relief is to postpone the charge on the gain accruing on disposal of the old assets until disposal of the new assets. Even then, if the trader again invests the proceeds in replacements, he may claim relief a second time; and this process may be continued indefinitely. Only when the assets are disposed of without being replaced will the day of reckoning have arrived: the trader will then in effect be taxed on the accumulated gains that would have been charged on each of the earlier disposals, but for roll-over relief, as well as on the gain accruing to the assets finally disposed of.

Relief is available in respect of five classes of assets, of which the first four are specified in s. 33(6) and the fifth was added by F.A. 1969 Schedule 19 para 17:

Class 1: A. Any land, building, part of a building, or structure in the nature of a building occupied solely for the purposes of the trade (except where the claimant's trade is that of dealing in or developing land, or of providing services for the occupier of land in which the claimant has an interest).

B. Fixed plant or machinery which does not form part of a building or of a structure in the nature of a building.

Class 2:   Ships.
Class 3:   Aircraft.
Class 4:   Goodwill.
Class 5:   Hovercraft.

F.A. 1971 s. 60(1)(a) removed the restriction that both the old and the new assets should fall within the same class. Replacements acquired on or after 20 April 1971 must fall within one, but no particular one, of the five classes. Relief is no longer denied where, for example, the proceeds of selling a ship are invested in a hovercraft.

Another cardinal requirement is that the new assets be acquired, or an unconditional contract for their acquisition be entered into, within the period beginning twelve months before and ending three years [twelve months if the acquisition took place before 6 April 1973] after the disposal of the old assets, unless the time limit is extended or restricted by the Board by notice in writing (s. 33(3), as amended by F.A. 1973 s. 37).

Example 3

Ivor Fortune runs a fleet of ships. He bought the S.S. *Amnesia* in 1966 for £50,000 and sold it in 1969 for £120,000, applying this money towards the purchase of the S.S. *Hysteria*, costing £130,000, a few months later. In 1972 he sold the *Hysteria* for £160,000, which he applied towards the purchase of the S.S. *Deliria* shortly afterwards for £180,000. He has now sold the *Deliria* for £270,000, with which he has bought an Andy Warhol painting.

Under s. 33 Ivor may claim relief in respect of the 1969 and 1972 disposals so as to postpone his charge to capital gains tax until now. The 1969 disposal consideration is deemed to be £50,000 (the amount which secures neither gain nor loss); and the *Hysteria*'s acquisition consideration is deemed to be £60,000 (£130,000 minus the difference between £120,000 and £50,000). Similarly the 1972 disposal consideration is deemed to be £60,000 and the *Deliria*'s acquisition consideration £80,000 (£180,000 minus the difference between £160,000 and £60,000). Ivor's chargeable gain on selling the *Deliria* is therefore £190,000 (£270,000 less £80,000).

Limited relief is available even where the claimant does not strictly comply with the requirements of s. 33(1):

S. 33(1) requirement	*Nature of partial relief*
(1) *All* the proceeds on disposal of the old assets must have been applied in the purchase of replacements.	Where part of the disposal consideration has been invested in the new assets, s. 33(2) provides for relief on the excess of the gain over the part *not* so invested. (*See* example below.)
(2) The old assets must have been 'used, and used only, for the purposes of the trade'.	Where a building or structure has been only partly used for the purposes of a trade, the part so used (together with any land occupied for purposes ancillary to the occupation of that part) may, by virtue of s. 33(7), be treated as a separate asset and the consideration on disposal of the whole building or structure apportioned.
(3) The old assets must have been used only for the purposes of the trade throughout the period of the trader's ownership.	Where the old assets were not used for the purposes of the trade throughout the period of ownership, relief is available under s. 33(8) for the time and extent to which the old assets were so used.

Example 4 (see s. 33(2) in table above)

Robin Widdows bought a bingo hall in 1966 for £10,000, which he sold in 1973 for £25,000, of which he has now applied £18,000 in the purchase of a second bingo hall.

If Robin claims relief under s. 33(2) the gain of £15,000 will be treated as reduced to £7,000 (excess of £25,000 over £18,000), and the acquisition consideration for the new hall reduced by the same amount from £18,000 to £10,000. (Note that s. 33(2) does not apply unless the part of the disposal consideration not invested in replacements does not exceed the gain, i.e. in this example s. 33(2) would not have applied if Robin had invested less than £10,000 of the £25,000 in his new hall.)

When it is necessary to apportion consideration under s. 33 (*see* (2) and (3) in table above), the apportionment must be 'in such manner as is just and reasonable' (s. 33(12)).

Roll-over relief may be claimed by a person carrying on two trades in different localities concerned with goods or services of the same kind who used the old assets in the one trade and uses the new assets in the other (s. 33(9)). Moreover, s. 33 applies with the necessary modifications not merely to trades but also to:

(*a*) the functions of a public authority,
(*b*) commercial woodlands,

(c) a profession, vocation, office, or employment (s. 33(10)), and
(d) the activities of non-profit-making bodies whose activities are directed to the promotion of the interests of their members (added by F.A. 1972 s. 118).

In cases of a partnership, each of the partners must claim relief separately.

S. 33 is displaced by special provisions contained in F.A. 1969 Schedule 19 para 16 in cases where the replacement is a depreciating asset, defined as an asset with a predictable life not exceeding sixty years.

(c) Assets lost or destroyed

As we have seen (3.31 § 4 above) the occasion of the entire loss or destruction of an asset constitutes a deemed disposal by virtue of s. 23(3). A loss claim does not always ensue, however, because any capital sum received by way of compensation or under an insurance policy is treated as consideration for the disposal (s. 22(3): see 3.31 § 2 above). On the other hand, if the capital sum is applied towards a replacement within one year of the loss or destruction (or such longer period as the Inspector may allow), the owner may claim to treat:

(a) the disposal consideration as reduced to the allowable expenditure on the asset; and
(b) the acquisition consideration of the replacement as reduced by the excess of the capital sum, together with any residual or scrap value, over the allowable expenditure on the old asset (Schedule 6 para 13(3)).

Schedule 6 para 13(3) applies only where the whole of the capital sum is applied towards a replacement. Para 13(4) provides for partial relief in cases where part only of the sum was so expended: the claimant is entitled to be treated as if (a) the gain accruing on the disposal of the old asset were reduced to the amount of the part not expended on the replacement; and (b) the acquisition consideration of the new asset were reduced by the same amount as the gain. Partial relief is available only if the part not expended on the replacement is less than the amount of the gain. (It will be appreciated that para 13(4) corresponds to s. 33(2): see para (1) of the table on p. 202 above and the example immediately below it.)

It is interesting to compare the above provisions with those governing the receipt of a capital sum in respect of an asset *which is not lost or destroyed*. Where the whole or a substantial part of the capital sum was applied in restoring the asset, or where the sum is small as compared with the value of the asset, the recipient may claim under Schedule 6 para 13(1) that receipt should not be treated as a disposal of the asset. If the receipt is not treated as a disposal, the capital sum, and any other amount which would have been treated as disposal consideration, must be deducted from the allowable expenditure in the capital gains computation on a subsequent disposal of the asset (ibid.).

These provisions, relating both to assets lost or destroyed and assets not lost or destroyed, do not apply to wasting assets (ibid. para 13(5)).

§ 4 Consideration payable by instalments

When an asset is sold for payments to be made by instalments, the general rule is that the disposal consideration is deemed to be the capitalized value of those payments (Schedule 6 para 2(3)) with no discount for deferred gratification or for risk. If any part of the sum brought into account is later shown to be irrecoverable, an adjustment is made (ibid. para 14(5)). However, Schedule 6 para 14(1) enabled the disponer to spread the capital sum over the instalment period, provided this exceeded eighteen months. Widespread avoidance ensued, especially by means of very long leases with premiums payable by small yearly instalments and a final large instalment near the end of the lease, say in 999 years' time. F.A. 1972 s. 116(1), (2) therefore substituted a new provision for Schedule 6 para 14(1) with effect from 11 April 1972: where payments are to be made over more than eighteen months, the capital gains tax may be paid by such instalments as the Board may allow over a period not exceeding eight years and not longer than the instalment period, but *only if* the disponer satisfies the Board that he would otherwise suffer undue hardship.

In *Coren* v. *Keighley* [1972] 1 W.L.R. 1556 a contract made in 1969 for the sale of a house in Islington for £3,750 provided that on completion the vendor would advance to the purchaser the sum of £2,250 repayable over ten years. The vendor unsuccessfully challenged his assessment for 1968–69 on a chargeable gain of £890 on the ground that the sale was for a consideration payable in instalments, and taxable in each year as a capital gain arose, under Schedule 6 para 14. Ungoed-Thomas J. held that, in the circumstances, the consideration had not been payable by instalments; rather the relationship between vendor and purchaser had, on completion, been extinguished and replaced by that of lender and borrower, so that there were in effect two transactions, not one.

§ 5 "Allowable expenditure"

As explained earlier (pp. 194–5), the chargeable gain or allowable loss on a disposal is arrived at by deducting from the disposal consideration "allowable expenditure", a concept which now falls to be considered and which is exhaustively defined in Schedule 6 para 4(1) as comprising:

(a) The cost of acquisition

This comprises consideration which the disponer or some other person on his behalf gave wholly and exclusively for the acquisition, together with any incidental costs. If the disponer did not acquire but created the asset, he may deduct expenditure wholly and exclusively incurred by him in its creation.

(b) Expenditure after acquisition

Two types of outlay are included in this category. The first is expenditure wholly and exclusively incurred by the disponer or on his behalf for the purpose of enhancing the value of the asset, provided the expenditure is reflected in the state or nature of the asset at the time of the disposal. The second is expenditure wholly and exclusively incurred by the disponer in establishing, preserving, or defending his title to, or to a right over, the asset.

(c) Incidental costs of disposal

Incidental costs, whether of acquisition or disposal, must in general satisfy two criteria. First they must be incurred wholly and exclusively for the purposes of the acquisition or disposal, as the case may be. Second they must take the form either of (a) fees, commission, or remuneration paid for the professional services of any surveyor, valuer, auctioneer, accountant, agent, or legal adviser, or (b) the cost of transfer or conveyance (including stamp duty). However, certain incidental costs are allowable regardless of these criteria, namely:

(a) in the case of the acquisition, the cost of advertising to find a seller; and
(b) in the case of the disposal, the cost of advertising to find a buyer and also any costs reasonably incurred in making any valuation required for purposes of the capital gains tax computation (Schedule 6 para 4(2)).

A legatee, or a person who becomes absolutely entitled to settled property as against the trustees, may deduct, on his disposal of the asset concerned, any expenditure within Schedule 6 para 4(2) incurred by him in connection with its transfer to him by the personal representatives or trustees (ibid. para 16(2)).

The statute disallows a number of items that might otherwise fall within Schedule 6 para 4(1):

(1) Any expenditure allowable in computing trading, or other income, for income tax or corporation tax purposes (Schedule 6 para 5(1)).

(2) Expenditure of a revenue nature (ibid. para 5(2)).

(3) Premiums or other payments made under a policy of insurance against the risk of any kind of damage to, or loss or depreciation of, the asset (ibid. para 12).

(4) Contingent liabilities that may be enforced against the disponer after the disposal in one of three situations:

(a) An assignment of a lease of land or other property under which the assignor retains a liability in the event of default by the assignee. (An assignor normally remains liable to his immediate lessor for breaches of covenant by his or subsequent assignees.)

(b) A disposal of land by a vendor or lessor after which he remains liable for breaches of any covenants for quiet enjoyment or the like.

(c) A sale or lease of property other than land after which the seller or lessor remains liable on his warranties or representations. (A seller of goods is liable for breaches of the implied terms as to title, fitness, merchantability, etc, contained in ss. 12 to 15 of the Sale of Goods Act 1893 as amended by the Supply of Goods (Implied Terms) Act 1973 (ibid. para 15(1)).

These contingent liabilities are left out of account altogether. If, however, it is subsequently shown to the satisfaction of the Inspector that any such liability has become enforceable, and is being or has been enforced, an appropriate adjustment will be made (ibid. para 15(2)).

(5) Any expenditure which has been or is to be met out of public money (ibid. para 17).

(6) Any payment of interest (except for interest allowed under TA s. 269 as charged to capital by a company in the *Chancery Lane* sort of situation (*see* pp. 133–4 above) (ibid. para 4(3)).

To round things off, we are cutely apprised by Schedule 6 para 2(1) that no deduction is allowed more than once from any sum or from more than one sum. Two small crumbs of comfort for the taxpayer. The Revenue are apparently prepared to treat as allowable any expenditure on initial repairs to a property (including decorations) if incurred to put the property in a fit state for letting. More significantly, the taxpayer has enjoyed a good run in litigation on the meaning of "allowable expenditure". In *IRC* v. *Chubb's Settlement Trustee* [1971] T.R. 1971 "incidental costs of disposal" was held to include not merely the costs of an actual disposal but also those of a deemed disposal such as on the occasion of a beneficiary's absolute entitlement against his trustee. In *IRC* v. *Richards' Executors* [1971] 1 W.L.R. 571 solicitors' fees incurred by executors in making valuation for estate duty purposes were held to have been expended in establishing their title within Schedule 6 para 4(1)(*b*) (*see* p. 205 above) and were therefore deductible in computing the extent of their liability on subsequently disposing of the assets in the course of administration. The Crown had urged that the fees had been incurred to enable the executors (1) to pay estate duty, and (2) to obtain probate. Their Lordships' rejection of this "dual purpose" argument ('It depends for its success,' commented Lord Guest (ibid. at 582), 'upon a very strict reading of the words of paragraph 4(1)(*b*)') is an important landmark in the current judicial retreat, which we noted at pp. 82–3 and 113–14 above, from the stringency of the earlier income tax decisions on the meaning of "wholly and exclusively" in its various contexts. Over the next few years, the author ventures to predict, the taxpayer can look forward to further successes against the grain of prevailing authority.

§ 6 Part disposals

On a part disposal (as to the meaning of which *see* 3.31 § 1 above) the chargeable gain or allowable loss is arrived at by deducting from the consideration the appropriate proportion of allowable expenditure (Schedule 6 para 7(1)). This is done in two stages. First the total of allowable expenditure on the asset must be divided into two parts, comprising:

(i) expenditure wholly attributable either to the part disposed of or to the part retained; and

(ii) expenditure not wholly attributable to either part.

The second stage is to apportion (ii). Para 7(2) provides us with a formula for doing so. The proportion attributable to the part disposed of is $A/(A + B)$, where A is the amount or value of the consideration for the part disposed and B is the market value of the part retained.

The two stages can be melded into a single formula, as follows:

Chargeable gain or allowable loss on a part disposal =

$$A - \left[E(1) + \left\{ \frac{A}{A+B} \times E(2) \right\} \right],$$

where $E(1)$ is the expenditure wholly attributable to the part disposed of (which always includes any incidental costs of disposal: *see* para 7(1)), and $E(2)$ is the expenditure not wholly attributable to either part.

The need to value the part retained makes the part disposal formula inconvenient in practice. The Revenue are prepared, in the case of part disposal of land, to allow an alternative method of computation. The part disposed of may be treated as a separate asset and any "fair and reasonable" method of apportioning the allowable expenditure may be adopted, e.g. a valuation of the part disposed of at its acquisition date or at 6 April 1965. In the case of quoted shares or securities also, the Revenue do in practice dispense with the part disposal formula (see p. 216 below).

§ 7 Restriction of losses by reference to capital allowances

The fact that an asset qualifies for capital allowances is irrelevant for capital gains tax purposes if a gain accrues on its disposal. In other words, expenditure within Schedule 6 para 4(1) is allowable regardless of whether capital allowances have been given for that expenditure (Schedule 6 para 6(1)).

If, however, there is a loss on disposal of the asset, any expenditure covered by capital allowances must be excluded from the computation (ibid. para 6(2)).

For the purposes of these provisions "capital allowances" are defined as including initial allowances, writing-down allowances, balancing allowances, and renewals allowances as well as similar allowances for expenditure on sea walls or cemeteries (ibid. para 6(4)). Balancing charges must also be taken into account (ibid. para 6(6)).

§ 8 Some special cases

(a) Assets derived from other assets

If and so far as the value of an asset ("A") is derived from another asset ("B") in the same ownership, an appropriate proportion of expenditure allowable under Schedule 6 para 4(1)(a) and (b) (see p. 205 above) must be attributed to A on its disposal; and if B remains in existence the same proportion must be attributed to A on the disposal of B (Schedule 6 para 8). This applies where assets have been merged or divided, or have changed their nature, or where rights over assets have been created or extinguished. One situation of this kind seems to arise where a lessee acquires the freehold or leasehold reversion to his lease. The value of the reversion would then derive in part from the former lease and, presumably, the appropriate proportion of any allowable expenditure in respect of the lease attributable to the reversion would normally be the whole. See [1972] B.T.R. 4-5 (P.L.).

No method of apportionment is specified in para 8, so that we are forced back on the residual provision that an apportionment for capital gains tax purposes is to be made in the manner that appears to the Inspector or, on appeal, to the Commissioners to be just and reasonable (Schedule 6 para 21(4)).

(b) Wasting assets

Schedule 6 paras 9 to 11 contain special rules for determining the chargeable gain or allowable loss accruing on a disposal of a wasting asset, defined in para 9(1) as 'an asset with a predictable life not exceeding fifty years'. The overall effect of these provisions is to exclude a proportion of allowable expenditure from the computation on the assumption that a wasting asset depreciates evenly by equal daily amounts throughout its useful life.

Paras 9 to 11 do not apply to:

(a) leases (which are governed by a separate set of rules considered at pp. 211–14 below);

(b) wasting chattels disposed of after 19 March 1968 (which are exempted from capital gains tax: see p. 236 below); or

(c) assets which have qualified in full for capital allowances (which are governed by the rules in para 6: see p. 208 above. Where an asset has qualified in part but not in full for capital allowances, both the allowable expenditure and the disposal consideration must be apportioned. The portions relating to the part that has qualified are then dealt with under para 6, while the other portions are dealt with under paras 9 to 11).

Plant or machinery is always to be regarded as having a predictable life of less than fifty years and in estimating that life it must be assumed that the plant or machinery will be used throughout its life in the normal manner and to the normal extent (para 9(1)(d)). On the other hand, freehold land and buildings are not wasting assets (para 9(1)(a)); nor is a life interest in settled property until the predictable life expectancy of the life tenant—ascertained from actuarial tables approved by the Board—is fifty years or less (para 9(1)(e)).

The basic rule, contained in para 10(1), is that on disposal of a wasting asset allowable expenditure must be reduced on the assumptions:

(a) that expenditure falling within para 4(1)(a) (see p. 205 above), after deducting any residual or scrap value, wastes away to nothing over the predictable life of the asset; and

(b) that expenditure falling within para 4(1)(b) (see p. 205 above) wastes away to nothing between the time when the expenditure is first reflected in the state or nature of the asset and the end of its predictable life.

The residual or scrap value of an asset is the predictable value, if any, which the asset will have at the end of its predictable life, which, in the case of plant or machinery, will come when it is finally put out of use as being unfit for further use (para 9(2), (1)(d)). Predictions must be made in the light of facts known or ascertainable at the time when the asset was acquired by the disponer (para 9(3)).

Para 10(2) obligingly provides two formulae for effectuating the basic rule set out in the preceding paragraph but one:

(a) The proportion of para 4(1)(a) expenditure to be excluded is $T(1)L$, where $T(1)$ is the period of ownership of the asset and L is its predictable life; and

(b) The proportion of para 4(1)(b) expenditure to be excluded is
$L - \dfrac{T(2)}{[T(1) - T(2)]}$, where $T(2)$ is the period between the time when the
para 4(1)(b) expenditure was first reflected in the state or nature of the asset and the time of disposal.

If para 4(1)(b) expenditure increases the scrap value of the asset, this must be taken into account under para 10(1)(a), set out in the preceding paragraph but one (para 10(3)); and if the asset is not a wasting asset at the time of acquisition, or of incurring expenditure, the periods taken into account are those commencing from the time when the asset became a wasting asset.

Example 5

In 1970 Peter Dowt, a tailor, bought a machine for making belts and cummerbunds (a wasting asset) for £4,800 incurring incidental costs of £200. Its predictable life was then 20 years and its predictable scrap value £920. In 1978 he spent £900 on improvements to the machine (which were immediately, and have continued since to be, reflected in the state of the machine), thereby increasing its scrap value by £80. In 1982 he sold the machine for £9,000, incurring £400 in incidental costs.

Peter's chargeable gain is computed as follows:

Disposal consideration		£9,000
Deduct: cost of acquisition	£5,000	
Less: proportion excluded		

$$= \frac{T(1)}{L} \times (\text{cost} - \textit{revised} \text{ scrap value})$$

$$= \frac{12}{20} \times (\pounds5,000 - \pounds1,000) \qquad\qquad \pounds2,400 \quad \pounds2,600$$

Deduct: enhancement expenditure   £900
Less: proportion excluded

$$= \frac{T(2)}{L - [T(1) - T(2)]} \times £900$$

$$= \frac{4}{20 - (12 - 4)} \times £900 \qquad\qquad £300 \quad £600$$

Deduct: incidental costs of disposal   £400   £3,600

Chargeable gain   £5,400

(c) Short leases

A lease having fifty years or less to run (a "short" lease) is a wasting asset. A lease with more than fifty years to run becomes a wasting asset from the time it has fifty years to run. Nevertheless short leases are governed not by the special rules for wasting assets but by an even more specialized set of provisions contained in Schedule 8 and F.A. 1968 Schedule 12 para 7, which give rise to some of the trickiest of capital gains tax computations.

The basic assumption: curved-line depreciation

On the disposal of a short lease acquisition and enhancement expenditure is deemed to waste, not on a straight-line basis as with other wasting assets, but on a curved-line basis. The rate of wastage is prescribed in a table contained in Schedule 8 para 1; it is slow when the lease has almost fifty years to run but becomes progressively quicker as the end of the term approaches. Here is an extract from the table:

Years	*Percentage*
50 (or more)	100
49	99·657
48	99·289
47	98·902
..	......
..	......
40	95·457
..	......
..	......
30	87·330
..	......
..	......

Years	Percentage
20	72·770
..	......
..	......
10	46·695
..	......
..	......
3	16·959
2	11·629
1	5·983
0	0

Between any two points next to each other in the table the rate of wastage follows a straight line month by month. For this purpose fourteen days or more count as a full month.

The table is used in conjunction with formulae contained in Schedule 8 para 1(4) which exclude:

(a) from expenditure within Schedule 6 para 4(1)(a) (*see* p. 205 above) a fraction equal to $\dfrac{P(1) - P(3)}{P(1)}$; and

(b) from expenditure within Schedule 6 para 4(1)(b) (*see* p. 205 above) a fraction equal to $\dfrac{P(2) - P(3)}{P(2)}$,

where P is the percentage derived from the table for the duration of the lease (1) at the beginning of the period of ownership, (2) at the time when any item of para 4(1)(b) expenditure was first reflected in the nature of the lease, and (3) at the time of disposal.

Sub-leases out of short leases

Granting a lease constitutes a part disposal. If the lease is granted out of a freehold the normal part disposal rules apply, but if out of a short lease the normal part disposal rules are displaced by provisions contained in Schedule 8 para 4(2) which restrict the allowable acquisition and enhancement expenditure to the proportion attributable to the period of the sub-lease. Had the draftsmen supplied us with formulae, which they did not, para 4(1)(a) and para 4(1)(b) expenditure would probably have been reduced to the fractions $\dfrac{P(3) - P(4)}{P(1)}$ and $\dfrac{P(3) - P(4)}{P(2)}$ respectively, where $P(4)$ is the percentage derived from the table for the duration of the lease at the time when the sub-lease comes to an end.

The acquisition and enhancement expenditure has to be scaled down yet further in cases where a sub-lease is granted at a rent higher than the grantor is himself paying and where therefore the grantor takes a smaller premium than if the rent he charged were the same as the rent he paid. After applying the two formulae in the preceding paragraph, the resultant reduced amounts of para 4(1)(a) and para 4(1)(b) expenditure must be reduced further to the fraction A/B, where A is the premium received and B is the premium that would have been received had the rents been the same.

Lease premiums

A person who takes a premium on granting a short lease is treated as receiving in each year of that lease an amount of rent (additional to any actual rent) equal to the premium reduced by one-fiftieth for each complete year (less one) of the short lease granted (*see* pp. 152–3 above). If the premium is payable to the grantor himself, he is charged under Schedule A (TA s. 80(1)), if to a person other than the grantor, that person is charged under Case VI (ibid. s. 80(5)).

Any element of double taxation is scrupulously avoided by omitting from any capital gains tax computation the portion of the premium chargeable to income tax. This result is achieved by rules which vary according to whether the lease is granted out of (a) a freehold or long lease, or (b) another short lease.

On the grant of a short lease out of a freehold or long lease, the normal part disposal rules apply. Any part of the premium chargeable under Schedule A or Case VI is excluded:

(i) from the disposal consideration (F.A. 1967 Schedule 13 para 8); and
(ii) from the consideration in the numerator of the part disposal fraction (Schedule 8 para 5(1)).

The part disposal formula becomes:

Chargeable gain or allowable loss =

$$(A - X) - \left[E(1) + \frac{A}{A\,B} \times E(2) \right],$$

where X is the part of the premium chargeable under Schedule A or Case VI and A, B, $E(1)$, and $E(2)$ are as stated at p. 207 above.

On the grant of a sub-lease out of a short lease, the chargeable gain or allowable loss must first be arrived at by applying the rules contained in Schedule 8 para 4(2) (*see* p. 212 above). The part of any premium chargeable under Schedule A or Case VI may then be deducted from the chargeable gain, if there is one, but cannot create a loss, nor, if there is an allowable loss, can it be used to increase that loss.

Leases of property other than land

The above provisions, apart from those applicable to the assignment of short leases and to lease premiums, govern leases of property other than land as well as leases of land, subject to any necessary modifications (Schedule 8 para 9(1)).

Duration of leases

Since 1968 the capital gains tax rules for determining the duration of a lease, whether of land or of property other than land, have differed from those used for purposes of Schedule A (*see* 2.74 § 3 above). The capital gains tax rules are these (four are to be found in F.A. 1968 Schedule 12 para 7 and the fifth in Schedule 8 para 9(3)):

(1) where the terms of the lease include provision for the determination of the lease by notice given by the landlord, the lease is treated as granted for a term not longer than one ending at the earliest date on which it could be determined by notice given by the landlord;

(2) where any of the terms of the lease or any other circumstances render it unlikely that the lease will continue beyond a date falling before the expiration of the term of the lease, the lease is treated as having been granted for a term not longer than one ending on that date;

(3) where the terms of the lease include provision for the extension of the lease beyond a given date by notice given by the tenant, the term of the lease is treated as extending for as long as it could be extended by the tenant, subject to any right of the landlord by notice to determine the lease;

(4) duration is decided by reference to facts known or ascertainable at the time when the lease was acquired or created; and

(5) the lease of a wasting asset which is movable property is treated as terminating not later than the end of its predictable life.

(*d*) Transfer of business to a company

There are special provisions, contained in F.A. 1969 Schedule 19 para 15, designed to enable a person to incorporate his business without incurring liability to capital gains tax. This result is achieved by a rather complicated "roll-over" rule. Where a person who is not a company transfers to a company a business as a going concern, together with the whole of its assets (but not necessarily the cash), wholly or partly in exchange for shares, the net aggregate amount of chargeable gains accruing to that person on the transfer must be reduced by the lower of:

(a) the cost price of the shares issued to the transferor; or
(b) the proportion of the aggregate net gains that (a) bears to the total consideration for the transfer (ibid. para 15(1), (2), (4)).

When the transferor ultimately disposes of the shares issued to him, the amount allowed as a deduction in the capital gains tax computation must be reduced by the amount by which the net chargeable gains on the transfer of assets were reduced, or, on a part disposal of the shares, by the proportionate amount of that reduction (ibid. para 15(3)).

(e) Shares, securities, or commodities

Shares of the same class held by one person in one capacity are regarded as indistinguishable parts of a single asset, known as a "holding" or "pool", growing or diminishing on the occasions on which additional shares of the class in question are acquired, or some of the shares of the class in question are disposed of (Schedule 7 para 2(1)). This *grundnorm*, and the consequences which flow from it, apply not merely to shares but to all assets of a nature to be dealt in without identifying the particular assets disposed of or acquired, such as debentures or commodity futures (ibid. para 2(7)). The term "shares" includes units in an authorized unit trust scheme (s. 45(8)). Shares are of the same class if they are treated as belonging to the same class by the practice of a recognized Stock Exchange or would be so treated if dealt with on such an Exchange (Schedule 7 para 2 (3)).

Shares held in different capacities are not part of the same holding: shares held, say, as trustee would constitute a holding separate from any shares of the same class held beneficially. Schedule 7 para 2(5) requires that shares held by a person to whom they were issued as an employee on terms which restrict his right to dispose of them must be treated as held by that person in a capacity different from that in which he holds other shares of the same class. The result is that shares issued to a person *qua* employee on restrictive terms form a separate pool of "clogged" shares while the restriction remains in force. Once the restriction comes to an end the clogged shares are pooled with any other shares of the same class held by the employee or ex-employee.

It follows that a disposal of shares in a holding is regarded as a part disposal unless it is a disposal of the entire holding (Schedule 7 para 2(2)).

Strictly, therefore, the part disposal formula should be used in apportioning any allowable expenditure (*see* p. 207 above). However, since the formula involves the inconvenience of valuing shares remaining in the pool, it is common practice simply to treat the cost of acquisition as averaged out over the holding.

There are two special rules which derogate from Schedule 7 para 2. Firstly, F.A. 1971 Schedule 10 para 6 makes provision for the situation where a person acquires and disposes of securities on the same day and in the same capacity. All securities acquired on the same day are treated as acquired by a single transaction and all securities disposed of on the same day are treated as disposed of by a single transaction. The securities so disposed of, as far as possible, are identified with (i.e. are deemed to be) the securities so acquired.

The second set of special rules deals with the situation where a holder of shares or securities finds himself, as a result of some form of company reorganization, with a partly or entirely new holding. This situation can arise in various ways:

(*a*) On a reorganization of share capital, e.g. when a company makes a rights (= to be paid for) or bonus (= gratis) issue of shares or debentures in proportion to existing holdings.

(*b*) On a reduction of share capital (other than by paying off redeemable capital), perhaps by altering the rights attaching to shares of a particular class.

(*c*) On a conversion of securities. "Conversion" includes exchanges of shares or securities for others as well as the conversion of a company's securities into shares; and "securities" includes any secured or unsecured loan stock of a government or public authority as well as of any company.

(*d*) On an exchange of shares or debentures in one company for those in another in connection with a take-over.

(*e*) Under a scheme for the reconstruction of a company or companies or for the amalgamation of one company with another.

The governing principle in all these circumstances is that the new holding is to be regarded as having been acquired at the same time and for the same consideration as the old holding. The holder is treated as having neither disposed of his original holding nor acquired the new holding but as retaining the same asset he had before (Schedule 7 para 4(2)).

Any consideration which the holder gives or becomes liable to give is treated as having been given for the original holding (Schedule 7 para 4(3)). Conversely, if the holder receives or becomes entitled to receive any consideration other than the new holding, such as a capital distribution, or a cash payment by a company effecting a take-over, he is treated as having made a part disposal of his original holding (ibid. paras 3(1) and 4(4)). More particularly, where the holder in the case of a rights issue receives or becomes entitled to receive a provisional allotment of shares, and he disposes of his rights, any consideration he receives must be treated as a capital distribution (F.A. 1966 Schedule 10 para 8). As to capital distributions, *see* 3.31 § 6 above; and notice that F.A. 1967 Schedule 13 para 4(2) contains the same rule where a sum received in addition to the new holding on a conversion of securities is small as is applied to small distributions by Schedule 7 para 3(2), set out on p. 189 above.

(f) Options

An option is a chargeable asset (s. 22(1)(*a*)) governed by special rules contained in Schedule 7 para 14, which apply to options of all kinds, whether binding the grantor to sell, to buy, or to enter into any other transaction (sub-para (7)).

The grant of an option that is not exercised (i.e. is abandoned) constitutes a disposal by the grantor (sub-para (1)), though the abandonment of an option (except of the two types mentioned in the ensuing paragraph) does not constitute a disposal by the grantee (sub-para (3)). A forfeited deposit of purchase money for a transaction which is abandoned is treated as equivalent to a consideration for an option which is not exercised (sub-para (8)); and may therefore give rise to a chargeable gain in the hands of the person receiving it. If an option is exercised, both the option and its exercise are treated as a single transaction in which:

(*a*) if it is an option binding the grantor to sell, the grantor treats the option consideration as part of the sale consideration (sub-para (2)(*a*)), while the grantee treats the cost of the option as part of the cost of acquiring what is sold (sub-para (3)(*a*)); and

(*b*) if it is an option binding the grantor to buy, the grantor deducts the option consideration from the cost of acquiring what is bought (sub-para (2)(*b*)), while the grantee deducts the cost of the option as an incidental cost of disposal (sub-para (3)(*b*)).

In the case of a double option, binding the grantor both to sell and to buy, the option consideration is divided equally and the rules apply as if there were two separate options (sub-para (6)).

F.A. 1971 s. 58(1), (2) provides, by way of exception, that there *is* a disposal on abandonment after 19 April 1971 of:

(*a*) an option to subscribe for shares in a company, or
(*b*) an option to acquire assets intended for use in a trade carried on by the grantee.

In practice, by far the most numerous species of option are those dealt in on Stock Exchanges as though they were shares, i.e. "call" options (which bind the grantor to sell quoted shares or securities) and "put" options (which bind him to buy them). A put or call option is—quite illogically—treated as a wasting asset, the life of which ends when the right to exercise it ceases, or when the option becomes valueless, whichever is the earlier (sub-para (4)). (Note that options to *subscribe* for shares, discussed in the preceding paragraph, are not normally dealt in on Exchanges.)

(*g*) Appropriations to and from stock-in-trade

Where an asset acquired by a person otherwise than as trading stock is appropriated by the trader for the purposes of his trade, he is treated as having sold the asset for its market value (Schedule 7 para 1(1)). The trader may, however, elect that the market value at the time of appropriation be treated, in computing his trading profits, as reduced by the amount of any chargeable gain or allowable loss accruing on the notional disposal (ibid. para 1(3), as restricted by F.A. 1969 Schedule 19 para 14). The effect of such an election is to avoid any immediate charge to capital gains tax, but on the subsequent sale of the asset or cessation of the trade any profit or loss will be included in the computation of trading profits.

Conversely, if at any time an asset forming part of trading stock is appropriated by the trader for any other purpose, or is retained by him on his ceasing to carry on the trade, he is treated as having acquired it at that time for a consideration equal to the amount brought into the accounts of the trade in respect of it for tax purposes (Schedule 7 para 1(2), as amended by F.A. 1969 Schedule 19 para 14).

Schedule 7 para 1(1) applies only if, had the trader sold the asset at the time of appropriation for its then market value, a chargeable gain or allowable loss would have accrued to him. The provision therefore does not apply where the asset is tangible movable property and either (*a*) its market value is £1,000 or less, or (*b*) it is a wasting asset. As we shall see later (pp. 235–6 below), a gain accruing on the disposal of tangible movable property which falls within (*a*) or (*b*) is not a chargeable gain.

(B) THE SPECIAL RULES FOR ASSETS HELD ON 6 APRIL 1965

§ 1 The general principle: straight-line time apportionment

Capital gains tax was not intended to operate retroactively. 'On the disposal of assets by a person whose period of ownership began before 6 April 1965,' Schedule 6 para 24(2) assures us, 'only so much of any gain accruing on the disposal as is . . . to be apportioned to the period beginning with 6 April 1965 shall be a chargeable gain'. Unfortunately, the architects of the 1965 Act, being legislatively but not actually omnipotent, could accurately effectuate this rule only by requiring all chargeable assets to be valued on 6 April 1965, clearly a practical impossibility. They were forced therefore—except in the case of quoted shares or securities and land reflecting development value—to rely on the assumption that the gain or loss on disposal after 6 April 1965 had accrued at a uniform rate from nothing at the beginning of the period of ownership to its full amount at the time of disposal; or, in other words, that the fraction of the gain or loss which represents the chargeable gain, or allowable loss, as the case may be is, $T/(P + 1)$, where, of the full period of ownership, T is the portion from 6 April 1965 and P is the portion before that date (ibid. para 24(3)). P is limited to a maximum of twenty years (ibid. para 24(6)).

A more complicated time apportionment formula is called for where one or more items of additional expenditure within Schedule 6 para 4(1)(b) (*see* p. 205 above) have been incurred on an asset held on 6 April 1965:

Chargeable gain or allowable loss =

$$E(0)\frac{T}{P + T} + E(1)\frac{T}{P(1) + T} + E(2)\frac{T}{P(2) + T} \text{ and so on,}$$

where P = period of ownership before 6 April 1965 (up to a maximum of twenty years),

$P(1)$ = period of ownership from the time when the first item of additional expenditure was reflected in the value of the asset until 6 April 1965 (up to a maximum of twenty years),

$P(2)$ = as for $P(1)$, substituting "second" for "first",

and so on; and

$E(0)$ = proportion of whole gain attributable to the original expenditure

i.e. $\left(\dfrac{\text{original expenditure}}{\text{total allowable expenditure}} \times \text{whole gain}\right)$,

$E(1)$ = proportion of whole gain attributable to the first item of additional expenditure

i.e. $\left(\dfrac{\text{first item of expenditure}}{\text{total allowable expenditure}} \times \text{whole gain} \right)$,

$E(2)$ = as for $E(1)$, substituting "second" for "first",

and so on; and

T = period of ownership from 6 April 1965.

The disponer is given the right to elect that the computation be made by reference to the value of the asset on 6 April 1965 rather than under the time apportionment rules, in which case the asset will be treated as having been disposed of and immediately re-acquired by him at market value on 6 April 1965 (ibid. para 25(1)). The election—which is irrevocable (ibid. para 25(3))—must be made by notice in writing to the Inspector within two years of the end of the year of assessment (or, in the case of a company, the accounting period) in which the disposal was made or such further period as the Board may by notice in writing allow (F.A. 1968 Schedule 12 para 5(1)). Thus the disponer would normally elect for a 6 April 1965 valuation where that would yield a smaller gain than the time apportionment rules. On the other hand, where the 6 April 1965 valuation would yield a greater loss, he can claim only the smaller loss under the time apportionment rules; and if there is a gain one way and a loss the other —whichever way—the disposal is treated as giving rise to neither gain nor loss (Schedule 6 para 25(2)). An election cannot be made in relation to an asset which has been valued since 6 April 1965 for purposes of a part disposal apportionment (ibid. para 25(4)). Thus in effect an election can be made only on the first disposal or part disposal after 6 April 1965; if not made then, it cannot subsequently be made in relation to that asset and, once made, binds all subsequent part disposals of the same asset.

Unquoted shares held on 6 April 1965 are not pooled (ibid. para 26(2)). Instead, on disposals after 5 April 1965, unquoted shares held on 6 April 1965 are identified on a f.i.f.o. basis (first in, first out) with unquoted shares of the same class acquired before 6 April 1965 (ibid. para 26(3)). The chargeable gain or allowable loss is then computed in the usual way, i.e. by applying the time apportionment rules, unless the disponer elects for a 6 April 1965 valuation.

Example 6

Hunter Divi buys and sells the following shares in U.R. Nuts Ltd:

Purchases:	1952	100
	1957	300
	1962	500
	1967	700
	1972	900
Sales:	1966	200
	1970	400
	1974	600

The 200 shares sold in 1966 are identified with 100 bought in 1952 and 100 of the shares bought in 1957. The 400 shares sold in 1970 are identified with the remaining 200 bought in 1957 and 200 of the shares bought in 1962. The 600 shares sold in 1974 are identified with the remaining 300 bought in 1962 and 300 of the pool of 1,600 acquired after 5 April 1965.

§ 2 **An exception: quoted shares or securities**

The assumption of uniformity referred to on p. 219 above is unnecessary in the case of quoted securities held on 6 April 1965, for which the general rule is that they should be notionally sold and re-acquired by their owners at that date at market value (ibid. para 22(2)); as to market value, *see* 3.34 § 2 above). "Quoted securities" means shares or securities quoted on a recognized UK Exchange on, or at any time during the six years before, 6 April 1965: and units in any authorized unit trust scheme whose prices are published daily by the managers (ibid. para 22(1)). The general rule does not apply, however, where it would result in (*a*) a greater gain than the actual gain, or (*b*) a greater loss than the actual loss, or (*c*) where there would be a gain one way and a loss the other. In the case of (*a*) or (*b*), the computation is based on the actual expenditure incurred rather than on market value; and in the case of (*c*) the disposal is deemed to give rise to neither gain nor loss (ibid. para 22(4)). It seems fair that, if the disponer is to be taxed on the smaller gain, the Revenue should be able to restrict him to the smaller loss. This is an illusion: in practice the holder of quoted securities who wishes to displace a 6 April 1965 valuation must go to the trouble and expense of searching his records (if he has kept any) for years when capital gains tax was not so much as a twinkle in the Chancellor's eye. A measure of relief has been given him by F.A. 1968 Schedule II para 1. On a disposal after 19 March 1968 of quoted securities held on 6 April 1965 the disponer may irrevocably elect that they be treated as acquired on 6 April 1965 at market value. Although made on the occasion of a disposal, the election must cover either:

(a) *all* his fixed-interest securities and preference shares; or
(b) *all* his other securities (ordinary shares, unit trusts, etc), or both (ibid. para 1(3)).

An election covering shares held in one capacity, e.g. beneficially, does not extend to shares held in another, e.g. as trustee (ibid. para 1(5)); and must be made within the same time limit after the first relevant disposal as an election under Schedule 6 para 25(1) (*see* p. 220 above) (ibid. para 1(6)). The election does not cover disposals between husband and wife or between members of a group of companies unless the transferor has actually made an election covering securities of that class (ibid. para 1(4)). An election for companies in a group must be made by the principal company of the group (ibid. para. 2).

It follows that there are two sets of rules for computing the chargeable gain or allowable loss in respect of disposals after 19 March 1968 of quoted shares or securities held on 6 April 1965:

(a) Where the securities disposed of are not covered by an election under F.A. 1968

Where the securities disposed of were acquired at different times, they are identified with securities of the same class acquired before 6 April 1965 on the basis of f.i.f.o. (first in, first out) (Schedule 6 para 22(6)), while securities of the same class acquired on or after 6 April 1965 are pooled (*see* p. 215 above). It is then necessary to make two separate computations, one using 6 April 1965 value as the cost of acquisition, the other using the actual cost of acquisition. If there is a gain both ways, or a loss both ways, only the smaller gain is chargeable or the smaller loss allowable; and if there is a gain one way and a loss the other, a nil assessment results on the basis of no gain no loss.

Example 7

Hunter Divi buys the following ordinary shares in U.R. Mugs Ltd:

1960	100 shares for £200
1962	200 shares for £500
1964	300 shares for £900
1966	400 shares for £1,400

Their market value on 6 April 1965 was £3.25 a share.

In 1970 Hunter sold 500 of the shares for £3,000 and in 1973 sold a further 400 for £3,200.

The capital gains tax computation in respect of the 1970 disposal is as follows:

(a) On the basis of the actual acquisition cost:

Disposal consideration	£3,000
Deduct: cost of acquisition (identifying on a f.i.f.o. basis)	£1,300
Chargeable gain	£1,700

(b) On the basis of the 6 April 1965 value:

Disposal consideration	£3,000
Deduct: cost of acquisition	£1,625
Chargeable gain	£1,375

The chargeable gain is therefore £1,375.

On the 1973 disposal, the computation is as follows (using the averaging method, not the part disposal formula: *see* p. 216 above):

(a) On the basis of the actual acquisition cost:

Disposal consideration	£3,200
Deduct: cost of acquisition	
= £300 (remaining 100 shares acquired in 1964) + £1,050 (300 of the shares acquired in 1966 at average cost of £3.50)	£1,350
Chargeable gain	£1,850

(b) On the basis of the 6 April 1965 value:

Disposal consideration	£3,200
Deduct: cost of acquisition	
= £325 (remaining 100 shares at 6 April 1965 value) + £1,050	£1,375
Chargeable gain	£1,825

The chargeable gain is therefore £1,825.

(b) Where the securities disposed of are covered by an election

The computation is simply made on the basis that the acquisition cost of securities acquired before 6 April 1965 is their market value at that date.

All securities of the same class, whether acquired before or after 6 April 1965, are pooled in the normal manner.

Thus, returning to Example 7, were Hunter Divi to make an election under F.A. 1968 Schedule II para 1, the capital gains tax computation on the 1970 disposal would look like this (again using the averaging method rather than the part disposal formula):

Disposal consideration £3,000

Deduct: cost of acquisition (no. of shares × average cost per share)

$$= 500 \times \frac{£3,500 \ (600 \ @ \ £3 \cdot 25 \ \text{per share} + £1,400}{1,000 \ (\text{total no. of shares in pool})} \qquad £1,675$$

Chargeable gain £1,325

On the 1972 disposal the computation would be:

Disposal consideration £3,200

Deduct: cost of acquisition

$= 400 \times £3 \cdot 35$ £1,340

Chargeable gain £1,860

§ 3 A second exception: land reflecting development value

A set of provisions similar to those governing quoted shares or securities held on 6 April 1965 is applicable to disposal of land in the UK reflecting development value owned on that date. The owner is deemed to have acquired the land at its market value on 6 April 1965 (Schedule 6 para 23(2)), unless this would result in a larger gain or a larger loss than actually accrued (ibid. para 23(4)). If the 6 April 1965 value yields a gain where there is actually a loss, or a loss where there is actually a gain, the disponer is treated as having made neither gain nor loss (ibid. para 23(4)). These provisions required modification, in the case of disposals between 6 April 1967 and 22 July 1970, to take account of betterment levy (*see* pp. 19, 185–6 above).

(c) LOSSES

The rules for losses are plain and simple. S. 23(1) provides that: 'The amount of a loss accruing on a disposal of an asset shall be computed in the same way as the amount of a gain accruing on a disposal is computed', to which s. 23(2) adds the complementary proposition that a loss is allowable if a gain similarly computed would have been chargeable. It follows that: 'A loss accruing to a person in a year of assessment during no part of which he is resident or ordinarily resident in the United Kingdom shall not be an allowable loss' unless the corresponding gain accruing to him would have been chargeable under s. 20(2) (*see* p. 190 above).

The net allowable loss (as to which, *see* p. 186 above) for a year of assessment from 1956–66 onwards may be carried forward and set against net chargeable gains of subsequent years indefinitely (s. 20(4)). It cannot be carried back (except in one situation: *see* p. 228 below). Nor, up to 1970–71, could the loss be set against short-term gains. Furthermore, a loss is not available against gains accruing to a non-resident individual, nor to a trustee or personal representative, nor accruing on a disposal of assets acquired less than two years before disposal from a connected person (s. 21(5): *see* pp. 226–7 below). In the case of a husband and wife living together, the net allowable loss of one may be set against the net chargeable gains of the other for that year of assessment (s. 20(5)), unless either spouse elects, by application to the Inspector before the following 6 July, that s. 20(5) should not apply (s. 20(5) proviso).

A loss accruing on the disposal of an asset to a connected person is deductible only from a chargeable gain accruing to the disponer on a subsequent disposal to the same connected person (Schedule 7 para 17(3)), unless the disposal was:

(1) made after 5 April 1969,
(2) by way of gift in settlement,
(3) of an asset, or of income from an asset, which is (*a*) wholly or primarily applicable for educational, cultural or recreational purposes, (*b*) for persons who are members of an association for whose benefit the gift was made, and (*c*) most of whom are not connected persons in relation to the settlor (Schedule 7 para 17(3) proviso, added by F.A. 1969 Schedule 19 para 12).

A loss on the disposal of an option acquired from a connected person is an allowable loss only if it is disposed of at arm's length to a non-connected person (Schedule 7 para 17(4)).

3.35 THE RATE OF CHARGE

§ 1 Normal basis

Capital gains tax is normally levied on the net chargeable gains of a year of assessment (as to which, *see* p. 186 above) at a flat rate of 30% (s. 20(3)).

§ 2 Alternative basis

There is, however, an "alternative basis of charge"—known as "the half-income rule"—for individuals resident or ordinarily resident in the UK. The alternative basis, enacted in s. 21, takes effect only if its application reduces the amount of tax payable on the normal basis. There is no need for the taxpayer to claim or make an election for the alternative basis, since only the smaller of the two amounts is legally chargeable.

The half-income rule operates in two stages. First, the amount of the chargeable gains is reduced:

(a) if it does not exceed £5,000, by one-half; and

(b) if it does exceed £5,000, to £2,500 plus the excess over £5,000,

and second, the reduced amount is subjected to income tax under Case VI of Schedule D. If the resultant amount of tax payable is less than would have been paid at the normal rate of 30%, then the taxpayer is charged in the lesser amount (s. 21(1)).

The assumptions made about the reduced amount are that:

(1) It is the top slice of the individual's income.

(2) It is unearned income.

(3) It is available for person reliefs (except life assurance relief), but not for any other reliefs.

(4) It is not available for set-off against any loss, or against any payments (e.g. annual payments) which may be made out of profits or gains brought into charge for tax (s. 22(2)).

The half-income rule does not apply:

(1) to an individual neither resident nor ordinarily resident in the UK;

(2) to a company;

(3) to a trustee or personal representative; or

(4) to an individual whose chargeable gains accrue from the disposal of an asset acquired (otherwise than as legatee) less than two years before the disposal from a connected person (s. 21(5): for the definition of connected persons, see pp. 193–4 above).

These exclusions are especially significant in relation to the rule that a loss —whether the net allowable loss of a particular year of assessment or an unallowed loss carried forward from some previous year—can only be set against gains that would qualify for the alternative basis (s. 21(5)). The object of this rule is to prevent the exploitation of the alternative basis by means of arrangements under which gains would be made to accrue in the hands of connected persons having small or moderate means and therefore in a position to obtain the maximum benefit.

It should be appreciated that the taxpayer is not entitled to have *some* of his gains during the year of assessment taxed on the alternative basis and the others at 30%. Only the net chargeable gains of a year of assessment are assessable on the alternative basis, if that proves more favourable than the normal rate. Clearly the alternative basis will tend in practice to favour those with small incomes and small gains: it is equivalent, for an individual liable at basic rate only whose gains do not exceed £5,000, to a flat rate of 15% (half the basic rate).

Husband and wife

The half-income rule requires modification in the case of a husband and wife living together to take account of the fact that the wife's gains are assessed and charged on her husband (*see* pp. 192-3 above). Where the wife has chargeable gains but the husband does not, her gains are treated as the top slice of the joint income. If both have chargeable gains, the gains are aggregated and treated as the top slice of the joint income: any reduction in tax on the alternative basis is then apportioned between husband and wife in proportion to the respective amounts of their gains (s. 21(4)).

Unit and investment trusts

Until 1 April 1972 the tax treatment of unit and investment trusts was rather clumsy and inequitable. The rate of tax on gains accruing to unit and investment trusts was 30%. To prevent double taxation in the hands both of the trust and of the unit holder the gains of the trust (less tax) were apportioned each year between the unit holders. On ultimate disposal of the units a unit holder was entitled to deduct from the disposal consideration any amount apportioned to him during his period of ownership. The result was that a unit holder might pay more capital gains tax than he would have had he managed his own portfolio. F.A. 1972 ss. 112-114 provided that gains realized by an authorized unit trust or approved investment trust should be taxed at the rate of 15%. When the unit holder disposes of his units he is liable to tax but in computing his liability is entitled to a tax credit of 15% of the amount of his chargeable gain. A unit holder to whom the half-income rule applies (whose effective rate of tax is 15%) therefore pays no capital gains tax on disposal of his units.

3.4 Death

On a death before 31 March 1971 the deceased was deemed to have disposed of, and his personal representatives to have acquired, all the assets of which he was competent to dispose at their market value at the date of death (s. 24(1)). Death therefore gave rise to a charge to capital gains tax as well as to estate duty; but double taxation was avoided by allowing any capital gains tax chargeable in consequence of a death to be deducted in valuing the estate for estate duty purposes (s. 26(1), (2)).

On a death after 30 March 1971 assets of which the deceased was competent to dispose are deemed to be acquired by his personal representatives (or other person on whom they devolve) at their market value at the date of death, but *there is no deemed disposal* (s. 24(1), as amended by F.A. 1971 Schedule 12 para 1). Death is no longer a chargeable occasion for capital gains tax purposes. The rule is retained, however, that any net allowable loss of the year of assessment in which a death occurred may be carried back and set against chargeable gains accruing in the three previous years of assessment, taking a later year before an earlier one (s. 24(5)).

If the personal representatives dispose of an asset otherwise than to a legatee, e.g. in order to pay estate duty, they are chargeable on any gains that might accrue; and, moreover, are not entitled to offset their losses against gains of the deceased or of the beneficiaries. On the other hand, if the personal representatives dispose of an asset to a legatee, no chargeable gain accrues to them, although the legatee is treated as if their acquisition of the asset had been his (s. 24(7)). "Legatee" includes 'any person taking under a testamentary disposition or on an intestacy or partial intestacy, whether he takes beneficially or as trustee' (s. 45(1)). When it was provided in F.A. 1971 Schedule 12 para 3 that 'no chargeable gain shall accrue to any person on his making a disposal by way of donatio mortis causa', the s. 45(1) definition required extension. After the words quoted above there was added: 'and a person taking under a donatio mortis causa shall be treated (except for purposes of section 24 of this Act) as a legatee and his acquisition as made at the time of the donor's death' (s. 45(1), as extended by F.A. 1971 Schedule 12 para 4).

3.5 Settled property

"Settled property" is defined in s. 45(1) as 'any property held in trust other than property to which section 22(5) of this Act applies'. S. 22(5), we recall from p. 188 above, applies to assets held by a person as nominee or as bare trustee.

3.51 THE SETTLOR

The creation of a settlement constitutes a disposal of the settled property by the settlor. 'A gift in settlement,' s. 25(2) informs us, 'whether revocable or irrevocable, is a disposal of the entire property thereby becoming settled property notwithstanding that the donor has some interest as a beneficiary ... [or as] ... a trustee.' A settlor and trustee of a settlement fall within the list of connected persons (*see* pp. 193–4 above), from which we are entitled to deduce that the disposal consideration on creation of a settlement is market value at the date of creation.

3.52 THE TRUSTEE

Generally capital gains tax on disposals of settled property is assessed on the trustees, who are excluded from the benefit of the half-income rule and therefore always pay tax at the rate of 30%. All the usual types of disposal are occasions of charge but, in addition, trustees are chargeable on the occasion of *deemed* disposals in two important situations.

The first is clearly set out in s. 25(3): 'On the occasion when a person becomes absolutely entitled to any settled property as against the trustee all the assets forming part of the settled property to which he becomes so entitled shall be deemed to have been disposed of by the trustee, and immediately re-acquired by him in his capacity as a trustee within section 22(5) of this Act [*see* p. 188 above], for a consideration equal to their market value.' Thereafter the trustee's acts are treated as acts of the beneficiary (s. 22(5)), so that on any subsequent disposal of the assets by the trustee only the beneficiary will be chargeable.

When a trustee transfers an asset to a beneficiary absolutely entitled to settled property, any allowable loss in respect of the asset transferred, or in respect of the asset from which it derived (e.g. if the bare trustee sells one asset at a loss, buys another with the proceeds, and transfers that asset to the beneficiary), is treated as if it were an allowable loss accruing to the beneficiary at the time of becoming absolutely entitled—provided the trustee is unable to deduct the loss from chargeable gains accruing to him in the year of assessment in which the beneficiary became absolutely entitled (s. 25(8)). (The trustee then loses the right to use the loss.) It is immaterial whether the loss accrued in the year of absolute entitlement or was carried forward from a previous year.

If tax assessed on trustees in respect of a chargeable gain accruing to them is not paid within six months of the due date, and the asset in respect of which the chargeable gain accrued, or any part of the proceeds of sale, is transferred by the trustee to a person absolutely entitled as against the trustees to it, that person may be assessed and charged in the name of the trustees (s. 25(9)). The assessment must be made within two years of the time when the tax became payable by the trustees and is limited in amount to the chargeable gain which accrued to the trustees or, if part only of the assets or the proceeds was transferred, to the proportionate part of the chargeable gain (s. 25(9)).

The second situation in which trustees are deemed to dispose of settled property is provided for by s. 25(4) as amended by F.A. 1971 Schedule 12 para 7: 'On the termination at any time after 6 April 1965 of a life interest in possession in all or any part of settled property, the whole or a corresponding part of each of the assets forming part of the settled property and not ceasing at that time to be settled property, shall be deemed . . . at that time to be disposed of and immediately re-acquired by the trustee for a consideration equal to the whole or a corresponding part of the market value of the asset.'

In relation to deaths after 30 March 1971, no chargeable gain arises on a deemed disposal under either s. 25(3) or s. 25(4) brought about by a death (F.A. 1971 Schedule 12 paras 6 and 9). If, on the death, property reverts to the disponer (e.g. an asset settled on X for life, remainder to the settlor), the disposal and re-acquisition under s. 25(3) are deemed to be for a consideration securing neither gain nor loss to the trustee (ibid. para 6(b)). The explanation for this rule lies in the general intention of the 1971 Act that, on death, no capital gains tax should be chargeable, but where an asset deemed to be disposed of attracts estate duty, the allowable expenditure in respect of that asset should be notionally raised to its market value at the date of death (i.e. its dutiable value). Where the asset escapes estate duty (e.g. by reverter to disponer), the allowable expenditure should remain unchanged. Gifts are another illustration of this general intention. Estate duty is not chargeable on property given away more than seven years before the donor's death: if the donor dies in the seventh year after the gift, 40% of the property is dutiable, if he dies in the sixth year after the gift, 70% is dutiable, if he dies in the fifth year, 85% is dutiable, and only if he dies in the fourth or earlier year is full duty payable. F.A. 1971 Schedule 12 para 11(a) therefore provides that where a life interest is terminated by the death of a person not entitled to the life interest at the time of his death but entitled to it at some time within the seven years ending with the death, no chargeable gain accrues to the trustees if full estate duty is payable in respect of the life interest. If the reduced amounts of estate duty are payable (60%, 30% and 15% respectively), any chargeable gain or allowable loss accruing by virtue of s. 25(3) or s. 25(4) must be reduced by the complementary percentage (i.e. 40%, 60%, or 85% respectively).

Formerly in the case of a settlement with no life interest, in possession, there was a deemed disposal by the trustees every fifteen years, starting with the date of creation of the trust (s. 25(6), (7), (13)). This rule has been repealed in relation to any fifteen-year period ending after 30 March 1971 (F.A. 1971 s. 59(2) and Schedule 14 Part V).

3.53 THE BENEFICIARIES

No chargeable gain accrues on the disposal of an interest in a settlement (Schedule 7 para 13(1)). This applies in particular to an annuity or life interest, and the reversion to an annuity or life interest. It does not apply to an interest which has been transferred (i) to the person making the disposal or to a previous beneficiary, (ii) for valuable consideration other than another interest in the settlement (ibid.). Thus, if property is settled upon trust for Hughie for life, remainder to Louis absolutely, no chargeable gain would arise on the sale by Louis of his reversionary interest to Dewey. If Dewey were to dispose of the reversionary interest to Bluey, Dewey would be chargeable in respect of any gain. Even if Dewey were to retain the reversionary interest, he would be deemed to dispose of the settled property at market value under Schedule 7 para 13(2) on the occasion of becoming absolutely entitled to it as against the trustees, i.e. on Hughie's death, which would therefore be the occasion for a deemed disposal by Dewey under Schedule 7 para 13(2) as well as by the trustee under s. 25(3).

3.6 Exemptions

Exemption from capital gains tax takes one of three forms:

(1) Certain *assets* are not chargeable assets.
(2) On certain disposals the *gains* are not chargeable.
(3) Certain *persons* or *bodies* are not chargeable in respect of their gains.

3.61 NON-CHARGEABLE ASSETS

These are:

(1) Motor vehicles of a type commonly used for private purposes and suitable for use as private vehicles (s. 27(1)).

(2) Savings certificates and non-marketable securities issued under the National Loans Act 1939 or any corresponding Northern Ireland enactment (s. 27(4), (9)), e.g. Premium Bonds, Defence Bonds, National Development Bonds.

(3) Winnings or prizes from betting, lotteries, or gaming (including any pool betting or lottery or game) (s. 27 (7)).

Any disposal of a non-chargeable asset gives rise neither to a chargeable gain nor to an allowable loss (s. 27(10)).

3.62 EXEMPTED GAINS

(1) Small gifts

A gain accruing to an individual on a disposal of gift of an asset whose market value at the date of the gift does not exceed £100 (s. 27(2)). Exemption is lost if the total value of gifts made by that individual during the year of assessment exceeds £100 (s. 27(2)).

(2) Foreign currency

A gain accruing on the disposal by an individual of currency of any description acquired by him for the personal expenditure abroad of himself or his family or dependants, including expenditure on the provision or maintenance of a residence abroad (s. 27(5)).

(3) Medals

A gain on the disposal of a decoration for valour or gallant conduct acquired by the disponer otherwise than for money or money's worth (s. 27(6)).

(4) Damages

A sum received by way of compensation or damages for any wrong or injury suffered by an individual in his person or in his profession or vocation (s. 27(8)).

(5) Insurance policies

A gain on the disposal of the rights under a life assurance policy or deferred annuity contract (s. 28(2); see pp. 188–9 above), or on the disposal of the rights of the insurer or insured under an insurance policy other than a policy of insurance on human life (Schedule 7 para 10(1), (3)).

(6) Private residences

A gain accruing to an individual on the disposal of a dwelling-house or part of a dwelling-house which is, or has at any time in his period of ownership been, his only or main residence (s. 29(1)(a)). The exemption extends to any land which the individual has for his own occupation and enjoyment with that residence as its garden or grounds up to an area (inclusive of the site of the house) of one acre or such larger area as the Commissioners concerned may in any particular case determine, on being satisfied that, regard being had to the size and character of the house, the larger area is required for the reasonable enjoyment of it (or of the part in question) as a residence (s. 29(1)(b)).

The whole of the gain is exempt if the house, or part of the house, has been the only or main residence of the individual throughout his period of ownership, or for the entire period other than any part of the last twelve months (s. 29(2)); if not, the exemption is limited to the proportion of the gain that the actual period of residence (including the last twelve months, whether resident or not) bears to the entire period of ownership (s. 29(3)). The period of residence is deemed, provided two conditions are satisfied, to include:

(a) one period or aggregate periods of absence not exceeding three years;
(b) any period of absence throughout which the individual worked in any employment or office abroad; and
(c) any period or aggregate periods of absence not exceeding four years throughout which the individual was prevented from residing in the house in consequence of the situation of his place of work or of any condition imposed by his employer requiring him to reside elsewhere, being a condition reasonably imposed to secure the effective performance by the employee of his duties. The conditions are (i) there must have been a time both before and after the period when the house was the individual's only or main residence; and (ii) the period of absence must be a period during which the house was not the individual's only or main residence and throughout which he had no other residence eligible for exemption (s. 29(4)).

With one exception, an individual is entitled to exemption for one residence only. An individual with more than one residence may give written notice indicating which is to be treated as his main residence for any period. The notice must be given within two years from the beginning of the period and may be varied by a further notice. In the absence of notice, the Inspector must decide on the main residence: the individual has thirty days within which to appeal to the Commissioners against the decision (s. 29(7)). A husband and wife living together are allowed one main residence only, and any notice which affects them both must be made jointly (s. 29(8) (*a*)).

The exceptional case in which an individual is entitled to exemption in respect of a second residence is where he disposes of a house or part of a house which at any time in his period of ownership was the sole residence of a dependent relative of his, occupied by that relative rent-free and without any other consideration (s. 29(10)). The dependent relative exemption can be claimed for one residence only (s. 29(10)(*a*)).

Exemption applies also to a gain accruing to a trustee on the disposal of settled property which, during the period of ownership of the trustee, has been the only or main residence of a person entitled to occupy it under the terms of the settlement (s. 29(9)). Any notice under s. 29(7) must be given by the beneficiary and trustee jointly (s. 29(9)(*b*)).

THE TIMES

"Since no part of the house is used exclusively for business purposes we are rather hoping to avoid capital gains tax if and when we sell"

There must be an apportionment of the gain to exclude from exemption any part of a house used exclusively for the purposes of a trade or business, profession or vocation (s. 29(5)). "Exclusively" is probably a draftsman's error: the implication is, for example, that a study in which an author does all his work remains within the exemption if he occasionally entertains friends in it. Apportionment of the gain is also necessary where part of the house has not been used by the individual as his residence, e.g. a basement flat let to tenants (s. 29(12)).

No exemption is available at all where the residence was acquired 'wholly or partly for the purpose of realizing a gain from the disposal of it'; or in respect of the proportion of a gain relating to expenditure subsequent to the acquisition of the residence which was incurred for that purpose (F.A. 1968 Schedule 12 para 2(1)). This is an all too common anti-avoidance formula which, in the author's view, puts an unwarranted discretion in the hands of the Inspectorate. Nowadays how many houses are not bought partly for the purpose of realizing a gain?

(7) Chattels sold for £1,000 or less

A gain accruing on the disposal of an asset which is tangible movable property for a consideration in amount or value not exceeding £1,000 (s. 30(1)). If the consideration exceeds £1,000, marginal relief restricts the amount of tax chargeable to half the difference between the consideration and £1,000 (s. 30(2)). Conversely, if the consideration is less than £1,000, the consideration must be deemed to be £1,000 so as to restrict any allowable loss (s. 30(3)).

Example 8

Baron Landscape bought a painting—'Les Pieds Sales' by Guy Vassaire —in 1967 for £200, and another painting in 1969 for £1,700. In 1971 he sold the first painting for £1,200 and in 1973 he sold the second painting for £700.

The Baron's tax bill in respect of 'Les Pieds Sales' (£300 on the normal basis, perhaps less on the alternative basis) cannot exceed £100. His allowable loss in respect of the second painting is restricted to £700.

S. 30(3) is an important provision; without its protection the Revenue might be inundated with loss claims for every broken teacup, lost wristwatch, or torn up tax law textbook in the land.

The disposal of a set, or part of a set, of articles to the same person, or to persons acting in concert, or to connected persons, whether on the same or different occasions, is treated as the disposal of a single article (s. 30(4)). Any restriction under s. 30(2) or s. 30(3) must be based on the aggregate consideration in amount or value. An article disposed of between 11 November 1964 and 7 April 1965 is taken into account for the purpose of ascertaining the aggregate consideration for the set to which that article belongs, but the gain on that article is not a chargeable gain (s. 30(4)).

This exemption does not apply to any disposal of commodities on a terminal market or to any disposal of currency of any description (s. 30(6)).

(8) Chattels which are wasting assets

A gain accruing on the disposal after 19 March 1968 of tangible movable property (or of an interest therein) which is a wasting asset. (F.A. 1968 Schedule 12 para 1(1)). Exemption does not apply:

(*a*) to any asset which has qualified for capital allowances, e.g. an asset used solely for the purposes of a trade, profession or vocation throughout the disponer's period of ownership (ibid. para 1(2));
(*b*) where an asset has only partially qualified for capital allowances, to the proportion of the gain which relates to the expenditure which *has* so qualified (ibid. para 1(3)); or
(*c*) to a disposal of commodities on a terminal market (ibid. para 1(4)).

(9) Works of art etc

A gain accruing on the disposal of an asset by way of a gift or bequest which qualifies for remission of estate duty under F.A. 1894 s. 15(2) (s. 31(1)). F.A. 1894 s. 15(2) provides that: 'It shall be lawful for the Treasury to remit the Estate duty . . . in respect of any such pictures, prints, books, manuscripts, works of art of scientific collections, as appear to the Treasury to be of national, scientific, or historic interest, and to be given or bequeathed for national purposes, or to any university, or to any county council or municipal corporation.'

A disposal by way of gift, including a gift in settlement, or a deemed disposal under s. 25(3) or s. 25(4), is treated as being for such consideration as would secure neither gain nor loss to the disponer, provided two conditions are satisfied:

(i) the asset disposed of must be an object of national, scientific, historic or artistic interest within F.A. 1930, s. 40; and
(ii) an undertaking must be given, by the person the Treasury think appropriate in the circumstances of the case, in the terms of F.A. 1950 s. 48, i.e. that the object will be kept permanently in the UK, reasonable steps will be taken for its preservation, and reasonable facilities for examining it will be allowed to any person authorized by the Treasury (s. 31(3), (4)).

(10) Gilt-edged securities

A gain accruing on the disposal after 15 April 1969 of Government securities specified in F.A. 1969 s. 41(2) and Schedule 18 and in Orders made by the Treasury (F.A. 1969 s. 41(1)).

(11) Funds for reducing the National Debt

A gain which accrues on the disposal by trustees of settled property held on trusts to provide funds for the reduction of the National Debt (TA s. 364).

3.63 EXEMPT PERSONS OR BODIES

A gain which accrues to a charity is not a chargeable gain if it is applicable and applied for charitable purposes (s. 35(1)). When property held on charitable trusts ceases to be subject to charitable trusts the trustees must be treated as if they had disposed of, and immediately re-acquired, the property at market value (s. 35(2)(*a*)). Any subsequent gain will therefore fall into charge.

Formerly disposals *to* a charity were normally chargeable. Now the position is governed by F.A. 1972 s. 119, which provides that:

(*a*) any disposal, including a deemed disposal under s. 25(3) or s. 25(4),
(*b*) made after 21 March 1972,
(*c*) otherwise than under a bargain at arm's length,
(*d*) to

    (i) a charity, or
    (ii) The National Gallery, The British Museum, The Royal Scottish Museum, The National Museum of Wales, any other similar national institution, any museum or art gallery in the UK maintained by a local authority or university in the UK, any university library, The National Art Collections Fund, or The National Trust,

should be treated as giving rise to no gain or allowable loss. On subsequent disposal by the charity or other body, the acquisition by the original disponer is treated as the acquisition of the charity or other body (ibid. s. 119(2)(*b*)), unless the charity can take shelter under s. 35(1).

The exemptions for High Commissioners, Agents-General, and their staff under TA s. 372 and for visiting forces under TA s. 367 apply for capital gains tax as well as for income tax. Consular officers and employees exempt from income tax under Case IV or Case V of Schedule D under TA s. 374(1) are also exempted by TA s. 374(2) from capital gains tax in respect of any gain on the disposal of assets situated outside the UK.

A gain is not chargeable if it accrues to a person from his disposal of investments held by him as part of a superannuation fund approved under TA s. 208 (TA s. 208(2)). Where part only of a fund is approved, the capital gains tax exemption is correspondingly reduced (ibid. s. 208(2) proviso). Gains are also not chargeable which accrue from the disposal of assets held as part of those funds whose income is exempt from income tax, namely:

(a) Parliamentary pension funds (TA s. 211(3));
(b) National Insurance supplementary schemes (TA s. 212(4));
(c) the Royal Seamen's Pension Fund (TA s. 212(4));
(d) Indian family pension funds (TA s. 213(2));
(e) Indian, Pakistan, and colonial pension funds (TA s. 214(4));
(f) the Central Africa Pension Fund (TA s. 216(3));
(g) the Overseas Service Pensions Fund (TA s. 217(3));
(h) pension funds for overseas employees (TA s. 218(2)); and
(i) approved retirement annuity contracts and trust schemes (TA s. 226(6)).

3.7 Reliefs

A number of reliefs have already been dealt with:

(1) Roll-over relief on the replacement of business assets (pp. 200–3 above).
(2) Relief in respect of delayed remittances of gains (p. 191 above).
(3) Payment of capital gains tax by instalments (p. 204 above).

Several reliefs remain to be considered.

3.71 TRANSFER OF BUSINESS ON RETIREMENT

Relief is available under s. 34 to an individual aged sixty years or more on the disposal of his business. The nature of this relief is set out in the following propositions:

(1) The disposal must be by way of sale or gift.
(2) The disposal must comprise either:

    (a) the whole or part of a business which he owned throughout the period of ten years ending with the disposal; or
    (b) shares or securities of a company which, throughout the period of ten years ending with the disposal, was:
        (i) a trading company;

(ii) his family company (i.e. a company in which at least 25% of the voting rights were exercisable by him or in which, if at least 75% of the voting rights were exercisable by him *or* a member of his family, at least 10% of the voting rights were exercisable by him alone: "family" in this context means spouse, relative, or spouse's relative, and "relative" means brother, sister, ancestor or lineal descendant); and

(iii) a company of which he was a full-time working director.

(3) The amount of relief cannot exceed £10,000; the relief is £2,000 for a man of sixty, and increases by £2,000 for every year by which his age exceeds sixty (and a corresponding part of £2,000 for every fraction of a year) up to the maximum for a man of sixty-five.

(4) Relief is given only in respect of "chargeable business assets": these are assets (including goodwill but excluding assets held as investments) used for the purposes of a trade, profession, vocation, office, or employment other than assets on the disposal of which no chargeable gain accrues, or, in the case of the disposal of shares or securities in the family company, on the disposal of which no chargeable gain *would* accrue if the family company disposed of the asset at the time of the disposal of the shares or securities.

(5) The relief takes the following form. On a disposal within (2)(*a*) above, the gains (and losses) in respect of chargeable business assets are aggregated and only so much of the aggregate as exceeds the amount available for relief ranks as chargeable gains. On a disposal within (2)(*b*) above, the gains in respect of the shares or securities are aggregated and then the aggregate sum is reduced to the proportion corresponding to the proportion that the company's chargeable business assets bear to its total assets (including cash). Only so much of this reduced sum as exceeds the amount available for relief constitutes chargeable gains.

(6) Any balance of relief can be carried forward and used on a subsequent disposal, but the total reliefs must not exceed the maximum amount available to the individual according to his age on the last relevant disposal. The reliefs are applied in the order in which disposals take place.

3.72 DOUBLE TAXATION RELIEF

TA s. 497 (double taxation relief by agreement with other countries) and TA s. 498 (unilateral double taxation relief) apply to capital gains tax in the same way as they apply to income tax (s. 39(1)), as does TA s. 518 (disclosure of information for purposes of double taxation) (s. 39(4)). Foreign capital gains tax available for relief against UK capital gains tax is not also available for relief against income tax (s. 39(3)). Where foreign capital gains tax has been paid and double taxation relief is not available, the disponer is entitled to treat the foreign tax paid as an allowable deduction in any computation necessary for purposes of UK capital gains tax (Schedule 6 para 20).

3.73 SMALL DISPOSALS

F.A. 1971 belatedly put an end to a great deal of administrative and personal inconvenience by providing that: 'An individual shall not be chargeable to capital gains tax for a year of assessment if the aggregate amount or value of the consideration for all the disposals of assets made by him in that year does not exceed £500' (ibid. s. 57(1)). Where the aggregate consideration exceeds £500, marginal relief is given by limiting the amount of tax payable to one half of the difference between £500 and the aggregate consideration (ibid. s. 57(2)). On the other hand, where the aggregate consideration does not exceed £500 in a particular year of assessment, allowable losses of that year can be carried forward only to the extent that they exceed chargeable gains of that year (ibid. Schedule 11 para 2(1)); and, in the case of a married woman living with her husband, the excess of allowable losses over chargeable gains of one spouse must be reduced by any excess of chargeable gains over allowable losses of the other (ibid. para 2(2)).

In calculating the aggregate consideration for purposes of these provisions, the consideration for a disposal must be disregarded if:

(a) it falls to be excluded from the computation of a gain arising on the disposal; or

(b) a gain accruing on the disposal is not a chargeable gain (ibid. para 8(1)).

3.74 POSTPONEMENT OF PAYMENT OF TAX

Under Schedule 10 para 4 personal representatives and trustees were, under certain circumstances, entitled to pay their capital gains tax over a period of eight years. F.A. 1972 s. 117 substituted a broader provision enabling *any* person, at his option, to pay capital gains tax by eight equal yearly instalments or sixteen half-yearly instalments (with interest at the rate of 6%), provided two conditions are satisfied:

(1) the disposal in respect of which the tax is payable must be by way of gift or deemed disposal under s. 25(3) or s. 25(4); and

(2) the assets disposed of must be:

(a) land or an estate or interest in land;

(b) any unquoted shares or securities; or

(c) any assets used exclusively for the purposes of a trade, profession, or vocation carried on, immediately before the disposal, by the disponer, i.e. business assets.

The first instalment is normally due twelve months after the disposal. Any outstanding tax, together with interest, may be paid at any time; and *must* be paid if:

(1) the disposal was by way of gift to a connected person or was a deemed disposal under s. 25(3) or s. 25(4); and

(2) the assets are subsequently disposed of for valuable consideration (ibid. s. 117(3)).

4

Corporation Tax

In my last year's Budget speech I announced my intention to reform the structure of corporation tax in order to remove the present discrimination between retained and distributed profits. I explained that this discrimination distorts the capital market, tends to misallocate scarce investment resources, impedes companies that need to raise equity capital, and lessens the pressure for efficiency. *Anthony Barber* Budget Speech 21 March 1972.

4.1 Historical background

For two decades after the War, a company was liable to two distinct taxes—income tax on its undistributed profits and profits tax (originally the war-time National Defence Contribution: *see* pp. 17, 19 above) on its total profits. In 1965–66, the last year for which companies were taxed under this system, the rate of income tax was 41·25% and the rate of profits tax was 15%. The combined rate of charge—56·25% in 1965–66—applied both to distributed and undistributed profits. Where a company chose not to distribute any of its profits, those profits suffered tax at the rate of 56·25% directly. Where part or all of its profits were distributed, the company deducted or was deemed to have deducted income tax at the rate of 41·25% but was entitled to retain any deduction as an offset against any income tax payable by the company on the profits out of which the distribution had been made. Indeed, the deduction could be retained even where no income tax was paid, e.g. because the company's profits were relieved from tax by losses carried forward from previous years. Each shareholder was treated as having already suffered income tax in respect of the distribution and was therefore liable only to surtax on the grossed-up amount received by him.

The "classical" system of company taxation introduced in 1965 also involved the imposition of two taxes on a company—corporation tax and income tax—but with the important difference that distributed profits were to be taxed twice—once in the hands of the company and a second time in the hands of the shareholders. This was achieved by effecting a complete separation between a company and its shareholders. A company was to be liable to corporation tax on its total profits, i.e. both income and capital gains, and was to be required under a new Schedule F not only to deduct income tax at the standard rate but also to account for the tax deducted to the Revenue. The shareholder's position was to remain unchanged. The distribution in his hands was still to be regarded as having borne income tax at the standard rate. Thus if he were exempt or liable to income tax at less than the standard rate he was to be entitled to claim the appropriate repayment, if he were a standard rate taxpayer no further payment was to be required of him, and if he were a surtaxpayer the grossed-up amount of the distribution was to be included in his total income for surtax purposes. One effect of the classical system was to encourage companies to raise capital by loan issue (e.g. of debentures) rather than by share issue; interest payments but not distributions, were deductible from total profits.

In 1972–73, the last year for which the 1965 system applied, the rate of corporation tax was 40% and the standard rate of income tax was 38·75%. A company's tax position under the classical system, as compared with the pre-1965 system, therefore depended, all other things being equal, upon the extent to which the company distributed its profits. To pay the same effective rate of tax in 1972–73 that it would have paid in 1956–66, a company would have had to distribute about 42% of its (pre-tax) profits: if it distributed any more than that, its effective rate of tax would begin to climb above 56·25%.

The primary justification for the classical system was the desirability of providing, in Mr Callaghan's words, 'a strong incentive to all companies to plough back more of their profits for expansion' (Hansard 6 April 1965 col. 255). Economists had even then begun to doubt the wisdom of a retentionist policy. Later their opposition to retentionism grew. A number of countries abandoned retentionist systems. Finally in the 1971 Budget Speech Mr Barber announced the Government's intention of reforming the structure of corporation tax so as to remove the element of discrimination against distributed profits. Two alternative methods for doing so (apart from the pre-1965 system) suggested themselves—the "two-rate" and the "imputation" systems. A Select Committee appointed to consider them reported in October 1971 in favour of the "imputation" system. F.A. 1972 implemented this system with effect from 1 April 1973. The introduction of a new system of corporation tax has been the occasion for substantial amendment, but not abandonment, of the 1965 provisions. The basic structure of the 1965 corporation tax legislation has been retained.

4.2 General description of corporation tax

A company resident in the UK is chargeable to corporation tax on all its profits, both income and chargeable gains. Chargeable gains accruing to a company are in effect taxed twice—once to corporation tax in the hands of the company and, since gains increase the value of a company's shares, a second time to capital gains tax in the hands of shareholders disposing of their shares. The imputation system has not affected this form of double taxation.

Corporation tax is an annual tax levied for "financial years". "The financial year 1973" is the year to 31 March 1974. The rate of corporation tax is fixed in arrear: see TA s. 243(5), (6). Thus the rate for 1973–74 is to be announced in the 1974 Budget Speech—and even then there is a possibility that it will be changed in the 1974 Act. However, the Government have announced that the rate for 1973–74 may be assumed—"for illustrative purposes only"—to be 50%.

The tax is charged on a current year basis. Assessments are made by reference to the profits of "accounting periods". Where an accounting period straddles 31 March, the profits of that period are apportioned between the two financial years on a time basis (TA s. 243(3)). Thus if a company were to make up its accounts for calendar years, disclosing profits in 1973 of £12,000 and in 1974 of £24,000, its profits liable to corporation tax in the financial year 1973 would be £15,000 (£9,000 + £6,000). Normally an "accounting period" is the period for which a company chooses to make up its accounts; but may not in any event exceed twelve months.

The basic rule for the computation of profits chargeable to corporation tax is that the amount of income is to be ascertained in accordance with income tax law and practice as if accounting periods were years of assessment (TA s. 250(1)), while the amount of chargeable gains for an accounting period is the net figure arrived at after deducting from the total amount of chargeable gains accruing to the company in that period any allowable losses, whether also accruing in that period or carried forward from previous accounting periods (TA s. 265(1)).

Companies under the control of five or fewer persons or under the control of their directors—known as "close companies"—are subject to a number of disadvantages relative to other companies.

Corporation tax assessed for an accounting period must generally be paid within nine months of the end of that period or, if this is later, within

one month of the making of the assessment (TA s. 243(4)). The two
exceptions to this rule are considered at pp. 251-2 below.

4.3 Elements of the imputation system

Under the imputation system a company continues to pay corporation
tax at a uniform rate—illustratively 50%—on all its profits, whether
distributed or undistributed. However, the new system imposes a lower
effective rate on a company's chargeable gains than on its income by
requiring a fraction only of the company's net gains (chargeable gains less
allowable losses, including losses brought forward) to be included in the
computation of its total profits. For illustrative purposes, the fraction is
three-fifths, which means that the lower effective rate is 30% (50% of
three-fifths)—the same, we notice, as the normal rate of capital gains tax
levied on individuals. Another innovation is the reduced rate of charge—
illustratively 40%—on the income of small companies.

A company will make its distributions in the same way as before but a
new terminology has been introduced. Under the old system a company
making a distribution would have deducted tax at the standard rate, paid
over the net amount of the distribution to its shareholders, and accounted
for the deduction to the Revenue. Under the imputation system, a company
making a distribution to its shareholders is required to pay to the Revenue,
over and above the amount of the distribution, "advance corporation tax"
(hereafter "ACT") equal to three-sevenths of the amount of the distribution. Three-sevenths is the grossing-up fraction equivalent to a deduction
of 30%: £100 less a deduction of 30% is £70, £70 grossed-up by three-
sevenths is £100. The result is simply that, whereas before 1973–74—
assuming the standard rate then to have been 30%—a company with a
fund of £100 to distribute would normally have declared a dividend of
£100 and deducted and paid over to the Revenue £30, now a company
with £100 to distribute will normally declare a dividend of £70 and pay
ACT to the Revenue of £30. In short, the changes required by the new
system are firstly that dividends be declared in the net rather than the
gross amounts available for distribution and, secondly, that ACT payments
be made in lieu of standard rate deductions. To speak of deduction in
relation to distributions under the new system would be, in the Churchillian
phrase, a terminological inexactitude.

The key substantive change wrought by the new system is this. Every
resident shareholder in receipt of a distribution in respect of which ACT

has been paid is entitled to a tax credit equal to the ACT paid in respect of his share of the distribution. Thus if a company with ten equal shareholders were to declare a dividend of £700, paying £70 to each shareholder, the company would be required to pay ACT of £300 to the Revenue and each shareholder would be entitled to a tax credit of £30. These credits may be set against the shareholders' liability to income tax. A shareholder who is a basic rate taxpayer pays no tax in respect of the distribution because his tax credit exactly matches his income tax liability. In a sense the company has paid tax for him. A shareholder who is exempt from income tax may claim his credit from the Revenue. A shareholder subject to excess liability must include his share of the distribution plus his credit in his total income for excess liability purposes.

The imputation system introduces a distinction between "qualifying" and "non-qualifying" distributions. Qualifying distributions are dividends and similar payments. Non-qualifying distributions are bonus redeemable shares and bonus debentures. The point of distinction is that, while qualifying distributions constitute income in the hands of the shareholders at the time of receipt, non-qualifying distributions represent merely the right to receive *future* income (usually in the form of annual fixed-interest payments). Only qualifying distributions give rise to liability to ACT and hence only qualifying distributions confer tax credits on the shareholders.

The amount of a qualifying distribution *made* by a company, together with the relative ACT, is referred to as a "franked payment" (F.A. 1972 s. 84(3)). The amount of a qualifying distribution *received* by a company, together with the relative tax credit, is known as "franked investment income" (F.A. 1972 s. 88(1)). Thus if company A were to pay a dividend of £70 to company B, company A would be said to have made a franked payment of £100 and company B to have received franked investment income of £100. Company B is not chargeable to corporation tax in respect of franked investment income, which it may set against its franked payments for the purposes of reducing accountability for ACT. Surplus franked investment income may be used to obtain relief at the end of the accounting period in respect of four items and, if still not exhausted, may be carried forward and treated as franked investment income of later accounting periods. Company A's position is more complicated, as we shall now see.

A company's liability to corporation tax on its profits is called its "mainstream" liability. ACT paid in respect of qualifying distributions made during an accounting period may be set against the company's mainstream liability on the income of its profits for that period—but never against mainstream liability in respect of chargeable gains. The maximum ACT set-off is 30% of income. This amount represents the ACT that would have been payable had the entirety of the company's income in that accounting period been made available for distribution. Surplus ACT may, if the company so elects, be carried back against tax on the income of the previous two accounting periods and, if the ACT is still not fully exhausted, may be carried forward indefinitely against tax on income of subsequent periods. Thus if a company with profits of £10,000, comprising income of £8,000 and gains of £2,000, has made a distribution of £7,000 and paid ACT of £3,000 to the Revenue, the company may offset £2,400 (30% of £8,000) of the ACT against its mainstream liability on income of £4,000 (50% of £8,000) so as to reduce its mainstream corporation tax on income to £1,600, and may then claim to carry back the surplus ACT of £600 against its corporation tax on income of the previous accounting period, then of the accounting period before that, then of successive subsequent accounting periods. The expression "mainstream corporation tax" is used to denote the company's corporation tax bill as reduced by any ACT set-off.

Under the 1965–73 system a company accounted to the Revenue for income tax in respect of its distributions on a monthly basis. More precisely, every month the company added up the amounts of income tax for which it was accountable to the Revenue—not only in respect of distributions but in respect also of interest payments, patent royalties, and annual payments—and subtracted amounts of income tax it had suffered by deduction from its franked investment income, annual payments, and other taxed receipts. The net balance of income tax was either payable or repayable to or from the Revenue. Any necessary adjustments were made at the end of the year of assessment.

Under the new system it was decided to improve the liquidity of companies to the extent of requiring them to account to the Revenue on a quarterly rather than a monthly basis. Every company must now account to the Revenue, normally within fourteen days of the end of every calendar quarter, for the excess of ACT payable in respect of franked payments over tax credits in respect of franked investment income. The company must also account to the Revenue, within the same period, for income tax in respect of interest, annual payments, and other payments it has made under deduction of tax, although it may reduce its accountability by the amount of any payments received under deduction of tax, e.g. interest from other companies or on Government securities. The main difference is that under the new system a company cannot set income tax suffered by deduction against ACT, nor can it use its tax credits to reduce its accountability for income tax on payments it has made under deduction of tax.

4.4 Detailed account of the tax

The rules of company taxation may be seen as a three-tiered pyramid. The lowest tier consists of those rules applicable to companies generally, in the middle lie the special rules governing close companies, and at the top there are several even more specialized sets of rules for those classes of company thought to require special attention, e.g. small companies, building societies, life assurance companies, etc.

4.41 SCOPE OF THE CHARGE

The *grundnorm* is contained in TA s. 238(1): 'Corporation tax shall be charged on profits of companies.' What, we must not be too proud to ask, is a company and what are profits?

"Company," TA s. 526(5) tells us, means 'any body corporate or unincorporated association, but does not include a partnership, a local authority or a local authority association'. A company for tax purposes is therefore a much larger animal than for purposes of company law. Moreover, the corporation tax definition is extended by TA s. 354(1), which requires that the trustees of an authorized investment trust be treated as if they were a company and as if the rights of unit holders were shares in the company. On the other hand, the corporation tax definition of a company does not apply to TA ss. 486 to 489 (anti-avoidance), 497 to 499 (double taxation relief), 533 (connected persons), or Schedule 12 (double taxation relief: Republic of Ireland). Moreover, the provisions relating to groups of companies apply only to bodies corporate. The expression "unincorporated association" is not defined for corporation tax purposes. In income tax cases it has been held to include the Old Monkland Conservative Association ((1905) 5 T.C. 189), the Glamorgan Quarter Sessions ((1910) 5 T.C. 537), the Carlisle & Silloth Golf Club ((1913) 6 T.C. 198), and the National Association of Local Government Officers ((1934) 18 T.C. 499).

"Profits," we are informed by TA s. 238(4)(*a*), 'comprise both income and chargeable gains.' Elsewhere in the Corporation Tax Acts, the word is used in a more restricted sense to mean "profits chargeable to corporation tax", i.e. *income other than franked investment income and group income* plus chargeable gains (*see*, for example, ss. 243(1), (2), (3) and 247(1)). Unless the income accrues to a company in a fiduciary or representative capacity, the Income Tax Acts do not apply to the income of a company resident in the UK (TA s. 238(2)(*a*)), nor to such income of a non-resident company as falls within the definition of chargeable profits under TA s. 246(2) (TA s. 238(2)(*b*)). (We will be taking a look at TA s. 246(2) in the next paragraph but one.) Similarly, a company is not liable to capital gains tax in respect of those chargeable gains accruing to it which are within the charge to corporation tax or would fall into charge but for an exemption from corporation tax (TA s. 238(3)).

A company resident in the UK is chargeable to corporation tax on all its profits wherever arising (TA s. 243(1)). A company is chargeable on profits accruing for its benefit under any trust, or arising under any partnership, to the extent that it would have been chargeable had the profits accrued to it directly (TA s. 243(2)); and, s. 243(2) continues, is chargeable too on profits arising in the course of its winding up—but, s. 243(2) concludes, 'not otherwise . . . on profits accruing to it in a fiduciary or representative capacity except as respects its own beneficial interest (if any) in those profits'. Professor Wheatcroft has pointed out (in [1966] B.T.R. 2, 3; in *Talbot and Wheatcroft* 3–01, and in *Wheatcroft and Park* 5–24) that the use of "otherwise" in s. 243(2), coupled with the exception of income accruing in a fiduciary or representative capacity from the general exemption of companies from income tax in TA s. 238(2), suggests that both income tax and corporation tax may be chargeable on income arising to a company as trustee during the period of its winding up. This was presumably not the intention of the legislature and it is regrettable that the opportunity has not yet been taken to clarify a point of such manifest practical significance.

A company not resident in the UK is within the charge to corporation tax only if it carries on a trade in the UK through a branch or agency and, even if it does, the charge is limited to its "chargeable profits" (TA s. 246(1)). "Branch or agency" means 'any factorship, agency, receivership, branch or management' (TA s. 527(1)). "Chargeable profits" are defined in TA s. 246(2) as:

(*a*) any trading income arising directly or indirectly through or from the branch or agency and any income from property or rights used by, or held by or for, the branch or agency; and

(*b*) such chargeable gains accruing on the disposal of assets situated in the UK as would be chargeable to capital gains tax on an individual neither resident nor ordinarily resident in the UK. Thus a non-resident company is chargeable:

    (i) to corporation tax in respect of income accruing to a branch or agency carrying on a trade in the UK on behalf of the company;

(ii) to income tax in respect of any other income accruing to the company from sources within the UK; and
(iii) where the company carries on a trade in the UK through a branch or agency, to corporation tax in respect of chargeable gains accruing on the disposal:

(a) of assets situated in the UK and used in or for the purposes of the trade at or before the time when the gain accrued; or
(b) of assets situated in the UK and used or held for the purposes of the branch or agency at or before that time, or assets required for use by or for the purposes of the branch or agency (see F.A. 1965 s. 20(2)).

4.42 BASIS OF, AND PERIODS FOR, ASSESSMENT

'Corporation tax is assessed and charged on the full amount of the profits arising in a company's accounting period' (TA s. 247(1)). Normally this is the period for which a company chooses to make up its accounts (TA s. 247(3)(b)), with the important qualification that an accounting period can never exceed twelve months (TA s. 247(3)(a)). An accounting period begins when the company first comes within the charge to corporation tax (TA s. 247(2)(a)), and whenever the company's accounting period ends without the company then ceasing to be within the charge to corporation tax (TA s. 247(2)(b)). An accounting period ends on the first occurrence of (a) the expiration of twelve months from its beginning, (b) the end of the period for which the company has chosen to make up its accounts or for which the company has chosen not to make up accounts, (c) the company beginning or ceasing to trade or to be, in respect of its trade or all its trades, within the charge to corporation tax, (d) the company beginning or ceasing to be resident in the UK, and (e) the company ceasing to be within the charge to corporation tax (TA s. 247(3)). These rules have no application to a company resident in the UK whose income is wholly derived from distributions from other resident companies and therefore not within the charge to corporation tax. Consequently a company in this situation is treated, for the purpose of getting its accounting periods under way, as coming within the charge to corporation tax at the time when it commences to carry on business (TA s. 247(4)).

The Inspector is empowered, if he considers the beginning or end of any accounting period is uncertain, to make an assessment for such period not exceeding twelve months as appears to him appropriate: see IRC v. Helical Bar Ltd [1972] A.C. 773. That period will then be treated as an accounting period of the company unless the Inspector sees fit in the light of further facts to revise it or, on appeal against the assessment in respect of some other matter, the company shows the true accounting periods (TA s. 247(8)).

4.43 COMPANIES IN LIQUIDATION

The practice of fixing the rate of corporation tax in arrear formerly resulted in a prudent liquidator having to hold back his final distribution until the following Budget, since only then would he know the rate of corporation tax for the company's final year. ("Final year" means the financial year in which the company's affairs are completely wound up (TA s. 245(1)).) F.A. 1967 therefore provided that corporation tax should be charged on the profits of a company arising in the winding up in its final year at the rate fixed for the penultimate year (F.A. 1967 Schedule 11 para 5(1), (2), now consolidated in TA s. 245(2)). Thus if a liquidator completed a liquidation by, say, 30 November 1972, the profits arising in the course of winding up during the eight months from 1 April 1972 would be charged to corporation tax at the rate of 40%, i.e. the rate fixed by F.A. 1972 s. 64 for the financial year 1971.

The commencement of a winding up marks the end of one accounting period and the beginning of a new one. Thereafter accounting periods run until the prior occurrence of (a) the expiration of twelve months, and (b) the completion of the winding up (TA s. 247(7)).

4.44 DUE DATE FOR PAYMENT

As we have seen (pp. 244–5 above), the due date is generally nine months after the end of the accounting period or, if this is later, one month after the making of the assessment (TA s. 243(4)). There are two exceptions, the one of considerable practical importance, the other much less so.

The first exception applies to companies which were trading before the financial year 1965 and have continued the same trade since then. Their corporation tax—not merely on trading profits but on all profits—must be paid within the same interval from the end of the accounting period for which it is assessed as there was between the end of the basis period of the trade for the year 1965–66 and 1 January 1966 or, if later, within one month of the assessment (TA s. 244(1)). Thus, for example, a company which commenced trading on 1 July 1960 has made up its accounts for regular periods of twelve months, and has continued the same trade throughout, is required to pay corporation tax within eighteen months of the end of each

K

accounting period (or within one month of the assessment, if this is later). (The company's basis period for the year 1965–66 was the year to 30 June 1964 and the gap between 30 June 1964 and 1 January 1966 was eighteen months.) The intention was to protect companies trading at the time when corporation tax was introduced against any hardship that might have resulted had their due date for payment been brought forward. The provision is therefore excluded in cases where the interval is less than nine months (TA s.244(1) proviso).

The second exception applies to any building society which entered into arrangements with the Revenue for 1965–66 under which the assessment which would have been made by reference to a period ending before that year was made by reference to a period ending in that year. The time for payment of corporation tax by a building society of this description is specified in TA s. 344(2).

4.45 COMPANY DISTRIBUTIONS

"Distributions" are defined in TA ss. 233–7, as amended by F.A. 1972 Schedule 22. There are two kinds—qualifying and non-qualifying. The class of non-qualifying distributions has two occupants only, namely bonus redeemable shares and bonus securities issued in respect of shares in or securities of the company (TA s. 233(2)(c) and F.A. 1972 s. 84(4)(a)). "Security" in this context includes unsecured loans as well as debentures (TA s. 237(5)). All of the other types of distribution rank as qualifying distributions (F.A. 1972 s. 84(4)). The most important is of course a dividend, but before we have a look at a detailed list of qualifying distributions, let us consider the tax treatment of distributions generally. The list may then make better sense.

The taxability of a distribution varies according to whether it is qualifying or non-qualifying and whether it is made to an individual or to another company. There are therefore four possibilities, which will be examined successively.

Permutation 1: qualifying distribution to an individual

The company's position: F.A. 1972 s. 84

A resident company which makes a qualifying distribution after 5 April 1973 is liable to pay ACT (F.A. 1972 s. 84(1)) at a rate which, for the year 1973–74, is three-sevenths of the amount or value of the distribution (ibid. s. 84(2)).

The time and manner in which ACT for a company's accounting period is to be paid are regulated by F.A. 1972 Schedule 14 (F.A. 1972 ss. 84(5), 89(4)). A company must make returns to the Collector within fourteen days of the end of each "return period" (Schedule 14 para 1(1), (3)). Any complete calendar quarter within the accounting period is a return period (ibid. para 1(2)(*a*)). Any odd bits left at the beginning and/or end of the accounting period are also return periods (ibid. para 1(2)(*b*)). Thus a company which makes up its accounts for periods of twelve months from 1 February each year has five return periods in each of its accounting periods: 1 February to 31 March, the three calendar quarters ending 30 June, 30 September, and 31 December, and finally 1 January to 31 January.

The return a company makes must show:

(*a*) the amount of its franked payments in that period;
(*b*) the amount of franked investment income it has received in that period; and
(*c*) the amount of any ACT payable (ibid. para 2(1)).

ACT is payable on the excess of a company's franked payments in an accounting period over its franked investment income (F.A. 1972 s. 89(2)). Thus, at the end of each return period within its accounting period, a company must account to the Revenue for the excess of ACT payable in respect of qualifying distributions it has made over any tax credits in respect of qualifying distributions it has received. If, in that return period, the company's franked investment income is greater than its franked payments no ACT is payable (ibid. s. 89(1)), but the excess of franked investment income may be carried over to later return periods within the same accounting period so as to frank later qualifying distributions, i.e. to reduce the amount of ACT payable in respect of franked payments made in later return periods.

Where a return has been made of franked payments made in a return period and ACT has been paid in respect of them, any franked investment income received by the company in later return periods within the same accounting period may be carried back so as to frank the earlier distributions, thereby entitling the company to a repayment of ACT (ibid. Schedule 14 para 4(1), (2)).

If at the end of an accounting period, there remains franked investment income which has not been exhausted in franking distributions, the residue is called a "surplus of franked investment income" (ibid. s. 89 (6)), this being a term of art. As we shall see (pp. 257–8 below), a surplus of franked investment income may be used to obtain certain kinds of immediate relief and, if still not exhausted, may be treated as franked investment income of later accounting periods. For the purpose of (*b*) in the preceding paragraph but one, franked investment income received by a company in a return period must include the excess, if any, of:

(*a*) any surplus franked investment income carried forward from a previous accounting period; and

(*b*) any excess of franked investment income received in earlier return periods of that accounting period over franked payments made in those earlier periods (ibid. Schedule 14, para 2(3)).

Any ACT paid by the company in respect of any distribution made by it in an accounting period may be set against its liability to corporation tax on the income component of its profits (ibid. s. 85(1)). The maximum ACT set-off is 30% of the company's income (ibid. s. 85(2)). In arriving at a company's "income" for this purpose it must be assumed that any reliefs available against total profits (e.g. charges on income, management expenses, trading losses) are set against income before chargeable gains (ibid. s. 85(6)).

Where there is surplus ACT in any accounting period, the surplus is treated as if it were ACT paid in respect of distributions made by the company in successive later accounting periods (ibid. s. 85(4)), i.e. it is carried forward and set successively against corporation tax on income of subsequent accounting periods until eventual exhaustion. The company may, however, make a claim under F.A. 1972 s. 85(3) within two years of the end of the accounting period in which the surplus ACT has arisen, in which case the surplus will be carried back and set against corporation tax on income of accounting periods beginning in the two years preceding that period, taking more recent before more remote periods.

There are circumstances in which surplus ACT cannot be carried forward under s. 85(4) beyond a change in the ownership of a company (F.A. 1972 s. 101(3)). The circumstances are these (TA s. 101(1)):

(*a*) where, within any period of three years, there is both a change of owner-ship and a major change in the nature or conduct of a trade or business carried on by the company; or

(*b*) where, at any time after the sale of the activities in a trade or business carried on by a company has become small or negligible, and before any revival of the trade or business, there is a change in the ownership of the company.

The individual's position: Schedule F: F.A. 1972 ss. 86, 87

Where a company resident in the UK makes a qualifying distribution after 5 April 1973 to an individual resident in the UK, he becomes entitled to a tax credit (F.A. 1972 s. 86(1)) equal in amount to the ACT payable by the company in respect of that distribution (ibid. s. 86(2)). Thus a company declaring a dividend in 1973–74 of £700 to ten equal shareholders must pay ACT of £300, thereby conferring on each shareholder a tax credit of £30. The individual may claim to have the credit set against his liability to income tax or, where the credit exceeds that income tax, to have the excess paid to him (ibid. s. 86(4))

An individual in receipt of a dividend or other distribution made by a company resident in the UK is chargeable to income tax under Schedule F on the aggregate of the amount or value of the distribution and his tax credit (Schedule F paras 1 and 2, as substituted in TA s. 232(1) by F.A. 1972 s. 87(2)).

Example of a qualifying distribution to an individual

Findem & Fleecem Ltd, a debt-collecting company, makes up its accounts for financial years. Its pattern of profitability is as follows:

financial year 1974: profits of £40,000, comprising £30,000 income and £10,000 chargeable gains
financial year 1975: profits of £50,000, comprising £32,000 income and £18,000 chargeable gains
financial year 1976: profits of £111,000, comprising £80,000 income and £30,000 chargeable gains

In June 1976 the company declares a dividend of £140,000, of which £2,100 is received by Will D. Fault, one of its major shareholders. From a fiscal viewpoint, Will's circumstances in 1976–77 are these: he is a married man whose sole source of income is his salary of £8,040 p.a. as managing director of Spineless Bookbinders Ltd and whose only child is a full-time Bar Finals student at The College of Law.

The taxability of Findem & Fleecem Ltd

The company account to the Revenue for ACT of £60,000 in respect of the distribution (three-sevenths of £140,000). This may be set against the company's corporation tax liability on income (£40,000). But the maximum set-off is £24,000 (30% of £80,000). Therefore surplus ACT remains of £36,000 (£60,000 – £24,000). This is treated as if it were ACT paid in respect of distributions made by the company in later years, unless the company claims to carry

Will's taxability

Salary		£8,040
Dividends received	£2,100	
relative tax credit (three-sevenths)	£900	£3,000
Total income		£11,040
Less personal relief	£775	
child relief	£265	£1,040
Assessable income		£10,000

The taxability of Findem & Fleecem Ltd.

it back first, so as to obtain immediate relief. If the company were to make a claim, the surplus ACT of £36,000 would be set against corporation tax on income in 1975 of £16,000, leaving £20,000 of surplus ACT to be set against corporation tax on income in 1974 of £15,000. The unexhausted surplus ACT—£5,000—is carried forward to set against the corporation tax on income in later accounting periods.

Thus, if the company were to make no claim under F.A. 1972 s. 85(3), its corporation tax bills would be:

1974 £18,000 [£15,000 on income, £3,000 on chargeable gains]
1975 £21,400 [£16,000 on income, £5,400 on chargeable gains]
1976 £25,000 [£16,000 on income (£40,000 – maximum ACT set-off of £24,000), £9,000 on chargeable gains]

and surplus ACT of £36,000 would be available to carry forward.

Alternatively, if the company were to make a claim under F.A. 1972 s. 85(3), its corporation tax bills would be:

1974 (revised) £9,000 [£6,000 on income (£15,000 – maximum ACT set-off of £9,000), £3,000 on chargeable gains]
1975 (revised) £11,800 [£6,400 on income (£16,000 – maximum ACT set-off of £9,600), £5,400 on chargeable gains]
1976 (revised) £25,000 [£16,000 on income (£40,000 – maximum ACT set-off of £24,000), £9,000 on chargeable gains]

and surplus ACT of £17,400 (£36,000 – £9,600 – £9,000) remains unexhausted and available to carry forward.

Will's taxability

Unified tax payable:	
on first £5,000 at basic rate	£1,500
on next £1,000 at 40%	£400
on next £1,000 at 45%	£450
on next £1,000 at 50%	£500
on next £2,000 at 55%	£1,100
£10,000	£3,950
Investment income surcharge on excess over £2,000: £1,000 at 15%	£150
	£4,100
Less tax credit on divis received	£900
Total tax payable	£3,200

Permutation 2: qualifying distribution to a company

The company making the distribution is in the same position irrespective of whether its distribution is received by an individual or a company. We are therefore concerned in the ensuing paragraphs solely with the recipient company's taxability. It may be as well to remind ourselves at the outset that the distribution plus the relative tax credit in the hands of the recipient company are its "franked investment income" (*see* p. 246 above).

Franked investment income is not chargeable to corporation tax. TA s. 239 enacts that: 'corporation tax shall not be chargeable on dividends and other distributions of a company resident in the United Kingdom, nor shall any such dividends or distributions be taken into account in computing income for corporation tax'. A company's franked investment income received in an accounting period may be used to frank its distributions of that period, in the manner explained on pp. 253–4 above.

Normally, a company resident in the UK is not entitled to any repayment of income tax in respect of any surplus franked investment income it may have in a year of assessment (TA s. 240(1)). However, a company may make a claim under TA s. 254(1) requiring, for a specified purpose, that the amount of the surplus be treated as if it were profits chargeable to corporation tax. The purpose is to obtain relief on the notional profits in respect of (*a*) trading losses which may be offset against total profits under TA s. 177(2) (as to which *see* pp. 267–8 below), (*b*) charges on income, (*c*) management expenses, and (*d*) certain capital allowances available against total profits (under the Capital Allowances Act 1968 s. 74(3): *see* pp. 269–70 below) (TA s. 254(2)). The effect of a claim is to reduce or extinguish the surplus of franked investment income. Income tax is repayable accordingly (TA s. 254(1)). (One refers to repayment of *income* tax because the tax credit represents basic rate income tax.)

Where the four items mentioned in the previous paragraph do not exhaust the surplus of franked investment income, or where the company has not made a claim under TA s. 254(1), the unrelieved amount of surplus franked investment income may be carried forward to successive subsequent accounting periods and treated as franked investment income received by the company in those later periods (F.A. 1972 s. 89(3)).

Instead of or in addition to making a claim under TA s. 254(1), a company may make a claim under TA s. 255(1) requiring that surplus franked investment income be taken into account for relief under TA s. 177(1) (relief for trading losses carried forward) or s. 178(1) (carry-back relief for terminal losses). A claim under s. 255(1) relating to s.177(1) must be made within six years from the end of the year of assessment for which the claim is made (TA s. 255(6)(*a*)). A claim under s. 255(1) relating to s. 178(1) must be made within six years of the time when the company ceases to carry on the trade (TA s. 255(6)(*b*)). The surplus franked investment income to be taken into account for a year of assessment under s. 255(1) does not include any part carried forward from an earlier year of assessment (TA s. 255(7)).

We have seen (p. 257 above) that a company in receipt of franked investment income cannot normally claim payment of its tax credit from the Revenue (TA s. 240(1)). Under F.A. 1972 s. 86(3), however, a company resident in the UK which is entitled to a tax credit in respect of a distribution may claim to have the amount of the credit paid to it if:

(*a*) the company is wholly exempt from corporation tax or is only not exempt in respect of trading income; or
(*b*) the distribution is the subject of some express exemption under the Tax Acts (other than TA s. 239; as to which *see* p. 257 above).

No such payment may be made in respect of franked investment income which has been used to frank distributions of the company (ibid. s. 89(5)); and, conversely, if an amount of tax credit has been paid to a company under F.A. 1972 s. 86(3), the relative franked investment income cannot be used to frank its distributions (ibid.) nor for purposes of a claim under TA s. 254(1) (as to which *see* p. 257 above) (TA s. 254(8), substituted for its predecessor by F.A. 1972 s. 90(1) and Schedule 15).

These principles are modified in relation to dividend payment made between companies within the same group where an election is made to treat the dividends as "group income": *see* p. 272 *et seq.* below.

Permutation 3: non-qualifying distribution to an individual

A company making a non-qualifying distribution is not required to pay ACT in respect of the distribution, nor is the recipient entitled to any tax credit in respect of the distribution. This is because bonus redeemable shares and bonus securities are not income at the time of receipt, merely the right to receive future income. When interest is paid in respect of the bonus shares or securities, the payment ranks as a qualifying distribution (under TA s. 233(2)(*d*)(i): *see* p. 260 below).

Thus logically a non-qualifying distribution should be ignored for tax purposes from the point of view of both company and recipient. As usual in tax matters, logic does not altogether prevail. While the company remains chargeable to corporation tax on its profits regardless of any non-qualifying distributions it may have made, the individual who receives bonus redeemable shares or bonus securities cannot ignore them totally for unified tax purposes. F.A. 1972 s. 87(5) provides for the taxability of an individual in receipt of a non-qualifying distribution in these propositions:

(a) he is not liable to basic rate income tax on the amount or value of the distribution;

(b) he is liable at the higher rates on the amount or value of the distribution, i.e. he must bring the amount or value of the distribution into the computation of his total income and, to the extent that his total income exceeds £5,000, he is liable at the higher rates after deducting basic rate tax in respect of the excess above £5,000 (the point being that, in theory, the higher rates include basic rate; and he is liable on the amount or value of a non-qualifying distribution only at the higher rates); and

(c) the amount or value of the distribution must be treated for purposes of our old friends TA ss. 52 and 53 as not brought into charge to income tax.

In determining the amount of the distribution constituted by a bonus issue of redeemable shares or securities, the value of redeemable shares is taken to be the nominal value of the shares plus any premium payable on redemption (or in any other circumstances), and the value of securities is taken to be the principal amount thereby secured (including any premium payable at maturity or in other circumstances) (F.A. 1972 Schedule 22 para 2(2)).

An individual in receipt of a non-qualifying distribution is left in an anomalous and rather unhappy position. He has as yet received no income, yet he is liable at the higher rates of tax on a notional sum. When he receives income in respect of his bonus shares or securities in the form of interest payments, the interest payments are taxed as qualifying distributions with the usual consequences. The statute offers him one small crumb of comfort. If he has paid higher rate tax on a non-qualifying distribution and later the company makes a repayment of the share capital or of the principal of the security which constituted the non-qualifying distribution, in respect of which he would be subject to excess liability, then he is entitled to deduct from his excess liability the amount of higher rate tax he originally paid (F.A. 1972 s. 87(6)).

The administrative régime for accounting to the Revenue in respect of non-qualifying distributions is much less rigorous than that applicable to qualifying distributions. A company resident in the UK which makes a non-qualifying distribution after 5 April 1973 must make a return to the

Inspector of that distribution within fourteen days from the end of the accounting period in which the distribution is made or, if it is made on a date not falling in an accounting period, within fourteen days from that date (F.A. 1972 s. 105 and Schedule 21 para 1(1)). The return must contain particulars of the transaction giving rise to the distribution as well as the name(s) and address(es) of the person(s) receiving the distribution and the amount or value of the distribution received by him or each of them (ibid. Schedule 21 para 1(2)).

Permutation 4: non-qualifying distribution to a company

In effect a non-qualifying distribution made by one company to another is outside the corporation tax system. The paying company's tax position is unaffected by the distribution; it pays no ACT and can make no deduction in respect of the distribution. The recipient company is not entitled to any tax credit and cannot use the distribution to frank any qualifying distributions it may have made. Moreover, if the recipient company passes on the non-qualifying distribution to its shareholders, directly or indirectly, the distribution by the recipient company will not rank as a qualifying distribution even if otherwise it might have come within the definition (F.A. 1972 s. 84(4)(b)).

Definition of a "qualifying distribution"

The statutory list includes the following types of payment:

(1) *Any dividend paid by the company, including a capital dividend* (TA s. 233(2)(a)). An example of (1): company sells factory for £100,000, declares dividend of £70,000.

(2) *Any other distribution out of the assets of the company (whether in cash or otherwise) in respect of shares in the company* except to the extent that it (i) represents a repayment of share capital, or (ii) is made for new consideration (TA s. 233(2)(b)). "New consideration" means consideration not provided directly or indirectly out of the assets of the company (TA s. 237(1)). An example of (2): a company distributes a cash bonus to its shareholders.

(3) *Any interest or other distribution out of assets of the company in respect of securities of the company*, except to the extent that it represents the principal thereby secured (TA s. 233(2)(d)). S. 233(2)(d) applies only to securities which are:

(i) bonus securities issued after 5 April 1965;
(ii) unquoted securities (a) convertible into shares in the company, or
    (b) carrying any right to receive shares in or securities of the company;

(iii) securities under which the interest payable by the company (*a*) depends to any extent on the results of the company's business, or (*b*) represents more than a reasonable commercial rate;

(iv) securities issued by:

(*a*) a 75% subsidiary company to its non-resident parent; or

(*b*) a company to a non-resident fellow subsidiary where both companies are 75% subsidiaries of the same *non-resident* parent; or

(*c*) a company to a non-resident fellow subsidiary where both companies are 75% subsidiaries of the same *resident* parent, unless 90% or more of the share capital of the company issuing the securities is owned by a resident company; or

(v) securities which are connected with shares in the company, where "connected with" means that it is necessary or advantageous for a person who has (or disposes of or acquires) any of the securities also to have (or to dispose of or acquire) a proportionate holding of the shares.

The underlying rationale appears to be that all the situations within s. 233(2)(*d*) involve the servicing, but not the repaying, of loan capital: payments made by the company in these situations are more akin to dividends than interest and are therefore treated as though they were dividends.

(4) Where there is a transfer of assets or liabilities between a company and its members, there is a distribution by the company to a member to the extent that the market value of the benefit received by that member exceeds the market value of any new consideration given by him (TA s. 233(3)). This rule does not apply where the company and the member are companies resident in the UK and the former is a subsidiary of the latter or both are subsidiaries of a third resident company (ibid. proviso). "Subsidiary" for this purpose is defined in TA s. 233(4).

There is some doubt as to whether s. 233(3) covers transfers between a company and one of its members as well as transfers between a company and its members as a whole. The better view, accepted by the Revenue, is that it does (*see Talbot & Wheatcroft* 9–16). An example of (4) might, on this view, be: company sells to a member for £10 a filing cabinet worth £15, is treated as making a distribution to him of £5.

(5) We have seen that a repayment of share capital does not normally constitute a distribution. Where, however, there is a bonus issue of shares (other than fully paid preference shares: TA s. 234(2)) at or after the repayment of share capital, the bonus issue is treated as a distribution (TA s. 234(1)). The amount of the distribution or, if there are several bonus

issues, the aggregate amount of the distributions, cannot exceed the amount of capital repaid (ibid.). Thus if a company has repaid £50,000 of share capital in year 1 and years 3 and 5 it issues bonus shares, the amount of the distribution in year 3 cannot exceed £50,000 and the amount of the distribution in year 5 cannot exceed the amount which remains after subtracting the year 3 distribution from £50,000.

(6) TA s. 235 provides for the converse contingency. Where there is a repayment of share capital preceded by a bonus issue of shares made after 6 April 1965, the repayment is to be treated as a distribution up to the amount of the bonus element (TA s. 235(1)). This does not apply where the bonus issue falls to be treated as a qualifying distribution. It therefore applies to an issue of bonus redeemable shares within TA s. 233(2)(c) but not to a bonus issue treated as a distribution under TA s. 234(1).

● The aim of s. 235 is to prevent a company from escaping the distribution provisions by making a distribution out of reserves in the guise of a bonus issue. For example, if a company with an issued share capital of 100 ordinary shares of £1 each were to make a bonus issue of 200 ordinary shares and were to convert the original 100 ordinary shares into 100 preference shares of £1 each, any repayment of either the preference or the ordinary shares would, up to a maximum of £200, be treated as a distribution. Any excess over £200 would rank as a genuine repayment of capital—though it might cause a later bonus issue to rank as a distribution under TA s. 234.

Where share capital is issued at a premium representing new consideration, the amount of the premium is to be treated as forming part of that share capital for the purpose of determining whether any distribution made in respect of the shares is to be treated as a repayment of share capital (TA s. 235(4)). Subject to this, premiums paid on redemption of share capital are not treated as repayments of capital (ibid. s. 235(5)). Thus if a company were to issue 100 ordinary shares at £1·10 per share, were later to capitalize the premium of £10 together with £40 of reserves in order to make a bonus issue on a 1 : 2 basis of ordinary shares, and finally were to resolve to reduce its capital by repaying 50p per share, the company would be regarded as having distributed 40p per share and as having repaid share capital to the extent of 10p per share. On the other hand, were a company to issue 100 £1 shares at par for cash, redeemable at £1·10, it would be regarded on redemption as having made a distribution of 10p per share.

4.46   THE COMPUTATION OF A COMPANY'S PROFITS

A company's profits are ascertained by aggregating its income (computed under the like Schedules and Cases as apply for income tax purposes and in accordance with the provisions applicable to those Schedules and Cases) with its chargeable gains to arrive at its total profits (TA s. 250(3)).

§ 1 Income

The amount of income is computed in accordance with income tax principles, all questions of taxability being determined *prima facie* in accordance with income tax law and practice as if accounting periods were years of assessment (TA s. 250(1)). In relation to a company's accounting period, the "income tax law" to which TA s. 250(3) refers means the law applying, for the year of assessment in which the accounting period ends, to the charge to income tax on individuals, exclusive of those enactments of the Income Tax Acts making special provision for the taxability of individuals (TA s. 250(2)).

Two special rules for the computation of income are worth a mention. A provision of the Income Tax Acts conferring an exemption from income tax applies *prima facie* for purposes of corporation tax (TA s. 250(4)). Where a company begins or ceases to carry on a trade, or to be within the charge to corporation tax in respect of a trade, the company's income should be computed as if that were the commencement or discontinuance, as the case may be, of the trade, whether or not the trade was in fact commenced or discontinued (TA s. 251(1)).

§ 2 Chargeable gains

A company's chargeable gains must be computed in accordance with the principles applying for capital gains tax, all questions of taxability being determined in accordance with the provisions relating to capital gains tax as if accounting periods were years of assessment (TA s. 265(2)). The amount of chargeable gains to be included in the computation of a company's total profits for an accounting period is the net amount of chargeable gains accruing to the company in that period after deducting any allowable losses, whether of the same or earlier accounting periods (but not earlier than 1965–66) (TA s. 265(1)). However, in order to achieve a lower effective rate of corporation tax on a company's chargeable gains than on its income, F.A. 1972 s. 93(1) provides that only such fraction of the net amount referred to in TA s. 265(1) as Parliament may determine is to be included in the company's total profits. This provision took effect from 1 April 1973 (F.A. 1972 s. 93(1)(*a*)). For the year 1973–74 the specified fraction is (illustratively) three-fifths, which reduces a company's effective rate of tax on its chargeable gains to 30% (assuming a corporation tax rate of 50%). Where a company's accounting period straddles March 31—so that it falls partly in one financial year and partly in another—and the specified fractions for the two financial years are different, the gains of the accounting period are apportioned to each financial year on a time basis and the specified fractions separately applied (F.A. 1972 s. 93(3)); and there is a time apportionment too when an accounting period straddles 1 April 1973 except of course that no fraction is applied to reduce the gains apportioned to the period before that date (ibid. s. 93(4)).

§ 3 Deductions from total profits

The Corporation Tax Acts draw an important distinction between those items which are deductible in computing income from each source (e.g. a company's wages bill), or from chargeable gains (e.g. an allowable loss of an earlier accounting period), and those which are deductible from total profits, namely:

   (i) charges on income;
   (ii) trading losses;
   (iii) management expenses of an investment company; and
   (iv) the minor capital allowances.

A case which illustrates the importance of this distinction is *Willingale* v. *Islington Green Investment Co.* [1972] 3 A.E.R. 849.

TA s. 251(2) provides that, unless expressly authorized, no deduction may be made in computing income from any source:

(*a*) in respect of dividends or other distributions; nor
(*b*) in respect of any yearly interest, annuity, or other annual payment or in respect of any such other payment as is mentioned in TA s. 52(2).

But this provision is by no means so formidable as it appears. In the first place, there are two exceptions to s. 251(2)(*b*):

   (i) sums which are, or but for an exemption would be, chargeable under Schedule A (s. 251(2)(*b*)); and
   (ii) yearly interest, incurred wholly and exclusively for the purposes of a trade, payable in the UK on an advance from a bank carrying on a bona fide banking business in the UK (s. 251(3)).

Secondly, the words "in computing income from any source" in s. 251(2) make it plain that the prohibition does not extend to deductibility from total profits. Let us now consider successively the four items which are deductible from total profits.

(1) Charges on income

"Charges on income" comprise the following payments:

(a) any yearly interest, annuity, other annual payment and any such other payments as are mentioned in TA s. 52(2) (other than sums which are chargeable under Schedule A or would be but for an exemption); and

(b) any other interest payable in the UK on an advance from a bona fide bank (as to which, see *United Dominions Trust Ltd* v. *Kirkwood* [1966] 2 Q.B. 431), member of The Stock Exchange, or UK discount house (TA s. 248(3), as amended by F.A. 1973 s. 50(1)). We recall (from p. 264 above) that these payments are among those disallowed as deductions in computing income from any source by TA s. 251(2).

However, even a payment which falls within this definition will not rank as a charge on income if it is:

(1) payable otherwise than out of profits brought into charge to corporation tax; or

(2) a dividend or other distribution of the company, e.g. within TA s. 233(2)(d) (see pp. 260–2 above) (TA s. 248(2)); or

(3) deductible in computing any description of profits (presumably chargeable gains as well as income) for purposes of corporation tax (TA s. 248(2)); or

(4) charged to capital (TA s. 248(5)(a)); or

(5) not ultimately borne by the company (ibid.); or

(6) not made under a liability incurred for a valuable and sufficient consideration (unless payment takes the form of a covenanted donation to charity) (see *Ball* v. *National and Grindlay's Bank* [1972] 3 W.L.R. 17) (TA s. 248(5)(b)); or

(7) in the case of a payment by a non-resident company, incurred wholly and exclusively for the purposes of a trade carried on by it in the UK through a branch or agency (unless payment takes the form of a covenanted donation to charity) (ibid.).

Moreover, by TA s. 248(4), a payment within TA s. 248(3)(a) made by a company to a non-resident will not qualify as a charge on income unless:

(i) the company is resident in the UK; and

(ii) either

    (a) the company deducts income tax from the payment under TA s. 53 or s. 54 and accounts for it to the Revenue under TA

Schedule 9 (or is authorized to make payment in full to a non-resident under the provisions of a double taxation agreement: *see* Statutory Instrument 1970 No. 488): or

(b) the payment is made out of income brought into charge to tax under Case IV or V of Schedule D; or

(c) the payment is a payment of interest falling within TA s. 249.

S. 249 covers interest paid outside the UK by a trading company, where:

(a) under the terms of the contract, the interest is to be paid, or may be required to be paid, outside the UK; and

(b) either:
   (i) the liability to pay was incurred wholly or mainly for the purposes of activities of the company's trade carried on outside the UK; or
   (ii) the interest is payable in a non-sterling currency and the liability to pay the interest was incurred wholly or mainly for the purposes of activities of the company's trade, wherever carried on (TA s. 249(1)).

To the extent that charges on income made wholly and exclusively for the purposes of a trade carried on by the company exceed the amount of the profits against which they are deductible, they may be taken into account in computing a loss for purposes of carry-forward loss relief under TA s. 177(1) (TA s. 177(8)) or of terminal loss relief under TA s. 178(1) (TA s. 178(4)).

Thus yearly interest incurred wholly and exclusively for trading purposes may be deducted in computing trading income. Other charges on income may be deducted, not in computing income, but from total profits. The corporation tax rules as to charges on income are plainly modelled on those of the income tax system.

(2) Trading losses

The income tax blueprint shows through even more clearly in the corporation tax rules relating to trading losses. A trading loss is computed in the same way that trading income would have been computed (TA ss. 177(6) and 178(4)). A company which has incurred a trading loss in an accounting period may use that loss in one or more of three ways. Let us consider each in turn.

(i) *Carry-forward against trading income of the same trade: TA s. 177(1)*

A company may make a claim under TA s. 177(1) requiring that a trading loss of one accounting period be carried forward indefinitely and set against trading income from the same trade in succeeding accounting periods. The claim must be made within six years after the end of the accounting period in which the loss was sustained (TA s. 177(10)). Relief is given against earlier accounting periods before later (TA s. 177(1)).

TA s. 177(7) provides that, where trading income of a later accounting period is insufficient to absorb the entire loss carried forward from an earlier period, the loss may be offset also against any interest or dividends on investment which would have fallen to be taken into account as trading receipts of the later period but for the fact that they are subjected to tax under other provisions. This provision will apply only to a banking or financial company which deals in the securities or shares which yielded the interest or dividends. A company may also make a claim under TA s. 255(1) to set a loss carried forward against surplus franked investment income of the later period (see pp. 257–8 above).

(ii) *Set-off and carry-back against total profits: TA s. 177(2)*

A company may make a claim under TA s. 177(2) requiring that the trading loss of an accounting period be set off against total profits of that period—chargeable gains included. If the company wishes, the claim may require too that the loss also be carried back against total profits, provided the company was then carrying on the trade (TA s.177(2)). The carry-back cannot be for a time greater than the length of the accounting period in which the loss was sustained (TA s. 177(3)). If that time embraces more than one accounting period, the profits of a more recent period are to be relieved before those of a more remote period (TA s. 177(2)) and, to the extent that an accounting period falls partly within and partly outside the carry-back time, the profits of that period are to be apportioned (TA s. 177(3)).

A claim under s. 177(2) must be made within two years from the end of the accounting period in which the loss was incurred (TA s. 177(10)). A loss which is the subject of a claim under s. 177(2) may be set also against surplus franked investment income under TA s. 254 (see p. 257 above). On the other hand, a claim under s. 177(2) does not apply to trades falling within Case V of Schedule D (TA s. 177(4)). Furthermore, a loss cannot be relieved under s. 177(2) unless it is shown that for the accounting period in question the trade was being carried on on a commercial basis and with a view to the realization of gain (ibid.). A loss sustained in an accounting period by a company carrying on the trade of farming or market gardening is excluded from s. 177(2) if the trade sustained a loss—computed without regard to capital allowances—in each of the prior five years (TA s. 180(2)).

To the extent that a trading loss is due to any 100% first year allowance on machinery and plant (under F.A. 1971 s. 42(1), as amended by F.A. 1972 s. 67), the carry-back period is extended from twelve months to three years (TA s. 177(3A), added by F.A. 1971 Schedule 8 para 16(6)).

(iii) Carry-back of terminal losses: TA s. 178(1)

Where a company ceasing a trade has suffered a trading loss in any accounting period falling wholly or partly within the twelve months prior to cessation, the company may make a claim under TA s. 178(1) requiring that the loss be set off against trading income of the same trade for accounting periods falling wholly or partly within the three years preceding those twelve months. Apportionments are made as necessary (TA s. 178(2)). Relief is given for later before earlier accounting periods (TA s. 178(1)). Moreover, relief under s. 178(1) is only available in so far as the loss cannot be relieved under any other provision, e.g. TA s. 177(2) (ibid. proviso).

A claim under s. 178(1) must be made within six years from the time of cessation (TA s. 178(5)). Relief for a terminal loss may be given also against:

(1) interest or dividends on investments not chargeable as trading income (TA s. 177(7)—considered at p. 257 above—is applied to carry-back as well as to carry-forward relief by TA s. 178(4)); and

(2) surplus franked investment income (TA s. 255(1): *see* pp. 257–8 above). Moreover, a company may make a claim under TA s. 178(3) that those capital allowances which fall to be made to the company by way of discharge or repayment of tax (as opposed to those which are deductible from total profits) be taken into account so as to create or augment a terminal loss.

Losses other than trading losses

A company which incurs a Case VI loss in an accounting period may make a claim under TA s. 179(1) requiring that the amount of the loss be set off against any income arising from transactions in respect of which the company is assessed to corporation tax under Case VI for the same or any subsequent accounting period. The claim must be made within six years after the end of the accounting period in which the loss was sustained (TA s. 179(3)).

Allowable capital losses may be set only against chargeable gains of the accounting period in which they are sustained and of subsequent successive accounting periods.

(3) Management expenses of an investment company

An investment company resident in the UK is entitled to deduct its expenses of management. A more restricted form of relief is available in respect of the management expenses of insurance companies. Investment and insurance companies will be considered later (*see* pp. 289–90 below).

(4) The minor capital allowances

The major capital allowances, those covering capital expenditure incurred for the purposes of a trade, are treated as trading expenses of the accounting period for which they are given (Capital Allowances Act 1968 s. 73(2)). Any corresponding balancing charge is treated as a trading receipt of that period (ibid.). In other words, the major capital allowances and charges are given in taxing a trade. The allowances and charges within this category are those given in respect of industrial buildings or structures, machinery and plant, mines and oil wells, patents, and scientific research.

The minor capital allowances and charges—those in respect of farm or forestry buildings and works, those given to the lessor of industrial buildings or structures or of machinery and plant, and those given to a person who licenses patent rights in return for royalties—are given by way of discharge or repayment of tax. Their corporation tax treatment is governed by Capital Allowances Act 1968 s. 74, which may be broken down into the following propositions:

(1) a minor allowance available for an accounting period is given effect by deducting it from the class of income against which it is primarily available (ibid. s. 74(1)), i.e. income from farming or letting, as the case may be, and any corresponding balancing charge is treated as an addition to the appropriate class of income (*see* ibid. ss. 6(6)(*b*), 12(2)(ii), 46(3)(*b*) and F.A. 1971 s. 48(2)); and

(2) if the appropriate class of income is insufficient to absorb the allowance, then (*a*) the amount unrelieved may be carried forward indefinitely against the appropriate class of income in succeeding accounting periods (Capital Allowances Act s. 74(2)); unless (*b*) the company makes a claim under Capital Allowances Act s. 74(3) (within two years from the end of the accounting period for which the allowance falls to be made: ibid. s. 74(5)) that the amount unrelieved be offset against total profits of that accounting period and then against total profits of a previous period not greater in point of time than the accounting period for which the allowance falls to be made (Capital Allowances Act s. 74(3), (4)). The claim under s. 74(3) does not apply to expenditure in respect of patent rights. These are given

effect for corporation tax purposes under provisions corresponding to (1) and (2)(*a*) above (see TA s. 385(3), 5(*b*)).

(5) The order in which deductions from total profits may be made

The relief for charges on income is given after all the other reliefs except group relief (as to which *see* 4.48 § 4 below) (TA s. 248(1)).

(6) Company reconstructions without change of ownership: TA s. 252

Relief from losses and the right to capital allowances may be carried over from one company ceasing a trade to another taking up that trade, provided the companies are in substantially the same ownership.

TA s. 252 applies where, on a company ("the predecessor") ceasing to carry on a trade, another company ("the successor") begins to carry it on, and:

(*a*) at any time within two years after that event at least a three-fourths share of the trade belongs to the same persons as it belonged to at some time within a year before that event; and

(*b*) the trade is not, within the period taken for comparison under paragraph (*a*), carried on otherwise than by a company chargeable to corporation tax in respect of it (TA s. 252(1)).

The "period taken for comparison" is interpreted by the Revenue to mean the period between the latest time at which paragraph (*a*) is satisfied by the predecessor and the earliest time at which it is satisfied by the successor (*see* Revenue booklet I.R. 18 on *Corporation Tax* December 1972 para 83).

Where s. 252 applies, the consequences are these:

(1) The successor receives any capital allowances and is subject to any balancing charges that would have been made to or on the predecessor had it continued the trade (TA s. 252(2)).

(2) No sale or transfer of the assets which is made on the transfer of the trade gives rise to any allowance or balancing charge (ibid.).

(3) The successor is entitled to bring forward any trading losses which the predecessor has not used under TA s. 177(2) (TA s. 252(3)). (For unsuccessful attempts, *see Wood Preservation* v. *Prior* [1969] 1 A.E.R. 364 and *J. H. & S. (Timber) Ltd* v. *Quirk* [1973] S.T.C. 111.)

(4) The predecessor is not entitled to any terminal loss relief (ibid.), except as provided by TA s. 252(5), under which the predecessor is given an entitlement to terminal loss relief in the event of the successor itself discontinuing the trade within four years of succeeding to it.

(5) Special (and barely comprehensible) provision is made for the situation in which, within the period taken for comparison under TA s. 252(1)(*a*),

the successor ceases to carry on the trade and thereupon a third company begins to carry it on.

4.47 PAYMENTS BY A COMPANY WHICH ARE NOT DISTRIBUTIONS

F.A. 1972 Schedule 20 regulates the time and manner in which a company resident in the UK:

(a) is to account to the Revenue for income tax in respect of payments made after 5 April 1973 which are not distributions but from which tax is deductible under TA s. 53 or 54; and

(b) is to be repaid income tax in respect of payments received by the company after that date (F.A. 1972 s. 104). A payment within s. 104 is described as a "relevant payment" (F.A. 1972 Schedule 20 para 1).

The payments covered by TA s. 53 are, broadly, these:

(a) any annuity or other annual payment;

(b) any patent royalty;

(c) payments which, under TA s. 156 or 157, are treated as if they were patent royalties (mining and cable rents and royalties).

TA s. 54 covers certain types of yearly interest, unless payable on a bank loan (*see* p. 130 above).

A company is required, for each of its accounting periods, to make returns to the Collector of any relevant payments in that period (ibid. para 2(1)). The return must be made within fourteen days of the end of each return period (ibid. para 2(3)). The return periods are the same as for ACT purposes (*cf.* ibid. para 2(2) with F.A. 1972 Schedule 14 para 1(2), considered at p. 253 above). The return must show the amount of any relevant payments made by the company in the return period and the income tax in respect of those payments for which the company is accountable (ibid. para 3). Where in any accounting period a company receives any payment on which it has borne income tax by deduction, the company may claim to have that income tax set against the income tax it is liable to pay on relevant payments made by it in that period (ibid. para 5(1)). Income tax in respect of any payment required to be included in a return is due at the time by which the return is to be made and is payable without the making of any assessment (ibid. para 4(1)). Where a company makes a relevant payment on a date which does not fall within an accounting period, the company must make a return of that payment, and income tax in respect of the payment is due, within fourteen days of that date (ibid.

para 9). If the Inspector issues a notice of assessment earlier than either of these due dates, the income tax assessed is due within fourteen days of the issue of the notice (ibid. para 19(2)).

4.48 GROUPS AND CONSORTIA

§ 1 Group income: TA s. 256(1)

● Where a subsidiary pays dividends to its parent or to a fellow subsidiary of a resident parent, the paying and receiving companies may jointly elect under TA s. 256(1) that the dividends be treated as "group income", in which case:

(1) the paying company will not have to account for ACT in respect of the dividends; and

(2) the recipient company will receive no tax credit in respect of them, nor will the dividends be available to frank distributions of the recipient (since they are not to be included in references to its franked investment income unless the Corporation Tax Acts specifically say so). For this purpose one company is a subsidiary of another if the other company holds directly or indirectly more than 50% of its ordinary share capital.

TA s. 256(1) applies also where the paying company is a trading or holding company owned by a consortium the members of which include the recipient company. "Trading or holding company" means a trading company or a company the business of which consists wholly or mainly in the holding of shares or securities of trading companies which are its 90% subsidiaries (TA s. 256(6)(a)). A company is owned by a consortium if at least 75% of its ordinary share capital is beneficially owned by five or fewer resident companies of which none beneficially owns less than 5% of that capital (TA s. 256(6)(c)). Those companies are the members of the consortium (ibid.).

The right of election under TA s. 256(1) is subject to several important limitations:

(1) it may be claimed only if both companies are bodies corporate resident in the UK (TA s. 256(1));

(2) it applies only to dividends, including capital dividends, but not to other distributions (ibid.) (*see also* 4.48 § 3 below).

§ 2 Charges on income: TA s. 256(2)

A paying and a receiving company within the scope of TA s. 256(1) are given a further right under TA s. 256(2) to jointly elect that charges on income paid by the former to the latter shall be without deduction of tax. The election is available also where the recipient is a 51% subsidiary of the paying company.

§ 3 Elections: TA s. 257

An election, whether under TA s. 256(1) or (2), must be made by notice in writing to the Inspector setting out the facts showing the companies' entitlement to make it (TA s. 257(1)) and has no effect in relation to dividends or other payments paid within three months of the election or until the Inspector is satisfied, and has notified the companies concerned, that the election is validly made (TA s. 257(2)). Either company making the election may at any time revoke it by notice in writing to the Inspector (TA s. 257(4)); and the election loses its force at any time the companies cease to be entitled to make it (TA s. 257(3)).

● Neither election applies to dividends received by a company on investments held as trading stock, or to dividends in respect of which, if s. 256(1) and s. 256(2) do not apply to it, the recipient company would be entitled by virtue of any exemption to claim payment of the tax credit (TA s. 256(3), as extended by Finance Bill 1973 cl. 23).

An election under s. 256(1) is invariably advantageous to companies which qualify to make it. Even while the election is in force, the paying company can pay ACT in respect of "any amount of dividends" (TA s. 256(1) proviso). In the Revenue view, this enables a company not only to account for ACT in respect of one dividend and not in respect of the next, but also to account for ACT in respect of *part* of a dividend and not the remainder (*see* Revenue booklet I.R. 18 *Corporation Tax* para 133). Thus, where a subsidiary or jointly-owned company, as the case may be, has franked investment income as well as income chargeable to corporation tax, the group or consortium may agree to account for ACT only on the part of the dividend referable to the franked investment income, i.e. to make a franked payment equal to the franked investment income. This part of the dividend will arrive in the hands of the recipient company as franked investment income and may be put to use in franking its own distributions.

The benefit of an election under s. 256(2) is more equivocal. There is no equivalent in s. 256(2) of the proviso to s. 256(1). Hence no great advantage. One drawback is that while the election remains in force, charges on income *must* be paid without deduction. On the other hand, if no election is made in respect of charges, a group or consortium is faced with the inconvenience of having to account to the Revenue for deductions and then obtaining relief or repayment of the tax.

§ 4 Group relief: TA ss. 258–64

● There is a scheme called "group relief" by which certain kinds of relief, e.g. for trading losses, may be surrendered between members of a group or consortium. The companies involved are called "the surrendering company" and "the claimant company" (TA s. 258(1)). Both must be bodies corporate resident in the UK (TA s. 258(7)).

Two companies are deemed to be members of a group if one is the 75% subsidiary of the other or both are 75% subsidiaries of a third company (TA s. 258(5)(a)). In determining whether one company is a 75% subsidiary of another, the other company is treated as not being the owner of any share capital which it owns directly or indirectly:

(a) if a profit on a sale of the shares would be treated as a trading receipt of its own or another body corporate's trade, or

(b) in a body corporate not resident in the UK (TA s. 258(7)).

A company is owned by a consortium if all of the ordinary share capital of that company is directly and beneficially owned between them by five or fewer companies (TA s. 258(8)(a)). Those companies are called the members of the consortium (ibid.). Group relief within a consortium is available where the claimant company is a member of the consortium and the surrendering company is:

(a) a trading company which is owned by a consortium and which is not a 75% subsidiary of any company, or

(b) a trading company which is a 90% subsidiary of a holding company and not a 75% subsidiary of any other company and the holding company is owned by the consortium, or

(c) a holding company which is owned by the consortium and which is not a 75% subsidiary of any company (TA s. 258(2)).

Group relief consists in allowing the following items to be set off against the total profits of the claimant company for its corresponding accounting period:

(1) a trading loss incurred by the surrendering company in an accounting period (TA s. 259(1));

(2) any excess of the minor capital allowances (as to which *see* pp. 269–70 above) which fall to be made to the surrendering company for an accounting period over the appropriate class of income arising in that period (TA s. 259(2));

(3) any excess of management expenses disbursed by the surrendering company (being an investment company) for an accounting period over the company's profits of that period (TA s. 259(3)); and

(4) any excess of charges on income paid by the surrendering company in an accounting period over its profits of that period (TA s. 259(6)).

A "corresponding accounting period" is any accounting period of the claimant company which falls wholly or partly within an accounting period of the surrendering company (TA s. 261(1)). Where the accounting periods do not coincide the amount which may be set off is appropriately reduced (TA s. 261(2)).

There are two important differences in the operation of group relief as between a group and a consortium. In the first place, whereas within a group, relief may be passed from parent to subsidiary, from subsidiary to parent, or from one subsidiary to another, within a consortium relief may be passed upwards only. The diagrams below and overleaf indicate the constitution of a group and of the two types of consortium and the arrows indicate the possible ways of surrendering reliefs:

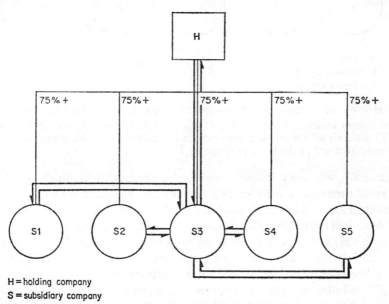

H = holding company
S = subsidiary company

MODEL OF A GROUP

The arrows indicate the ways of surrendering relief available to S3 *vis-à-vis* both H and the other subsidiaries. All the other subsidiaries are in the same position as S3

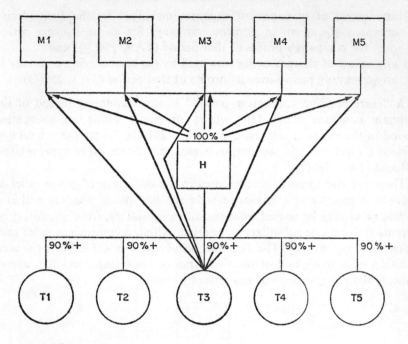

H = holding company
M = member company
T = trading company

MODEL OF A CONSORTIUM—INCLUDING A HOLDING COMPANY

The arrows indicate the ways of surrendering relief available to both H and T3 *vis-à-vis* all the other companies in the consortium. All other trading companies are in the same position as T3

Secondly, whereas a fellow member of a group may claim the whole of the relief surrender, a member of a consortium may claim only the fraction proportionate to its share in the consortium.

TA s. 260(1) requires that a claimant company's total profits against which it may deduct any group relief are to be determined by disregarding any relief derived from a subsequent accounting period but after deducting any other relief from tax. It will be no surprise to learn that "any other relief" includes charges on income—no surprise because we will recall (from p. 270 above) that TA s. 248(1) relieves charges against total profits as reduced by any other relief *other than group relief*.

Group relief is normally available only where both the claimant company and the surrendering company are members of the same group or satisfy the

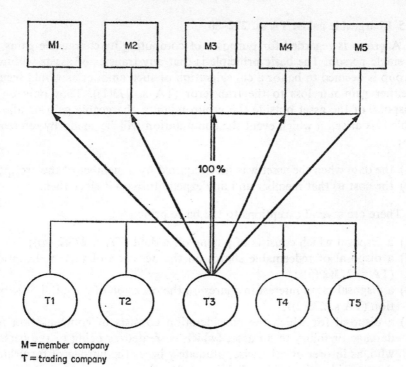

M = member company
T = trading company

MODEL OF A CONSORTIUM—WITHOUT A HOLDING COMPANY

The arrows indicate the ways of surrendering relief available to T3 *vis-à-vis* all other companies in the consortium. All the other trading companies are in the same position as T3

conditions for a consortium *throughout* the surrendering company's accounting period to which the claim relates (TA s. 262(1)). However, s. 262(2)–(4) does make provision, where a company leaves or joins a group or consortium, for time apportionment of the surrendering company's losses (or whatever) and the claimant company's total profits on the assumption that for both companies an accounting period then ends and a new accounting period begins.

A claim for group relief must be made within two years from the end of the surrendering company's accounting period to which the claim relates (TA s. 264(1)(c)). The claim requires the consent of the surrendering company (TA s. 264(1)(b)) and, within a consortium, the consent also of each member other than the claimant company (TA s. 264(2)).

§ 5 Chargeable gains: TA ss. 272–80

A group is regarded for purposes of computing its chargeable gains as a single person. The basic principle is that any transfer of assets within a group is deemed to be for a consideration of such amount as would secure neither gain nor loss to the transferor (TA s. 273(1)). Thus only on a disposal of the asset outside the group might a chargeable gain or allowable loss arise, in which event the computation will be made by reference to:

(a) the date when the asset was first acquired by a member of the group;
(b) the cost to that member and any expenditure on it since then.

There are several exceptions to the basic principle:

(1) a disposal which consists of paying off a debt (TA s. 273(2)(a));
(2) a disposal of redeemable shares on the occasion of their redemption (TA s. 273(2)(b));
(3) a disposal of an interest in shares on the occasion of a capital distribution (TA s. 273(2));
(4) a disposal for which the consideration consists of compensation for damage or injury to an asset (which is treated as being to the person who, as insurer or otherwise, ultimately bears the burden of furnishing that consideration (TA s. 273(3)); and
(5) any *deemed* disposal (see the concluding part of TA s. 273(1), which appears to limit the basic principle to actual disposals: *see* further *Talbot & Wheatcroft* 4–30).

The provisions relating to the chargeable gains of groups apply to bodies corporate resident in the UK (*see* TA s. 272(1)(a), (2)) and a few other specified entities, such as nationalized industries, the constituent bodies of which are treated as forming a group under TA s. 272(5).

4.49 CLOSE COMPANIES

§ 1 Prefatory

For over fifty years special restrictions have been placed on companies under the control of a family or small group of individuals—originally known as "director-controlled companies", later as "close companies"—with a view to curtailing the fiscal abuses to which these incorporated pocket-books, as Transatlantic company lawyers call them, lend themselves. Thus between 1922 and 1966 companies controlled by five or fewer persons were required to make a "reasonable" distribution of their income within a "reasonable" time. If not, a surtax direction and apportionment might be made subjecting the controllers to surtax on the entirety of the company's income as though they had received it in the form of a dividend. From 1937 limits were placed on the deductions which companies of this kind could make for remuneration or other sums paid to controlling directors in arriving at their income liable to profits tax.

F.A. 1965 greatly extended the range of disadvantages applicable to close companies. A large chunk of the Act was devoted to setting up an entire micro-system of special rules. The crucial terms and concepts—"close company", "participator", "associate", "loan creditor", "director", "whole-time service director", "control", and a host of others—were rigorously defined. There followed a sharp decline in the number of applications to Companies House for incorporation.

The disadvantages to which close companies were subjected between 1965 and 1973 were these:

(1) Limits were placed on the remuneration payable to directors other than whole-time service directors.

(2) Any loan made otherwise than in the ordinary course of the company's business, e.g. as a bank, to a participator or his associate, was made the occasion of a Draconian assessment on the company to what the Act describes (as only a statute would) as an amount of income tax equal to income tax on the grossed-up equivalent of the loan. To translate, this meant that, with standard rate at 41·25%, a loan of £100 to a participator or his associate would bring down on the company's head an assessment of £70 odd (41·25% of £170·21).

(3) The same result flowed from any payment for a restrictive covenant made to a participator or his associate.

(4) The definition of "distribution", already by no means uncomprehensive, was extended to include the following additional items:

   (i) interest paid by the company to a director other than a whole-time service director for money advanced by any person;

  (ii) any annuity or other annual payment paid by the company to a participator;

 (iii) with certain exceptions, any rent or other consideration paid or given by the company to a participator for property other than money; and

 (iv) expenditure incurred by the company in providing for a participator or his associate any living accommodation or other benefits in kind, so far as not reimbursed by the participator or associate.

(5) The "company surtax" provisions were recast and, to some extent, formalized. The main changes were threefold. Firstly, administration, previously in the hands of the companies section of the Controller of Surtax, was handed over to the Inspectorate and thereby decentralized. Second, the concept of reasonableness in relation to levels of distribution was abandoned. In its place, the legislation set up a maximum "required standard" of distribution—60% of income in the case of a trading company or property investment company, 100% in the case of an investment company other than a property investment company. Any amount by which distributions fell short of the required standard—called a "shortfall" —could be apportioned to the members for the purposes of both income tax and surtax. The third change was more subtle. Under the company surtax provisions it had been for the Revenue to show that the level of distribution was unreasonable. Under the shortfall system, it was for the company to show that its business requirements prevented a higher level of distribution.

Widespread misgivings were held about the close company rules. It seemed curiously inconsistent to institute a system of corporation tax whose main economic justification lay in the desirability of discouraging distributions and yet to nurture at its bosom a sub-system, applicable to the vast majority of companies, designed to discourage retentions. Moreover, the close company rules clearly operated as a strong disincentive to incorporation.

Measures were therefore enacted in the 1971 and 1972 Acts which effect a considerable relaxation and simplification of the close company rules. The overall result has been to exclude some 80% of the trading companies which originally came within these rules. Only three disadvantages remain for close companies. One is the extended definition of "distribution" (though it now includes only two additional items, namely loan interest and benefits in kind). The second is the necessity of maintaining an adequate level of distributions. Once again the terminology has changed. Instead of "shortfall" we must refer to "an excess of relevant income over distributions". More important, the idea seems to be to return to the pre-1965 situation, in which ongoing negotiations between the company and the Revenue ensured an adequate level of distributions, rather than the more formal régime of the 1965–73 era. The third is the restriction placed on loans to participators or their associates.

§ 2 Defining our terms

(1) "Close company"

A close company is one which is under the control of:

(a) five or fewer participators, or

(b) participators who are directors (however many there may be) (TA s. 282(1)).

A company is also a close company if it satisfies the apportionment test contained in TA s. 282(2) (as amended by F.A. 1972 Schedule 17 para 1(2)), i.e. if, on the assumptions (i) that the company is close, and (ii) that all the company's income is apportioned (a concept we will examine later at para 3), more than half of the income falls to five or fewer participators. Certain companies cannot be close:

(a) any non-resident company (TA s. 282(1)(a));

(b) any registered industrial and provident society or building society (ibid. (b));

(c) any company controlled by the Crown and not otherwise a close company (ibid. (c));

(d) any company (i) controlled by one or more open companies, and (ii) not controlled by five or fewer participators who are not open companies (TA s. 282(1)(d), applying TA s. 282(4)(a), as amended) (to prevent abuse, TA s. 282(5) defines "open company" for this purpose to mean any non-close company other than one which is not close solely by virtue of non-residence: *see* (a) above);

(e) any company in which (i) shares carrying not less than 35% of the voting power (not being shares entitled to a fixed rate of dividend, whether with or without a further right to participate in profits) have been allotted unconditionally to, or acquired unconditionally by, and are beneficially held by, the public; and (ii) those shares have been quoted and dealt in on The Stock Exchange within the preceding twelve months (TA s. 283(1), as amended by F.A. 1973 s. 50).

(2) "Participator"

A participator is, in general, any person having a share or interest in the capital or income of the company, including:

(a) any person who possesses, or is entitled to acquire, share capital or voting rights in the company,

(b) any loan creditor of the company,

(c) any person who possesses, or is entitled to acquire, a right to receive or participate in distributions of the company or any amounts payable by the company to loan creditors by premium on redemption, and

(*d*) any person who is entitled to secure that income or assets (whether present or future) of the company will be applied directly or indirectly for his benefit (TA s. 303 (1)).

(3) "Associate"

An associate is defined by TA s. 303(3), (4), in relation to a participator, to mean:

(i) his relatives, i.e. husband or wife, parent or remoter forebear, child or remoter issue, or brother or sister;

(ii) his partner(s);

(iii) the trustee(s) of any settlement in relation to which the participator is, or any relative of his is or was, a settlor; and

(iv) where the participator has an interest in any shares or obligations of the company which are subject to any trust (except superannuation and other trusts for exclusive benefit of employees), or are part of the estate of a deceased person, any other person having an interest in those shares or obligations (e.g. co-executors: *Willingale* v. *Islington Green Investment Co.* [1972] 3 A.E.R. 849).

(4) "Director"

"Director" includes:

(i) any person occupying the position of director by whatever name called;

(ii) any person in accordance with whose directions or instructions the directors are accustomed to act; and

(iii) any person who is concerned in the management of the company's trade or business and is, either on his own or with one or more associates, the beneficial owner of, or able directly or indirectly to control 20% or more of the company's ordinary share capital (TA s. 303(5), as amended by F.A. 1972 Schedule 17 para 6).

(5) "Control"

A person is taken to have control of a company if he exercises, or is able to exercise or is entitled to acquire, control, whether direct or indirect, over the company's affairs and, in particular, if he possesses or is entitled to acquire:

(*a*) the greater part of the share capital or issued share capital of the company or of the voting power in the company; or

(b) such part of the issued share capital as would, if the whole of the company's income were in fact distributed among the participators (excluding the rights of loan creditors), entitle him to receive the greater part of the amount so distributed; or

(c) such rights as would, in the event of the winding up of the company or in any other circumstances, entitle him to receive the greater part of the assets of the company which would then be available for distribution among the participators (TA s. 302(2), as amended by F.A. 1972 Schedule 17 para 5). TA s. 302(4) reads like something from Gilbert and Sullivan: a person must be treated for this purpose as entitled to acquire anything which he is entitled to acquire at a future date, or will at a future date be entitled to acquire.

§ 3 Apportionment: F.A. 1972 Schedule 16

● Where the "relevant income" of a close company for an accounting period exceeds its distributions for that period, the excess may be apportioned by the Inspector among the participators (F.A. 1972 Schedule 16 para 1(1), (2)) according to their respective interests in the company (ibid. para 4(1)).

Any sum apportioned to an individual must be included in the computation of his total income as its top slice, received by him at the end of the accounting period to which the apportionment relates (ibid. para 5(2)(a)). He is treated as having paid basic rate tax on the sum (ibid. para 5(2)(b)) but is not entitled to any repayment of the income tax treated as having been paid (ibid. para 5(2)(c)), nor is the sum treated as brought into charge to income tax for purposes of TA ss. 52 and 53 (ibid. para 5(2)(d)). So far as the company is concerned, there are provisions in ibid. para 7 designed to ensure that apportionment is no less advantageous than the making of a qualifying distribution.

Where an apportionment is made among the participators in a company, one of which is itself a close company, the sum apportioned may be sub-apportioned to the participators of that company, and the same process repeated until all the sub-apportionments are made to individuals (ibid. para 1(4)).

The Inspector also has power under para 2 to apportion *the whole* of the relevant income of a non-trading company for an accounting period, whether or not there is any excess. An apportionment cannot be made of the income of either a trading company or a member of a trading group (defined as a company which exists mainly for the purpose of co-ordinating

L

the administration of a group of trading companies: ibid. para 11(2)(*a*)) unless the excess is more than £1,000 (ibid. para 1(3)).

In determining whether there is an excess of relevant income, distributions for an accounting period are taken to consist of:

(*a*) any dividends which are declared in respect of the period and are paid during the period or within a reasonable time thereafter, and
(*b*) all other distributions made in the period except dividends within (*a*) attributable to a previous period (ibid. para 10(1)).

The relevant income of a company depends upon its "distributable income". A company's distributable income for an accounting period is the aggregate of:

(i) (*a*) the amount on which the company has to pay corporation tax, less the corporation tax payable on that amount; minus (*b*) the amount of the company's chargeable gains liable to corporation tax, less the corporation tax attributable to those gains;
(ii) the amount of the qualifying distributions comprised in any franked investment income (excluding franked investment income relieved under TA s. 254 or 255: *see* pp. 257–8 above); and
(iii) any group income (F.A. 1972 Schedule 16 para 10(2)).

Thus if in an accounting period a close company has total profits of £1,000 comprising income of £500 and chargeable gains of £500, receives franked investment income of £200 and group income from a fellow subsidiary of £110, its distributable income will be £500 ((i) [(*a*) (£1,000 less £400)— (*b*) (£500 less £150)] + (ii) [£140] + (iii) [£110]).

Distributable income for an accounting period falls into one of two categories:

(i) "estate or trading income", i.e. (*a*) income which, if the company were an individual, would be earned income; (*b*) income chargeable to tax under Schedule A or Schedule B; and (*c*) income chargeable to tax under Schedule D and which arises from the ownership or occupation of land or from furnished lettings (ibid. paras 10(4), 11(1)); and
(ii) "distributable investment income", i.e. the amount of the distributable income, excluding the part attributable to estate or trading income, less the smaller of:
(*a*) 10% of the estate or trading income, and
(*b*) £500 or, if the accounting period is of less than twelve months, a proportionately reduced amount (ibid. para 10(3)).

By way of exception, in the case of companies carrying on the trade of insurance, banking, money lending, financing of hire purchase or similar transactions, or dealing in securities, income incidental to the trade is treated as estate or trading income even where it satisfies the definition in (ii) above (ibid. para 10(5)). In determining any description of income referred to in this and the preceding paragraph, any deductions from total profits for charges on income, management expenses, or other amounts must be treated as made first from the company's investment income charged to corporation tax, next from estate or trading income, and finally from chargeable gains (ibid. para 10(8)).

The relevant income of a company for an accounting period is:

(a) for a trading company or member of a trading group (as defined in ibid. para 11(1) and (2) respectively), so much of its distributable income for that period as can be distributed without prejudice to the requirements of the company's business; and

(b) for any other company (which will be referred to in this book as a "close investment company", although the statute wisely avoids the term "investment company" so as to rule out the possibility of confusion with the creature of that name to which TA s. 304 (relief for management expenses) applies), all of its distributable investment income for that period plus, if it has any estate or trading income, so much of the estate or trading income as can be distributed without prejudice to the requirements of the company's business so far as concerned with the activities or assets giving rise to estate or trading income (ibid. para 8(1)).

The maximum relevant income is determined by two provisions. Firstly, in no case is the relevant income to exceed 100% of the company's distributable investment income for the accounting period plus 50% of the estate or trading income for the period (ibid. para 9(1)). Secondly, a trading company with (a) estate or trading income for an accounting period of twelve months of £5,000 or less and (b) no associated company in the accounting period, is entitled to disregard that estate or trading income in determining the maximum relevant income (ibid. para 9(2), (3)). Sub-paras 9(2) and (3) provide also (1) tapering abatement where the estate trading income is between £5,000 and £15,000; and (2) that, where there are one or more associated companies, the figures of £5,000 and £15,000 should be divided by one plus the number of associated companies. Para 9(6) adds that, if the accounting period is less than twelve months, the figures of £5,000 and £15,000 must be proportionately reduced.

Any close company, other than a close investment company with no estate or trading income, may after the general meeting at which its accounts are adopted make a request to the Inspector for a clearance in relation to any accounting period comprised in that period of account (ibid. para 18(1)). The Inspector must, within three months after receipt of the request, intimate to the company whether or not he proposes to make an apportionment in respect of the company for that accounting period (ibid. para 18(2)). The request for clearance must be accompanied by a copy of the company's accounts, a copy of the directors' report for that period (if any), and such further information as it may think fit (ibid. para 18(1)). Where the Inspector does not, within the time limit, intimate his intention to make an apportionment, no apportionment may be made unless the information supplied to the Inspector was incomplete or inaccurate, or the company ceases to carry on its main activity or goes into liquidation within twelve months of the end of the accounting period concerned (ibid. paras 18(4), (13)).

§ 4 Extended definition of "distribution"

For close companies the definition of "distribution" is widened to include the following items:

(1) (a) any loan interest,
    (b) in excess of 8% per annum of the lesser of the loan or the issued share capital,
    (c) paid by a close company to:
        (i) a director of (aa) that company, or
                (bb) any company which controls or is controlled by the close company
      who has a material interest in (aaa) the close company, or
                        (bbb) a company which controls the close company, or
      (ii) an associate of a director within (i) (TA s. 285); and
(2) any expense incurred by a close company in or in connection with the provision for any participator or associate of a participator of living or other accommodation, of entertainment, of domestic or other services, or of other benefits or facilities of whatever nature, so far as not made good to the company by the participator or associate (TA s. 284(2), (7)).

§ 5 Loans to participators or associates: TA ss. 286, 287

Where a close company makes a loan or advance to a participator or associate, the company is assessed, as if it were an amount of corporation tax chargeable on the company for the accounting period in which the loan or advance is made, on 'an amount equal to such proportion of the amount of the loan or advance as corresponds to the rate of advance corporation tax in force for the financial year in which the loan or advance is made' (TA s. 286(1) as substituted by F.A. 1972 Schedule 17 para 3(1), (2)). A company is to be regarded for this purpose as making a loan to a person where:

(*a*) that person incurs a debt to the close company, or
(*b*) a debt due from that person to a third party is assigned to the close company (TA s. 286(2)).

In either case the company is regarded as making a loan of an amount equal to the debt (ibid.).

These provisions do not apply:

(1) where the loan or advance is made in the company's ordinary course of business, e.g. as a money lender (TA s. 286(1)); or
(2) where the loan does not exceed £15,000 and the borrower, being a director or employee of either the close company or an associated company, works full-time and does not have a material interest in the close company or in any associated company (TA s. 286(3)).

A person has a material interest in a company (for the purpose of (2) as well as of 2.54 above):

(*a*) if he, either alone or with one or more associates, or if any associate of his, is the beneficial owner of, or able, directly or indirectly, to control more than 5% of the company's ordinary share capital; or
(*b*) if, on an amount equal to the whole distributable income of the company falling to be apportioned, more than 5% of that amount could be apportioned to him together with his associates (if any), or to his associate(s) (TA ss. 285(6), 286(9)).

If any part of the loan or advance is repaid to the company after the company has been assessed to tax under s. 286(1), relief must be given from a proportionate part of that tax by discharge or repayment (TA s. 286(5)). Conversely, where the company has made a loan or advance and subsequently releases or writes off the whole or part of the debt in respect of it, the person to whom the loan or advance was made must include the amount released or written off, grossed-up at the basic rate, in the computation of his total income (TA s. 287(1)(*a*) as substituted by F.A. 1971 Schedule 6 para 32(1)).

4.40 SPECIAL CLASSES OF COMPANIES

§ 1 Small companies: F.A. 1972 s. 95

A special "small companies rate"—an illustrative 40%—is enacted by F.A. 1972 s. 95(1) for resident companies whose income in an accounting period does not exceed a "lower relevant maximum amount", with tapering relief where the income is between the lower and the "upper relevant maximum amount". Where a company has no associated company in the accounting period these amounts are £15,000 and £25,000 respectively (ibid. s. 95(3)(a)). Where the company has one or more associated companies in the accounting period, the lower relevant maximum amount is £15,000 divided by one plus the number of those associated companies and the upper relevant maximum amount is £25,000 divided by one plus the number of those associated companies (ibid. s. 95(3)(b)).

Thus a company with income in an accounting period of £15,000 or less pays corporation tax on that income at the rate of 40% rather than the normal 50% and, like any other company, pays corporation tax on its chargeable gains at an effective rate of 30%. Where the company's income for an accounting period is between £15,000 and £25,000, the corporation tax to be paid on its income—applying the normal rate (illustratively 50%) —is reduced by a fraction to be determined by Parliament of the following amount:

$$(M - P) \times \frac{I}{P},$$

where M is the upper relevant maximum amount, P is the amount of the profits, and I is the amount of the income (ibid. s. 95(2)). The fraction is taken for illustrative purposes to be three-twentieths. In the result, a company with, say, income of £24,000 and no gains will pay corporation tax of £12,000 (50% of £24,000) minus £150 (three-twentieths of (£25,000 — £24,000)).

For accounting periods of less than twelve months the relevant maximum amounts are reduced proportionately (ibid. s. 95(6)).

§ 2 Industrial and provident societies, housing associations, and building societies

A special rate—again an illustrative 40%—applies to the income, but not the chargeable gains, of:

(a) any registered industrial and provident society as defined in TA s. 340 and any co-operative association as mentioned in TA s. 340(8);

(b) any housing association approved for purposes of TA s. 341; and
(c) any building society as defined in TA s. 343 and any similar company within TA s. 343(9) (ibid. s. 96(1), (2)).

The special rate does not apply to any body under the control of one or more companies which fall outside s. 96 (ibid. s. 96(2)).

Share or loan interest paid by a registered industrial and provident society is not treated as a distribution (TA s. 340(1)). Share or loan interest paid in an accounting period of the society is deductible in computing its trading income for the period or, if the society is not carrying on a trade, is deductible from total profits as a charge on income (ibid.). It is normally paid without deduction of income tax (ibid. s. 340(2)).

Where for any year of assessment a building society has entered into arrangements with the Revenue under TA s. 343, dividends or interest payable in respect of shares in, or deposits with or loans to, s. 343(2) prescribes the rules to be applied to the society for corporation tax purposes. No part of the dividends or interest may be treated as a distribution of the society or as franked investment income of any resident company (TA s. 343(2)). The society is entitled, in computing its total profits for any accounting period ending in the year of assessment, to deduct the actual amount paid in the accounting period together with any income tax deducted in respect of that amount and accounted for to the Revenue. A recipient company which is paid or credited with any such dividends or interest is treated as having received the grossed-up equivalent of the amount actually received, and is entitled to a set-off or repayment of tax accordingly.

§ 3 Investment and insurance companies: TA ss. 304–6

An investment company resident in the UK is entitled, in computing its total profits for any accounting period, to deduct its expenses of management (including commissions) for that period (TA s. 304(1)).

"Investment company" means any company whose business consists wholly or mainly in the making of investments and the principal part of whose income is derived therefrom, and includes any savings bank (TA s. 304(5)). "Expenses of management" do not include any expenses deductible in computing income for the purposes of Schedule A (TA s. 304(1)), and must be reduced by the amount of any income derived from sources not charged to tax other than franked investment income and group income (ibid. proviso). Where the management expenses of an accounting period, together with any charges on income paid in that period wholly and exclusively for purposes of the company's business, exceed total profits, the excess may be carried forward to the succeeding period and treated as management expenses of that period (ibid. s. 304(2)). Alternatively, the excess may be set against surplus franked investment income under TA s. 254 (*see* p. 257 above).

The provisions relating to investment companies contained in TA s. 304 are applied, with certain modifications, to life assurance companies by TA s. 305. The corporation tax provisions with regard to capital allowances apply with any necessary adaptations to machinery or plant provided for use or used for the purposes of an investment or life assurance company's business, in the same way they apply to machinery or plant provided for use or used for the purposes of a trade (TA s. 306(1)). Any capital allowances or balancing charges made by virtue of s. 306(1) must be treated as made in taxing a trade (ibid.).

§ 4 Authorized unit trusts and approved investment trusts

An authorized unit trust is treated for corporation tax purposes as if it were an investment company (TA s. 354(1)). An authorized unit trust or approved investment trust (as defined in TA s. 359) has, since 1 April 1972, paid corporation tax on its chargeable gains at an effective rate of 15% i.e. in 1972–73 only three-eighths of its chargeable gains had to be included in the computation of its total profits chargeable to corporation tax (three-eighths of 40% = 15%), while for 1973–74 the fraction is taken for illustrative purposes to to be three-tenths (three-tenths of 50% = 15%) (F.A. 1972 s. 93(1)(*b*), (2)(*b*)).

§ 5 Companies carrying on mutual business, or not carrying on a business: TA s. 346

Distributions made either by:

(*a*) a company which carries on any mutual business; or
(*b*) a company which does not carry on, and never has carried on, a trade or a business of holding investments and whose objects do not include the carrying on of a trade or of a business of holding investments,

are treated as distributions subject to the normal rules, but only to the extent to which the distributions are made out of profits of the company which are brought into charge to corporation tax or out of franked investment income (TA s. 346(1), (4)).

§ 6 Company partnerships: TA s. 155

● Special rules contained in TA s. 155 apply to partnerships which include at least one company. Here is a brief summary of those rules, straight from the horse's mouth (Revenue booklet I.R. 18 *Corporation Tax* December 1972 para 263): 'The general approach of the legislation is to ascertain the partnership trading income for an accounting period as if the whole partnership were a company and from that to find the shares appropriate to the company partners. These shares are then taken out and the companies are each assessed to corporation tax on the basis of their accounting periods. Where the partnership includes one or more individuals the balance left after the companies' shares are taken out represents their shares and is assessed to income tax on the partnership.'

5
Value Added Tax

SUNDAY EXPRESS

Alice in Wonderland might have commented:

> *How cheerfully he seems to grin,*
> *How neatly spread his claws*
> *And welcomes little fishes in,*
> *With gently smiling jaws!*

5.1 Basic schema of the tax

As we should all be aware by now, unless recently back from a protracted holiday in the Outer Hebrides, selective employment tax and purchase tax were jettisoned as from 1 April 1973 in favour of a new indirect tax called value added tax ("VAT"). At the same time, another new tax, known as car tax, came into force, levied at the rate of 10% of the wholesale value of all chargeable vehicles made or registered in the UK. We are concerned in the ensuing pages solely with VAT.

The progenitor of our VAT was the French *Taxe sur la Valeur Ajoutée* (TVA), introduced into France in 1954 and now operative in one form or another in no less than twelve European countries. The EEC adopted VAT as the system of indirect taxation least likely to cause distortions in the flow of trade between member countries, a decision which committed Great Britain, as an intending member, to the adoption of a VAT herself. Two directives of the EEC Council, dated 11 April 1967, provide in some detail for the VAT framework to be adopted throughout the Community. The conceptual foundation for our own VAT is well expressed in Article 2 of the first of those Directives (67/227/EEC): 'The principle of the common system of value added tax involves the application to goods and services of a general tax on consumption exactly proportional to the price of the goods and services, whatever the number of transactions which take place in the production and distribution process before the stage at which the tax is charged. On each transaction, value added tax, calculated on the price of the goods or services at the rate applicable to such goods or services, shall be chargeable after deduction of the amount of value added tax borne directly by the various cost components.'

The basic UK legislation on VAT is to be found in the elegantly drafted F.A. 1972 Part I, as supplemented by a daunting body of Orders and Regulations made thereunder, and amended by F.A. 1973. In this chapter of the book, all statutory references are to F.A. 1972 unless otherwise stated; and references to "the General Regulations" should be construed as references to the Value Added Tax (General) Regulations 1972 (S. I. 1972 No. 1147), which have been amended by the Value Added Tax (General) (Amendment) Regulations 1973 (S.I. 1973 No. 244), referred to hereafter as "the Amendment Regulations".

The basic charging provisions is s. 1(1): 'A tax, to be known as value added tax, shall be charged in accordance with the provisions of this Part of the Act on the supply of goods and services in the United Kingdom (including anything treated as such a supply) and on the importation of goods into the United Kingdom.' The tax is quietly assigned to the care and management of the Commissioners of Customs and Excise by s. 1(2). Unlike other VATs the UK tax is charged at a single standard rate of 10% (s. 9(1)) which, as the Government frequently remind us, is the lowest rate in Europe. By s. 9(3), the Treasury are empowered to make an Order increasing or decreasing the rate of VAT by up to 20%. Any such Order will lose its force at the expiration of one year from the date on which it takes effect, unless continued in force by a further Order under s. 9(3). There are two exceptions to the standard rate—zero-rating and exemption. The former is the provision that the supply of certain goods and services should be charged at the rate of 0%, the latter that the supply of certain goods and services should not be chargeable at all. It is important not to confuse one with the other. Exemption is deceptive in that, contrary to one's intuitive expectation, it is less beneficial to the taxpayer than zero-rating. Indeed there are circumstances in which exemption may even be less beneficial than chargeability; but by now, dear reader, you must have become inured to that kind of shock.

Essentially the idea is that each trader should pay tax on the "value added" at his stage of the production and distribution chain; he then passes the tax onto the next trader in the chain, who in turn passes it on, until finally the consumer is left bearing the accumulated charges of all the traders in the chain. This is not to say that VAT is the type of tax whose burden increases according to the number of stages of production and distribution, i.e. a "cascade" tax. Each trader in the chain is ordinarily able to reclaim all the tax charged at prior stages of production and distribution—known as his "input tax" (*see* 5.26 below). Provided the final sale price remains unchanged, the VAT burden on the consumer will be constant however many stages of production and distribution may be involved. An example may help to clarify this point: let us trace the flow of a good through three stages of production and distribution, then through four stages, and compare our results: see opposite.

We notice that in these two hypothetical situations the total VATs charged on traders in the production and distribution chain equal the VAT borne by the customer. This is not necessarily the case. The assumption upon which these two analyses are based is perfect inelasticity of demand (*see* pp. 7–8 above). There is no legal or economic reason why, in the more realistic case of at least partly elastic demand, a trader should not absorb part or all of the tax burden.

One of the advantages claimed for the new tax concerns the export trade. Under the purchase tax and SET system, exports were not entirely free of tax; although manufacturers did not suffer SET or, on their exports, purchase tax, they were liable to purchase tax on ancillary items such as stationery and in effect also bore purchase tax and SET in the form of higher prices paid for services rendered to them by auditors, carriers, and the like.

Another advantage claimed for VAT is that it has broadened the base of

	Value of supply (selling price ex-VAT)	VAT charged	input tax (VAT credit)	VAT paid at each stage
Producer sells to manufacturer	100	10	nil	10
Manufacturer sells to shopkeeper	180	18	10	8
Shopkeeper sells to customer	230	23	18	5
				23
Producer sells to manufacturer	100	10	nil	10
Manufacturer sells to wholesaler	150	15	10	5
Wholesaler sells to shopkeeper	200	20	15	5
Shopkeeper sells to customer	230	23	20	3
				23

indirect taxation in the UK. Purchase tax was levied on a relatively narrow spectrum of goods, mostly luxuries; VAT applies to almost the entire spectrum, many necessaries included, as well as to services and imports. When purchase tax rates were raised, consumers tended simply to buy other goods, leaving the total volume of consumption more or less unaffected. The Chancellor therefore found it difficult under the old system to take effective deflationary action, i.e. in the laboured jargon of political journalism, to take the heat out of the economy. VAT enables the Chancellor to do so because, the tax being so broadly based, consumer expenditure cannot so easily be displaced into other channels. The broad base of VAT means too that a small increase in the rate of tax will produce a large yield: indeed it has been estimated that a rise of only 1% in the standard rate would result in additional revenue of £200 m. Of course there is another side to all this. Given that the yield from our indirect taxes is to remain roughly the same (purchase tax and SET in 1972–73 produced £2,384 m: VAT and car tax in 1973–74 are expected to produce £2,375 m), the more broadly based our system of indirect taxation becomes the more regressive will be its effects. On the basis of the Government's published list of VAT price changes, it would be a fair generalization to suggest that the prices expected to rise were those for necessaries or near-necessaries while those expected to fall were for luxury items which had previously borne high rates of purchase tax.

5.2 Principles of computation

The principles of computation are essentially an elaboration of a series of definitions. Let us examine the key concepts in turn.

5.21 TAXABLE PERSONS: S. 4

The concept of a taxable person is defined in F.A. 1972 s. 4(1): 'A person who makes or intends to make taxable supplies is a taxable person while he is or is required to be registered under this Part of the Act.' Broadly speaking, registration is required of all businesses other than those making taxable supplies not exceeding £5,000 a year, although a person making taxable supplies who is not liable to be registered may apply to the Commissioners to be registered if he considers it to his advantage. Registration is dealt with more fully at 5.51 below.

The existence of a taxable person is a prerequisite to chargeability on a supply of goods or services (not, however, on imports: see 5.24 below). S. 2(2) provides that: 'Tax on the supply of goods or services shall be charged only where . . . (b) the goods or services are supplied by a taxable person in the course of a business carried on by him; and,' the subsection adds, 'shall be payable by the person supplying the goods or services.'

Special provision has been made for a number of special classes of taxable person, some of which we will now consider.

§ 1 Groups of companies: s. 21

It would be administratively inconvenient for one member of a group to charge VAT on a supply to a fellow member, since the tax would have to be reclaimed by the fellow member as part of his input tax. S. 21 therefore enables two or more bodies corporate—provided they are eligible—to apply to be treated as members of a group (s. 21(4)). The prerequisite of eligibility is that one of the companies, one person (whether individual or corporate), or a partnership of individuals should be in control of all the applicant companies (s. 21(3), as extended by Regs. 1(1), 5(3) of S.I. 1973 No. 595, hereafter referred to as "the Isle of Man Order"). The Commissioners may refuse the application only if it appears to them necessary to do so for the protection of the revenue (s. 21(4)). If the application succeeds, the applicants are treated in effect as a single entity. One of them is constituted "the representative member"; all supplies within the group are disregarded, while supplies by or to a member of the group are treated as made by or to the representative member; and any tax paid or payable by a member of the group on imports is treated as paid or payable by the representative member (s. 21(1)).

We notice in passing that there is no need for *all* members of a group to be included in the election under s. 21(4). Indeed we shall come to realize that it may well be convenient for members to be excluded which make predominantly zero-rated or exempt supplies.

Conversely, a single company carrying on a business in several divisions may elect under s. 23(1) to be registered as several separate entities in the names of those divisions.

§ 2 The Crown: s. 19

The Crown is chargeable to VAT on its supplies in the same way as any other taxable person (s. 19(1)). Moreover, where the supply by a Government department of any goods or services does not amount to the carrying on of a business but it appears to the Treasury that similar goods or services are or might be supplied by taxable persons in the course of a business, then, if and to the extent that the Treasury so directs, the supply of those goods or services by that department will be treated for VAT purposes as a supply in the course of a business carried on by it (ibid. s. 19(2)).

§ 3 Local authorities: s. 20

A local authority which makes taxable supplies is liable to be registered, whatever the value of the supplies (s. 20 (1)).

§ 4 Partnerships: s. 22

The registration of persons carrying on a business in partnership may be in the name of the firm (s. 22(1)). Any change of partner is in effect ignored.

§ 5 Terminal markets: s. 26 and S.I. 1973 No. 173

These are not, as the name implies, slaughterhouses but certain com-modity markets, such as the London Metal Exchange, the London Rubber Market, and the Liverpool Barley Futures Market. Pursuant to the powers conferred on them by s. 26, the Treasury have made the Value Added Tax (Terminal Markets) Order 1973 (S.I. 1973 No. 173). This Order zero-rates certain supplies of goods and services in the course of dealings on the ten specified markets. The supplies zero-rated are: (i) those involving goods ordinarily dealt with on the market, provided the supplies are future trans-actions not leading to a delivery of goods by or to a member of one of the markets; and (ii) sales of physical goods between the members of a particular market, provided certain conditions are satisfied.

§ 6 Agents for non-residents: s. 24

Where a person who is accountable for any tax, or on whom any duties are imposed, is a non-resident of the UK or Isle of Man, the Commissioners are empowered by s. 24(1) (as extended by the Isle of Man Order) to direct, by notice in writing to any agent, manager, or factor resident here, that he be substituted for the non-resident as the person accountable or under the obligation in question. The agent etc must have acted on behalf of the non-resident in matters by reference to which the accountability or obligation arose (ibid.).

5.22 BUSINESS: S. 45

"Business" is defined in s. 45(1) to include any trade, profession, or voca-tion; and:

(a) the provision by the Independent Broadcasting Authority of broadcast-ing services;

(b) the provision by a club or by an association (other than a trade union within the Industrial Relations Act 1971 ss. 61 and 86) of the facilities available to its members;

(c) the provision by an organization of the advantages of membership, provided the organization is an organization of persons carrying on a trade, profession, or vocation which has made an election in writing to the Commissioners; and

(d) the admission, for a consideration, of persons to any premises.

The distinction between (b) and (c) is far from obvious: to the extent that they overlap, an election or non-election under (c) would be immaterial.

S. 45(3) deals with the *IRC* v. *Brander & Cruickshank* [1971] 1 A.E.R. 36 type of situation (*see* pp. 101–2 above). It provides that, where a person, in the course of carrying on a trade, profession, or vocation, accepts an office, other than a public office, any services supplied by him as holder of the office should be treated for VAT purposes as supplied in the course of a business carried on by him.

The words "in the course of a business" are of some importance. In respect of supplies they constitute one of the pre-conditions of chargeability, while certain special provisions with regard to imports apply only where the importation is carried out in the course of a business. Less important are the words "for the purpose of a business" considered subsequently.

5.23 SUPPLY: SS. 5–8

§ 1 Nature of a supply: s. 5

We have seen that "supply" has a central place in the charging provisions (*see* s. 1(1) at pp. 293–4 and s. 2(2) at p. 296 above). Nowhere is the concept specifically defined. S. 5, which shows early promise as a definition of supply, turns out to be more concerned with differentiating a supply of goods from a supply of services. The importance of this distinction emerges from s. 5(2), which tells us that a supply of goods may be taxable whether for a consideration or not, while a supply of services is taxable only if made for a consideration. The sub-section states: 'Supply of goods includes all forms of supply and, in particular, the letting of goods on hire and the making of a gift or loan of goods; but supply of services does not include anything done otherwise than for a consideration.' We will see that there are different rules for goods and services with regard to the time and place of supply (§§ 3 and 4 below); and that imported goods but not services are taxable, while exported goods are zero-rated and exported services only zero-rated if within Schedule 4 Group 9.

Mutual exclusivity of goods and services is provided for by s. 5(8) in the form of a negative definition of a supply of services: 'anything which is not a supply of goods but is done for a consideration (including, if so done, the granting, assignment or surrender of the whole or part of any right) is a supply of services'. The respective territories of supplies of goods and of services are delineated by s. 5 (3)–(6). A person who produces goods by applying to another person's goods a treatment or process is treated as supplying goods and not as supplying services (s. 5(3)). The supply of any form of power, heat, refrigeration, or ventilation is a supply of goods and not of services (s. 5(4)). The granting, assignment, or surrender of a major interest in land is treated as a supply of goods (s. 5(6)). "Major interest" is defined as the fee simple or a tenancy for a term exceeding twenty-one years (s. 5(6)). The grant of a lesser interest for a consideration is, by implication, a supply of services. S. 5(6) is of little practical importance, since the grant, assignment, or surrender of *any* interest in land, with a few stated exceptions, is exempt under Group I of Schedule 5.

S. 5(5) gives effect to Schedule 2, which specifies a number of matters to be treated as a supply of goods in the course of business, including:

(a) where goods acquired or produced by a taxable person in the course of a business carried on by him are applied by him to the personal use of himself or any other person (Schedule 2 para 1); and

(b) where a person ceases to be a taxable person, any goods then forming part of the assets of a business carried on by him, unless the business is transferred as a going concern to another taxable person (ibid. para 3).

(These are, respectively, the situations with which the principle in *Sharkey* v. *Wernher* (p. 71 *et seq.* above) and TA ss. 137–8 (pp. 74–5) are concerned for income tax purposes).

Another small indication of the nature of a supply may be gleaned from s. 7(2)(c), which implies that the sending or taking of goods on approval, or sale or return, or similar terms does not in itself constitute a supply.

The Treasury have power under s. 5(7) to make an Order with respect to any description of transaction that it is to be treated as:

(a) a supply of goods and not services;

(b) a supply of services and not goods; or

(c) neither a supply of goods nor services.

The first Order made under s. 5(7) (S.I. 1972 No. 1170) provides that a gratuitous loan of goods by a taxable person in the normal course of, and for the purpose of, a business carried on by him, e.g. a loan of knitting machines to housewives working part-time at home for a knitwear manufacturer, should be treated as neither a supply of goods nor a supply of services.

In determining whether goods or services are supplied to or by persons carrying on a business in partnership, no account may be taken of any change in the partners nor of any change from the business being carried on by the person on his own to its being carried on by him in partnership or vice versa (s. 22(1)).

§ 2 Self-supply: s. 6, S.I. 1972 No. 1970, and S.I. 1972 No. 1169

Under s. 6(1) the Treasury are empowered to make Orders securing that, where goods are acquired or produced in the course of a business carried on by him and:

(a) are neither supplied to another person nor incorporated in other goods produced in the course of that business; but

(b) are used by him for the purpose of a business carried on by him,

the goods should be treated as both supplied to him for the purpose of that business and supplied by him in the course of that business.

S. 6(2) is the corresponding enabling provision with regard to services. It empowers the Treasury to make Orders securing that, where:

(a) a person, in the course of a business carried on by him, does anything for the purpose of that business which is not a supply of services but would, if done for a consideration, be a supply of services; and

(b) such other conditions as may be specified in the Order are satisfied,

the services should be treated as being both supplied to him for the purpose of that business and supplied by him in the course of that business.

Two Orders have been made pursuant to s. 6(1) and (2), the one dealing with cars (S.I. 1972 No. 1168, later revoked and replaced by S.I. 1972 No. 1970), the other with stationery and other printed matter (S.I. 1972 No. 1169).

Perhaps it would be an idea to illustrate the operation of s. 6(1) and (2) by way of an example. We should bear in mind that the underlying rationale is to preserve the competitiveness of persons supplying these goods to businesses which make exempt or partly exempt supplies. Let us suppose that Hooten Holler & Co, soundproofing consultants, buy paper etc for £8,800 (including VAT of £800), from which they produce their own stationery. Had they bought it, the stationery would have cost them £11,000 (including VAT of £1,000). Hooten Holler & Co are liable to account for £200, i.e. output tax of £1,000 (on the supply *by* them *in the the course of* their business) less input tax of £800 (on the supply *to* them *for the purpose of* the business).

§ 3 Time of supply (the "tax point"): s. 7 and Part IV of the General Regulations as amended

At the inception of VAT the provisions relating to the time of supply were important in determining whether tax was chargeable at all. The provisions remain important in the event of any changes in the standard rate and, of more immediate practical significance, in determining the accounting period into which a supply falls for purposes of making returns.

The rules given pride of place in s. 7(2) and (3) are not necessarily the ones which apply in practice.

(i) The rules in pride of place

(a) Goods

A supply of goods is treated as taking place:

(a) if the goods are to be removed, at the time of removal;
(b) if the goods are not to be removed, at the time when they are made available to the person to whom they are supplied;
(c) if the goods (being sent or taken on approval, or sale or return, or similar terms) are removed before it is known whether a supply will take place, at the time when it becomes certain that the supply has taken place, but not later than twelve months after the removal (s. 7(2)).

(b) Services

A supply of services is treated as taking place at the time when the services are performed (s. 7(3)).

(ii) The rules in practice

The rules which normally apply in practice are those of s. 7(4)–(6). S. 7(7) and (8) make provision for certain special situations.

By s. 7(4), the supply is treated as taking place at the time when a tax invoice is issued or a payment is received, under these circumstances:

(a) if the person making the supply issues the invoice in respect of it before the time applicable under s. 7(2) or (3); or
(b) if he receives a payment in respect of the supply before the time applicable under s. 7(2)(a), 2(b), or (3).

S. 7(5) allows the person making a supply a limited right to choose the time of supply; if he issues a tax invoice in respect of it within fourteen days of the time applicable under s. 7(2) or (3), the supply is treated as taking place at the time the invoice was issued, unless he elects otherwise by notice in writing to the Commissioners. The Commissioners may, at the request of a taxable person, extend the period of fourteen days (s. 7(6)). F.A. 1973 s. 5 makes it clear that s. 7(4) is to take precedence over s. 7(5) to the extent of any conflict.

Where there is a deemed supply under Schedule 2 para 1 (*see* p. 300 above)

or under s. 6 (self-supply: *see* p. 301 above), the supply is treated as
taking place when the goods are applied or used in the manner specified in
those provisions (s. 7(7)). The Commissioners are empowered by s. 7(8) to
make Regulations overriding the other provisions of s. 7 by which:

(*a*) goods supplied on hire for any period are treated as being successively
   supplied on hire for successive parts of that period; and
(*b*) services supplied for any period are treated as being successively
   supplied for successive parts of that period.

Pursuant to their powers under s. 7(8), the Treasury have made Regulations
governing time of supply in Part IV of the General Regulations, as amended
by the Amendment Regulations. One Regulation of particular importance
relates to services supplied by a barrister, or in Scotland by an advocate: tax
is chargeable when the barrister or advocate issues a tax invoice or receives a
fee, whichever is the earlier (Reg. 4 of the Amendment Regulations, amending Reg. 20 of the General Regulations).

§ 4 Place of supply: s. 8

The place of supply is important in so far as goods and services are taxable
only if supplied, or deemed to be supplied, in the UK (s. 1(1): *see* p. 293
above). The provisions for goods and for services to some extent overlap.

(*a*) Goods

If the supply of any goods does not involve their removal from or to the
UK they are to be treated as supplied in the UK if they are in the UK and
otherwise they are to be treated as supplied outside the UK (s. 8(2)). If the
supply of any goods involves their removal from the UK they are to be
treated as supplied in the UK (s. 8(3)); and if it involves their removal to the
UK they are to be treated as supplied outside the UK (ibid.). To remove
doubt, s. 8(8) provides that, where goods, in the course of their removal from
a place in the UK to another place in the UK, leave and re-enter the UK,
the removal is not to be treated as a removal from or to the UK.

(*b*) Services

Services are treated as supplied in the place where they are rendered. However, if services might be considered as supplied either in or outside the UK
or as supplied both in and outside the UK, they are to be treated as supplied
in the UK if the person supplying them has his place of business or principal
place of business in the UK and otherwise as supplied outside the UK
(s. 8(4)). For this purpose any person carrying on a business through a

branch or agency in the UK must be treated as having his principal place of business here (ibid.). Where services consist of transport between two places, one in the UK, the other abroad, so much of the services as consists of transport within the UK is to be treated as supplied here, the remainder as supplied abroad (s. 8(5)).

The Treasury are empowered by s. 8(6) to substitute for s. 8(4) and (5) such other provisions as to the place of supply of services as they see fit.

(c) Goods partly in and partly outside the UK

Where a supply of goods is such that s. 8(2) and (3) cannot be applied to it, s. 8(4) and (6) are to apply to it as though it were a supply of services (s. 8(7)).

§ 5 Relief on supply of certain second-hand goods: s. 14

As a general rule second-hand goods are taxable on the full selling price. The effect of this rule is to place non-taxable persons selling second-hand goods, perhaps privately, in a favourable position relative to taxable persons, usually dealers in those goods. The Treasury are therefore empowered by s. 14(1) to make Orders reducing the tax chargeable on the supply of specified goods. This has been done for cars (S.I. 1972 No. 1970), works of art, antiques, and scientific collections (S.I. 1972 No. 1971), motor cycles (S.I. 1973 No. 328), and caravans (S.I. 1973 No. 329). Tax on the supply of second-hand goods of these kinds is chargeable, not on the full selling price, but on the seller's margin only. For details, *see* H.M. Customs & Excise Notices Nos. 711, 712, and 713. *See also* F.A. 1973 s. 6.

5.24 IMPORTS: SS. 2(3), 16–18

We recall from the words of s. 1(1) (pp. 293–4 above) that there are two occasions of charge. One is the supply of goods and services in the UK. The importation of goods into the UK is the other.

By s. 2(3), tax on the importation of goods is to be charged and payable as if it were a duty of customs. The implication of this provision, together with certain qualifications, is spelled out in s. 17. S. 17(1) tells us that the Customs and Excise Act 1952 and, except where the contrary intention appears, any other enactments relating to customs generally (including Regulations or other statutory instruments), are to have effect, subject to any exceptions and adaptations the Commissioners may by Regulations prescribe, as if all goods imported into the UK were liable to duties of customs and as if those duties included VAT chargeable on the importation of goods. S. 17(2) excepts certain enactments from the operation of s. 17(1), namely:

(a) ss. 34(4), 35, and 36 (reimportation);
(b) s. 37 (importation of goods from the Channel Islands);
(c) s. 43(a) (relief from duty of antiques);
(d) s. 221(2) (exemption of certain mechanical lighters);
(e) s. 259 (charge of duty on manufactured or composite articles);
(f) s. 260(1)(b) (declaration as to duty payable);
(g) s. 272 (supply of goods without payment of duty to Her Majesty's ships); and
(h) ss. 308-11 (Isle of Man).

The Treasury are empowered by s. 16(1) to make Orders giving relief from tax chargeable on the importation of goods, subject to such conditions as may be imposed by the Order, if relief appears to them necessary or expedient having regard to any international agreement or arrangements. The VAT (Imported Goods) Relief (No. 1) Order 1973 S.I. 1973 No. 327, made pursuant to s. 16(1), provides for the admission without payment of VAT of certain goods imported for use or demonstration at exhibitions and the like held in the UK. Under s. 16(2) the Commissioners may by Regulations make provision for remitting or repaying tax chargeable on the importation of goods shown to their satisfaction to have been previously exported from the UK; and s. 16(3) gives them a similar power where they are satisfied that the goods have been or are to be re-exported. There are Regulations made under s. 16(2) and (3) to be found in the General and in the Amendment Regulations.

S. 18 empowers the Commissioners to make Regulations for enabling goods imported by a taxable person in the course of a business carried on by him to be delivered or removed, subject to such conditions or restrictions as the Commissioners may impose for the protection of the revenue, without payment of the tax chargeable on the importation; and for that tax to be accounted for together with the tax chargeable on the supply of goods or services by him. There are also Regulations under s. 18 in the General Regulations. The idea is to do away with unnecessary administrative work. We shall see later that tax chargeable on the importation *is* the importer's input tax in respect of the imported goods. It would be silly to have the importer pay VAT in respect of the importation only to claim back an equal amount as his input tax.

Where goods subject to a duty of customs are supplied while warehoused and before payment of the duty, the supply must be disregarded for VAT purposes (s. 27(1)). (Under the bonded warehousing system imported goods may be deposited in public warehouses at a reasonable rent without payment of customs duties until the goods are withdrawn for home consumption, or at all if they are to be re-exported.)

5.25 VALUE: SS. 9(1), 10, 11, AND SCHEDULE 3

VAT is charged at the standard rate:

(a) on the supply of goods or services, by reference to the *value* of the supply; and

(b) on the importation of goods, by reference to the *value* of the goods (s. 9(1)).

"Value" under (a) above is to be determined in accordance with the provisions of s. 10 (s. 10(1)), and under (b) above in accordance with s. 11.

(a) Value of supply

The basic rule is contained in s. 10(2): 'If the supply is for a consideration in money its value shall be taken to be such amount as, with the addition of the tax chargeable, is equal to the consideration.' Thus if a taxable supply is made for a consideration of £110, the value of the supply would be £100, the remaining £10 representing VAT. The statutory terminology may be expressed as a simple equation:

VALUE OF SUPPLY + VAT (charged on that value) = CONSIDERATION

Where a supply of any goods or services is not the only matter to which a consideration in money relates, the supply is deemed to be for such part of the consideration as is properly attributable to it (s. 10(4)). If the supply is not for a consideration at all, or is for a consideration not consisting or not wholly consisting of money, the value of the supply must be taken to be 'its open market value' (s. 10(3)). Presumably s. 10(3) applies only to exchanges, since gifts are subject to a special rule contained in Schedule 3 para 6.

We will recall (from pp. 196–9 above) that the architects of the capital gains tax legislation, when faced with the problem of defining market value, simply borrowed the rules of estate duty law and practice lock, stock, and barrel. The draftsmen of Part I of F.A. 1972 have not taken this easy way out. Instead they have given us an entirely new code of rules. The general rule, contained in s. 10(5), is that the open market value of a supply is taken to be the amount which would be its value if the supply were 'for such consideration in money as would be payable by a person standing in no such relationship with any person as would affect that consideration'. However, a number of special rules are enacted in Schedule 3 which override those of s. 10 to the extent of any conflict (s. 10(6)).

Where it appears to the Commissioners that:

(a) a taxable person has made a supply for a monetary consideration fixed with a view to reducing liability to VAT, and

(b) it is likely that goods or services will be similarly supplied by him,

they may, if it is necessary for the protection of the revenue, give that person directions for securing that the value by reference to which tax is charged on any future supply by him is not less than the open market value of the supply (Schedule 3 para 1). Para 2 contains a similar power enabling the Commissioners to counteract the avoidance device of a taxable person supplying non-taxable persons with goods to be sold retail, either by them or by others, except that under para 2 the value of the supply is to be determined as if the consideration given by the non-taxable persons for the supply were the retail price obtained for those goods. Para 3 deals with hire-purchase: the consideration for goods supplied on hire-purchase under an agreement governed by the Hire-Purchase Act 1965 (or the equivalent Scottish or Northern Irish enactment) is deemed to be the cash price stated in the agreement. (Thus the finance charge, i.e. the interest component, escapes VAT.) Para 4 provides that where goods or services are supplied for a monetary consideration which is to be reduced if payment is made immediately or within a specified time (i.e. at a discount), the consideration must be taken to be so reduced whether or not payment is so made. Para 5 deals with book tokens and the like: where a right to receive goods or services for an amount stated on any token, stamp, or voucher is granted for a consideration, the consideration is to be disregarded for VAT purposes except to the extent that it exceeds the stated amount. (Thus the only chargeable occasion will normally be the exchange of the token etc for goods or services.) By para 7, where a supply of services consists in the provision of accommodation in a hotel, inn, boarding house, or similar establishment for a period exceeding four weeks, the value of so much of the supply as is in excess of four weeks must be taken to be reduced to such part thereof as is attributable to facilities other than the right to occupy the accommodation. That part cannot be less than 20% (para 7(b)).

Tucked away in Schedule 3 para 6 is the important provision that where a supply is a gift of goods or a deemed supply within Schedule 2 para 1 (the *Sharkey* v. *Wernher* situation: *see* p. 300 above), the value of the supply must be taken to be the cost of the goods to the person making the supply; except that if that cost does not exceed £10 and the supply is a gift its value must be taken to be nil. The architects of our VAT were clearly unimpressed by the solution adopted for income tax purposes by their Lordships in *Sharkey* v. *Wernher* (*see* p. 71 above). The dissentient view in that case, held by a numerical majority, has to this extent been vindicated.

(b) Value of imported goods

The value of imported goods, says s. 11, must be taken to be the aggregate of:

(a) the amount that would fall to be taken as their value under the Customs and Excise Act 1952 s. 258 if VAT were a duty of customs;
(b) the amount of any customs duty; and
(c) the amount (i) of any surcharge under the Sugar Act 1956 s. 7, or (ii) of any levy under the Agriculture and Horticulture Act 1964 s. 1, or (iii) payable under the European Communities Act 1972 s. 6(5) (which deals with Community agricultural levies).

The Customs and Excise Act 1952 s. 258(1) (as substituted by the European Communities Act 1972 s. 4 and Schedule 4 para 2(1), (8)) provides that, for purposes of any *ad valorem* customs duty, the value of goods is to be taken according to the rules applicable in the case of Community customs duties. (Unfortunately space precludes any considerations of these rules.)

5.3 Accounting for and payment of the tax

5.31 CONTENT: WHAT IS TO BE ACCOUNTED FOR: S. 3 AND PART V OF THE GENERAL REGULATIONS AS AMENDED

A taxable person is liable to account, at the end of each "prescribed accounting period" (as to which, *see* para 5.32 below), for the excess of any tax chargeable on supplies by him ("output tax") over his "input tax" (s. 3(1)). "Input tax" is defined as:

(a) tax on the supply to a taxable person of any goods or services for the purpose of a business carried on or to be carried on by him; and
(b) tax paid or payable by a taxable person on the importation of any goods used or to be used for the purpose of a business carried on or to be carried on by him (ibid.).

In the converse situation where the amount of a person's input tax exceeds his output tax—which may arise because he has made zero-rated supplies—the excess must be paid over to him by the Commissioners (s. 3(2)).

If all the goods or services supplied by a taxable person rank as taxable supplies, he is entitled to deduct the whole of his input tax (s. 3(3)(a)). On the other hand, if all his supplies are exempt, none of his input tax is deductible. However, difficulties arise where some of his supplies rank as taxable supplies and the remainder are exempt. S. 3(3)(b) provides that only such part of his input tax as is attributable to the taxable supplies may be deducted. S. 3(4) requires the Commissioners to make Regulations for securing a "fair and reasonable" attribution of input tax to taxable supplies. These Regulations are to be found in Part V of the General Regulations as amended by Regs. 5–7 of the Amendment Regulations. Reg. 24(1) of the General Regulations gives us two mutually exclusive methods for apportioning input tax to taxable supplies. The more important, Method 1, allows the person making the mixed supplies to deduct the fraction of his input tax which bears the same ratio to his total input tax as does the value of his taxable supplies to the value of all his supplies. Method 2 is of limited scope. Reg. 24(2) empowers the Commissioners to allow or direct the use of a method other than one of the two specified in para (1). Just as well, the author is inclined to think. Reg. 24(1) leaves plenty of room for avoidance. For example, a person making mixed supplies is able, by taking a large mark-up on his taxable supplies relative to his exempt supplies, to obtain a deduction in respect of a proportion of his exempt supplies. To illustrate this point, let us suppose that a hotelier runs two establishments, one providing holiday accommodation (an exempt supply: Schedule 5 Group 1 Item 1(a)), the other providing normal hotel accommodation (a taxable supply). In a given period his inputs in respect of each establishment (laundry, furniture, stationery, etc) are £110 (including VAT of £10). In this period he supplies hotel accommodation for £330 (including VAT of £30) and holiday accommodation for £200 (on which no VAT is chargeable). The ratio of the value of taxable to total supplies is 3:5. He is therefore entitled to a deduction of £12 in respect of input tax (three-fifths of his total input tax of £20). Effectively he has obtained a deduction of £2 in respect of the input tax on his exempt supply. (Curiously, this is a point which is not discussed in the standard books on VAT.)

S. 3(6) empowers the Treasury to make Orders disallowing the deduction of input tax in respect of the supplies or importations specified in the Order. 'All countries with a VAT', the White Paper explains, 'have found it necessary to restrict the right to claim credit for tax on inputs in the case of certain goods and services, in particular those which are likely to be used for both business and private purposes' (Cmnd. 4929 para 25). The Orders made to date disallow deductions of input tax in respect of:

(a) hardware, sanitary ware, or other articles of a kind ordinarily installed by builders as fixtures which are incorporated in any part of a building by a taxable person constructing the building for the purpose of granting a major interest in it (Input Tax (Exceptions) (No. 1) Order 1972 S.I. 1972 No. 1165);

(b) motor car, unless *inter alia* the car is unused and is supplied or imported for the purpose of being sold (VAT (Cars) Order 1972 S.I. 1972 No. 1970 Reg. 4, replacing the Exceptions (No. 2) Order (S.I. 1972 No. 1166), revoked by S.I. 1972 No. 1534: Reg. 5 of the Cars Order extends the disallowance to cars self-supplied by taxable persons for their own use); and

(c) business entertainment expenditure, unless on overseas customers (Input Tax (Exceptions) (No. 3) Order 1972 S.I. 1972 No. 1167, as amended by the Isle of Man Order Regs. 1(1), 11).

The Treasury are given power by s. 28(1) to provide by Order for the giving of relief from tax paid on the supply or importation for the purpose of any business carried on by any person of machinery or plant in cases where some or all of that tax cannot be deducted under s. 3.

5.32 A SPECIAL RELIEF: REFUND OF INPUT TAX TO CERTAIN BODIES: S. 15

Where tax is chargeable on the supply of goods or services to, or on the importation of goods by, certain bodies and the supply or importation is not for the purpose of any business carried on by the body, the Commissioners are bound, on a claim made by the body at such time and in such form and manner as the Commissioners may determine, to refund to it the amount of the tax so chargeable (s. 15(1)). The bodies in this fortunate position include local authorities and a wide variety of public bodies.

5.33 METHOD: HOW TAX IS TO BE ACCOUNTED FOR: s.30 AND PART VII OF THE GENERAL REGULATIONS

Tax on the supply of goods or services must be accounted for and paid by reference to "prescribed accounting periods" at such time and in such manner as may be determined by or under Regulations made by the Commissioners (s. 30(1)). Claims in respect of input tax must also be made in the manner so determined (ibid.). Under s. 30(2) Regulations may require the keeping of accounts and the making of returns in the form and manner specified in the Regulations and may require taxable persons supplying goods or services to other taxable persons to provide them with invoices (known as "tax invoices") containing particulars of the supply, the tax chargeable on it, and the persons by and to whom the goods or services are supplied.

The Regulations made pursuant to s. 30 are to be found in Part VII of the General Regulations. The idea is that the standard accounting period should be three months but that accounting periods should be allocated among taxable persons by the Customs and Excise in such a way as to ensure a more or less even monthly flow of payments. Where a taxable person expects his input tax to regularly exceed his output tax—because he makes zero-rated supplies—he may be entitled to a shorter accounting period of one month so as to improve his cash flow position. Accordingly Reg. 46(1) provides that every registered person must, on a prescribed form contained in the Schedule to the Regulations, furnish the Controller (i.e. the Controller, Customs and Excise, VAT Central Unit: Reg. 2(1)) with a return showing the amount of tax payable by or to him in respect of each period of three months ending on dates notified in the certificate of registration issued to him, or otherwise, and containing full information in respect of all other matters specified in the form. The return must be made not later than the last day of the month following the end of the period to which it relates (ibid.). The Commissioners are empowered by proviso (a) to Reg. 46(1) to direct or allow a registered person to furnish returns in respect of periods of one month and by proviso (c) to vary the length of any accounting period or the date on which any return is to be furnished to meet the circumstances of any particular case. Reg. 48 requires that a registered person furnishing a return must account therein for all his output tax as well as for all his import tax in respect of the period to which the return relates and at the same time pay any amount of tax appearing by that return to be due.

S. 30(3) allows for Regulations making special provision for specified taxable supplies by retailers of any goods or services or of any particular description of goods or services. These Regulations may *inter alia* permit the value which is to be taken as the value of the supplies to be determined by any special method described in any Notice. The VAT (Supplies by Retailers) Regulations 1972 S.I. 1972 No. 1148 lost no time in giving statutory effect to the four methods set out in Notice No. 707 entitled *VAT: Special schemes for retailers.*

5.34 ENFORCEMENT: SS. 31–41 AND PART VIII OF THE GENERAL
REGULATIONS

The Commissioners are given extensive powers to assist them in securing
compliance with the requirements of the VAT legislation. We only have
space to run through them quickly. S. 31(1) gives the Commissioners a wide
power to make estimated assessments. Under s. 32(1) the Commissioners
may, as a condition of allowing or repaying any input tax, require the
production of documents relating to the tax; and may, as a condition of
paying over the excess of input tax over output tax, require appropriate
security for the amount of the payment. S. 35 enables them to compel the
furnishing of information and production of documents, while s. 37 makes
provision for entry and search of premises and for the searching of persons
by authorized personnel (though, recognizing that discretion is the better
part of valour, s. 37(3) insists that: 'no woman or girl shall be searched
except by a woman').

S. 34(1) imposes on every taxable person the duty to keep such records
as the Commissioners may require. By s. 34(2), the Commissioners may
require any records kept in pursuance of s. 34(1) to be preserved for such
period not exceeding three years as they may require.

There are provisions of the usual stringency with regard to the recovery
of tax. S. 33(1) declares that: 'Tax due from any person shall be recoverable
as a debt due to the Crown.' S. 33(2) adds that any amount shown in an
invoice as tax chargeable on a supply is to be recoverable as tax due from
the person issuing the invoice. The Commissioners are empowered by
s. 33(3) to make Regulations authorizing distress to be levied (or, in Scotland, diligence to be done: s. 33(4)) on the goods and chattels of any defaulter. Regulations made pursuant to s. 33(3) and (4) are to be found in
Part VIII of the General Regulations. S. 41 gives VAT first place in the
priority queue in the event of bankruptcies, windings-up, etc. These provisions are supplemented by the various penalties and offences contained
in s. 38. In particular, any person knowingly concerned in, or in the taking
of steps with a view to, the fraudulent evasion of tax by him or any other
person, is liable under s. 38(1) to a penalty of £1,000 or three times the
amount of the tax, whichever is the greater, or to imprisonment for a term
not exceeding two years, or to both.

On the other hand, the taxpayer is given a right of appeal to a VAT
tribunal against the decision of the Commissioners with respect to any one
of a number of specified matters (s. 40(1)). However, his appeal will not
be entertained unless he has made all the returns he is required to make

and has paid the amounts shown in those returns as payable by him (s. 40(2)). The further conditions surrounding his right of appeal are laid down by s. 40(3)–(5).

5.4 Zero-rating

5.41 GENUS: NATURE OF THE BEAST: S. 12

Where a taxable person makes a zero-rated supply, the supply is treated as chargeable at the rate of 0%—a zero rate (s. 12(1)). Consequently, no tax is charged on the supply, *whether or not tax would otherwise be chargeable*, but the supply is treated in all other respects as a taxable supply (ibid.). The basic principle is therefore that a taxable person making zero-rated supplies is in the enviable position of not having to account to the Controller for any output tax but none the less being able to reclaim the whole of his input tax. The italicized words above—a paraphrase, not the exact words, of s. 12(1)—carry the important implication that zero-rating prevails not merely over standard rating but also over exemption.

Zero-rated supplies are specified in Schedule 4 (s. 12(2)) (*see* 5.42 below). The statutory list of zero-rated items does to some extent overlap with the list, contained in Schedule 5, of exempted items. Notably, Schedule 4 Group 8 Item No. 1 (the granting by a person constructing a building of a major interest in, or in any part of, the building or its site) overlaps with Schedule 5 Group 1 Item No. 1 (the grant, assignment, or surrender of any interest in, or right over, land or of any licence to occupy land, subject to certain exceptions). The conundrum arises: what is the position of a person making only exempt supplies, some of which are zero-rated? An example would be someone whose sole occupation consists in building houses and selling them. The essence of the conundrum lies in the rule that a person making exempt supplies only is not a taxable person (*see* 5.21 above) and therefore, technically, is incapable of making zero-rated supplies within s. 12(1), considered in the preceding paragraph. We are left, to borrow Churchill's phrase, with a riddle wrapped in a mystery inside an enigma.

Relief by way of zero-rating in respect of the items specified in Schedule 4 is extended by s. 12(3) to cover their importation. By s. 12(4), the Treasury are empowered—subject to obtaining Parliamentary approval (s. 43(4)(c))—to make Orders varying Schedule 4 by adding to or deleting from it any description specified therein or by varying any such description. Pursuant to their powers under s. 12(4), the Treasury have made Orders in respect of supplies by charities (S.I. 1973 No. 385), food (S.I. 1973 No. 386), and young children's clothing and footwear (S.I. 1973 No. 387), and a miscellany of other goods and supplies (S.I. 1973 No. 324).

One of the most important categories of zero-rating—exported goods—is not contained within the list in Schedule 4. S. 12(6) provides that a supply of goods is to be zero-rated if the Commissioners are satisfied that the person supplying the goods has either exported them or shipped them for use as stores on a voyage or flight to an eventual destination outside the UK or as merchandise for retail sale to passengers on such a voyage or flight. S. 12(7) empowers the Commissioners to make Regulations zero-rating supplies of exported goods, presumably with a view to enabling them to annex restrictive conditions to the granting of zero-rating in respect of particular classes of exported goods. Regulations governing exports are to be found in Part VI of the General Regulations as amended by the Amendment Regulations. These provisions apply only to goods; services supplied to overseas traders or for overseas purposes are zero-rated only if they fall within Schedule 4 Group 9.

S. 12(8) gives us the Draconian provision that where the supply of any goods has been zero-rated under Regulations made pursuant to s. 12(7) and either the goods are found in the UK after the date on which they were supposed to have been exported or any condition specified in the Regulations or imposed by the Commissioners is broken, the goods are liable to forfeiture under the Customs and Excise Act 1952. (A dramatic extension of the *nemo dat* principle—not only can a man not give what he does not have, he cannot, we now learn, give what he does have but has not paid the tax on. Perhaps this new principle might be included in the standard textbooks on the Sale of Goods!) Moreover, the tax that would have been chargeable on the supply but for the zero-rating becomes payable forthwith by the person to whom the goods were supplied or by any person in whose possession the goods are found in the UK (s. 12(8)). The legislature are clearly taking no chances. However, the Commissioners have a discretion to waive payment of the whole or part of that tax (s. 12(8)). It will be interesting to see how they exercise it.

5.42 SPECIES: THE BEAST'S SPECIFIC CHARACTERISTICS: SCHEDULE 4

As has been stated earlier, zero-rated items are listed in Schedule 4. S. 46(2) provides that Schedules 4 and 5 (the latter, we recall, containing the list of exemptions) are to be interpreted in accordance with the notes contained therein. We must bear in mind that, by s. 46(3), the descriptions of Groups in Schedules 4 and 5 are for ease of reference only and do not affect the interpretation of the descriptions of items in those Groups.

The Groups in Schedule 4 are these:

SCHEDULE 4: ZERO-RATING

Group 1—Food

The supply of anything which:

(a) is comprised in the general items set out below; and
(b) is not comprised in the excepted items set out below, except a supply in the course of catering.

General items

Item No.

1. Food of a kind used for human consumption.
2. Animal feeding stuffs.
3. Seeds or other means of propagation of plants comprised in item 1 or 2.
4. Live animals of a kind generally used as, or yielding or producing, food for human consumption.

Excepted items

Item No.

1. Beverages chargeable with any duty of customs or excise specifically charged on spirits, beer, wine, or British wine and preparations thereof, but not including mixtures which may be sold by retail without licence.
2. Pet foods, canned, packaged, or prepared; packaged foods (not being pet foods) for birds other than poultry or game; and biscuits and meal for cats and dogs.

Group 2—Water

Item No.

1. Water other than:
    (a) distilled water, deionized water, and water of similar purity; and
    (b) water comprised in the excepted items set out in Group 1.

Group 3—Books, etc.

Item No.

1. Books, booklets, brochures, pamphlets, and leaflets.
2. Newspapers, journals, and periodicals.

M

3. Children's picture books and painting books.
4. Music (printed, duplicated, or manuscript).
5. Maps, charts, and topographical plans.
6. Covers, cases, and other articles supplied with items 1 to 5 and not separately accounted for.

Note: This Group does not include plans or drawings for industrial, architectural, engineering, commercial or similar purposes.

Group 4—Talking Books for the Blind

Item No.
1. The supply to the Royal National Institute for the Blind of—
   (*a*) magnetic tape specially adapted for the recording and reproduction of speech for the blind;
   (*b*) tape recorders designed for the reproduction of sound from such tape;
   (*c*) parts and accessories for goods comprised in paragraphs (*a*) and (*b*) above.

Group 5—Newspaper Advertisements

Item No.
1. The publication in any newspaper, journal, or periodical of any advertisement.
2. The preparation of any advertisement intended for publication solely or mainly in one or more newspapers, journals, or periodicals.
3. The supply of services for the purpose of securing such a publication or a preparation as is mentioned in item 1 or 2.

Group 6—News Services

Item No.
1. The supply to newspapers or to the public of information of a kind published in newspapers.

Note: This item does not include the supply of photographs.

Group 7—Fuel and Power

Item No.
1. Coal, coke, and other solid mineral fuels.
2. Coal gas, water gas, producer gases, and similar gases.
3. Petroleum gases and other gaseous hydrocarbons, whether in a gaseous or liquid state.

4. Hydrocarbon oil, petrol substitutes, and power methylated spirits (within the meaning of the Hydrocarbon Oil (Customs and Excise) Act 1971).
5. Electricity, heat, and air-conditioning.
6. Lubricating oils other than those included in item 4.

Group 8—Construction of Buildings, etc.

Item No.

1. The granting, by a person constructing a building, of a major interest in, or in any part of, the building or its site.
2. The supply, in the course of the construction, alteration, or demolition of any building or of any civil engineering work, of any services other than the services of an architect, surveyor, or any person acting as consultant or in a supervisory capacity.
3. The supply, in connection with a supply of services falling within item 2, of materials or of builder's hardware, sanitary ware, or other articles of a kind ordinarily installed by builders as fixtures.

Group 9—Services to Overseas Traders or for Overseas Purposes

Item No.

1. Any services supplied by an agent to his principal if the principal is an overseas trader or overseas resident.
2. The application of any treatment or process to goods imported on behalf of an overseas trader or overseas resident for subsequent re-export and in fact re-exported.
3. The preparation, publication, or dissemination of any advertisement in the UK or the Isle of Man on behalf of an overseas trader or an overseas authority.
4. The supply of any services for the purpose of securing the preparation, publication, or dissemination of any advertisement in the UK or Isle of Man on behalf of an overseas trader or an overseas authority.
5. The supply, in such circumstances as may be specified by order of the Treasury, of such services comprised in Group 2 or Group 5 of Schedule 5 to this Act as may be so specified.
6. The supply to an overseas trader or overseas resident of any services not used in the UK or Isle of Man and not included in items 1 to 5 of this Group nor in any Group in Schedule 5 to this Act.
7. The supply to an overseas authority of any services not comprised in item 5 of this Group nor in any Group in Schedule 5 to this Act.
8. The supply to an overseas trader of services consisting of the storage

at, or transport to or from, a port or customs airport (within the meanings of the Customs and Excise Act 1952) of goods which respectively are to be exported or have been imported, or of the handling or storage of such goods in connection with such transport.

9. The preparation of plans and specifications for construction operations outside the UK and the Isle of Man.

10. The granting, assignment, or surrender of any right solely exercisable or exercised outside the UK and the Isle of Man.

Group 10—Transport

Item No.

1. The supply, repair, or maintenance of any ship which is neither—
   (a) a ship of a gross tonnage of less than 15 tons; nor
   (b) a ship designed or adapted for use for recreation or pleasure.

2. The supply, repair, or maintenance of any aircraft which is neither—
   (a) an aircraft of a weight of less than eighteen thousand pounds; nor
   (b) an aircraft designed or adapted for use for recreation or pleasure.

3. The supply to and repair or maintenance for the Royal National Life-boat Institution of any lifeboat.

4. Transport of passengers—
   (a) in any vehicle, ship, or aircraft designed or adapted to carry not less than twelve passengers; or
   (b) by the Post Office; or
   (c) on any scheduled flight.

5. Transport of passengers or freight outside both the UK and the Isle of Man or to or from a place outside both the UK and the Isle of Man.

6. Any services provided for the handling of ships or aircraft in a port or customs airport, or for the handling, in a port or customs airport, or on land adjacent to a port, of goods carried in a ship or aircraft.

7. Pilotage services.

8. Salvage or towage services.

9. Any services supplied within or outside the UK for or in connection with the surveying of any ship or aircraft or the classification of any ship or aircraft for the purposes of any register.

10. The making of arrangements for the supply of, or of space in, any ship or aircraft or for the supply of any services included in items 1 to 8.

11. The supply on hire of any container solely for the transport of freight outside both the UK and the Isle of Man or to or from a place outside both the UK and the Isle of Man.

Group 11—Caravans

Item No.

1. Caravans exceeding the limits of size for the time being permitted for the use on roads of a trailer drawn by a motor vehicle having an unladen weight of less than 2 tons.

Group 12—Gold

Item No.

1. The supply of any gold bullion.
2. The supply of gold coins by an authorized dealer in gold to another such dealer.

Group 13—Bank Notes

Item No.

1. The issue by a bank of a note payable to bearer on demand.

Group 14—Drugs, Medicines, and Appliances Supplied on Prescription

Item No.

1. The supply of any goods dispensed, by a person registered in the register of pharmaceutical chemists kept under the Pharmacy Act 1954 or the Pharmacy and Poisons Act (Northern Ireland) 1925, on the prescription of a person registered in the register of medical practitioners, the register of temporarily registered medical practitioners, or the dentists' register.

Group 15—Imports, Exports, etc.

Item No.

1. The supply of imported goods before the delivery of an entry (within the meaning of the Customs and Excise Act 1952 s. 28) under an agreement requiring the purchaser to make such entry.
2. The transfer of goods or services from the UK or the Isle of Man by a person carrying on a business both inside and outside the UK or the Isle of Man to his place of business outside both the UK and the Isle of Man.
3. The supply to or by an overseas authority, overseas body, or overseas trader, charged with the management of any Defence project which is the subject of an international collaboration arrangement or under direct contract with any Government or Government sponsored international body participating in a Defence project under such an

arrangement, of goods or services in the course of giving effect to that arrangement.

Group 16—Charities
Item No.
1. The supply by a charity established primarily for the relief of distress of any goods which have been donated for sale.
2. The export of any goods by a charity.

Notes: (1) Where the goods have been donated from his stock in trade by a taxable person item 1 shall only apply to the extent of the exception contained in Schedule 3 para 6. (2) Item 1 shall apply only if the supply is a sale by the first donee of the goods.

Group 17—Clothing and Footwear for Young Children
Item No.
1. Articles designed as clothing or footwear for young children and not suitable for older persons.

Note: "Clothing" includes hats and other headgear.

5.5 Exemption

5.51 GENUS: NATURE OF THIS OTHER BEAST: S. 13

A supply of goods or services is an exempt supply if it is of a description for the time being specified in Schedule 5 (s. 13(1)). While, as we have seen (para 5.41 above), zero-rating and exemption are partially overlapping categories, the categories of chargeability and exemption are mutually exclusive. S. 46(1) defines a taxable supply as any supply of goods or services in the UK other than an exempt supply. As with zero-rating the Treasury are empowered to make Orders varying Schedule 5 (s. 13(2)).

5.52 SPECIES: THE CHARACTERISTICS OF OUR OTHER BEAST: SCHEDULE 5

The Groups specified in Schedule 5 are these:

SCHEDULE 5: EXEMPTIONS

Group 1—Land

Item No.

1. The grant, assignment, or surrender of any interest in or right over land or of any licence to occupy land, other than—
   (a) the provision of accommodation in a hotel, inn, boarding house, or similar establishment or of holiday accommodation in a house, flat, or caravan;
   (b) the granting of facilities for camping in tents or caravans;
   (c) the granting of facilities for parking a vehicle;
   (d) the granting of any right to take game or fish; and
   (e) the granting of any right to fell and remove standing timber.

Group 2—Insurance

Item No.

1. The provision of insurance of any description.
2. The making of arrangements for the provision of any insurance.

Group 3—Postal Services

Item No.

1. The conveyance of postal packets by the Post Office.
2. The supply by the Post Office of any services in connection with the conveyance of postal packets.

Note: "Postal packet" has the same meaning as in the Post Office Act 1953, except that it does not include a telegram.

Group 4—Betting, Gaming and Lotteries

Item No.

1. The provision of any facilities for the placing of bets or the playing of any games of chance.
2. The granting of a right to take part in a lottery.

Group 5—Finance

Item No.

1. The issue, transfer, or receipt of, or any dealing with, money, any security for money, or any note or order for the payment of money.

2. The making of any advance or the granting of any credit.
3. The making of arrangements for any transaction comprised in item 1 or 2.
4. The issue, transfer, or receipt of, or any dealing with, any security or secondary security within the definition in the Exchange Control Act 1947 s. 42.
5. The operation of any current, deposit, or savings account.

Group 6—Education

Item No.
1. The provision of education if—
   (a) it is provided by a school or university; or
   (b) it is of a kind provided by a school or university and is provided otherwise than for profit.
2. The supply of any goods or services incidental to the provision of any education included in item 1.
3. The provision of any instruction supplemental to the provision of any education included in item 1.
4. The provision by a youth club of the facilities available to its members.

Group 7—Health

Item No.
1. The supply of services and, in connection with it, the supply of goods, by a person registered or enrolled in any of the following—
   (a) the register of medical practitioners or the register of temporarily registered medical practitioners;
   (b) the dentists' register;
   (c) either of the registers of ophthalmic opticians or the register of dispensing opticians kept under the Opticians Act 1958 or either of the lists kept under s. 4 of that Act of bodies corporate carrying on business as ophthalmic opticians or as dispensing opticians;
   (d) any register kept under the Professions Supplementary to Medicine Act 1960;
   (e) the register of nurses or the roll of nurses maintained in pursuance of the Nurses Act 1957 s. 2(1) or kept under the Nurses (Scotland) Act 1951 s. 2 or s. 3 or the Nurses and Midwives Act (Northern Ireland) 1970 s. 17(1);

(f) the roll of certified midwives kept under the Midwives Act 1951 s. 2, the Midwives (Scotland) Act 1951 s. 3, or the Nurses and Midwives Act (Northern Ireland) 1970 s. 17(1);

(g) any roll of ancillary dental workers established under the Dentists Act 1957 s. 41.

(h) the register of dispensers of hearing aids and the register of persons employing such dispensers maintained under the Hearing Aid Council Act 1968 s. 2.

2. The supply of any goods or services by a dental technician.

3. The supply of any services by a person registered in the register of pharmaceutical chemists kept under the Pharmacy Act 1954 or the Pharmacy and Poisons Act (Northern Ireland) 1925.

4. The provision of care or medical or surgical treatment and, in connection with it, the supply of any goods, in any hospital or other institution approved, licensed, registered, or exempted from registration by any Minister or other authority.

Group 8—Burial and Cremation

Item No.

1. The disposal of the remains of the dead.

2. The making of arrangements for or in connection with the disposal of the remains of the dead.

5.53 OUR TWO BEASTS FACE TO FACE

One important point of distinction between zero-rating and exemption is that, whereas zero-rating attaches not merely to supplies of goods or services in the UK but also to importations, and indeed to exports, exemption is available in respect of supplies of goods or services only. Narrowing our focus to supplies of goods or services, the essential difference in principle between zero-rating and exemption is that a zero-rated supply ranks as a taxable supply while an exempt supply *ex hypothesi* does not. It follows that on a zero-rated supply the person making the supply charges no output tax and yet is entitled to reclaim his input tax, while on an exempt supply he is entitled neither to charge output tax nor to reclaim input tax. The result is that, all other things being equal, the person making a zero-rated supply is better placed from a fiscal point of view than the person making an exempt supply.

Some further implications of the distinction between zero-rating and exemption may be highlighted by an example. Let us postulate a trader wishing to maintain a profit of £10 in respect of a particular supply:

	Ignoring VAT	If supply is zero-rated	If supply is exempt	If supply is standard-rated
Trader pays	£10	£11	£11	£11
Trader charges	£20	£20	£21	£22
Trader (reclaims)/ pays to the Commissioners	—	(£1)	—	£1
Profit margin	£10	£10	£10	£10

The critical figure is the price the trader must charge to maintain the same level of profitability. We notice that where the supply is zero-rated he need charge no more than he would have charged had VAT not existed. On the other hand, where the supply is exempt he must raise his sale price to £21 to cover the input tax charged on him. We also notice, perhaps with a measure of surprise, that a taxable person would be better off purchasing a standard-rated rather than an exempt supply since (on these figures), although the standard-rated supply will cost him £22 as against £21 for the exempt supply, he will be entitled to reclaim £2 as against nil in respect of *his* input tax. The reverse would be true for a non-taxable person (who is not entitled to reclaim his inputs). To complete our analysis, we should observe that both a taxable and a non-taxable person would do better to acquire a zero-rated rather than an exempt supply; and that a non-taxable person would even do better acquiring a zero-rated as against a standard-rated supply. Of course to a taxable person it makes no fiscal difference whether a supply is zero- or standard-rated.

5.6 Registration: Schedule 1

S. 4(2) tells us that registration is governed by the provisions of Schedule 1. The basic obligation to register is prescribed by para 1, which provides that a person making taxable supplies is liable to be registered:

(a) if there are reasonable grounds for believing that the value of his taxable supplies in any future period of one year will exceed £5,000; or

(b) after the end of any quarter, if the value of his taxable supplies in the period of one, two, three, or four quarters then ending has exceeded the amount shown in the following Table as applicable to that period:

TABLE

Number of quarters comprised in period	Amount applicable
1	£1,750
2	£3,000
3	£4,250
4	£5,000

By way of exception, a person is not liable to be registered by virtue of (b) above if he is able to satisfy the Commissioners that the value of his taxable supplies over the entire year will not exceed £5,000 (para 1).

If any person fails to comply with the requirements of Schedule 1, he is liable to a penalty of £1,000 or, if greater, three times the amount of the tax evaded by the failure (s. 38(5)). Moreover, if an unregistered person issues an invoice showing an amount as tax or as attributable to tax, he is liable on each issue to a penalty of the same amount as under s. 38(5) (s. 38(6)). Thus a person who should be registered but is not has the worst of both worlds: he remains accountable for tax on his supplies but is unable to invoice the tax on to his customers or to claim repayment of any input tax. On 19 February 1973 Mr Terence Higgins, Financial Secretary to the Treasury, announced that a million of Britain's businesses had sent in their VAT registrations.

A registered person who makes taxable supplies ceases to be liable to be registered:

(a) after the end of any quarter, if he has been registered for the whole of the two years then ending and the value of his taxable supplies in each of those years has been £4,000 or less, or the value of his taxable supplies in each of the quarters comprised in those years has been £1,250 or less; and

(b) at any time, if the Commissioners are satisfied that the value of his taxable supplies in the period of one year then beginning will be £4,000 or less (para 2).

Notwithstanding the rules contained in paras 1 and 2:

(a) where a person who makes or intends to make taxable supplies satisfies the Commissioners that any such supply is zero-rated or would be zero-rated if he were a taxable person they may, if he so requests and they think fit, exempt him from registration; and

(b) where a person who makes or intends to make taxable supplies is not and will not be liable to be registered the Commissioners may, if he so requests and they think fit, treat him as so liable, subject to such conditions as they think fit to impose;

until it appears to the Commissioners that the request should no longer be acted upon or the request is withdrawn (para 11).

Recent Developments

As explained in the Preface, this section is intended to provide an opportunity for discussion of developments not included in the text. The discussion is in two parts, the first dealing with decisions of the Courts, the second with legislative activity, principally of course with F.A. 1973. The cases and statutory provisions are considered in roughly the order in which they relate to the text. Page references in heavy type are of course to the text. The section is concluded by a few extra notes arising in further elucidation of some passages of text.

Case-law

The first case to claim our attention is *Arranmore Investment Co.* v. *IRC* [1973] S.T.C. 195 which, happily, reinforces the comments made at **p. 27** about TMA s. 33, described there as a "cardboard castle". Arranmore was a land investment company which had paid £1,815 odd in tax after its accountants had agreed computations with the Revenue on the basis that the company's lettings of building sites constituted disposals for purposes of short-term capital gains tax. Later, in a quite separate case, the Special Commissioners decided that a letting by an investment company of a plot of land did not amount to a Case VII disposal. Arranmore's accountants thereupon put in a formal claim under the predecessor to TMA s. 33 for the £1,815. The Commissioners thought the claim barred by the proviso to s. 33(2). The Court of Appeal in Northern Ireland went even further, holding that the point of law did not arise "in connection with the computation of profits" within s. 33(4). 'I do not think,' said Lowry L.C.J., 'that a point of law can be said to arise in connection with the computation of profits, merely because its decision will ultimately affect the existence or extent of the taxpayer's liability' (ibid. at 204). After discussing the narrowness of the taxpayer's right of appeal under s. 33, his Lordship concluded that: 'The time may well have come for Parliament to review the restriction which fetters the power to state a case on a point of law arising under s. 33' (ibid. at 205).

It is interesting to compare the taxpayer's right of appeal under s. 33 with his right of appeal under TMA s. 56 **(pp. 30–1)**.

S. 33 has existed since 1923 and has given rise to a fair amount of litiga-tion (e.g. *Rose Smith & Co.* v. *IRC* (1933) 17 T.C. 586, *Radio Pictures Ltd* v. *IRC* (1938) 22 T.C. 106, *Carrimore Six Wheelers* v. *IRC* [1944] 2 A.E.R. 503, etc.). On the other hand, s. 56 has had a place in our code since 1880, yet only in 1971 did the opportunity arise—in *R.* v. *H.M. Inspector of Taxes, ex p. Clarke* [1972] 1 A.E.R. 545, mentioned briefly at **p. 31**—for judicial elucidation. If *the Arranmore case* does nothing to reify the mirage of the taxpayer's right of appeal under s. 33, perhaps *Clarke's case* will serve to redress the balance. Not that Mr Clarke won his case—but the reasoning by which the Court of Appeal rejected Mr Clarke's appeal will no doubt be invoked by future generations of taxpayers against the Revenue. What happened in *Clarke's case* was this. In early 1970 the taxpayer had appealed against an assessment. On 9 March the assessment had been affirmed by the Commissioners. However, by an oversight in the office of their clerk, the Commissioners' decision had been notified, not to the Crown's re-presentative at the hearing (a Mr MacKeith), but to the Inspector handling the case. The decision was forwarded to Mr MacKeith on 23 March. He asked the Commissioners to state a case on 2 April. The taxpayer objected. The Court of Appeal held: (1) that the Crown *had* expressed immediate dissatisfaction since "immediate" meant 'with all reasonable speed con-sidering the circumstances of the case' (ibid. at 551 *per* Salmon L.J.); but (2) even if this conclusion were wrong, that the requirement of immediacy was directory and not mandatory. '[A]lthough non-compliance with a provision which is merely directory,' Salmon L.J. explained, 'may make the party in default liable to a penalty, if the statute says so, it cannot vitiate anything that follows' (ibid. at 553).

Murphy v. *Ingram* [1973] 2 A.E.R. 523 concerned the claim of a former Revenue official to child relief (**pp. 52–3**) in respect of his daughter. During the first ten weeks of the tax year 1969–70 she was a full-time student at the University of York. Her course finished on 19 June 1969 and on 19 July she married. Her income for 1969–70 prior to her marriage was £10 and subsequent to her marriage not less than £270. Megarry J. held the taxpayer entitled to full child relief for that year: although the daughter did not cease on her marriage to be the taxpayer's child, her post-nuptial income was deemed under the predecessor to TA s. 37 (*see* **p. 177**) to be her husband's. To the Crown's contention that this rule operated only between husband and wife and the Revenue, not *quoad* others, his Lordship replied: 'I can see no language in the section to support such a contention' (ibid. at 533). (His Lordship's comments on "deeming" provisions in general can be found at **p. 187**.) Megarry J.'s judgment is also valuable for his observations on a number of peripheral issues, including the judicial preference for the *Law Reports* over the Revenue's *Reports of Tax Cases,* which we noted at **p. 32.** Megarry J. (who heads the Incorporated Council for Law Reporting) must now have put the matter beyond doubt. Disapproving the citation of *Leitch* v. *Emmott* [1929] 2 K.B. 236; 14 T.C. 633 from the *Tax Cases* he stated his reasons for preferring the version in the *Law Reports:* 'First the headnote in the *Tax Cases* gives little or no indication of the process of reasoning involved in the decision: the *Law Reports* sets out the relevant statutory provision and the ratio decidendi, whereas although the catchwords in the *Tax Cases* mention r. 16, the headnote does not quote or even mention the rule, and it states the conclusion in seven words that give no indication of what the point was. . . . Second, the *Law Reports* version includes a report of the argument of counsel, which the *Tax Cases* lacks. Third, the language of the judgments appearing in the *Law Reports* differs in a number of respects from that in the *Tax Cases;* and almost certainly these revisions were made or approved by the judges' (ibid. 528–9).

It was also Megarry J. who, in *Ransom* v. *Higgs* (**pp. 63** (containing a résumé of the facts), **64, 82, 161**), delivered a striking judgment at first instance firmly repelling a series of planned raids on the Revenue (to borrow Lord Donovan's phrase: [1972] A.C. at 657). The Court of Appeal have now [1973] S.T.C. 330) partly affirmed and partly reversed Megarry J.'s decision. Their Lordships agreed with the Court below that Mr Higgs' part in the transactions amounted to trade or an adventure in the nature of trade; but held that the trustees, not Mr Higgs, were liable to be assessed on the profit of £170,000 since at no time had he received, nor was he entitled to, any part of that sum. 'To my mind,' ventured Roskill L.J., 'the crucial factor in this case is that the acts of the companies which were an essential prerequisite to the achievement of the scheme were not in any real sense acts of the companies carried out in those companies' own interests. They were acts forced on or enjoined on the companies by Mr Higgs and those acting with him against the companies' own interests but in the interests of those who controlled the companies. The dominating actor was Mr Higgs' (ibid. at 356–7). His Lordship made it abundantly clear that he was not relying on any doctrine of "the substance" (*see* **pp. 37–9**): 'I fully accept . . .,' he said, 'that it is not legitimate to disregard the separate legal entities involved. . . . [T]he reason why Mr Higgs is to be held to have been trading . . . is because of what he personally did and procured' (ibid. at 359). Russell L.J., in a much shorter judgment, put the matter more colourfully: 'The analogy may be, as analogies so often are, imperfect; but the conductor of an orchestra is responsible for the performance of the symphony although he plays no instrument. Even more so, if he happens to control the performing rights in the work' (ibid. at 372).

In *Taylor* v. *Good* [1973] S.T.C. 383 a different facet of the question of trade or no trade (pp. 63, 64) arose for decision. In 1959 Mr Taylor, a grocer in Cheltenham, attended an auction for a 17-room house on the outskirts of the town, where his father had once worked as a gardener. To his surprise, he was one of only two bidders; and had the house knocked down to him for £5,100. At the time he was undecided what to do with the property but had in mind the possibility of going to live in it with his wife. He abandoned this idea shortly afterwards: in view of the house's condition, his wife considered it impracticable. In 1962 he obtained planning permission and in 1963 sold the property to a developer for £54,500. He was assessed for 1963–64 under Case 1 of Schedule D in a sum representing the difference between the purchase and sale price. The Special Commissioners affirmed the assessment on the footing that the transaction represented an adventure in the nature of trade. On appeal, Megarry J. held, applying *Mitchell Bros* v. *Tomlinson* (1957) 37 T.C. 224, that although the transaction initially lacked the characteristics of trade, once the transactions relating to planning permission had begun, there came into existence material which might have supported the Commissioners' decision. 'For the taxpayer,' the learned judge pointed out, 'a non-trading inception may be a valuable asset: but it is no palladium' (ibid. at 392). However, the Commissioners' finding that there had been trading throughout the period from purchase to sale could not stand: 'I think the least unsatisfactory course would be to remit the case to the Special Commissioners to determine, consistently with this decision, when the trading . . . began, and what value (if not agreed) the property had when it became the subject of trading, so that the true profit derived from the trade may be determined' (ibid. at 397).

Clark v. *Follett* [1973] S.T.C. 240 also concerns a once-off transaction in land (pp. 62–3), though Mr Clark's appeal was by no means as promising as Mr Taylor's. Mr Clark had sold a farm to the Air Ministry in 1943. After the War, following the Crichel Down affair, Government policy was to give former owners an opportunity to buy back land no longer needed by the Ministries. In 1961 the Air Ministry offered the farm back to the taxpayer for £14,250. The day after taking a conveyance of the farm, the taxpayer sold it by auction for £39,000. Trying to make bricks without straw, he contended that the profit was derived, not from an adventure in the nature of a trade, but from the realization of a capital asset, namely the right of pre-emption acquired by him in 1943 under the Lands Clauses

Consolidation Act 1845. Not surprisingly, Goulding J. dismissed his appeal: even assuming the taxpayer had acquired a right of pre-emption under the 1845 Act, he had exercised that right in order to acquire the land with a view to profitable re-sale.

Let us now return to the duality argument. Leaving its broader implications aside for the moment, the argument in its narrow form runs like this: where an enactment requires that, to be allowable, expenditure must be "wholly and exclusively" incurred for a particular purpose, an admission or finding that an item was incurred partly for that and partly for another purpose disqualifies the item in its entirety. This argument won the support of the House of Lords in *Ricketts* v. *Colquhoun* (**p. 81**). However, a number of judges have sought ways round it. Indeed the author was able at **pp. 81–3** (Schedule D), **113–14** (Schedule E), and **207** (capital gains tax) to point to such cases as *Bowden* v. *Russell & Russell*, *Elwood* v. *Utitz*, *Owen* v. *Pook*, *Horton* v. *Young*, and *IRC* v. *Richards' Executors* as creating 'a climate of liberality in which the efficacy of some of the older decisions must be regarded as doubtful' (**p. 114**). An important link in this growing chain of authority was Pennycuick V.-C.'s decision in *Taylor* v. *Provan* (a summary of which, together with the facts, appears on **p. 114**). The Court of Appeal have now ([1972] 2 W.L.R. 675), in a single judgment delivered by Russell L.J., removed that link by reversing Pennycuick V.-C.'s decision. The Court held that:

(1) The expenses reimbursed to Mr Taylor fell within what is now TA s. 195 (*see* **p. 115**) as emoluments of a director. He was not entitled to differentiate expenses paid to him as a director from those paid to him in respect of his special assignment. 'We say at once that this may well be considered to be, to say the least, unfair, but one is by now familiar with systems of fiscal legislation which, in order to prevent avoidance devices, cast the net so wide as to ensnare the innocent' (ibid. at p. 679).

(2) The travelling expenses were not deductible within what is now TA s. 189(1) (*see* **p. 111**). 'It is clear that if regard is to be had to the personal position of the taxpayer, ordinarily resident as he was across the Atlantic and required by the nature of his special assignment to come from time to time to the United Kingdom, then these expenses would come within [s. 189(1)]. But this approach, which found favour with Warrington L.J. in his dissenting judgment in *Ricketts* v. *Colquhoun* [1926] A.C. 1; 10 T.C. 118, is clearly established on authority to be wrong: see, for example, the same case. The test is an objective one: it must be established that the expenditure was necessitated by the nature of the office and the duties involved in it without reference to the personal circumstances of the particular holder of

M*

that office (ibid. at 681). Pennycuick V.-C.'s two-places-of-work conclusion was 'a misreading of the situation' (ibid. at 682).

We may not have seen the end of *Taylor* v. *Provan*. On 16 April 1973 the Appeal Committee of the House of Lords granted the taxpayer leave to appeal. Now that the House no longer regards itself as bound by its own previous decisions, the opportunity may arise to take up Lord Pearce's suggestion in *Owen* v. *Pook* that *Ricketts* v. *Colquhoun* be considered afresh.

Incidentally, another appeal from a decision of Pennycuick V.-C. in *Fall* v. *Hitchen* (**p. 102**) will have been heard by the Court of Appeal by the time this book is published.

Finally, let us take a look at *Aplin* v. *White* [1973] S.T.C. 322 which raises a short point on the meaning of "interest of money" within Case III of Schedule D. (Some rather more difficult cases on the subject are discussed at **pp. 139–40**.) Mr Aplin was an estate agent in Tooting. He collected rents on behalf of clients and deposited the moneys at a bank in the name of his firm. As it would have been difficult to divide the interest among his clients, Mr Aplin had not accounted to them for it. He was assessed under Case III in respect of the interest and challenged the assessment on the basis that the interest belonged really to his clients or, alternatively, that it should have been assessed under Schedule D Case II. Megarry J. rejected these contentions: the interest fell squarely within Case III and the fact that the taxpayer was not beneficially entitled to the money was beside the point, since he had "received" it within what is now TA s. 114(1).

Statutory provisions

Let us kick off with stamp duties, not in fact dealt with in this book, but which our high-flying bird gave us a glimpse of at **p. 4**. Formerly, stamp duties included *capital duty*, payable on the formation of a limited company at the rate of 50p for every £100 of nominal capital, and *loan capital duty*, exigible at the same rate whenever a company borrowed money, e.g. by issuing debentures, unless the loan took the form of a bank overdraft or purely temporary arrangement. In order to harmonize our law with the EEC directive on company taxation, we have had to get rid of *loan capital duty* and restructure *capital duty*. The new system, implemented by F.A. 1973 ss. 47–50 and Schedule 19, comes into operation on 1 August 1973. The key concepts are "capital companies", "chargeable transactions", and "relevant documents": the basic idea is that, whenever a chargeable transaction is carried out by a capital company, the relevant document is to be charged with *ad valorem* stamp duty of £1 for every £100 of the amount determined in relation to that document under Part II of Schedule 19.

Turning now to income tax, where our high-flying bird came to ground, we recall that one of the less salutary effects of the new system of unified tax (**pp. 49** *et seq.*) would have been that charities receiving income under covenants expressed as a net sum after deduction of tax were able to reclaim from the Revenue only £30 in every £100 rather than £38·75 as in the days of standard rate. In his 1973 Speech the Chancellor confessed to having received a number of representations that the resultant drop in the income of charities would cause considerable hardship, since they were in many cases committed to long-term expenditure which they had anticipated meeting out of covenanted donations before the basic rate of 30% was announced in 1971. He therefore proposed a scheme for transitional relief whereby a charity making a repayment claim would be able also to claim a supplementary payment for the years 1973–74 to 1976–77. This payment would be based on the tax repaid to the charity concerned in respect of its net covenants for the year 1971–72. For 1973–74 it would be the difference between that amount and what would have been repaid had the standard rate been 30% in 1971–72: for 1974–75 it would be 75% of that difference: for 1975–76 it would be 50%: and for 1976–77 25%. Thereafter the supplementary payments would cease: by then most seven-year covenants would have ceased and all new covenants would be made in awareness of the implications of the new system. Mr Barber's scheme has now been implemented in F.A. 1973 s. 52.

Another of Mr Barber's proposals, designed to tighten up the régime governing incentive schemes instituted by F.A. 1972 s. 79 and Schedule 12 (outlined at **pp. 105–7**), was implemented in F.A. 1973 s. 19 and Schedule 8.

An account of Part II of Schedule 8, which establishes a framework for savings-related share incentive schemes, was given at **pp. 107–8**; but space precluded consideration of Part I of that Schedule, which deals with profit-sharing schemes. The ensuing three paragraphs represent an attempt to supply that deficiency.

To make sense of the provisions in Part I of Schedule 8, we must first appreciate that, under s. 79 of the 1972 Act, the two Schedule E charges contained in s. 79(4) and (7) (*see* **p. 107**) are excluded not only if the scheme meets the conditions laid down in Schedule 12 but also if the shares (or interest therein) were acquired under profit-sharing arrangements (s. 79(2)(*b*), (3)(*b*)), defined as 'arrangements under which employees of a body corporate receive as part of their emoluments shares or interests in shares of that body or of a body controlling it to an extent determined in advance by reference to the profits of either body' (s. 79(8)). Paras 1–3 of Schedule 8 provide that, where the arrangements were made or modified after 22 March 1973, s. 79(2)(*b*) and (3)(*b*) will no longer be sufficient to exclude the Schedule E charges, unless:

(*a*) the arrangements allow all full-time employees of the company concerned who have been full-time employees for a continuous period of not less than two years to acquire shares or interests in shares on similar terms;

(*b*) the shares are not subject to restrictions which may or will result in the acquirer obtaining a benefit through an increase, subsequent to the acquisition, in the value, or the value to him, of the shares or interest; and

(*c*) the shares cannot be exchanged for or converted into shares which are subject to restrictions of the kind mentioned in (*b*).

Para 4 of Schedule 8 substitutes a complicated new s. 79(2)(*c*). S. 79(2)(*c*) formerly provided for three situations, any one of which would oust the charge under s. 79(4). One such situation was an ordinary acquisition of shares not subject to any special restrictions. The new s. 79(2)(*c*) narrows down this situation by attaching to it a number of additional requirements:

(1) the shares must not be subject to any restrictions:
    (*a*) not attaching to all shares of the same class; or
    (*b*) liable to cease at some time after the acquisition; or
    (*c*) depending on the shares being or ceasing to be held by directors or employees; and
(2) they must not be exchangeable for, or convertible into, shares subject to such restrictions; and
(3) immediately after the acquisition, a majority of such of the shares of the same class as were not held by or for the benefit of an associated company of the body in which they were held, must have been acquired:
    (*a*) otherwise than *qua* director or employee or by virtue of a public offer; or
    (*b*) by persons who were or had been directors or employees.

Para 5 lays down a rule of construction. The rule specifies what is to be regarded as a restriction in determining whether, for purposes of (almost all) the share incentive schemes legislation, shares (or interests therein) acquired or to be acquired after 18 October 1972 are subject to any restrictions. The answer is: 'any contract, agreement, arrangement or condition by which [the acquirer's] freedom to dispose of the shares on any interest in them or to exercise any right conferred by them is restricted'. There is one exception, namely where the restriction is imposed as a condition of a loan which is not a "related" loan. The concept of a related loan is spelled out in para 6.

Whilst on the subject of Schedule E, we might pause to take note of a statement made on 29 June 1973 by Mr John Nott, the Minister of State at the Treasury, in reply to a Parliamentary Question as to the taxability of long service awards to employees (as to which *see* **pp. 109, 117–19**). 'In law,' said the Minister, 'all such awards are taxable and where they are made in cash tax must be deducted under the normal PAYE procedure. By concession, however, the Inland Revenue will not seek to charge tax in respect of long service awards which take the form of tangible articles of reasonable cost when the award is in respect of a period of service of not less than 20 years and no similar award has been made to the recipient within the previous 10 years.' By way of explanation, Mr Nott added that: 'An article may be taken to be of "reasonable cost" where the cost to the employer does not exceed £2 for each year of service. This figure has been adopted in the expectation that it will not need revision for a considerable time to come.' No doubt this concession will shortly find its way into Revenue booklet I.R.1. ("Extra-Statutory Concessions").

F.A. 1973 s. 14(1) provides that a lump sum paid to a person on his retirement from an office or employment is not chargeable under Schedule E if:

(*a*) (i) it is paid under a scheme or fund exempted either by TA s. 221(1), (2) or by F.A. 1970 s. 24(1); and

    (ii) it is neither a payment of compensation to which F.A. 1972 s. 73 applies nor a payment chargeable to tax under F.A. 1971 Schedule 3 para 9; or

(*b*) (i) it is a benefit paid under a scheme or agreement within TA s. 220 or under a retirement benefits scheme within F.A. 1970 s. 25; and

    (ii) the person to whom it was paid was chargeable to tax under TA s. 220 or under F.A. 1970 s. 23 in respect of the sums paid, or treated as paid, with a view to providing the benefit.

By s. 14(2), this provision is deemed always to have had effect. S. 14 may seem clearer when the statutory provisions referred to in it are explained. TA s. 220 (mentioned at **p. 125**) contains a charge under the old code (*see* lower down **p. 125**) on retirement benefits etc provided for directors and employees of bodies corporate. F.A. 1970 s. 23 is the parallel charge under the new code (*see* again **p. 125**). TA s. 221(1), (2) contains a set of exceptions to the charge under s. 220, which apply under the old code: F.A. 1970 s. 24(1) (p. 125) enacts a similar set of exceptions from s. 23 for purposes of the new code. (The exceptions are, briefly, approved schemes, statutory schemes, and schemes set up by foreign Governments for the benefit of their employees.) F.A. 1972 s. 73 is designed to keep within the charge on golden handshakes (contained in TA s. 187: see p. 118) payments of compensation for premature retirement etc not due to ill-health, while F.A. 1971 Schedule 3 para 9 brings into charge to tax certain unauthorized payments and payments after cessation of tax exemptions made under approved retirement and superannuation schemes.

F.A. 1973 s. 15(a) effects a slight relaxation in the conditions of approval under the new code by striking out F.A. 1970 s. 19(2)(f). These conditions, including s. 19(2)(f), are set out at p. 126.

We have already discussed (at pp. 165-6) the background to, and general import of, the provisions enacted in F.A. 1973 s. 38 and Schedule 15 in order to bring into charge to UK tax profits arising from the exploitation of the UK part of the Continental Shelf. We now have the opportunity to examine those provisions in greater detail.

S. 38(1) sets the scene with the provision that: 'The territorial sea of the United Kingdom shall for all purposes of income tax, capital gains tax, and corporation tax . . . be deemed to be part of the United Kingdom.' S. 38(2) proceeds to define the central concepts, including these:

(a) "exploration or exploitation activities" means activities carried on in connection with the exploration or exploitation of so much of the seabed and subsoil and their natural resources as is situated in the UK or a designated area;

(b) "exploration or exploitation rights" means rights to (inter alia) assets to be produced by exploration or exploitation activities;

(c) "designated area" means an area designated by Order in Council under the Continental Shelf Act 1964 s. 1(7) (so far three such Orders have been made).

The first charging provision is s. 38(3), which subjects to UK tax any profits or gains from exploration or exploitation activities carried on in a designated area or from exploration or exploitation rights. S. 38(4) supplements this with a more limited charge on non-residents: any profits or gains arising to a non-resident from exploration or exploitation activities carried on in the UK or in a designated area or from exploration or exploitation rights, are deemed for purposes of corporation tax to arise from a trade carried on in the UK through a branch or agency, and any gains accruing to such a person on disposal of such rights are deemed to accrue on disposal of assets used for the purposes of a trade carried on in the UK through a branch or agency. The final charge is contained in s. 38(5): any emoluments from an office or employment in respect of duties performed in a designated area in connection with exploration or exploitation activities are to be treated for income tax purposes as emoluments in respect of duties performed in the UK (i.e. as taxable under Schedule E Case I if they accrue to a resident and under Schedule E Case II if they accrue to a non-resident). S. 38 takes effect for income tax and capital gains tax purposes from 1973–74 and for corporation tax purposes from the financial year 1973.

F.A. 1973 s. 16 is an important provision which will have the effect in many cases of calling into question the desirability of resorting to a device which has hitherto been an essential part of the tax planner's stock-in-trade —the accumulation settlement (see pp. 169–70). The section applies to income arising to trustees in any year of assessment which is to be accumulated or is payable at the trustees' (or anyone else's) discretion (s. 16(2)(a)). The section also applies to income of a close company apportioned to trustees under F.A. 1972 Schedule 16 para 1 (see p. 283) (s. 16(3), (4)). It does not apply to income which:

(i) (before being distributed) is the income of any person other than the trustees (s. 16(2)(b));
(ii) is treated for any income tax purpose as income of the settlor (s. 16(2)(b));
(iii) is exempted as being income of a charity or of an approved retirement benefits scheme (s. 16(2)(c)); or
(iv) is applied in defraying the trustees' expenses (s. 16(2)(d)).

The section's sting comes in the tail: sub-section (6) provides in effect that for 1973–74 and subsequent years of assessment, undistributed income arising under a settlement should be taxed at both the basic and the additional rate, in other words at 45% (basic rate of 30% plus the surcharge of 15%). This result is achieved by amending TA s. 451(2)(e), (5). We recall from pp. 173–4 that under TA s. 451 capital sums paid by trustees to the settlor or his wife are treated as income of the settlor to the extent that they are covered by available undistributed income arising under the settlement: s. 16(6) requires the trustees in each year of assessment to deduct from total undistributed income arising under the settlement for that and previous years 45% of that total less the aggregate of the income arising in that year and certain other items. There is a small mitigating factor: in s. 16 "trustees" does not include personal representatives (s. 16(5)).

F.A. 1973 s. 17, dealing with payments under discretionary trusts, is an attempt to cope with one of the consequences of the charge under s. 16. By s. 17(1), where in any year of assessment trustees make a payment to any person in exercise of a discretion vested in them or any other person, then, if the sum paid is treated as income of the payee, e.g. under any of the provisions discussed at **pp. 170–5** (TA ss. 434–59), the payment is to be governed by s. 17(2)–(5) and not by TA s. 52 or 53. S. 17(2) requires that the payment be treated as a net amount from which the tax has been deducted *both at the basic and any additional rate*; and that the notional deduction be treated:

(a) as income tax paid by the person to whom the payment is made; and
(b) so far as not set off under s. 17(3), as income tax assessable on the trustees.

S. 17(3) allows as an offset against the trustees' liability under s. 17(2)(b):

(a) any tax charged on the trustees at the additional as well as the basic rate pursuant to s. 16;
(b) the investment income surcharge on any close company apportionment **(pp. 283–6)** treated as income of the trustees; and
(c) tax in respect of income available to the trustees for distribution at 5 April 1973 (assumed to be two-thirds of the net amount of that income—an approximation to the truth, since income taxed at 38·75% is assumed to have suffered tax of $61·25 \times \frac{2}{3} = 40·83\%$).

Where a payment is made from which tax has been deducted under s. 16, the payer must supply the recipient with a certificate of deduction under TA s. 55 **(p. 136)** if requested in writing so to do (s. 17(4)). As with s. 16, "trustees" does not include personal representatives (s. 17(5)).

Finally let us turn our attention to companies. The slimline F.A. 1973 contrives to devote more space to corporation tax than to any other whilst effecting no very significant changes to its structure. Most of the new provisions are anti-avoidance measures aimed at potential abuses, though some take a fairly developed imagination to appreciate and, one would have thought, would have called for a great deal of ingenuity to perpetrate. However, it has to be admitted that that sort of ingenuity, as the cases show, is in plentiful supply.

The first set of provisions, contained in ss. 22–4, is apparently intended to strike at the possibility of using the tax credits which attach to distributions under the imputation system so as to fashion sinister new forms of dividend stripping not covered by TA s. 460 **(p. 29)**. (The tax treatment of distributions under the new system is dealt with at **pp. 252–62**.) The general approach of these provisions is to place restrictions on the right to use the tax credit conferred by a distribution on its recipient. S. 22 applies to any qualifying distribution made after 5 April 1973 other than amounts treated as such by reason of TA ss. 234, 235 (*see* **pp. 261–2**) or F.A. 1972 Schedule 22 para 3(3) (which provides that no amount is to be regarded for purposes of TA s. 233(2)(*d*) (*see* **pp. 260–1**) as representing the principal secured by a security issued after 5 April 1972 in so far as it exceeds any new consideration received by the company for the issue of the security—the idea being to tighten up s. 233(2)(*d*) by closing off one of the ways of escaping its clutches) (s. 22(5)). Where a person (whether individual or corporate) (i) receives a qualifying distribution within the scope of s. 22, (ii) is entitled to a tax credit on it, and (iii) holds—with associated holdings, as defined in F.A. 1973 Schedule 10 para 2—at least 10% of any class of shares giving rise to the distribution, then the income represented by the distribution (i) is not exempt, (ii) is treated as not brought into charge to income tax for the purposes of TA ss. 52 and 53, and (iii) interest paid cannot be relieved against it under F.A. 1972 s. 75 (*see* **p. 131**) (s. 22(1), (3)). S. 22 does not apply so far as the distribution comes from (*a*) profits arising after the shares were acquired, or (*b*) shares acquired before 6 April 1965 (s. 22(1)).

S. 23 disallows certain reliefs in respect of bonus issues. There are two pre-conditions to its operation. Firstly, s. 23 applies only where, on or after 6 April 1973, a person receives an amount which is treated as a distribution by virtue of:

(*a*) TA s. 234 (bonus issues following repayment of share capital);
(*b*) TA s. 235(1) (matters not treated as repayments of share capital); or
(*c*) F.A. 1972 Schedule 22 para 3(3) (distributions in excess of new consideration received: (*see* **p. 262**) (s. 23(1)).

Secondly, s. 23 applies only in so far as these distributions exceed a normal return to the recipient on what he has paid for the shares in respect of which the distribution is made (s. 23(6)); and for this purpose if the recipient paid more than the market value or nothing, he is assumed to have acquired them at their then market value (s. 23(7)(*a*)).

The effect of a distribution falling within s. 23 is this:

(i) no exemption can be claimed and no losses can be set off against the distribution and its corresponding tax credit (s. 23(2));
(ii) the recipient is assessable to income tax on the distribution plus tax credit at a rate equal to the rate of investment income surcharge in force when the distribution is made (s. 23(3));

(iii) a company cannot treat the distribution and tax credit as franked investment income (s. 23(4));

(iv) the tax credit cannot be set against income tax due on annual payments under TA ss. 52 and 53 (s. 23(5)(a)); and

(v) interest paid cannot be relieved against the distribution and tax credit under F.A. 1972 s. 75 (s. 23(5)(b)).

S. 24 is designed to prevent groups of companies from avoiding the effects of ss. 22 and 23. This is achieved by way of a small extension to TA s. 256(3) (see p. 273).

F.A. 1973 also makes a concerted attack on the sale of losses, especially losses arising from first-year allowances. This attack might have taken the form of a redefinition of ordinary share capital. Instead the idea is that the relationship of parent and subsidiary, and the size of a member's share in a consortium, are no longer to be determined simply by looking at the holding of ordinary share capital. Ownership of ordinary share capital may not accurately reflect one company's interest in another.

Accordingly F.A. 1973 s. 28 makes the qualifications for entitlement to group relief (pp. 274–1) more stringent. The additional requirements for the availability of group relief are that:

(a) the parent company must be beneficially entitled to not less than 75% or, as the case may be, 90% of any profits available for distribution to equity holders of the subsidiary company (s. 28(2)(a));

(b) the parent company must be beneficially entitled to not less than 75% or, as the case may be, 90% of any assets of the subsidiary company available for distribution to its equity holders on a winding-up (s. 28(2)(b)); and

(c) a member's share in a consortium must be taken to be the lowest of:
  (i) the percentage of ordinary share capital of the surrendering (or holding) company which is beneficially owned by that member;
  (ii) the percentage to which that member is beneficially entitled of profits available for distribution to equity holders of the surrendering (or holding) company; and
  (iii) the percentage to which that member would be beneficially entitled of any assets of the surrendering (or holding) company available for distribution to its equity holders on a winding-up (s. 28(3), (4)).

Ss. 29–31 are complementary measures. S. 29 is a complicated provision which excludes the group relief provisions where companies are moved from one group or consortium to another in order to obtain the benefit of group relief. S. 30 is designed to prevent exploitation of capital allowances given to lessors of plant or machinery by schemes under which a group of companies with taxable profits might take the benefit of a tax loss created by such first-year allowances and then arrange for the leasing contract (which will subsequently yield taxable profits) to be transferred to another group in a position to use these profits to relieve its (the transferee group's) losses. S. 31 strikes at the exploitation of group relief and first-year allowances by company partnerships (**pp. 290–1**).

By way of consolation, the right of a holding company to surrender ACT to its 51% subsidiaries under F.A. 1972 s. 92 is no longer limited to surplus ACT.

Finally, there are a number of amendments to the close company rules (**pp. 278** *et seq.*). F.A. 1973 s. 20 relaxes the restrictions on loans to participators or their associates imposed by TA ss. 286–7 (**pp. 286–7**) in cases where a loan is made after 5 April 1973 to a person who uses the loan to acquire shares or interests in shares under an approved share incentive scheme, provided that the person in question does not have a material interest in the company in which the shares are held or in any company controlling that company.

S. 21 introduces Schedule 9, which contains a number of detailed amendments to the apportionment provisions contained in F.A. 1972 Schedule 16 (**pp. 283–6**). The provisions affected include para 5 (*see* **p. 283**) and para 10 (*see* **pp. 284–5**). Fortunately, an explanation of these amendments falls outside the scope of this book.

Extra Notes to Text

(**p. 42**) Although TA s. 482(7) applies only 'for the purposes of this section' (these being the words missing from the quote), the rule has been accepted as generally applicable since its enunciation in Lord Loreburn L.C.'s judgment in *De Beers* v. *Howe* [1906] A.C. 455 at 458.

(**p. 51**) A married man making maintenance payments is entitled to the lower relief only. These are of two kinds—'small maintenance payments' not exceeding £12 per week or £52 per month (TA s. 651) and payments exceeding these amounts. The former are paid in full, the latter under deduction of tax. Both are deductible as charges on income (*see* **p. 56**): and this precludes any claim to the higher relief (*see* TA s. 8(1)(*a*)(ii)).

(**p. 72**) Note that in invoking the principle against the Revenue, *Ridge Securities* v. *IRC* [1964] 1 A.E.R. 275 suggests it is possible.

(**p. 91**) A claimant may, under s. 168(3) (as substituted by F.A. 1971 s. 16(1), (2)(*a*)), confine the relief to his/her income, excluding income of his/her spouse.

(**p. 98**) Notice that this change in the profit-sharing arrangement affects the partners' taxability for 1971–72: they will be assessed for 1971–72—on the basis of the partnership profits of the year to 31 January 1971—in the ratio 40:30:30 for the first eleven months and 80:10:10 for the remaining month.

(**p. 142**) Lord Denning (at 46 T.C. at 485); it was applied by Ungoed-Thomas J. in *McMann* v. *Shaw* [1972] 3 A.E.R. 732 in holding that long-term compensation payments for loss of office fell within Case III.

(**p. 170**) For the vested interest *see IRC* v. *Hamilton Russell's Executor* [1943] 1 A.E.R. 474.

(**p. 170**) As to the meaning of 'settlor', *see Crossland* v. *Hawkins* [1961] Ch. 537.

(**p. 170**) The draftsman of a settlement normally has two main objectives, the one positive (to effectuate the settlor's wishes in favour of the intended class of beneficiaries), the other negative (to fully alienate the property or income so as to leave the settlor free from further liability to tax). The reward for success is often dramatic. A settlor liable to high marginal rates is able to place income or income-bearing assets in the hands of persons subject to tax at much lower rates. (Even more dramatic, of course, where the beneficiaries are persons for whom the settlor would in any event have provided, e.g. his children.) The draftsman's task was once much easier that it is today. A number of complex provisions, contained in TA ss. 434–59, have now been enacted to counter the avoidance of tax by devices involving settlements.

(**p. 175**) If the settlor fails to divest himself absolutely, the consequences may be horrendous: *see Vandervell* v. *IRC* [1967] 2 A.C. 291 (if you have tears . . .).

(**p. 176**) For a taste of some of the difficulties that can arise in taxing the beneficiaries, *see Carlish* v. *IRC* [1958] 38 T.C. 37.

Index